POLITICS
AND **PUBLIC**
POLICY

POLITICS
AND PUBLIC POLICY

Second Edition

CARL E. VAN HORN
Rutgers University
DONALD C. BAUMER
Smith College
WILLIAM T. GORMLEY, JR.
Georgetown University

CQ
PRESS

A Division of Congressional Quarterly Inc.
Washington, D.C.

Printed in the United States of America
Second Printing

Library of Congress Cataloging-in-Publication Data

Van Horn, Carl E.
    Politics and public policy / Carl E. Van Horn, Donald C. Baumer, William T. Gormley, Jr.--2d ed.
        p.   cm.
    Includes bibliographical references and index.
    ISBN 0-87187-658-2
    1. United States--Politics and government. 2. Political culture--United States. 3. Pressure groups--United States. 4. Policy sciences. I. Baumer, Donald C., 1950-   . II. Gormley, William T., 1950-   . III. Title.
JK274.V33 1991
320.973--dc 20   91-37455
                                                                       CIP

TO

Evan and Ross Van Horn
Ben and Maggie Baumer
B.J. and Ken Gormley

Contents

Tables and Figures   xi
Preface   xiii

**PART I. THEMES, PERSPECTIVES,
AND THE POLICY ENVIRONMENT**   1

1   **American Politics and Public Policy**   5
    Policy Makers   7
    A Federal System   13
    Policy Influences Outside Government   15
    The Scope of Conflict   19
    Politics and Policy   23

2   **Political Culture, the Economy, and Public Policy**   29
    A Durable Political Culture   29
    The Problematic Economy   37
    A Comparative Perspective   44
    Summary   48

PART II. SIX POLICY DOMAINS   53

3   **Boardroom Politics**   57
    Corporate Concerns   59
    Corporate Governance   65
    Strategies and Policies   70
    After the Board Has Met   74
    Summary   81

4   **Bureaucratic Politics**   87
    The Low Game   88
    The Cross-Pressured Bureaucracy   93
    Rules and Regulations   101
    Protected Beaches, Unprotected Workers   109
    Summary   117

5   Cloakroom Politics   123
The Crowded Agenda   124
Entrepreneurial Politics   130
Rites of Passage   137
Shaky Ground Rules, Unreliable Watchdogs   144
Summary   150

6   Chief Executive Politics   155
Rulers of the Agenda   156
The Power to Persuade   163
The Buck Stops Here   172
Promise and Performance   179
Summary   184

7   Courtroom Politics   189
Cases and Controversies   189
Judicial Coalitions   194
New Wine in Old Bottles   200
Unity and Continuity   201
Innovative Decisions   201
Minorities as Beneficiaries   203
The Long Road to Justice   208
Real Solutions and Solutions as Problems   212
The Paradoxical Decree   215
Summary   217

8   Living Room Politics   223
Bystanders and Activists   224
Citizens, Politicians, and Journalists   229
The Power of Public Opinion   240
A Potent Weapon of Democracy   250
Summary   255

**PART III. FROM POLICY DOMAINS
TO POLICY RESULTS   261**

9   Institutional Performance   265
An Analysis of Conventional Political Institutions   266
Alternatives to Conventional Politics   271
Performance Appraisal   272
Summary   287

10   Political Feasibility   293
Alternative Perspectives on Institutions   293
Inclusionary Strategies   298

Exclusionary Strategies   300
Persuasive Strategies   303
Forum Shifting   305
Summary   307

11 **Assessing American Public Policy**   311
Choosing Yardsticks   311
Defend the Nation   315
Achieve Sustained Economic Growth   319
Ensure Equal Opportunity   324
Provide a Safety Net   328
Protect the Environment   333
Summary   337

Index   343

Tables and Figures

TABLES

1-1 The Policy-Making Spectrum: The Scope of Conflict   21
1-2 Domains of the Policy Process   25
2-1 Government Expenditures and Tax Revenues in
       Selected Countries, 1988   46
3-1 Public Employment in Six Western Nations   59
3-2 Most Important Objectives of Chief
       Executive Officers (CEOs)   61
3-3 The Public-Private Spectrum: Degree
       of Government Influence   64
4-1 Outlays and Employees of Federal Departments
       and Selected Agencies, 1989   89
5-1 Some Issues Considered in the
       102d Congress, 1991-1992   125
5-2 Subcommittees of Two Congressional Committees   132
6-1 Issues, Agendas, and Chief Executive Discretion   159
6-2 Presidential Promises, Action, and Policy   174
8-1 Tax and Spending Cut Initiatives
       and Referenda, 1976-1984   246

FIGURES

4-1 The Department of Justice   90
7-1 Branches of Law   191
7-2 The Structure of the Judicial System   196

Preface

How and why certain problems are selected for attention while others are ignored, how policy makers design and implement policies, and how those policies ultimately influence the nation in which we live—these are the focus of this book. Digging into the who, what, when, and where of American public policy requires diligence and patience. The practice of politics and policy making is complicated, involving thousands of people in government institutions and the private sector, but it can be understood by those who are willing to make the effort.

In *Politics and Public Policy* we go beyond conventional analyses that focus narrowly and exclusively on presidents and members of Congress to offer a more comprehensive and realistic view of policy making in the United States. Laws, regulations, administrative rulings, and corporate decisions ensue from the efforts of judges, bureaucrats, corporate officials, journalists, and voters, as well as legislators and chief executives. Moreover, state and local governments are playing an important and expanding role in the design and conduct of public policies.

Politics and Public Policy uses a unique framework to explore the roles of the various people and institutions that make public policy. Differences in the politics within these arenas result in different policies and outcomes. To facilitate an understanding of such variations, we describe six domains of public policy:

1. *Boardroom politics:* decisions by business leaders and professionals that have important public consequences
2. *Bureaucratic politics:* rule making and adjudication by administrators who consider the interests of clients, legislators, and the chief executive, as well as their professional judgment
3. *Cloakroom politics:* law making by legislators who weigh the competing demands of constituents, interest groups, and presidents or governors
4. *Chief executive politics:* decision making dominated by presidents, governors, mayors, and their advisers
5. *Courtroom politics:* court orders by judges, influenced by interest groups and their competing adversaries

6. *Living room politics:* the consequences of public opinions expressed by and through grass-roots movements, political activists, voters, and the mass media

Naturally we prefer the "policy domain" approach over the traditional "policy process" approach, with its focus on the stages of agenda setting, policy formulation, implementation, and evaluation. We should emphasize, however, that the two approaches are not incompatible. Although the book was designed to stand on its own in public policy and American government courses, many colleagues tell us that they use it in conjunction with a more traditional policy process text to broaden students' perspective on the politics of policy making in the United States.

What we offer is a road map for negotiating the twists and turns of the public policy landscape. We hope that readers will come away with a better understanding of how policies are made and implemented, who is powerful and who is not, and how public policies influence American citizens. We also hope that readers will be better equipped to judge the performance of the nation's political institutions and their leaders.

The book integrates discussions of policy making with a look at real policies and their effects. How policies are chosen and implemented is important, but so is what is decided and what it means for citizens and society. Policy makers are constantly faced with difficult and unpleasant choices. Budget deficits, the homeless, toxic waste, and a plethora of other problems pose severe tests for political institutions and their leaders. Understanding more about how institutions process decisions and make policy will help readers better evaluate their leaders' performance on issues that matter most to them.

The second edition of *Politics and Public Policy* includes some important changes that have been made to incorporate new scholarship and to strengthen arguments made in the first edition. The entire book has been updated to reflect issues of the 1990s and the new pressures faced by political institutions.

Part I introduces the actors and institutions that shape policies and the distinctively American context in which those public solutions to problems are demanded. Shortened in this edition, the first two chapters also identify for students some of the normative concerns to which we return in the concluding chapters. In Part II, we explain our unique approach to organizing the study of public policy through the perspective of six policy domains; each domain has different power centers, different arenas for struggle, different participants, and often different outcomes.

After describing and analyzing the policy domains in Part II, we turn to more normative and evaluative concerns in Part III. Chapters assessing American political institutions and political change have been retained, while a new chapter on political feasibility that identifies strategies that help and hinder political success has been added. This new chapter underlines a central theme: a keener understanding of political institutions is essential to effective policy action.

We appreciate the support and encouragement we have received from many people in the production of this book. Those who helped with the original volume have been acknowledged in the first edition. We are pleased to recognize several others who have helped us prepare the second edition. Several colleagues commented on the first edition and made suggestions for changes, including Daniel Mazmanian, Charles Pyles, Mark Aldrich, and anonymous reviewers. Undergraduate and graduate students who enrolled in our courses provided especially valuable feedback. They encouraged us to conclude that the framework used in this book provides a provocative and appealing method for teaching public policy. Joanne Pfeiffer of the Eagleton Institute of Politics at Rutgers University once again provided excellent secretarial support.

We are especially appreciative of CQ Press for its continuing support of this project. Brenda Carter was very helpful in steering us through the revision process. This edition also reflects the careful attentions of Lydia Duncan, the manuscript editor, and Ann O'Malley, who saw the book through the production process.

Finally, we are most grateful to our families for their support and encouragement. We have dedicated this second edition to six family members who may improve public policy in the future.

THEMES, PERSPECTIVES, AND THE POLICY ENVIRONMENT

PART I

Before exploring the finer points of politics and public policy, readers need to be reminded of the background against which policies are made and implemented. Part I provides a brief overview of American political institutions and the policy process. Some of the material will be familiar to those who have studied American government, but the emphasis here is not on the structure of political institutions, but on how they perform their functions. Part I also introduces readers to the themes and perspectives that shaped the authors' approach to *Politics and Public Policy*.

Chapter 1 identifies those who influence public policy. Chief executives, legislators, bureaucrats, and judges all shape policy; but corporate executives, journalists, lobbyists, and citizens also participate in significant ways. Chapter 1 also examines the role played by state and local governments in the conduct of public affairs and shows that the very nature of politics and the policy outcomes differ according to which political actors and institutions are involved.

Chapter 2 examines the particular economic, social, and political forces that structure U.S. politics and public policy. Historical and contemporary political and economic conditions that influence public policies are identified. This chapter begins to make the connection between phenomena such as resource scarcity, increasing international economic competition, changing social mores, media influence, and the policy responses of American political institutions.

1 American Politics and Public Policy

When Iraq invaded Kuwait in 1990, President George Bush faced a formidable array of obstacles—a Congress controlled by the opposition party, a moribund United Nations, financially strapped allies, and a wily adversary adept at manipulating the mass media. Nevertheless, the president was able to galvanize widespread support for a massive troop deployment, spearheaded by the United States but strongly backed by the United Nations and an improbable assortment of Middle Eastern allies. Once the war began, Bush faced equally formidable problems—a shaky coalition linking some bitter enemies, a military whose battlefield skills were untested, and a mass media poised to cover shrill protests against spilling American blood on foreign soil. Despite these obstacles, he brought the war to a swift and successful conclusion. House Speaker Thomas Foley introduced the president to assembled members of Congress after the cease-fire and, departing from custom, congratulated him on a "brilliant victory" in the Persian Gulf.

Many analysts marveled openly at President Bush's success. Could this be the same president who had bungled budget discussions so badly that members of his own party abandoned him on a key vote? Could this be the same president who infuriated voters by converting his famous position on taxes ("Read my lips. No new taxes.") into a poor pun while pointing to his jogging shorts ("Read my hips!")? Others expressed amazement at the adeptness of the American military, the bipartisanship of Congress, and the supportiveness of the press corps. Could this be the same government that ignored a major savings and loan disaster until it had cost taxpayers $500 billion, and that offered little help to stem the rising tide of child poverty and violent crime? Could this be the same press corps that highlighted political conflicts during a previous war?

In this book, we attempt to explain these apparent contradictions by focusing on political institutions as critical but changing elements of the policy-making process. We develop a balanced view of political feasibility, stressing both constraints and opportunities. In addition, we move beyond the politician-centered view so often found in textbooks on American politics. Indeed, we extend our institutional analysis beyond the traditional branches of government to encompass corporate executives at one extreme, and ordinary citizens at the other. In doing so, we advance a broader view of what constitutes public policy.

To explain President Bush's success in the Persian Gulf, we stress the interplay between the man and his institutional surroundings. First, Bush recognized that the United Nations, so often overlooked, presented an opportunity to demonstrate international solidarity. Second, he worked hard at coalition building, deploying trusted aides to foreign capitals at key junctures. Third, he avoided micromanagement, allowing generals to make tactical and even strategic decisions. Fourth, he recognized that the war would be fought simultaneously in the deserts of the Middle East and in America's living rooms. The president and his close advisers had obviously learned many lessons from that military and political debacle, the Vietnam War. They devoted considerable attention to public relations.

Success was fleeting in the Persian Gulf and elsewhere. Military victory was followed by a bitter civil war, between troops loyal to Sadaam Hussein and Kurdish dissidents. Also, as the media's spotlight shifted back to domestic issues, the weaknesses of the Bush administration became more apparent. All of this confirms E. E. Schattschneider's observation that the choice of conflicts is critical to the determination of political success or failure.[1] But we need a better understanding of how policy domains differ, how settled or unsettled they are, and how they shape the choices we face.

Our primary aim in this book is to develop a conceptual framework for thinking about the relationship between politics and public policy. That framework stresses the importance of political institutions, which we have defined broadly to include structures and norms associated with different policy-making settings. Such a perspective yields six policy domains that form the core of the discussion in this book. Although we generalize about different political institutions, we also emphasize that political institutions can be changed. We cite examples of such changes and spell out their implications for public policy. We have tried to move away from the view that policy making is a sequential, linear process. We have also eschewed the perspective that voters and public officials are profit-maximizers whose behavior can be predicted on the basis of rational expectations. Thus our approach to the "new institutionalism" is to stress the importance of political institutions without reducing them to quantities in abstract mathematical formulas. The world of politics is messier than all that, but it is not so chaotic as to preclude some generalizations.

This book is organized so that the connection between politics and public policy remains in view. It is important to be able to see the forest *and* the trees. To that end, this chapter introduces several important themes and perspectives. We begin with a discussion of the public officials authorized by the national and state constitutions to make policy. Next, we turn to the subject of how governments interact with other governments in a federal system. Then the influence of lobbyists and journalists on public policy is examined. We subsequently illustrate the remarkable elasticity of policy making in the United States by focusing on the two ends of the policy-making spectrum: private decision making and public decision making. Last, we introduce the six policy domains, and attempt to show how complex and interdependent the process is. The six policy domains will be explored in depth in Part 2.

Policy Makers

At all levels of American government, power over public policy is shared by different institutions—legislatures, chief executives, and courts. The U.S. Constitution gives Congress the authority to make laws, the president the responsibility to administer them, and the Supreme Court the right to interpret and enforce them. The separation of powers is designed to make each institution independent of the others. Each delegation of authority is qualified by other constitutional provisions, however, so that legislative, executive, and judicial powers are shared to some extent. The same phenomenon is apparent at the state and local levels. Government institutions are as interdependent as they are independent.

The functioning of these institutions over time has accentuated this sharing and interdependence, although a considerable degree of separateness and independence still exists. In addition, a variety of bureaucratic institutions has been created that, independently, wield substantial power over public policy. In subsequent chapters it will be demonstrated that there is more to public policy than public officials. Here, however, the focus is on legislators, chief executives, bureaucrats, and judges.

Legislators

Under the Constitution and its state-level counterparts, legislators are the principal lawmakers in the political system. To become a law, a proposal, in the form of a bill, must be approved by Congress, a state legislature, or a city council. Approval depends on coalition building, the aim of which is to obtain the support of a legislative majority. Without legislative approval, no taxes can be raised, no money can be spent, and no new programs can be launched. The constitutional assumption is that the people's elected representatives should play the leading role in making public policy.

To ensure a high degree of responsiveness, legislators are accountable to the electorate every two, four, or six years. In practice, however, electoral accountability does not always result in the adoption of policies favored by the voters. One reason is that individual legislators can escape responsibility for policies adopted or not adopted by the legislature as a whole. Through casework, or constituency service, legislators can cultivate a hard core of grateful constituents who will support their legislator because he or she has performed some useful service for them, such as expediting the delivery of a Social Security check or arranging a tour of the Capitol. These norms enable legislators to pursue their own preferred policies, subject, of course, to certain constraints. A tobacco state senator probably would not tempt the Fates by leading the fight against tobacco advertising or "passive" smoking.

Legislative observers would find this mode of behavior more acceptable if legislators were responsive to the chief executive or to legislative party leaders, who may take a broader view. Such responsiveness could help to integrate legislative policy making. But legislative bodies are notoriously decentralized and fragmented, at least in the United States. In Western Europe, it is common to find parliamentary systems, in which the chief executive is also the leader of the parliament or legislative body, and "responsible party" systems, in which legislative members of the same party vote together on major issues. The United States, in contrast, has separate legislative and executive branches, weak political parties, and legislators with king-sized and queen-sized egos. Legislators in the United States enjoy a freewheeling, swashbuckling style that makes legislative coalition building difficult.

Another problem confronting legislative coalition builders is the concentration of power in legislative committees. Often referred to as "little legislatures," committees are the workshops of legislative bodies where bills are hammered out, amendments are drafted, and deals are struck. But here, too, many ideas are condemned to the dustbin of history. For that reason, committees are known as legislative graveyards; most bills die in committee without coming to the floor for a vote.

Despite these obstacles, legislators pass an amazing number of measures. Every year, for example, state legislatures in the United States approve about 40,000 bills.[2] In general, legislative bodies prefer to pass bills that distribute benefits rather than bills that impose penalties or bills that redistribute the wealth across social classes.[3] Legislative bodies prefer bills that delegate authority to the chief executive or the bureaucracy, although they may complain about executive "usurpation." By

delegating authority to others, legislators escape responsibility for difficult policy problems and for solutions that upset people. Delegation has
become rampant since Franklin Roosevelt's New Deal, when the Supreme Court allowed Congress to delegate considerable authority to the
executive branch. This has led some observers to wonder whether a
system of checks and balances has in fact become a system of blank
checks.

Chief Executives

With individual legislators marching to their own drumbeats, chief
executives face a formidable task when they engage in the politics of
lawmaking. Legislative deference to chief executives is far from automatic. Legislative resistance is especially likely when the legislative and
executive branches are controlled by different political parties, which is
the situation in twenty-nine states,[4] and which has been the case at the
national level for twenty-six of the last thirty-eight years.

Regardless of which party controls the legislative branch, chief executives cannot take legislative cooperation for granted. Even under the
best of circumstances, the chief executive's power is the "power to
persuade." [5] Chief executives cannot simply tell legislators what to do.
Rather, they must wheedle and cajole, relying on good ideas, political
pressure, personal charm, public support, and a touch of blarney. Some
chief executives, such as Ronald Reagan, have made the most of the
power to persuade, at least for a time. Others, such as Jimmy Carter,
were far less effective at speech making and personal appeals.

If wit and wisdom facilitate persuasion, chief executives also possess
other important resources that come with the office. Perhaps the most
important of these resources is visibility. When the president of the
United States catches cold, it makes national news. A gubernatorial
runny nose is less newsworthy, but governors and mayors have no
difficulty making headlines. Because of this visibility, chief executives
have emerged as the leading agenda setters within the government.
Along with the mass media, they help to determine which issues the
public thinks about and which issues the government will address. Some
formal vehicles for this agenda-setting role are the president's State of
the Union address and a governor's State of the State address. But chief
executives can command an audience at any time, especially in time of
crisis.

Despite their best efforts, chief executives lose many legislative battles. For example, the legislature may adopt a bill, as requested by the
chief executive, but one with so many amendments that it is unacceptable. When this happens, the chief executive may veto the bill, in which
case the legislature may vote to override. In many states, governors have

what is known as the "line-item" veto for budget bills. This enables governors to delete particular line items or programs from the budget without vetoing the entire bill—a formidable power that some presidents have coveted. Even line-item vetoes may be overridden, however.

When chief executives get sufficiently frustrated with the legislative branch, they may resort to questionable means to pursue policy goals. For example, Arizona Governor Bruce Babbitt issued an executive order declaring Martin Luther King Day a state holiday after the state legislature failed to enact equivalent legislation. Babbitt's successor, Evan Mecham, promptly rescinded the holiday, also by executive order.[6] Both actions illustrate the breakdown of executive-legislative cooperation. President Reagan, frustrated by congressional requirements for reporting national security operations, issued a classified executive order instructing the head of the CIA to say nothing to Congress about the sale of arms to Iran, despite statutory requirements for congressional notification. Some chief executives, opposed by powerful legislators, have grown impatient with the constitutional system of checks and balances.

There are, however, perfectly legal ways for chief executives to have an impact on public policy when legislative cooperation diminishes.[7] As the legislative branch has delegated more authority to the bureaucracy, chief executives have recognized that they can make policy as effectively through their influence on management as through legislation. By appointing loyal, capable cabinet and subcabinet officials, they can influence bureaucratic policy making. According to one observer, governors now spend more time managing state government than they do working with the state legislature.[8] Some presidents have also demonstrated keen interest in the management side of policy making. Nixon attempted to create an "administrative presidency," with high-level bureaucrats who followed the president's lead on major issues. Nixon's administrative presidency was derailed by the Watergate affair, but the strategy was used effectively by Reagan.[9]

Bureaucrats

The bureaucracy's size, power, and discretion to make decisions have grown enormously. Since 1969 state bureaucracies have increased 62 percent to 4.2 million people, and local bureaucracies have expanded 44 percent to 10.2 million people.[10] Although the size of the federal bureaucracy has been more stable during this period, its influence has grown as it dispenses larger amounts of federal money. Federal bureaucrats have ample opportunities to structure the behavior of state and local governments by awarding or withholding federal grants-in-aid. Bureaucrats at all levels of government also award contracts to private sector firms for goods or services supplied to the government. There can be little doubt that the bureaucracy constitutes a "fourth branch of government."

One of the bureaucracy's jobs is to implement policy by designing programs to carry out laws. The Internal Revenue Service (IRS) implements policy when it designs tax forms to conform with congressional intent. Similarly, the Immigration and Naturalization Service (INS) implements policy when it warns employers not to hire illegal immigrants. If statutes were clear and airtight, the implementation of policy would be fairly routine, but few statutes fit that description.

The importance of the bureaucracy in policy implementation sometimes distracts attention from the role the bureaucracy plays in policy making. Many laws are in fact drafted by bureaucrats or by legislative aides with substantial assistance from bureaucrats. In addition, bureaucrats make policy openly and directly through what is known as "administrative rule making." For example, the Federal Communications Commission (FCC) voted to "deregulate" radio in 1981, dropping requirements that radio stations cover news and public affairs and allowing radio stations to run as many commercials as they wish. This policy, in the form of an administrative rule, was adopted without an explicit mandate from Congress.

The FCC is one of the independent regulatory commissions— multimember bodies that operate relatively independently of the chief executive. The president appoints the regulatory commissioners, but they serve until their terms expire. Independent regulatory commissions are responsible for licensing nuclear power plants, resolving labor relations disputes, regulating the money supply, and setting the rates charged by public utilities.

In contrast to independent regulatory commissions, most bureaucracies are nominally accountable to the chief executive, who has the power to appoint and to fire the top officials. Most bureaucrats, however, are civil servants with considerable job security. As a general rule, they are less committed to the president's policies than are cabinet and subcabinet officials. Moreover, agencies develop strong symbiotic relationships with constituents and client groups. The Agriculture Department may be more sympathetic to farmers than to a president who wants to reduce farm price supports. In addition, chief executives do not appoint all agency heads. In state government, the people elect some agency heads, which may include the attorney general, the treasurer, the secretary of state, the auditor, and the superintendent of education. Finally, bureaucrats are accountable to other public officials, including legislators and judges. It is fair to say that the bureaucracy has many masters.

Judges

When legislators, chief executives, and bureaucrats cannot agree on appropriate public policies, the controversies often must be settled in the courts. In the American system of government, judges are the ultimate arbiters of policy disputes. They decide whether a law is constitutional and whether an administrative rule is legal. They decide when the federal government may tell state and local governments what to do. They decide the meaning of phrases such as equal protection, freedom of speech, separation of powers, and due process of law.

Judges, particularly federal judges, play a central role in the policy process. Federal judges are not passive arbiters of narrowly defined disputes but active architects of public policy. They immerse themselves in the details of technology, methodology, and administration. Increasingly, they have moved from procedural reasoning to substantive reasoning, at times functioning as legislators and managers. In specific cases, federal judges have seized control of state prisons, mental health facilities, and public schools. In addition, they have directed state legislatures to spend more money on underfunded programs. Judge Frank Johnson required a host of costly reforms at Alabama's mental hospitals, on the grounds that under the Fourteenth Amendment the rights of patients and inmates were being violated.[11] Similarly, Judge Arthur Garrity took over much of the management of the Boston public schools to ensure that his school desegregation orders were faithfully carried out.[12]

Decisions by federal district court judges may be reversed by U.S. circuit courts of appeals or by the U.S. Supreme Court. Appellate judges, as they are sometimes called, generally defer to trial judges, such as federal district court judges, however. They also defer to judges who preceded them on the bench. It is rare for the Supreme Court to reverse an earlier Supreme Court decision, even if today's justices would have decided the case differently. This informal norm is known as the doctrine of *stare decisis* or adherence to precedent, from the Latin phrase, "let the decision stand."

Despite stare decisis, courts move in new directions as new problems, such as AIDS, arise and as society takes note of changes, such as the growing number of working women. Indeed, in many policy domains, judges have been the principal trailblazers in government. The Supreme Court under Chief Justice Earl Warren took the lead in securing rights for persons accused of a crime.[13] The Court under Chief Justice William H. Rehnquist, although widely viewed as conservative, has taken steps to ensure affirmative action and to limit sexual harassment. For example, in *Johnson v. Santa Clara County*, the Rehnquist Court upheld a local government decision promoting a qualified woman ahead of a qualified man, even though the man was slightly better qualified.[14]

When the Supreme Court interprets the Constitution, that interpretation is binding in other courts. State supreme courts are the ultimate arbiters of disputes covered by state constitutions, however. If the Supreme Court allows searches and seizures under certain circumstances, a state supreme court may strike down the same kinds of searches and seizures, based on its reading of the state constitution. As the Supreme Court has once again become more conservative on the subject of criminal justice, state supreme courts have found civil rights for criminal defendants in state constitutions.[15]

The vagueness of phrases such as equal protection and due process of law permits courts wide leeway and discretion. Constitutions constrain the behavior of judges but do not determine their behavior. Richard Neely, chief justice of the West Virginia supreme court, said:

> Since there is hardly any question which cannot be framed in such a way as to assume 'constitutional' dimensions, for all intents and purposes every conceivable question of public policy is up for review by the courts. Vested with this power to determine what is and what is not within the purview of their authority, courts can at will substitute their judgment for that of all the other agencies of government.[16]

Judges, however, cannot act unless a case is brought before them by litigants. Furthermore, appellate judges must reach a consensus before they can speak. But this process is far less complex for a panel of three judges or nine justices than it is for a legislative body consisting of dozens or hundreds of individuals who represent diverse constituencies. As a result, when legislators reach an impasse on controversies such as abortion, school busing, and capital punishment, judges are in a position to fill this power vacuum.

A Federal System

Federalism

Washington, D.C., has no monopoly over the making of public policy in the United States. State and local governments are policy institutions within the federal system of government and in their own right. They are responsible for implementing most federal domestic programs, which typically leave many basic aspects of policy to the discretion of state and local decision makers.

The United States has a truly multigovernmental system. For a number of issues, state governments are virtually immune from federal supervision and control. Banking regulation, insurance regulation, and occupational licensing remain firmly in the hands of state administrative agencies. Questions concerning divorce and child custody are handled almost exclusively by state courts. Even public utility regulation is controlled largely by the states, despite sharp increases in utility bills and growing public concern.

Considerable autonomy is also exercised at the local level. Zoning decisions, which shape the character of neighborhoods and the quality of everyday life, are made by local governments, without so much as a raised eyebrow from state government officials or federal court judges. Inspections of housing, restaurants, and buildings, all of which are necessary for public health, are controlled by local governments with little input from other levels of government.

Intergovernmental Relations

Despite the considerable discretion exercised by state and local governments, the federal government has extended its control over them by offering the "carrot" of federal grants-in-aid in return for certain concessions. President Lyndon Johnson's War on Poverty relied heavily on such grants-in-aid. President Nixon used a different approach, which he called the new federalism. Under Nixon, the flow of federal dollars increased dramatically, while federal restrictions were loosened somewhat. President Reagan also voiced support for a new federalism, but his version combined sharp cutbacks in federal support with new responsibilities for state governments. President Bush continued the Reagan approach, calling for less aid for transportation projects, for example, but new mandates in other areas.

About 80 percent of the federal aid to state and local governments comes in the form of categorical programs, which have narrowly defined objectives, distinct statutory and budget identities, detailed planning and operational requirements, and defined target populations. The nation's principal income support strategy for the poor, Aid to Families with Dependent Children (AFDC), is a categorical grant program. AFDC's purpose is to help poor families with children maintain a minimal standard of living. Cash assistance is provided to families if they meet explicit statutory and administrative standards and obey certain regulations. Even though the states fund one-half of the cost of AFDC, federal law governs its fundamental rules.

Block grant programs—the balance of federal aid—give states and localities money for broad purposes, such as health, housing, education, and employment, but do not require that all recipients offer a specific set of programs and services. State and local governments have wide discretion to invest federal dollars as they see fit, but the federal government remains responsible for ensuring that the funds are spent for their intended purpose. For example, under the Community Development Block Grant program, mayors, governors, and their staffs may select a mix of housing services that seems well suited to the particular needs of their community.

Categorical programs still predominate, but Presidents Nixon and Reagan accomplished a shift away from categorical programs and toward greater reliance on block grants.[17] A parallel shift took place in regulation, from direct orders and mandates to more indirect forms of federal control, such as partial preemptions and crossover sanctions. An example of a partial preemption is the Surface Mining Control and Reclamation Act of 1977, which grants states the option of running their own strip-mining program, provided that federal standards are accepted. If a state refuses the option, the federal government exercises full preemption, running the program out of a regional office. Examples of crossover sanctions include the federal government's ability to withhold highway funds from states that refuse to set the drinking age at twenty-one years or to conform to a certain maximum highway speed limit. The federal government usually bargains with the states in the hope of achieving federal objectives.

Policy Influences Outside Government

Interest Groups and Political Parties

The fragmented, decentralized policy system described so far is highly permeable by groups outside of government. Private interest group involvement in public policy is a widely recognized and long-standing fact of American government. Interest groups work closely with legislators and bureaucrats to develop mutually beneficial policies. The specialized committee structure of Congress, which is mirrored by most state legislatures, enables interest groups to focus their efforts on the individuals and groups with power over the issues of greatest concern to them.

Clusters of people interested in the same issue—members of legislative committees and subcommittees, bureaucratic agencies that administer the policies formulated by a committee, and the groups that are most directly affected by such policies—are often called subgovernments or issue networks. These networks wield considerable influence over many policy domains, such as the financial industry, agriculture, public works, and defense contracting. Interest groups are full-fledged partners in major policy-making circles.[18]

The number and variety of interest groups in the United States are enormous. Although no one has been able to count all of them, various sources provide a rough estimate of the size of the interest group population, which has grown rapidly since the 1960s. The following information was drawn from directories of interest groups and lobbyists compiled in the early 1980s.

—There are nearly 16,000 national voluntary membership organizations and more than 200,000 state and local community groups.[19]
—More than 100,000 lawyers serve as professional lobbyists for various clients.
—More than 12,000 lobbyists are based in Washington. More than half of them are employed by groups with an economic or occupational base, such as unions, trade and professional associations, farm groups, and individual corporations.[20]
—More than 500 corporations employ lobbyists in Washington.[21]

Given the strong representation of private economic interests, it is not surprising that citizen groups have gotten into the act. More than 1,200 citizen groups are represented in Washington. Environmental groups, civil rights organizations, antipornography groups, and gun owner organizations are all examples of such groups. Thousands of additional groups may be found in state capitals and other communities.

State and local government officials also hire staffs to represent them in Washington. The National Governors' Association, National Conference of State Legislatures, National League of Cities, U.S. Conference of Mayors, National Association of Counties, and other organizations actively lobby the national government on matters of concern to states and localities. They also press legislators and administrators to act favorably on requests for financial assistance and regulatory decisions.

There is tremendous diversity in the size, resources, leadership, cohesiveness, and prestige of interest groups that participate in the policy process. Those with substantial money, committed members, strong leadership, and a favorable reputation exert considerable influence. All other things being equal, having a large membership is desirable because a group's political clout is enhanced if it speaks for many voters. But large groups have difficulty maintaining a unified membership and directing their activity toward policy goals that excite members. Therefore, small, intense, single-issue groups may be more successful than large groups.

An interest group with few members but a good deal of clout is the Business Roundtable—an organization of a few hundred top corporate executives. Although its membership is small, the enormous wealth it represents enables it to compete effectively in policy arenas with labor unions, such as the American Federation of Labor-Congress of Industrial Organizations (AFL-CIO), representing nearly 14 million workers.

When interest groups approach elected officials and government administrators, they are lobbying for help either to get something done to benefit them or to stop something from happening that adversely affects them. Many people equate lobbying with corrupt contributions or pressure tactics of one sort or another. Although some of these practices do go on, the normal situation is considerably more complicated than that.

Effective lobbying rests on the use of information and money. When lobbyists meet with members of Congress, they supply facts about issues and political intelligence about the positions and strategies of others in Congress and the executive branch. Lobbyists testify at congressional hearings, observe committee deliberations, and perform other services for their clients. Groups sponsor professional and social gatherings to which elected officials are invited—and often paid a fee for appearing—to cement relationships. Interest groups may conduct public relations campaigns to convince voters in the member's district to support their cause. Advertising, press releases, and letter-writing campaigns are all used to build a climate of support for their positions and to secure favorable treatment from legislators. And, of course, groups contribute to congressional election campaigns—nearly $160 million in 1990.[22]

Interest groups also lobby executive agencies. Bureaucratic agencies are responsive to interest groups because they need political allies to advance their policy goals and to protect them from legislators or chief executives who may dislike their programs and policies. Lobbying bureaucratic agencies generally entails using the same techniques used with legislators, except that campaign contributions apply only to elected officials. All major agencies have one or more constituent groups with which they maintain close and mutually beneficial alliances.

Interest groups are active within the judicial arena, although there they are less visible. The direct contribution of money is rare because it is illegal to bribe judicial officials. But interest group budgets can be used to back legal cases that have policy significance. Suits seeking to overturn legislative or administrative decisions are a common outcome of practically all important policy disputes. These challenges come not just from businesses trying to protect their financial interests; civil rights groups and environmentalists have successfully pursued legal strategies that have advanced their causes. Even the selection of judges is not beyond the reach of interest groups. They lobby executives and legislators on behalf of certain court nominees, and in some states and localities interest groups try to influence election contests between candidates for the bench.

As interest groups have become more numerous and influential, political parties have declined in importance as "linkage mechanisms" between citizens and government. Political parties continue to play a vital role in recruiting candidates for office; they also provide cues to voters that continue to matter, especially in elections where other information is scarce. But party organizations lack the technical expertise that interest groups possess—a key weakness in complex policy debates. And candidates for office rely less and less on parties to bring their message to voters. Instead they have turned increasingly to the mass media to play that important role.

The Mass Media

Perceptions of public officials, public policies, and governments are shaped significantly by the mass media, especially television and newspapers. By focusing obsessively on the "horse race" aspects of presidential campaigns, the media do not give voters enough real help in their efforts to evaluate the candidates' issue positions. By devoting more attention to national and local politics than to state politics, the media limit public awareness of state politics. By oversimplifying and sensationalizing certain policy controversies, the media discourage rational decision making. On the positive side, the media can be credited with exposing public problems and errant public officials. Political scientists and other observers are devoting increased attention to the role of the media in politics, especially their impact on election campaigns. The outcome of electoral contests ushers in a new administration, with a new vision for the future. By influencing the outcome of elections, the media indirectly influence public policy as well.

Clearly, the media influence public perceptions of the candidates' character traits and thereby shape campaign issues. Election results frequently hinge on how well each side presents its case to the media or through the media. Jimmy Carter was unable to overcome a perceived lack of leadership ability in 1980, but Ronald Reagan did not seem to be hurt by reports that he invented or distorted facts in his political speeches. In his concession speech following an overwhelming defeat at the polls in 1984, Walter Mondale admitted that he was an anachronism—a candidate who felt uncomfortable on television in a television age. Former senator Gary Hart's 1988 presidential campaign was abruptly interrupted when newspapers ran stories suggesting marital infidelity. Senator Joseph Biden also withdrew from the presidential race following press accounts of plagiarism. For some candidates, character is the issue.

The media's influence on politics and public policy extends well beyond the electoral arena. It is pervasive, reaching citizens in the nation's heartland and the powerful in Washington. Ironically, the media's influence is often so strong and ubiquitous that it is not noticed. The readers of the *Tri-City Herald* live near a nuclear power plant and a high-level nuclear waste disposal site in Hanford, Washington. This newspaper, which has long promoted nuclear power, runs numerous stories about the safety, reliability, and economy of nuclear power, and few stories about the dangers and unanticipated costs of nuclear energy. Stories have carried headlines such as "Radiation Linked to Good Health" and "A-Plants Don't Taint Environment." The paper's editors refer to nuclear "storage sites" rather than nuclear "dumps." [23] Exposure to such pronuclear sentiment on a regular basis means that local citizens are primed to view nuclear power favorably. Unless local newspapers fairly present both sides of an issue, citizens will lack one source of information they need to make intelligent decisions.

In contrast, many newspapers encourage investigative reporting, much of it very thorough and effective. The *Washington Post*'s persistent investigation of the Watergate break-in helped bring about the resignation of President Nixon and ushered in a new era in campaign finance. The *Chicago Sun-Times*'s 1978 series on the bribes, kickbacks, and payoffs accepted by city building inspectors, health inspectors, and fire inspectors had a major impact on city practices. In its zeal to catch greedy inspectors, the *Sun-Times* purchased a tavern, dubbed The Mirage, operated it for several months, and documented numerous instances of corruption. Following the publication of the series, the Chicago Fire Prevention Bureau created an internal investigations unit to monitor the quality of fire inspections; the city initiated team inspections by building, fire, and health inspectors to discourage shakedown attempts; the U.S. Justice Department added new lawyers to deal with findings concerning tax fraud; the IRS assigned additional agents; and the Illinois Department of Revenue created a permanent task force, the "Mirage Unit," for systematic audits.[24]

Although the media's ability to shape public policy is rooted in the ability to shape public opinion, the elite media—the major television networks, the preeminent newspapers and weekly news magazines—shape public policy directly. Chicago's public officials reacted swiftly to the *Sun-Times*'s series on corruption, rather than waiting for public outrage to mount. One often sees the same phenomenon following reports on "60 Minutes" or, in some instances, in anticipation of such reports. As a public relations exercise, public officials often react to an investigative report rather than face the fire storm of public criticism it is expected to trigger. In the process, media influence is magnified. The mere threat of a public outcry may be sufficient to alter public policy.

The Scope of Conflict

In most textbooks on American politics and public policy, the United States is described as a "representative democracy" in which citizens elect representatives—legislators and chief executives—who in turn make public policy. Elected representatives, taking the public's views into account, pass laws and make other authoritative decisions. They also appoint bureaucrats and judges, who adopt rules and adjudicate disputes. But representative democracy is only part of the picture. Many decisions of the utmost importance are made by corporate elites who do not have to answer to the American people. Although nominally accountable to boards of directors or stockholders (or both), corporate managers are in fact free to make many decisions as they see fit. These decisions—concerning plant location, production, marketing, jobs, and wages—are private.

At the other end of the policy-making spectrum, some decisions are made not by public officials, but by the people. This is literally true when voters participate in "issue elections." It is also true, for all intents and purposes, when public opinion becomes so aroused that public officials are compelled to defer to citizens and their preferences.

What exists in the United States, therefore, is not representative democracy but "elastic" democracy. When the scope of conflict is exceedingly narrow, representative democracy gives way to private decision making, such as corporate governance. When the scope of conflict is exceedingly broad, representative democracy gives way to public decision making in the form of direct democracy (Table 1-1). The policy-making process can be thought of as a kind of rubber band, which stretches well beyond the original contours of representative democracy.

Private Decision Making

Although it is useful to view business groups as lobbyists or intervenors in the policy-making process, it is necessary to view them as policy makers as well. If one considers only pressure politics, one misses the more worrisome side of business influence—namely, the private sector's capacity to make decisions that affect large numbers of people and the private sector's lack of accountability. Technically, such decisions are private policies; they are made by private actors such as corporate chief executive officers, vice presidents, and board members. As a practical matter, however, such private decisions are sanctioned and legitimated by the government—for example, by court decisions upholding private property rights. Charles Lindblom has argued that business enjoys a "privileged position" in American politics.[25] The government, for better or for worse, has delegated to the private sector primary responsibility for mobilizing and organizing society's economic resources. It might be said that decisions by "private governments" are often as far-reaching as decisions by the government itself.

Table 1-1   The Policy-Making Spectrum: The Scope of Conflict

Narrow	Moderate	Broad
Private decision making (corporate governance, capitalism)	Representative democracy (candidate elections, conventional lawmaking)	Public decision making (issue elections, aroused public opinion)

Large corporations, the private governments under consideration here, have distinctive decision-making processes. The focal point for corporate decision making is the board of directors, which consists of top company executives and prominent business leaders from other companies. At some companies, workers have a representative on the board; at many others, however, labor is not directly represented. According to close observers, corporate boards are dominated by top corporate executives. Even if outsiders constitute a majority of the board members, the strategic decisions are made by insiders and then ratified by the rest of the board.[26] This phenomenon has been referred to as "managerial capitalism."[27]

Most large corporations are free to make policy as they wish, with a minimum of government control. If a steel company decides to shut down a factory and lay off 2,000 workers, it is free to do so. In most states, companies are not even required to give their workers advance notice if they make such a decision. Corporations are also free to set prices as they see fit. A privately owned monopoly, such as an investor-owned public utility, is not free to set prices. Under an arrangement that dates back to the early twentieth century, private monopolies, such as public utilities, must accept fairly close government regulation, including price controls, in return for their monopoly status. But public utilities are exceptional. In general, government control is weak and corporate exercise of discretion is pervasive.

Corporate executives argue, with some justification, that they are accountable to the public through the workings of the market. If companies are mismanaged, or their prices are too high, or their products are inferior, consumers "vote with their pocketbooks" and spend their money elsewhere. But markets do not function that perfectly. Information about companies, their products, and their finances is costly to obtain and not easily understood. Consumers are handicapped by inadequate information. Moreover, markets fail to take into account the social costs of "externalities," such as air pollution. Where externalities are substantial, market prices grossly understate the underlying costs of producing services. Finally, government subsidies disguise the real costs of producing some goods and services. It is difficult to know, therefore, whether oil companies are operating efficiently, considering the generous subsidies they receive from the federal government. Indeed, some industries, such as defense and aerospace, receive such huge subsidies that it is difficult to evaluate them at all.

Many companies, especially publicly held companies whose stock is traded in the various stock markets, are accountable to their stockholders, on whom they depend for capital. As a group, stockholders are becoming more aware and more astute. Mobilized by citizen activists, such as Ralph Nader, and by "corporate raiders," such as T. Boone Pickens, stockholders have put pressure on corporate managers and corporate boards to eliminate certain investments, award higher dividends, and change other practices. For the most part, however, stockholders routinely accept the policies of corporate managers. They also typically rubber-stamp the slate of corporate directors proposed by management. If stockholders are relatively weak, workers are even weaker. Although workers can bargain through their unions over wages, benefits, and working conditions, they have virtually nothing to say about the decisions that affect the company's future and theirs. Private corporations are profoundly undemocratic in their governing arrangements. By accepting private ownership of corporate enterprises, the United States government precluded economic democracy and allowed corporate oligarchies to develop. As Robert Dahl observed, "a system of government [that] Americans view as intolerable in governing the state has come to be accepted as desirable in governing economic enterprises." [28]

Public Decision Making

If private decision making epitomizes one end of the policy-making spectrum—a narrow scope of conflict, limited accountability, and government deference to corporations—public decision making epitomizes the other end—a broad scope of conflict, high accountability, and government deference to the public at large. Some decisions are made in "the court of public opinion." When public officials sense that an issue is too controversial to be handled through normal channels, public opinion comes into play and the views of public officials recede into the background. In E. E. Schattschneider's words, the "scope of conflict" expands.[29]

Public opinion is like a slumbering giant, which, when aroused, becomes intimidating. The effects on public policy may thus be considerable. Public opinion has been credited with ending the war in Vietnam, sustaining the environmental movement, promoting tax relief, halting the spread of nuclear power plants, cracking down on drunk driving, and forcing presidents Lyndon Johnson and Richard Nixon from office. Public opinion also has jeopardized civil rights and civil liberties, encouraging local governments to "exclude" poor people from the suburbs and to undermine efforts to achieve meaningful school desegregation. Public opinion is the stuff of which dreams and nightmares are made.

Public decision making means, for the most part, that public officials defer to public opinion when an issue is highly salient and controversial. But the people also make policy more directly from time to time, at least at the state and local levels. They do so through mechanisms, including the initiative and the referendum, popularized by the Progressives early in the twentieth century. A *referendum* is the practice by which a measure that has been passed by or proposed by a legislature is placed on a ballot for voter approval or disapproval. An *initiative* is the procedure by which a measure proposed by citizens becomes law if approved by a majority of voters or by the legislature. To get an initiative on the ballot, a significant number of state residents—usually 5 percent to 10 percent of those voting in the last statewide election—must sign petitions.

At this writing, thirty-seven state constitutions authorize referenda, and twenty-one state constitutions authorize initiatives.[30] Referenda outnumber initiatives by approximately three to one, but initiatives carry more weight because they enable citizens to adopt policies opposed by elected officials. Initiatives and referenda have been used sporadically since the early twentieth century, but they became popular during the 1970s, as citizens, disenchanted with government, attempted to participate more directly in the policy-making process. In 1988, 230 propositions appeared on a ballot.[31]

Public decision making, whether through initiatives and referenda or through government deference to public opinion polls, is more controversial than it might seem. Many politicians believe that they were elected to make these decisions and that ordinary citizens lack the knowledge to make public policy directly. Politicians also worry about the growing influence of the mass media, which contribute so significantly to the formation of public opinion. If public opinion mirrors the views of journalistic elites, it simply magnifies media influence—a far cry from what the Progressives had in mind.

Politics and Policy

Politics varies from one issue to another because politics reflects issue characteristics such as visibility and complexity. Differences in politics in turn result in different policies and outcomes. To understand such variations, it is useful to think of six policy domains in which political struggles take place. These domains are encompassed by representative democracies, but they also reflect the highly elastic nature of American democracy. They run the gamut from highly private to highly public decision making.

Following are brief descriptions of the six policy domains that can be used as a framework for analyzing the policy process.

1. *Boardroom politics:* decision making by business elites and professionals, but with important public consequences
2. *Bureaucratic politics:* rule making and adjudication by bureaucrats, with input from clients and professionals
3. *Cloakroom politics:* policy making by legislators, constrained by various constituencies
4. *Chief executive politics:* a policy process dominated by presidents, governors, mayors, and their advisers
5. *Courtroom politics:* the issuance of court orders, in response to interest groups and aggrieved individuals
6. *Living room politics:* the galvanization of public opinion, usually through the mass media

Each of these domains implies a different arena of combat, a different set of participants, and different rules of conduct. Each also implies a different set of outcomes, ranging from stagnation to incrementalism to innovation, and from limited responsiveness to symbolic responsiveness to policy responsiveness. In short, different institutions yield different sets of policy consequences.

The six policy domains serve as convenient bridges between issue characteristics and policy consequences. Each policy domain can be related to both issue characteristics and policy outcomes (Table 1-2). The effects of issue characteristics such as salience, conflict, complexity, and costs on policy making and the implications of various policy processes for change, responsiveness, and other outcomes—that is, the policy consequences—will be examined. The changes that occur in issue characteristics over time and the consequences of such changes will be highlighted.

The reason for integrating process and substance is the close relationship that exists between the kind of issue under consideration and the policy process. Consider the following propositions:

—Issues that concern large numbers of people are likely to stimulate intense public debate and draw more participants into the policy process than issues that concern only a small segment of the public.

Table 1-2   Domains of the Policy Process

Domain	Principal actors	Common issue characteristics	Common policy outcomes
Boardroom politics	business elites professionals	low salience high complexity hidden costs	stagnation limited responsiveness
Bureaucratic politics	bureaucrats professionals clients	low to moderate salience low to moderate conflict disputed costs	incrementalism limited responsiveness
Cloakroom politics	legislators interest groups executive officials	moderate to high salience moderate to high conflict disputed costs	incrementalism symbolic responsiveness gridlock policy responsiveness
Chief executive politics	chief executives top advisers	high salience high conflict disputed costs	crisis management symbolic responsiveness
Courtroom politics	judges interest groups aggrieved individuals	high conflict manifest costs moderate to high salience	innovation policy responsiveness (to minorities)
Living room politics	mass media public opinion	high salience high conflict manifest costs	electoral change policy responsiveness innovation

—Complex policies and those that call for major changes in public or bureaucratic behavior are much more difficult to implement than policies that can be routinely carried out through established organizational networks.

—Issues involving hidden costs are handled by the private sector, whereas issues involving disputed costs or manifest costs require some governmental response.

Another reason for linking politics and policy is that substantive results flow from different policy-making processes. Consider, for example, the following: *15‑1, 539*

—Decisions made within the private sector and ratified by government agencies legitimate self-regulation, impose hidden costs on consumers, and preempt meaningful reform.

—Decisions made by low-level or middle-level bureaucrats tend to reflect professional norms, organizational imperatives, and standard operating procedures. Incrementalism, policy making that changes things only marginally, is the most likely result.

—Decisions made by politicians against a backdrop of public arousal occasionally provide opportunities for policy innovation. Highly conflictive issues that do not quite reach the crisis point often result in gridlock or stalemate, however.

—Politicians frequently make only symbolic responses to aroused citizens, or they may only address the problems of a few individuals, instead of taking broad policy action.

—Decisions made by judges may differ significantly from decisions made by other public officials, in that no effort need be made to dilute or disguise policy change. The Constitution, job security, and strong professional values protect judges from politicians, though not from politics. The courts are capable of addressing problems that paralyze other institutions of government.

An approach that highlights different policy domains has several advantages. First, the policy process is dynamic but disorderly. Issues move from one arena to another over time, but they do not follow the same sequence. This observation is fundamentally different from a leading point of view in the policy literature that assumes that issues proceed in a rather orderly fashion from the agenda-setting stage to the policy formulation stage to the policy adoption stage, and so on. Second, institutional settings matter, and they matter in somewhat predictable ways. For example, different branches of government and different levels of government present their own special opportunities and pitfalls. Successful political strategists are attentive to both. Third, the policy domains will demonstrate that the nontraditional areas of policy making deserve attention, for without them the picture is incomplete. The discussions of boardroom politics and living room politics will shed light on actors outside government, including business people, journalists, and citizens.

Overall, it will be established that issue characteristics constrain policy makers in significant ways, that there is no single policy process but rather there are several, that controversies shift from one arena to another over time, and that politics is a significant determinant of policy outcomes. This conception of politics involves not only the familiar institutions of government but also business elites, interest groups, the mass media, and public opinion.

Notes

1. E. E. Schattschneider, *The Semi-Sovereign People* (New York: Holt, Rinehart and Winston, 1960).

2. Richard Bingham, *State and Local Government in an Urban Society* (New York: Random House, 1986), 124.

3. Theodore Lowi, "American Business, Public Policy, Case Studies, and Political Theory," *World Politics* 16 (July 1964): 677-715.

4. Glen Craney, "Democrats Strengthen Hold on State Legislatures," *Congressional Quarterly Weekly Report*, November 10, 1990, 3843.

5. Richard Neustadt, *Presidential Power* (New York: John Wiley, 1976), 78.

6. Peter Goudinoff and Sheila Tobias, "Arizona Airhead," *New Republic*, October 26, 1987, 15-16.

7. Samuel Kernell, *Going Public: New Strategies of Presidential Leadership* (Washington, D.C.: CQ Press, 1986).

8. Coleman Ransone, Jr., *Governing the American States* (Westport, Conn.: Greenwood Press, 1978), 96.

9. Richard Nathan, *The Administrative Presidency* (New York: John Wiley, 1983).

10. Advisory Commission on Intergovernmental Relations, *Significant Features of Fiscal Federalism*, vol. 2 (Washington, D.C.: August 1990), 176-177.

11. Tinsley Yarbrough, *Judge Frank Johnson and Human Rights in Alabama* (University: University of Alabama Press, 1981).

12. J. Anthony Lukas, *Common Ground* (New York: Alfred A. Knopf, 1985).

13. *Gideon v. Wainwright*, 372 U.S. 335 (1963); *Miranda v. Arizona*, 384 U.S. 436 (1966).

14. *Johnson v. Santa Clara County*, 107 Sup. Ct. 1442 (1987).

15. Robert Pear, "State Courts Surpass U.S. Bench in Cases on Rights of Individuals," *New York Times*, May 4, 1986, 1.

16. Richard Neely, *How Courts Govern America* (New Haven, Conn.: Yale University Press, 1981), 7.

17. Randall Ripley and Grace Franklin, *Bureaucracy and Policy Implementation* (Homewood, Ill.: Dorsey Press, 1982), 62; Paul Peterson et al., *When Federalism Works* (Washington, D.C.: Brookings Institution, 1986), 218.

18. For more on subgovernments, see Randall Ripley and Grace Franklin, *Congress, the Bureaucracy, and Public Policy*, 3d ed. (Homewood, Ill.: Dorsey Press, 1984).

19. Graham Wootton, *Interest Groups, Policy, and Politics in America* (Englewood Cliffs, N.J.: Prentice-Hall, 1985), 91.

20. Arthur Close, ed., *Washington Representatives, 1990* (Washington, D.C.: Columbia Books, 1990), 3.

21. Jeffrey Berry, *The Interest Group Society* (Boston: Little, Brown, 1984), 20.

22. Charles Babcock, "PAC Donations at a Plateau," *Washington Post*, April 1, 1991, 17.

23. Cassandra Tate, "Letter from 'The Atomic Capital of the Nation,' " *Columbia Journalism Review* (May-June 1982): 31-35.

24. Pamela Zekman and Zay Smith, *The Mirage* (New York: Random House, 1979).

25. Charles Lindblom, *Politics and Markets* (New York: Basic Books, 1977),

170-188.

26. Lewis Solomon, "Restructuring the Corporate Board of Directors: Fond Hope—Faint Promise?" *Michigan Law Review* 76 (March 1978): 581-610; Victor Brudney, "The Independent Director—Heavenly City or Potemkin Village?" *Harvard Law Review* 95 (January 1982): 597-659.

27. Alfred Chandler, Jr., *The Visible Hand: The Managerial Revolution in American Business* (Cambridge, Mass.: Harvard University Press, 1977), 1-12.

28. Robert Dahl, *A Preface to Economic Democracy* (Berkeley: University of California Press, 1985), 162.

29. Schattschneider, *The Semi-Sovereign People*, 2-3.

30. Council of State Governments, *The Book of the States, 1988-1989* (Lexington, Ky.: Council of State Governments, 1988).

31. Austin Ranney, "Referendums," *Public Opinion* 11 (January-February 1989): 15.

2 Political Culture, the Economy, and Public Policy

American political institutions function as parts of the larger national cultural and socioeconomic system. The actions of political institutions and, therefore, the nature of public policy are greatly influenced by these cultural and economic forces, unique to the United States. The country, as a part of the global environment, is also affected by developments in other parts of the world. But the political agenda of U.S. policy makers is not the same as that of leaders in other industrialized nations, and it is fundamentally different from those of less-developed or socialist countries. The United States has the world's most powerful economy, which is greatly influenced by the actions of privately owned corporations. Government ownership of major industries, such as steel or transportation, is not even under consideration in the United States, but such ownership is common the world over. How to control the production of excess food is a contentious issue in the United States, but government officials in many other countries fret about how they are going to feed their citizens.

In this chapter we outline some of the underlying features and tendencies of the American cultural and economic environment. Before examining the specific arenas in which public policy is formulated and implemented, we should consider the broader context within which political institutions and actors function.

A Durable Political Culture

Political culture can be defined as the attitudes and beliefs of citizens about how political institutions and processes ought to work, about fellow citizens and their place in the political process, and about the proper rules of the political game.[1] Several enduring values of the American political culture have shaped public policy from the beginning of the Republic.[2] Individualism, the right of people to pursue their self-interest and to be responsible for their own well-being, is a fundamental American cultural value. Personal freedom, which is closely linked to individualism, has meant the right to pursue self-improvement and protection from government interference. Along with individualism, the sanctity of contracts and the right to acquire and own property contribute to the free market ideology that dominates the political and economic systems in the United States.

Americans also believe in democracy—the right of every citizen to participate in the political process. Support is widespread for equal treatment under the law, political equality, and equality of opportunity. In addition to these core political values, cultural values, including religion and the centrality of the nuclear family, have very significant political implications. It must be noted, however, that in many ways the United States does not live up to its political ideals, that it is a society with racist and sexist elements. As recently as 1950, black Americans did not have equal access to public schools or the voting booth. In the 1990s, though the government has for years expressed its commitment to breaking down racial barriers, there are few truly integrated communities. Women did not have the right to vote in elections until the beginning of the twentieth century, and they still earn considerably less money than men.

Conflicts and tensions between values and beliefs have frequently been the source of political struggle and debate in the United States. For example, the triumph of the Southerners and midwesterners, who rallied around Andrew Jackson, over the Eastern aristocratic cliques that controlled American government in the late eighteenth and early nineteenth centuries was accomplished by appealing to the public's belief in individualism, pragmatism, and equality of opportunity. Franklin Roosevelt's New Deal, which substantially expanded government management of the economy and publicly funded social welfare programs, represented a victory for democratic egalitarian values over uncompromising individualism and capitalism. Ronald Reagan's policies of the 1980s represented a swing back toward individualism, capitalism, and traditional family values. The dynamism of America's political culture stems in part from the inherent tensions between cherished, yet competing, cultural values. Political struggles that aim to change an existing balance between these values can have dramatic effects on the nature of public policy.

The Market Paradigm and Procedural Democracy

A towering presence in the American political culture is, and always has been, a world view that regards the so-called free market as the best allocator of society's goods and services. This viewpoint holds that government's role is primarily one of protecting certain economic, social, and political norms, or rules of conduct, such as competitive markets, private property, and representative government. This world view dominated the thinking of nearly all the Framers of the Constitution.

What is a free market? Or what is the market mechanism for allocating goods in a society? It is a system that relies on voluntary exchanges between autonomous individuals to allocate goods and services in an efficient manner. Efficiency can be defined as the maximum output technology can produce with the minimum use of resources. In free markets producers compete with one another to satisfy consumer demand for goods and services. Consumers are assumed to be willing to give up a certain amount of what they have, usually in the form of money, for various quantities of other goods and services—what economists call a demand function. When voluntary exchanges occur between producers and consumers, both parties are viewed as better off. A producer has given away something (a chair, for example) for something (say, $100) he or she values more. The consumer has given away something, the $100, for something he or she values more, the chair. As long as no coercion is involved, there is no reason to believe that these exchanges are not mutually beneficial.

In such a system those who provide the goods and services on the terms most consumers find attractive should naturally be involved in the most exchanges, whereas those who offer goods on unattractive terms should be involved in the least. Over time, the inefficient producers will fall out of the market. The efficiency of the system, the highest output at the lowest cost, is guaranteed by competition. Furthermore, many people benefit because their preferences ultimately determine what kinds of goods and services are provided and they buy them at the lowest possible cost.

This formulation was fully worked out in the eighteenth century and is usually credited to Adam Smith, who described his theory in his seminal work, *The Wealth of Nations*.[3] The free market formulation was enormously influential because it provided the justification for laissez-faire capitalism and representative democracy, advocates of which were fighting to free societies from the remnants of feudalism and curtail the privileges of the aristocracy. The free market paradigm forms the basis of the individualist ethic so central to American life. The logic of the free market is compelling—give people a chance to produce what they can and those who produce what is most wanted will obtain the greatest rewards. It is both democratic and meritocratic. This seems like a very desirable combination.

Before going further, however, it is necessary to carefully examine the free market paradigm. First, it is a theoretical construct, not an empirical reality. Often, a vast difference exists between actual markets and the free market ideal. Like any theoretical construct, it is based on a number of assumptions. One such assumption is that individuals and businesses behave on the basis of the rational pursuit of self-interest.

Rationality requires knowledge; therefore, to work properly, a market must include consumers who have "perfect knowledge" of what the market has to offer. That is, people must be aware of the alternatives to make rational choices about exchanges into which to enter. Otherwise, inefficient producers might be rewarded, and various other market distortions could occur.

Other necessary conditions are open entry into a market and fair competition among producers. If potential producers are excluded from offering their products to consumers, then innovation becomes less likely and efficiency is jeopardized. Similarly, if certain companies are able to engage in unfair behavior—terrorize competitors, produce at a loss for a long period of time, misrepresent their products to consumers—the free market dynamic is upset, and both production efficiency and consumer utility are compromised. The nature of a free market is quite specific, and actual markets are easily distorted.

Another essential point about the free market paradigm is that it does not prescribe outcomes. One cannot predict the mix of goods and services that will be available in a society using such a model. One can only assume that people know what they want and attempt to establish rules and procedures that will give society as many of the desired goods and services as is possible within the limits imposed by resources, technology, and individual productive capacity. If markets are free and open and people know what is available, goods and services should be allocated in a way that creates the greatest happiness for the greatest number. The desired outcome, happiness or what economists call "utility," is defined by the rules and procedures through which it is realized.

Under the free market paradigm individual freedom is defined as the opportunity that each person has to produce valued commodities and trade them to others for items of value. Giving every individual an equal opportunity to engage in such exchanges is recognized as being necessary if markets are to work properly. Clearly, equality of opportunity was not a reality when the Constitution was first designed, but the free market paradigm convinced many political philosophers and politicians of the validity of the idea of equality of opportunity. If markets were to operate optimally, entry into them had to be free and open; if societies were to be properly ordered, opportunities had to be open to all. When Thomas Jefferson wrote in the Declaration of Independence that "all men are created equal," he meant that all men, except slaves and the indentured, should be free to compete in society for the benefits that were available.

The basic point is that the free market paradigm dominates far more than the discipline of economics and the business sector of American society; it dominates the political and legal spheres as well. American democracy is procedural—it is defined by rules according to which political leaders are chosen by citizens in elections.[4] Its bedrock values— equality of opportunity, freedom of expression, the right to vote, the sanctity of property—spring directly from the free market paradigm. The Constitution elevates these procedural values above all others. Its logic is that justice is defined by procedural guarantees and that maintaining the integrity of procedures is the main task of government. Thus governments have an important but limited role to play in society. Other principal components of the Constitution—separation of powers, checks and balances, and federalism—were designed to limit governmental activity, and are best understood as attempts to protect markets from majority power and minority privilege (see *Federalist* 10).[5]

Procedural democracy is complex, amoral, antitraditional, and vague about certain questions, such as what happens when property rights conflict with other rights. Therefore, it should not be surprising that procedural democracy is not always implemented perfectly. Equality of opportunity, in particular, has been extremely difficult to realize because capitalist societies have allowed accumulated wealth, and the advantages that go with it, to be passed from one generation to the next. Cultural biases also have been stubbornly persistent in the United States. Nevertheless, the commitment of political elites and citizens to the values of procedural democracy has led to a gradual recognition that obvious contradictions to ideals such as equality of opportunity have to be confronted and resolved. Still, the ultimate goals are procedural. American democracy does not stand for equality of condition, only equality of opportunity; it is decidedly inegalitarian in this sense.

Participatory Democracy

Representative/procedural democracy does not place a great deal of value on direct citizen involvement in the making of policy decisions. For many democratic theorists this is a critical shortcoming. Jean-Jacques Rousseau, one of Adam Smith's contemporaries and acquaintances, said about representative government in England: "The people of England regards itself as free, but is grossly mistaken; it is free only during the election of members of parliament. As soon as they are elected, slavery overtakes it, and it is nothing." [6] He prescribed a much more classical form of democracy, in which citizens would make societal laws directly, submerging their self-interest in pursuit of the collective interest or "general will." Participatory democracy is an alternative to procedural democracy.

Interest in participatory forms of democracy is very much alive among contemporary democratic theorists.[7] Jane Mansbridge has written about what she calls "unitary" democracy, which envisions a common good that is separate and distinct from the outcome of the struggle between competitive interests in a political community.[8] Advocates of unitary democracy contend that community forums in which citizens meet face-to-face and work toward consensual solutions to the common problems they face are both feasible and highly desirable. In such settings issues can be framed in such a way as not to be easily divisible into "we" versus "they" dichotomies, and citizens learn how to work toward commonly desired ends.

A classic example of unitary democracy at work is a town meeting in which a question such as drinking water fluoridation is discussed. The issue affects nearly everyone in more or less the same way; advocates on both sides debate the issue face-to-face; most participants are looking for a consensual solution; and preferences are registered publicly without behind-the-scenes maneuvering. This form of democracy is still practiced in rural New England and holds considerable appeal for many Americans.

Participatory forms of democracy emphasize the importance of direct citizen involvement in the policy-making process. This idea is very much a part of American culture, even though relatively few citizens practice participatory democracy. It appeals to Americans in the abstract, but most take part in politics only by voting for representatives. Political reality is dominated by the pursuit of private interests, by affiliations with narrow interest groups, and by legal/adversarial processes and procedures.

Assessing Contemporary Political Culture

Debate about contemporary political culture usually centers on whether Americans in the 1980s and 1990s have become more conservative. Some observers have likened the 1980s to the 1950s, pointing out the prominence of free market, religious, and family-centered values in both eras. The evidence cited most frequently in making the case that the United States has turned to the right includes the presidential victories of Ronald Reagan in 1980 and 1984, and George Bush in 1988; the growing number of people who call themselves Republicans and the party's fund-raising ability; the pervasiveness of conservative policy proposals such as antiabortion legislation and tax limitation referenda; and the increased visibility of groups that espouse traditional values. The American people, it is claimed, tried liberalism in the 1960s and 1970s but found it wanting. During the 1980s they sought to establish a new equilibrium among leading political values, an equilibrium that was more traditional and conservative than that prevailing in the late 1960s and the 1970s.

This argument is backed by some empirical evidence, but it is not entirely persuasive. Conservative politicians and conservative policy ideas were more visible and successful in the 1980s than in the 1970s. The cultural changes taking place appear to be much more subtle and complex than suggested by the statement that Americans are becoming more conservative, however.

One widely cited reason for the rise of conservatism is the alleged collapse of liberalism and its political programs, which dominated the U.S. policy agenda from the 1930s to the 1970s. Modern American liberalism is closely associated with the Democratic party. Liberalism and the Democrats rose to power in the 1930s through New Deal legislation that expanded government involvement in social welfare and the economy. Uniting workers, intellectuals, Southerners, and various ethnic minorities, the Democrats implemented unprecedented social welfare programs and policies. The most conspicuous and enduring law, the Social Security Act, guarantees financial assistance to the elderly, the poor, and the disabled. During the 1960s and early 1970s large Democratic majorities in Congress worked cooperatively with Lyndon Johnson, and combatively with Richard Nixon, to design new government programs in housing, education, welfare, health, employment, civil rights, and environmental regulation.

Criticisms of these second-wave liberal Democratic policies were voiced by politicians, researchers, and citizens from the beginning and eventually grew stronger. Academic studies of social welfare, civil rights, and regulatory programs revealed many serious flaws of theory, design, and execution. Politicians and intellectuals also questioned the morality of liberalism, especially as it applied to abortion, school prayer, sex education, criminal justice, and the threat of communism. By the 1980s few politicians willingly identified themselves as liberals. Instead, they called themselves moderates, pragmatists, progressives, or neoliberals.

Although political leaders no longer labeled themselves liberal, Americans continued to support most liberal programs. Public trust in government institutions and public officials has declined since the 1960s, but support for government benefits remains high. The percentage of Americans who believe that the government will do "what is right" (always, or most of the time) slid from more than 70 percent to 25 percent between 1964 and 1982, but had risen to 42 percent by 1986-1988.[9] Public support for Social Security is very strong: nine Americans in ten cite at least one advantage of the program.[10] Despite years of chronic federal deficits of $200 billion or more, more than 95 percent of the public thought that either too little or about the right amount of money was being spent on Social Security in 1989.[11] By 1990, a majority of Americans (56 percent) favored a national health insurance system.[12]

Since the 1950s public opinion polls consistently have found that Americans like government benefits but do not like to pay for them. In the summer of 1990, 60 percent thought spending for domestic programs should increase, but 79 percent opposed raising federal income taxes.[13]

Some critics of modern liberalism argue that it is not the public's distaste for government spending that undermines liberal programs; rather, the public has become disillusioned with the social and moral values spawned by liberalism. If this argument is correct, it should be reflected in surveys about attitudes on abortion, school prayer, gun control, the death penalty, and racial integration. In fact, liberal attitudes have gained support in most of these areas. For example, support for the Supreme Court's stand on abortion, which guarantees a woman an unrestricted right to terminate a pregnancy during the first trimester, rose from 47 percent in the 1970s to 58 percent in 1989.[14] In 1988, most Americans—nearly 80 percent—opposed state laws prohibiting interracial marriages, but in 1965 only half the population opposed them. In 1988, more than 90 percent of Americans believed that blacks have a right to live anywhere they see fit; in 1960 only 70 percent recognized this right.[15]

The American public has hardened its attitude toward crime and criminals; the number endorsing the death penalty rose from 50 percent in the 1950s to more than 70 percent in 1990.[16] Support for gun control, however, fluctuated—it fell from 69 percent in the 1970s to 59 percent in the early 1980s, but had risen to 78 percent by 1990.[17] Moreover, the public remains committed to certain traditional ideas. Despite the rulings of the Supreme Court, approximately eight citizens in ten support prayer in public schools—a level that has remained constant for decades.[18] The proportion of the public that views religion as "very important" in their lives rose from 52 percent in 1978 to 55 percent in 1989, but remained far below the 70 percent level of the mid-1960s.[19] In a 1986 poll one-third of the respondents described themselves as born-again Christians.[20]

Detailed studies of American values reveal some generational differences on issues of political culture that are closely tied to life experiences and economic conditions. Americans born after World War II are more likely to exhibit what have been labeled "postmaterialist" values. They are more apt than their elders to believe that giving people a say in government decisions, protecting freedom of speech, and improving the environment are more important than curbing inflation, fighting crime, and expanding the economy.[21] These values were somewhat less popular among American youth under age twenty-five in the late 1980s than they were among youth of that age in the 1970s, however.[22] An annual survey of college freshmen in California showed that the percentage of those preparing for a career in business doubled from 12 percent to 24 percent between 1968 and 1987, and the percentage indicating that preserving the environment was important to them fell from 45 percent in 1972 to 16 percent in 1987. By 1990, however, the trend had changed again; interest in business had declined and interest in preserving the environment had increased.[23]

Americans' responses to direct questions about their ideological leanings reveal a very small conservative shift. Those who regard themselves as liberal (from slightly to extremely) declined from 31 percent in 1974 to 28 percent in 1989. Conservative self-identification rose from 30 percent to 33 percent during the same time span. Most Americans place themselves near the center of the ideological spectrum. In 1974, 70 percent of those surveyed saw themselves as moderates or slight liberals or conservatives; the percentage in these categories changed very little during the 1980s.[24]

Changes have occurred in the percentage of Americans calling themselves Republicans, Democrats, and independents. The number who regard themselves as Republicans rose from 23 percent in the mid-1970s to 28 percent after the 1980 election and to 33 percent by 1989. Democratic party affiliation declined from the 45 percent level that was maintained throughout most of the 1970s to 37 percent by 1989.[25] Change during the 1980s was most evident among voters under age thirty; they divided themselves equally (just under 30 percent) among the Democratic and Republican parties in 1988.[26]

Evidence suggests that there was some movement in a conservative direction during the 1980s, but there was no massive or unambiguous change in cultural and political values. The "new conservatism," to the extent that it exists at all as a cultural phenomenon, appears to consist largely of a resurgence of traditional American values, such as individualism, capitalism, distrust of government, and respect for law and order. The rapid cultural changes of the opposite sort—humanism, postmaterialism, permissiveness—that dominated the 1960s and 1970s have receded, but a number of liberal values, such as equal opportunity and concern for the environment, enjoy vast popularity.[27]

The Problematic Economy

The central economic objectives of U.S. policy makers are quite clear and have remained fairly constant for decades: to promote sustained economic growth without price inflation, to maintain low levels of unemployment and poverty, and to attempt to ensure a high standard of living for all American citizens. When unemployment and inflation rise, the cost of government also goes up. A rise of one percentage point in the number of unemployed Americans, for example, costs the Treasury roughly $25 billion in benefit payments and lost tax revenues. But keeping unemployment and inflation low is very difficult. Since 1950, the United States has experienced six recessions—periods when the economy failed to expand for several months or even several years, resulting in high levels of unemployment.

The task of managing the American economy today is growing more difficult. Whether and how government should intervene in the economy has always been a matter of great controversy in American politics—a central dividing line between liberals and conservatives, Democrats and Republicans. Moreover, the economic realities of the 1970s-1990s have shattered many of the old assumptions, increased the stakes of the game considerably, and multiplied the number and difficulty of choices policy makers face.

Government's Role in a Strong Economy

Government economic policy making was easier, and in some ways less critical, when the U.S. economy was expanding at a stable rate during the 1950s and 1960s. Consider the following indicators:

—The economy grew at a healthy rate of 4 percent annually, and per capita income increased by roughly 2 percent each year.

—Productivity growth—the measure of output per person per hour worked—was also impressive; the average annual increase was more than 3 percent.[28]

—Unemployment averaged about 4 percent, and annual inflation rates were seldom more than 2 percent.

—The cost of borrowing money, although gradually rising from a 2 percent interest rate in 1950, did not exceed 4 percent until 1965.

—The economy was running smoothly with slightly less than 60 percent of the adult population in the labor force—more than 85 percent of the men and 35 percent of the women.[29]

Government's role in the economy was fairly uncomplicated, by contemporary standards. When the economy slumped, the government enlarged the supply of money for investors and increased government spending to stimulate growth. Major recessions and accompanying unemployment were thus mitigated or avoided altogether. When a recession hit in 1957-1958, unemployment rose to a postwar high of nearly 7 percent; the federal government increased spending beyond revenues, resulting in a deficit of $13 billion at the end of 1958, also a postwar high. The unemployment rate had dropped to 5.5 percent by the following year.

The main purpose of macroeconomic policy—increasing or decreasing the money supply and the extent of deficit spending—was to maintain high levels of employment by stimulating demand for goods and services. With the economic depression of the 1930s and 1940s not far behind them, policy makers were preoccupied with the problem of unemployment. Joblessness was perceived as a male problem and was closely related to the condition of manufacturing firms, which employed one-third of the work force, compared with about one-sixth in today's economy.

The absence of strong competition for consumer markets by other nations was another fact of economic life in the 1950s and 1960s, when practically all products sold in the United States were manufactured domestically. U.S. exports accounted for one-fourth of all world exports and far exceeded imports.[30]

The American standard of living was the highest of any nation. In 1960 the nation's per capita gross national product (GNP), the monetary value of all goods and services produced in a year,[31] was roughly twice that of Western Europe and six times that of Japan.[32] The United States provided a model of economic strength and prosperity that the entire noncommunist world sought to emulate.

At the end of the 1980s, however, the U.S. economy was no longer the unchallenged economic powerhouse of the industrialized world. Many industrialized nations and several Third World nations had become important economic competitors. For example, in 1986 Japanese companies sold products worth more than $85 billion in the United States, while U.S. sales to Japan totaled only $27 billion.[33] The U.S. trade deficit—the difference between the value of imports and the value of exports—exceeded $160 billion in 1987. (By 1990 the trade deficit had been reduced to $110 billion.) The diminished autonomy of the American economy revealed more clearly than ever the intimate connection between government policy and economic performance. What American policy makers decide about trade and tax matters has a direct bearing on the ability of U.S. corporations to compete in the world market against corporations that are governed by different rules.

The 1950s and 1960s were not free of economic problems. Poverty was quite severe. For more than twenty years after World War II, roughly one American in five lived in poverty by U.S. government standards. In 1960, for example, 40 million Americans—22 percent of the population—were poor. By 1973 the poverty rate had fallen to half of the 1960 level, and it remained at 11 percent to 12 percent for the rest of the decade.[34] The average American's standard of living was much lower in the 1950s and 1960s than in the 1980s. Taking inflation into account, per capita income was roughly half the level achieved in the 1980s and 1990s.

By the 1960s various sectors of society, especially blue-collar workers, the elderly, and the middle class, began to demand a larger slice of the economic pie. The federal government initiated policies aimed at improving the economic well-being of various segments of society. The domestic portion of the federal budget burgeoned as programs for the elderly, the poor, the unemployed, students, veterans, military retirees, and many other groups were either created or enlarged. At the same time, billions of dollars were being spent to fight a war in Vietnam.

Expanding Government's Role

The late 1960s and early 1970s represent a watershed in American policy making, for hundreds of new spending and regulatory programs were established in that period. It was taken for granted that the economy would grow and that sufficient revenues would be produced to sustain these new government endeavors. Policy makers were not spending money lavishly; indeed, many of the new programs had meager budgets. But the political climate in Washington accepted, and in many ways encouraged, the practice of defusing conflicts by creating programs or regulations to satisfy interest groups and voters. The substantial reduction in poverty during the late 1960s and 1970s can be attributed in large part to federal income transfer programs, particularly Social Security.[35]

This flurry of policy initiatives enlarged the federal budget. In 1965 the budget was just under $120 billion—roughly double the 1952 level. Since then the federal budget has been doubling every six to eight years—in 1972, 1978, and 1986. As a percentage of GNP, federal spending rose from 14 percent in 1950 to 18 percent in 1960, to 20 percent in 1970, to 22 percent in 1980, and to 23 percent in 1990. Stimulated by the explosion of federal grant-in-aid programs, state and local government spending also shot up—from $50 billion in 1960 to more than $350 billion by 1980 to $760 billion in 1990. Government was spending more and relying more heavily on individuals to pay for it. Taxpayers began to feel the pinch. Personal income taxes and Social Security payroll taxes accounted for 64 percent of federal revenue in 1963, 77 percent in 1980, and 84 percent in 1990.

The growth in the Social Security program provides an excellent example of how spending can increase dramatically over time as policy makers adjust programs even in seemingly small ways. During the 1960s and 1970s the basic program for the elderly, known as Old Age Survivors Disability Insurance (OASDI), was amended several times. More people were made eligible; benefits were increased; a cost-of-living adjustment was added to offset the erosion in income caused by inflation; and other income security programs, including Supplemental

Security Income (SSI), were created for disadvantaged groups. At the time, these actions were not regarded as radical policy decisions. They were far less controversial than the creation of the Community Action Program, the passage of several civil rights acts, or the enactment of medical insurance programs for the poor (Medicaid) and elderly (Medicare, which became part of Social Security). The cumulative effect of these "modest" adjustments in Social Security became clear later on. The federal government allocated $25 billion to Social Security programs in 1965; by 1975 outlays for Social Security and Medicare had increased to nearly $78 billion. Social Security and Medicare expenditures had jumped to $150 billion by 1980, and were just under $350 billion in 1990.[36]

Changing Political-Economic Problems

Mounting public sector spending was only one dimension of the rapidly changing American economy. More Americans were working than ever before. The labor force expanded from 70 million in 1960 to 107 million in 1980 to nearly 120 million in 1990; and women's participation in the labor force increased dramatically, from just over 30 percent in 1960 to 50 percent by 1980 to 58 percent by 1990. The economy shifted away from the manufacturing of steel, automobiles, and heavy equipment and toward services, such as insurance, banking, and information. Between 1960 and 1990 employment in manufacturing remained fairly stable (17 million in 1960, rising to 20 million by 1980, then falling to 19 million in 1990), but service sector employment jumped to 28 million in 1990 from 7 million in 1960.

Economic troubles began to emerge during the 1970s, as revealed by the following indicators:

—Economic growth slowed to an annual rate of less than 3 percent.
—Annual productivity increases fell to just more than 1 percent.
—Unemployment averaged 6.2 percent—higher than in the 1950s and 1960s.
—Interest rates were just about twice as high as in the previous decade.
—Imports exceeded exports in seven of the ten years.
—Economic growth and productivity in West European countries and Japan were consistently higher than in the United States.
—The standard of living in several West European countries edged ahead of the United States for the first time in thirty years.[37]

Various sectors of the economy reacted to these unfavorable developments by seeking to protect their vital interests. An ever-expanding number of interest groups pressed lawmakers for more government subsidies or protective regulations. Underlying problems in the economy and their implications were ignored by national policy makers. By acceding to the demands of various interest groups, they shielded society from the negative effects of a sputtering, treadmill economy. Americans were running faster—more people working, more money in circulation, higher interest rates—but the economy was going nowhere. The Federal Reserve Board expanded the nation's money supply twice as fast in the 1970s as it had in the 1960s. Government spending consistently exceeded revenues, and the budget deficits mounted. The administrations of Richard Nixon, Gerald Ford, and Jimmy Carter adopted various government policies aimed at curbing spiraling inflation, including outright controls on wages and prices.

The unprecedented combination of high unemployment, rising prices, and mounting interest rates brought economic hardship to millions of Americans and gave rise to a new economic term—stagflation. Inflation became the most dreaded malady in this economy of sorrows, and for good reason. Prices increased by an average of 7.5 percent per year in the 1970s compared with only 2 percent per year during the 1960s. Americans shifted their concern from unemployment to inflation and its effect on their standard of living. Everyone wanted to be protected from the negative effects of inflation: unions bargained for inflation-adjusted wages; senior citizens demanded cost-of-living increases in Social Security programs; management passed price increases along to consumers; and landlords raised rents to offset rising utility bills.

Conditions were ripe for change as the 1980 presidential election approached. The extent of the nation's economic deterioration was clear: inflation surpassed 13 percent; interest rates approached 20 percent; productivity was declining; and 7 percent of the labor force was jobless. In this economic climate, any president would have been hard pressed to achieve reelection. Reagan and the Republicans proposed tax and expenditure reductions that the American middle class found understandable and appealing, and President Jimmy Carter was easily defeated.

Ironically, several of the building blocks in the Reagan administration's economic and government reform program had already been put in place during the last two years of the Carter administration. The Federal Reserve Board, under Chairman Paul Volcker, instituted a stricter monetary policy to choke off inflation. The Carter administration began to loosen government regulations in various sectors of the economy, including the telecommunications and transportation industries. Carter tightened efficiency measures in federally funded welfare programs. His spending priorities were a larger defense budget, freezes or cuts in domestic programs, and a balanced federal budget. These moderate policies reflected a consensus among national policy makers that a new economic order was needed.

There can be no doubt, however, that Reagan's election and the adoption of his economic policies by Congress in 1981 brought about major changes in American politics and the American economy. These policies and their consequences dominated the nation's economic policy agenda in the 1980s. The twin towers of Reagan's economic strategy were the Economic Recovery Tax Act, which slashed personal income taxes by one-quarter over three years, and the Omnibus Budget and Reconciliation Act, which increased defense spending and cut social spending in areas such as government jobs and training, education, and programs for the poor.[38]

This economic strategy was nothing less than audacious. Senate Republican leader Howard Baker called it a "river boat gamble." During the presidential primaries, rival candidate George Bush called it "voodoo economics." Reagan claimed that cutting taxes and domestic spending would invigorate the economy sufficiently to bring in the revenues needed for the continuation of other government programs and for the expansion in military spending.

These predictions were wrong. The economy plunged into the deepest recession in forty years; unemployment exceeded 10 percent in 1982, and the federal deficit increased from $60 billion in 1981 to nearly $200 billion two years later, reaching $220 billion in 1986 and again in 1990. The interest payments on the national debt alone exceeded $100 billion, or about 13 percent of all federal spending, by 1984. (By 1990 such payments had climbed to more than $180 billion.)

One positive result of the painful recession of 1981-1983 was that the inflation genie was put back into the bottle. Inflation fell from double digits in 1979-1981 to 6 percent in 1982 and averaged about 4 percent per year for the rest of the decade. By the end of 1983 an economic recovery was under way—productivity improved substantially and unemployment fell steadily. The American economy of the mid- to late 1980s looked healthy, but by 1990 another recession had set in. Furthermore, large federal deficits continued throughout the 1980s and into the 1990s, imposing a tremendous long-term burden on American citizens and policy makers.

Other problems, less obvious than the deficits, also lurked in the economy of the 1980s. By 1985, as a result of the recession of 1982, the poverty rate had risen to 15 percent (from 11 percent in 1979), which meant that there were 35 million poor Americans. In the remainder of the decade the poverty rate gradually declined, dipping below 13 percent in 1989. But the gap between rich and poor widened during the 1980s, as the more affluent households (top 20 percent) enjoyed a substantial increase in wealth, while the wealth of all others remained about the same. Wealth disparities were especially pronounced along racial lines; the median accumulation of property and other assets by white families in 1988 was more than $43,000, whereas the comparable figures for blacks and Hispanics were $4,200 and $5,500, respectively.[39]

Another problem was the persistence of high real interest rates—the difference between nominal interest rates and the rate of inflation—due in large part to the deficits. When individuals and corporations want to borrow money, they have to pay more for it in part because they are competing with the federal government, which is borrowing billions of dollars to pay for its activities. A significant portion—10 percent to 15 percent—of the government bonds and securities needed to finance the debt is owned by foreign investors. From 1981 to 1984, real interest rates in the United States were very high (more than 8 percent), which increased worldwide demand for the dollar and the value of the dollar relative to most other currencies. As a result, foreign imports were cheaper and U.S. exports more costly and therefore less competitive. This led to the high annual trade deficits ($150 billion to $160 billion) of the mid-1980s. Declining real interest rates in the late 1980s resulted in lower trade deficits, but the need to keep investment in government securities attractive to foreigners continues to limit the Federal Reserve Board's flexibility in adjusting interest rates to cope with changing economic conditions in the United States.

The Third World debt added another dimension to U.S. economic woes. During the 1970s American banks lent a great deal of money at interest rates ranging from 15 percent to 20 percent to many African and South American countries, whose main form of collateral was raw materials—in most cases, crude oil. At that time oil prices were high and had been projected to stay that way. But when the Organization of Petroleum Exporting Countries (OPEC) lost its control over crude oil supplies in the 1980s, oil prices fell precipitously, putting Third World debtor nations in a terrible position. Many of them could not even pay the interest on their loans, let alone the principal. Brazil and Mexico, for example, owed more than $100 billion each to foreign creditors by 1988, and a number of debt-dependent countries were spending more than 50 percent of their income from exports on debt repayment. Major U.S. banks had outstanding loans to developing countries of more than $43 billion in 1989 and were looking to the government for help in finding a solution to this problem.

A Comparative Perspective

The relationship between cultural values, economic conditions, and public policy is particularly apparent when we compare the United

States with other nations of the world. Western industrialized nations have quite different governmental operations and public philosophies that reflect diverse cultural and economic experiences. Consider the difference between the United States and Western Europe 100 years ago. In Europe desirable land had long been held by the wealthiest segments of society, economic mobility was minimal, and a large industrial working class had formed. In the United States the government was practically giving away large tracts of land in the West, frontiers remained to be settled, and large fortunes were being made and lost quickly. An industrial working class, composed mostly of European immigrants, was beginning to form, but most parts of the country remained primarily agrarian. American economic development was greatly influenced by the existence of a large property-owning segment of the population and an expanding middle class. These factors help account for some of the distinctive aspects of American politics and the American economy today: Its large, fairly autonomous private sector, its relatively modest government social welfare spending, and the widespread acceptance of the values of individualism and capitalism.

The social welfare state came relatively late to the United States. Programs to aid sick or injured workers, the elderly and disabled, the unemployed, and new parents were established in Western Europe several decades before they appeared in this country.[40] Nearly all West European countries have universal income support programs for the poor and unemployed and national health insurance systems; these have never taken hold in the United States. Although growth in American social welfare spending since the late 1960s has been comparable to that in Europe and Japan, other Western democratic governments are considerably more generous in providing housing assistance, unemployment benefits, vacation and maternity leaves, and income security for the elderly.[41] The data presented in Table 2-1 demonstrate that the U.S. government taxes its citizens less and spends less money on social welfare purposes—in the form of transfer payments—than most other developed nations.

Because the private sector/free market ethic continues to dominate the political culture and economy of the United States, American policy makers face choices very different from those in other countries. Unlike their European counterparts who may debate refinements in their national health care system, American policy makers are just beginning to take the idea of comprehensive health insurance seriously. Government planning and management are integral to the economies of Japan and many West European countries, but this approach is derided by business leaders and most government officials in the United States.[42]

Table 2-1   Government Expenditures and Tax Revenues in Selected Countries, 1988

Country	Government expenditures as percentage of GDP	Transfer payments as percentage of GDP[a]	Tax revenues as percentage of GDP
France	47	24	43
Japan	34	12	31
Netherlands	52	29	47
Sweden	62	21	55
United Kingdom	41	15	37
United States	32	11	29
West Germany	44	19	41

Source: United Nations, *National Accounts Statistics: Main Aggregates and Detailed Tables, 1988* (New York: United Nations, 1990), Parts 1 and 2.

Note: GDP = gross domestic product, the value of all goods and services produced for final use within each country.

[a]Includes Social Security, social assistance grants, and other social insurance benefits.

Although it is smaller than that of other industrialized nations, the public sector in the United States influences nearly every aspect of the nation's social and economic life. Especially influential is the burgeoning body of federal, state, and local regulatory law that governs public and private behavior. Between 1960 and 1980, the number of federal regulatory agencies doubled—from twenty-eight to fifty-six; their work force grew by 90,000; and their budgets increased threefold. The *Federal Register*, which is a compilation of all government regulations, grew from about 15,000 pages in 1946 to 87,000 pages in 1980.[43]

Similar increases occurred in most of the states. Spheres long regulated by the state and federal governments, such as transportation, food and drug quality, agriculture, occupational licensing, and banking, were joined in the 1960s and 1970s by consumer product safety, air and water pollution, workplace health and safety, automobile safety, and civil rights.

Beginning in the late 1970s, however, the federal government began to deregulate certain industries, including trucking, banking, broadcasting, and the airlines. The Reagan administration relaxed enforcement of strip-mining legislation, affirmative action statutes, and antitrust laws. Regulatory agencies were forced to cope with leaner budgets and fewer employees. The number of pages in the *Federal Register* declined dramatically, as the White House discouraged the passage of new administrative rules and regulations that were opposed by the business community. The regulatory surge of the 1970s was followed by a deregulatory trend in the 1980s that reaffirmed the strong appeal of the free market paradigm.

The sharing of policy responsibilities among different levels of government is characteristic of the American political system. States and localities dominate a number of important policy areas and share others with the federal government. Subnational governmental power is based on a tradition of local self-determination that is older than the country itself, protected by the Constitution, and sustained by individualistic cultural values.

American state and local governments are stronger and more autonomous than their counterparts in most other countries, but it would be a mistake to believe that only in the United States are power and authority vested in subnational governments. Canadian provincial governments have considerable constitutional authority, which gives them a certain measure of autonomy from the national government and superiority over the city governments. Britain and Sweden have unitary, rather than federal, systems, but local governments are important political institutions. In Sweden, large cities such as Stockholm have extensive taxing power. In Britain local powers come through less formal means, such as agreements recognizing local expertise and specifying institutionalized bargaining over certain policy matters. Central government leaders know that they must obtain the support of an extensive network of local public officials to finance and implement education, health, housing, and welfare programs, so they continually negotiate with local officials to secure their cooperation. In both nations the absence of a chief executive at the state or local level is probably the most significant contrast with American states and localities.[44]

Relationships between national and subnational governments undergo change. The independence of state governments from the federal government, which existed in nineteenth-century America, was significantly altered by the New Deal of the 1930s. The liberal Democratic programs of the Great Society in the 1960s and 1970s imposed a host of new national objectives on states and localities. With these sweeping programs, the federal government asserted itself as the leading actor in the intergovernmental system. Grant-in-aid programs and regulatory mandates gave the federal government leverage to alter traditional state and local services and to convince states and localities that they should provide many new ones.

The trend toward greater federal control of policy making and implementation abated during the 1980s. This change came about in part because of a nearly universal recognition that narrow-purpose federal grants led to fragmented and inefficient government services.

Too many programs were attempting to treat related problems without any effective means of coordination. Republican presidents Nixon and Reagan called for a "new federalism," in which states and localities would have more authority and responsibility. Many overlapping, but separately operating, federal aid programs were consolidated into block grant packages; still, most federal grant-in-aid money remained in the narrow-purpose programs known as categorical programs.

It is evident that state governments have grown in stature within the federal system. States have demonstrated their willingness and ability to raise money for public services, and state governments have become more innovative in policy making and in reforms aimed at improving management. It is evident that states have emerged from a long period of dormancy to become more equal partners in the federal system.

Summary

The purpose of this brief review has been to show how two broad forces in American society—political culture and the economy—influence politics, government, and public policy. Political culture determines what people expect of government and what role citizens and politicians play in politics. Economic well-being has been the most consistently important issue in American politics, and economic performance is both a cause and an effect of government policy. Political beliefs and expectations and the economy change over time, and these changes are reflected in the policy agenda of government.

Politics in the 1990s is markedly different from politics in earlier epochs in American history, and different politics means different policies. The United States seems to be entering an era in which limitations in the economy and trade-offs inherent in policy choices will have to be confronted more visibly, and one would hope, more candidly.

If the government tries to control inflation by employing strict monetary policies, for example, that move hurts the export market. Certain sectors of the economy, such as agriculture, feel the effects quickly and forcefully. If the government tries to alleviate the trade deficit by taxing or limiting foreign imports, American consumers pay higher prices for many products. If the government commits large sums of money to national defense or continues to run large deficits, less money will be available for housing, education, medical care, and public works programs. Americans have seen different priorities come and go. During the New Deal period federal government spending was seen as the key to prosperity; the private sector reemerged during Dwight Eisenhower's administration. The government came back with more spending and regulation in the late 1960s and 1970s, then drew back from regulation in the 1980s. Americans may begin to insist on more straight talk from politicians about which combinations of priorities are compatible and which are not.

The American government's response to the challenges of the present and the future will be shaped by cultural and economic developments and by the actions of policy-making institutions. Understanding the peculiarities of and the distinctions among the different domains of politics is central to the study of American public policy. These domains and their policy-making processes are the subject of Part 2.

Notes

1. See Lewis Lipsitz, *American Democracy* (New York: St. Martin's Press, 1986), 31.

2. For a more detailed discussion of American political values and beliefs, see Linda J. Metcalf and Kenneth M. Dolbeare, *Neopolitics: American Political Ideas in the 1980s* (New York: Random House, 1985).

3. Adam Smith, *The Wealth of Nations* (New York: Random House, Modern Library Edition, 1937).

4. The concept of procedural democracy is discussed at length in Ira Katznelson and Mark Kesselman, *The Politics of Power*, 2d ed. (New York: Harcourt Brace Jovanovich, 1979).

5. Alexander Hamilton, John Jay, and James Madison, *The Federalist Papers* (Cambridge, Mass.: Belknap Press, 1966).

6. Jean-Jacques Rousseau, *The Social Contract and Discourses*, trans. G. D. H. Cole (New York: E. P. Dutton, 1950), Book III, 94.

7. See Benjamin R. Barber, *Strong Democracy: Participatory Politics for a New Age* (Berkeley: University of California Press, 1984); and Philip Green, *Retrieving Democracy* (Totowa, N.J.: Rowman & Allanheld, 1985).

8. Jane J. Mansbridge, *Beyond Adversary Democracy* (Chicago: University of Chicago Press, 1983).

9. The 1964 and 1982 figures are from studies by the Center for Political Studies at the University of Michigan. They were also published in the *New York Times*, July 15, 1983, B6; and in William Crotty, *American Parties in Decline*, 2d ed. (Boston: Little, Brown, 1984), 67. The 1986 figure is from the *New York Times*, January 28, 1986, A1, A14. The 1988 figure is from *American National Election Survey: Pre- and Post-Election Survey*, Warren E. Miller, principal investigator, Center for Political Studies, University of Michigan, 1st ICPSR ed., Summer 1989.

10. See Paul Light, *Artful Work: The Politics of Social Security Reform* (New York: Random House, 1985), 59.

11. *General Social Survey, 1972-1989* (Chicago: National Opinion Research Center, University of Chicago, 1989).

12. *The Public Perspective*, ed. Everett C. Ladd, March-April 1991, 7.

13. *The Public Perspective*, ed. Everett C. Ladd, July-August 1990, 82.

14. George H. Gallup, *Gallup Poll 1972-1977* (Wilmington, Del.: Scholarly Resources, 1978), 247; *Gallup Report* no. 281, February 1989, 21.

15. See Crotty, *American Parties in Decline*, 67-68; *American National Election Survey*, Summer 1989.

16. Gallup, *Gallup Poll 1972-1977*, 583; CBS News/*New York Times* poll, September 13, 1990.

17. *The Gallup Poll Monthly* no. 300, September 1990, 34.

18. *Gallup Report* no. 177, April-May 1980, 11; *Gallup Report* no. 217, October 1983, 18; *American National Election Survey*, Summer 1989.

19. *Gallup Report* no. 259, April 1987, 12-14; *The Gallup Poll Monthly* no. 292, January 1990, 34.

20. *Gallup Report* no. 259, 28.

21. Ronald Inglehart, "Post-Materialism in an Environment of Insecurity," in *American Political Science Review* 75 (December 1981): 880-900.

22. Ibid., 888.

23. "More College Freshmen Plan to Teach," *New York Times*, January 12, 1987, A15; Larry Gordon, "College Poll Finds Spirit of Activism," *Los Angeles Times*, January 22, 1990, A3.

24. Depending on how the question is worded, different polling organizations come up with slightly different results regarding American ideological distribution. Overall, the findings of Gallup, the National Opinion Research Center, and the Center for Political Studies are quite similar. For an extended discussion, see *General Social Survey, 1972-1989*.

25. *General Social Survey, 1972-1989*.

26. *American National Election Survey*, Summer 1989.

27. For a thorough discussion, see Howard Gold, *Hollow Mandates: American Public Opinion and the Conservative Shift* (Boulder, Colo.: Westview Press, forthcoming).

28. *Business Week*, special issue, "The Reindustrialization of America," June 30, 1980, 10.

29. Unless otherwise indicated, the statistics provided in this section (including those for 1986-1988) were taken from tables in the appendixes to the *Economic Report of the President*, prepared annually by the Council of Economic Advisers. See *Economic Report of the President* (Washington, D.C.: Government Printing Office, 1986, 1987, 1988, 1991).

30. *Business Week*, "The Reindustrialization of America," 6-7.

31. Gross national product (GNP) differs from gross domestic product (GDP), another measure of national economic output, in that GNP includes the profits and income of American corporations and individuals that are operating abroad, but does not count the profits and income of foreigners or foreign-owned corporations operating in the United States. GDP includes the latter but does not include the former.

32. Robert B. Reich, in *The Next American Frontier* (New York: Penguin Books, 1983), cites Organization for Economic Cooperation and Development data on this point; see footnote, p. 285.

33. *New York Times*, January 17, 1988, E4.

34. See Harrell R. Rodgers, Jr., *The Cost of Human Neglect* (Armonk, N.Y.: M. E. Sharpe, 1982), 18.

35. See Lawrence E. Lynn, Jr., "A Decade of Policy Developments in the Income Maintenance System," in *A Decade of Federal Antipoverty Programs*, ed. Robert H. Haveman (New York: Academic Press, 1977), 88-95.

36. Figures are from *Economic Report of the President*, 1986; and Bureau of the Census, *Statistical Abstract of the United States 1975*, 95th ed. (Washington, D.C.: Government Printing Office, 1974).

37. Reich, *The Next American Frontier*, 285.

38. See Gregory B. Mills, "The Budget: A Failure of Discipline," in *The Reagan Record*, ed. John L. Palmer and Isabel V. Sawhill (Cambridge, Mass.: Ballinger, 1984), 111-114.

39. See Robert Pear, "Rich Got Richer in 80s; Others Held Even," *New York Times*, January 11, 1991, A1, A20.

40. Rodgers, *The Cost of Human Neglect*, 104-107.

41. Ibid., 57, 103-125; and Ira C. Magaziner and Robert B. Reich, *Minding America's Business* (New York: Harcourt Brace Jovanovich, 1982), 11-27.

42. The low regard for economic planning on the part of American policy makers is documented by Ross K. Baker in "The Bittersweet Courtship of Congressional Democrats and Industrial Policy" (Paper delivered at the annual meeting of the Midwest Political Science Association, Chicago, April 10-12, 1986).

43. Norman J. Ornstein, Thomas E. Mann, and Michael J. Malbin, *Vital Statistics on Congress, 1989-1990* (Washington, D.C.: CQ Press, 1990), 160.

44. Robert Lineberry and Ira Sharkansky, *Urban Politics and Public Policy*, 3d ed. (New York: Harper & Row, 1978), 33-44.

SIX POLICY
DOMAINS

PART II

Part II is the core of the book. We use six "domains" to illustrate the process, substance, and consequences of American public policy. The goal of these six chapters is to equip readers with analytical tools with which they can examine contemporary public policies and assess the behavior of political institutions. The chapters are arranged to take the reader from those institutional settings where issue salience is lowest and the scope of conflict most narrow—boardroom politics—to those where issue salience is highest and the scope of conflict most broad—living room politics. It may be useful to think of a spectrum, ranging from highly private decision making by corporate elites to highly public decision making by ordinary citizens, with decision making by government officials falling somewhere in between.

Chapter 3 develops the domain of boardroom politics as a metaphor for important policy decisions that are largely delegated to the private sector. In some cases, the existence of a government regulatory agency conceals the fact that the industry actually regulates itself with limited government oversight. In other instances, the illusion of government oversight is replaced by the illusion of competition, which conceals the existence of powerful oligopolies. Either set of circumstances means that hidden costs are imposed on consumers and workers. Low salience and high complexity of issues permit these costs without triggering a public outcry.

Chapter 4 introduces the domain of bureaucratic politics, decision making by the bureaucrats who work in and run the government's administrative agencies, both social service and regulatory. Although government agencies exist to carry out the laws, few administrative agencies are truly responsive to the general public. Instead they are most often responsive to clientele groups or to those agencies they are supposed to regulate. Indeed, responding to the public at large is less important to most bureaucrats than adhering to standard operating procedures and deeply ingrained professional norms.

Chapter 5 develops the domain of cloakroom politics as a metaphor for politics dominated by Congress, state legislatures, and city councils. Legislative politics is less predictable and more volatile than other forms of politics. At different times and in different issue areas, there is frequently evidence of symbolic responsiveness and policy responsiveness. Depending on the circumstances, one can observe incrementalism, small changes generally increasing government involvement in a policy area; gridlock, the failure to reach agreement on major public problems; and innovation, sometimes leading to substantial and sweeping policy change.

Chapter 6 focuses on chief executive politics as a metaphor for decision making by presidents, governors, mayors, and their advisers. The chief executive's special strengths include crisis management and policy initiation. That is not to say that chief executives consistently make good decisions in a crisis, only that they can and do make quick decisions. Chief executives' policy initiatives frequently are responsive to majority preferences, but they can encounter stiff opposition on the road to implementation. Chief executives try to shape majority preferences when possible, relying on symbolic responsiveness to provide a protective shield when their personal values do not coincide with the apparent values of the general public.

Chapter 7 develops the domain of courtroom politics or judicial policy making. Most court rulings are not policy-making actions but responses to grievances between two parties. Judges occasionally make policy, however, and when they do, their decisions are often innovative, creative, and costly. Unlike the legislative branch, courts are political institutions capable of redistributing benefits without concealing the magnitude of the costs, and capable of innovating without concealing the magnitude of change. Minorities frequently are the beneficiaries of judicial intervention, although it is worth noting that minorities may include not only women, blacks, and the handicapped, but also private corporations, criminals, and extremists.

Chapter 8 explores the domain of living room politics as a metaphor for the interplay between the mass media and public opinion on highly salient and highly conflictual issues. The argument will be advanced that public opinion, when aroused, must be satisfied. The termination of U.S. involvement in Vietnam and the resignation of President Richard Nixon are events that ultimately reflected public disenchantment with the behavior of the president of the United States. Ballot initiatives and referenda in pursuit of tax reductions or restraints on nuclear power show how citizens also can motivate significant state policy changes. Although living room politics is reserved for a select number of issues, it is a powerful force. Without living room politics, politicians would be less responsive to majority preferences than is currently the case.

3 Boardroom Politics

Social scientist Harold Lasswell once defined politics as "who gets what, when, and how." [1] By that definition, many private sector decisions are as political as those made by government officials. When a steel company shuts down a coke oven, the consequences for workers, their families, and the local community can be devastating. When a paper mill discharges poisonous chemicals into the atmosphere or a nearby stream, the consequences for public health may be severe. When a hospital decides to invest in expensive lifesaving equipment, such as emergency helicopters, the hospital may save many lives, but it may also raise its prices. When a business chooses to donate 5 percent of its pretax profits to charity, numerous nonprofit organizations may benefit, but the government may collect less tax money. In each of these cases, private organizations decide who gets what, when, and how.

To describe private decision making that has public consequences, the metaphor "boardroom politics" will be used here to refer to decisions made by private organizations, usually corporations, with limited government control. Some of these decisions are literally made in corporate boardrooms; others are made at lower levels by corporate managers, subject to constraints imposed by a board of directors. The private sector is not monolithic in its structure, norms, or purposes. There are important differences between publicly held and privately held companies, nonprofit and for-profit organizations, big corporations and small businesses, monopolies and competitive entities. Despite these differences, one statement is true of all private corporations: They have an enormous impact on the daily lives of all Americans. Charles Lindblom wrote that the role of the private sector is vital not just in the United States but in all market-oriented societies. "Corporate executives in all private enterprise systems . . . decide a nation's industrial technology, the pattern of work organization, location of industry, market structure, resource allocation, and, of course, executive compensation and status." [2]

The role of the private sector is especially significant in the United States. We can conclude from Table 2-1 in the previous chapter that the private sector accounted for about 68 percent of the gross domestic product in the United States in 1988, whereas in the United Kingdom the figure was 59 percent and in France it was 53 percent. The overwhelming majority of Americans, approximately 82 percent, are employed by the private sector. Other Western democracies are less reliant on private employment: in the United Kingdom, in the mid-1980s, almost 69 percent of all workers were privately employed; in Sweden, almost 62 percent were (see Table 3-1). In the United States, many vital industries are controlled primarily or exclusively by the private sector. These include railroads, airlines, electric companies, telephone companies, oil producers, automobile manufacturers, and mail delivery companies. In Western Europe many of these industries are controlled by government.

Moreover, the private sector in the United States is growing as a result of privatization and deregulation. Privatization, the transfer of service delivery functions from the public sector to the private sector, is spreading at the state and local levels. For example, approximately 35 percent of U.S. cities contract with private companies for refuse collection.[3] In some states, this practice is extensive. In New Jersey more than half of the municipalities contract for refuse collection; nearly as many arrange to have road construction and maintenance and solid waste disposal provided by private companies.[4] Contracting for social services, usually with nonprofit organizations, is also widespread. Almost half of the states contract for mental health services; in some states 90 percent of mental health funds are spent this way.[5] Other social services are also provided through contracts, including employment services, child abuse centers, nursing homes, day care centers, drug abuse clinics, and half-way houses for parolees. Privatization has advanced more slowly at the federal level, despite support from the Reagan and Bush administrations.

Deregulation, the relaxation of government standards and requirements, has proceeded much more rapidly at the federal level. During the Carter and Reagan administrations, Congress took steps to deregulate the airline, trucking, and financial industries. The Civil Aeronautics Board (CAB) was abolished, barriers to entry into the trucking industry were reduced, and savings and loan institutions were given greater freedom—for example, to issue credit cards and make consumer loans. Congress also deregulated the price of oil and natural gas. The Federal Communications Commission (FCC) relaxed government regulation of the broadcasting industry by eliminating limits on commercial time and by issuing licenses for longer periods of time. The FCC's role in regulating AT&T was reduced, as a result of an antitrust settlement that permits AT&T to compete with IBM and other computer companies in the lucrative data-processing market.

Table 3-1   Public Employment in Six Western Nations (in percent)

Country	Public employees/ all employees	Private employees/ all employees
France	32.6	67.4
Italy	24.4	75.6
Sweden	38.2	61.8
United Kingdom	31.4	68.6
United States	18.3	81.7
West Germany	25.8	74.2

Source: Richard Rose et al., *Public Employment in Western Nations* (New York: Cambridge University Press, 1985). Reprinted by permission.

More broadly, the Reagan and Bush administrations discouraged government regulation by requiring, for example, that administrative agencies submit cost-benefit studies to the Office of Management and Budget (OMB) before adopting major rules and regulations. This requirement has often been waived when an agency proposes a deregulatory rule. In this way, Republican administrations have discouraged administrative rule making except for the purpose of reducing controls on the private sector. As a result of these trends, the power of the private sector in American politics has grown.

Corporate Concerns

An agenda, whether corporate or governmental, consists of items or issues thought to warrant serious attention. The building blocks of corporate agendas differ from those of government agendas. The question that faces a private corporation is not whether to make changes in health policy or energy policy or transportation policy, but whether to focus most of its efforts on finance, management, or public relations. Within these broad categories, further choices must be made: whether to concentrate on diversification, modernization, product quality, expansion, or labor relations in order to achieve profit objectives; or to concentrate on advertising, customer relations, community relations, or government affairs. Although the typical business carries on all these activities at once, the emphasis given to one area or another varies considerably.

The Bottom Line

Corporate priorities may be inferred from corporate behavior, but executives also speak for themselves. When they do so, they reveal a preoccupation with profits, the proverbial "bottom line." As the editors of *Fortune* magazine discovered in their 1986 survey of 500 chief executive officers, corporate heads think mainly about financial matters and far less about product quality, customer relations, or employee relations (see Table 3-2).[6] They also think more about higher profits than about market share. These findings suggest that profitability is an overriding objective for most corporate executives, but that other issues can become priorities when they are seen as important means to the basic end of higher or sustained profits.

The fact that corporate executives care mainly about profits does not necessarily make their decisions easy. They must make complicated choices about how to juggle priorities in order to achieve their profit objectives. Corporate agendas are not limited to a single issue, any more than legislative, judicial, or executive agendas are. It should come as no surprise, then, that the priorities established by some corporations do not adequately anticipate all the difficulties they face down the road.

Consider the case of U.S. Steel, now known as USX. During the 1950s and 1960s, steel executives concentrated on profit margins and labor relations. Instead of opting for modern techniques, such as continuous casting and basic oxygen furnaces, U.S. Steel retained open-hearth furnaces and traditional production methods that were becoming obsolete. The Japanese, setting long-term goals, made the most of new technologies. U.S. Steel's ability to compete with the Japanese and other nations decreased to such an extent that company executives decided to concentrate more on oil and gas production than on steel manufacturing. Seventy-three percent of the company's revenues came from steel in 1978, but that figure dropped to 33 percent in 1985.[7] U.S. Steel, once the mightiest steel company in the world and a symbol of American know-how, is now only halfheartedly committed to the steel business.

Some companies neglect certain issues because they are preoccupied with other matters; other companies neglect issues because they doubt their importance or see no advantage in dealing with them. For example, many companies neglect the mental and physical health of their employees because they fail to perceive a connection between employee health and productivity. (The awareness of this connection is increasing as more commercial mental and physical health services try to sell the message that health and productivity are linked.) As union membership has declined, from approximately 19 million in 1977 to about 17 million in 1990, the ability of organized labor to sensitize companies to employee concerns has also diminished. Some companies neglect environmental impact, despite laws aimed at regulating it, because they do not wish to incur cleanup costs. As punishment, they may pay a fine, but only if the

Table 3-2   Most Important Objectives of Chief Executive
Officers (CEOs)

Objective	Percentage of CEOs citing objectives
Improve profits, earnings	36.7
Growth	21.9
Improve returns to shareholders	11.1
Employee development	8.8
Long-term planning, strategy	6.4
Control costs, improve productivity	4.5
Improve product/service quality	3.9
Restructure company	3.9
Provide for management succession	3.7
Other	27.8

Source: Maggie McComas, "Atop the Fortune 500: A Survey of C.E.O.s," Fortune, April 28, 1986, 29. Reprinted by permission.

government discovers the violation and vigorously enforces the law.

The mass media occasionally bring neglected issues to the public's attention because layoffs, environmental degradation, and threats to worker safety make good stories. But the media have shown less interest in exposing the potential shortcomings of the communications industry. Consider the question of cross-media ownership, the joint ownership of a newspaper and a broadcasting station in the same community. In January 1975 the FCC announced a major decision, allowing most newspaper-broadcasting combinations to remain intact despite concerns that cross-media ownership undermines diversity in the flow of news. Many of the nation's leading newspapers failed to report this story. Many of those that covered it failed to mention that their newspaper owned a local broadcasting station.[8] Clearly, some issues will remain buried if companies find it convenient to ignore them.

Agenda Determination

Corporate executives are the principal determiners of corporate agendas. As long as the company prospers, corporate managers are free to chart a course for the future. When earnings decline or a crisis erupts, board members intervene in an effort to get the company back on track. Board meetings can provide opportunities for members to establish new priorities, but this is often difficult, in part because top corporate executives usually sit on the board. The board meeting typically is the final step in a long, protracted process, however. Like a congressional debate, a board meeting is the culmination of a long series of discussions, of maneuvers and countermaneuvers, bargains, double crosses, and power plays. The meeting may be only a formality because the "decision" has been made. When the board of the Chrysler Corporation met in the spring of 1991, the company was in the midst of an eighteen-month sales slump, and desperately in need of a new loan from a group of thirty-eight banks from which it regularly borrowed. In order to convince the banks that the corporation was serious about reducing costs, the board voted to cut the dividend paid to investors in half (saving $33 million per quarter). Some weeks later the banks extended Chrysler a new $1.7 billion line of credit.[9]

Prior to important board meetings, managers may attempt to mobilize support to stave off a policy change or a coup d'état. An embattled Steve Jobs, then-chairman of Apple computers, threw a dinner party in the spring of 1985, with an influential board member as the guest of honor.[10] Jobs, whose position was in jeopardy, hoped to persuade the board member to rally to his cause. When the board member merely picked at his whole wheat pizza, Jobs began to see the handwriting on the wall. A Silicon Valley board member with no appetite for whole wheat pizza is like a steel worker who turns down a beer; it does not happen unless something is fundamentally wrong.

Corporate agendas are also influenced by the policies, schemes, and strategies of company rivals. In the early 1980s, Ford Motor Company decided to offer a five-year/50,000-mile warranty, and Chrysler had to swallow its pride or up the ante. Chrysler opted for one-upmanship, offering a seven-year/70,000-mile warranty. When one company hits upon a successful marketing strategy (as the Wendy's hamburger chain did by asking "Where's the beef?"), its competitors must react. Until they solve this problem by coming up with a snappy response or another scheme, marketing will be high on their agenda. Corporations have also thrown each other into a tizzy by staging takeover attempts. If unwelcome, they are referred to as "hostile" takeovers. Ted Turner proposed to take over CBS, forcing a transformation in the network's agenda. For weeks CBS was preoccupied with preventing the takeover. CBS eventually succeeded but later found it necessary to undertake a major management shake-up and massive layoffs.

Corporate agendas also may be shaped by government officials. President Lyndon Johnson issued Executive Order 11246 in 1965 and placed affirmative action on the agendas of businesses throughout the nation. Johnson's order prohibited discrimination by government contractors and established a compliance office to ensure cooperation. Because most sizable companies do some business with the government, Johnson's executive order guaranteed that affirmative action would receive serious attention in corporate boardrooms across the land. By offering lucrative contracts to companies willing to design and develop new weapons systems, the Defense Department also has been successful in shaping corporate agendas and in influencing university agendas. Corporate scientists and academics throughout the United States are engaged in research on space, defense, agriculture, energy, and environmental projects funded by the federal government.

Ordinary citizens do not play a significant part in setting corporate agendas, but they have been responsible for a number of highly visible agenda-setting efforts. By mobilizing activist shareholders, concerned citizens have attempted to shape corporate agendas through proxy resolutions that address important social issues—civil rights, corporate responsibility, apartheid in South Africa.[11] One highly publicized effort was Campaign GM, organized by Ralph Nader. With the support of the Securities and Exchange Commission (SEC), Campaign GM placed two proposals before the General Motors board: to increase the size of the board and to create a shareholders committee. The hope was that these reforms would increase consumer influence at GM. Neither proposal was adopted; indeed, no public interest proxy proposal opposed by management has ever passed. Nevertheless, in several instances, corporate managers have made modest concessions in return for an agreement by shareholder activists to withdraw their proxy resolutions.

The Public-Private Spectrum

Thus far corporations have been considered as a class. There are, however, differences among corporations, and these differences, apparent in policy making, are also apparent in agenda setting. Some businesses "affected with a public interest" [12] are more vulnerable to public pressure than most; other businesses, whose stock is not publicly traded, are less vulnerable than most. In between are those corporations with which the public is most familiar—corporations whose stock is traded but that are free to set prices as they please (see Table 3-3).

Public utilities, at one end of the spectrum, are businesses affected with a public interest. These are usually what some economists call "natural monopolies"—companies that supply services more efficiently if they face no competition. It is generally accepted that the rates natural monopolies charge for their services should be set by government officials to keep prices at a reasonable level. A classic example of a natural monopoly is a regional electric utility company; in nearly all parts of the country the rates such companies charge customers are determined by state public utility commissions. New ideas (like deregulation) and technologies have complicated the realm of so-called natural monopolies, however. In 1982, Congress decided that long-distance telephone services should no longer be monopolized by AT&T. Earlier

*Table 3-3   The Public-Private Spectrum: Degree of
             Government Influence*

Very low	Fairly low	Fairly high	Very high
privately held firms and foundations (Cargill, Inc., the Ford Foundation)	publicly held firms: competitive firms and oligopolies (the funeral industry, the auto industry)	publicly held firms: monopolies (investor-owned public utilities)	government corporations (TVA, U.S. Postal Service, municipal utilities, etc.)

Congress had decided there was enough competition in the energy industry and that natural gas companies should operate with less price regulation. A newer industry, cable television, was treated like a public utility, with city councils setting rates, until 1984, when Congress decided that cable television companies should be allowed to set their own rates.

The agendas of public utilities are subject to control by government officials because government regulators have considerable influence over their revenues, allowable costs, and profit margins. Regulators decide whether to grant a utility company's rate hike request in full or in part. A "stingy" public utility commission, in effect, places revenue requirement issues on a company's agenda; a "generous" commission enables a utility company to concentrate on other issues, such as expansion or diversification.

At the other end of the public-private spectrum are privately held companies, whose stock is not publicly traded but is held by family members or employees. These companies have considerable discretion in what they do and when they do it. In contrast to other companies, privately held companies need not hold an annual public meeting and need not submit extensive financial data to the SEC. Of course, most of these companies are quite small (fewer than twenty-five employees), but privately held companies account for approximately one-half of total employment in the United States.[13]

Foundations, which exist to dispense money to favored causes, constitute a small subset of private organizations that have extraordinary flexibility in setting their agendas. Although bequests sometimes impose constraints, foundations are usually free to set priorities and to change direction rapidly. The Ford Foundation, for example, announced in 1966 a major effort to promote equal opportunity for blacks in politics, education, employment, and housing. Over the next two decades, Ford supported civil rights litigation through grants to the Lawyers' Committee for Civil Rights under Law, the NAACP Legal Defense Fund, and other groups. Ford also supported a variety of educational and advocacy efforts aimed at improving conditions for black Americans.

Many citizen groups owe their origins to seed money from foundations. Political scientist Jack Walker noted that 39 percent of citizen groups formed during the postwar era received foundation grants at the time of founding.[14] Without the timely support of leading foundations, many civil rights groups and environmental groups probably would not exist; others would have vanished by now. Many conservative think tanks also depend upon foundation support. Think tanks such as the American Enterprise Institute, the Heritage Foundation, and the Reason Foundation helped to place deregulation, privatization, and a variety of other conservative causes on the government's agenda in the 1970s and 1980s. Through grants to nonprofit organizations, foundations also have transformed the agendas of city councils, state legislatures, and Congress, as nonprofit groups have promoted long-neglected political causes from civil rights to homelessness.

Corporate Governance

Boardroom politics is more hierarchical than cloakroom politics, more competitive than bureaucratic politics, and more volatile than courtroom politics. It is less visible than chief executive politics and living room politics but more pervasive than both. The scope of conflict—or the extent of public involvement—is relatively narrow, not because the stakes are low, but because the issues are regarded as being outside the government's jurisdiction and away from the public eye. As former White House chief of staff Donald Regan once put it, "Businessmen, for the most part, are not used to the glare of publicity." [15] In fact, there is a dramatic gap between the importance of boardroom politics and the degree of public involvement in it. Although boardroom politics has become more visible and more controversial since the 1960s, it is still largely private.

Who Has the Power?

American corporations wield considerable power and enjoy substantial autonomy. Nevertheless, no corporation is an island. Public utilities operate under constraints imposed by government regulators. Publicly held corporations take the interests and demands of their stockholders into account. All corporations and privately held companies must be sensitive to market forces. During times of upheaval, corporations find themselves responding to social movements, if only to deflect them. During times of crisis, corporations respond to appeals by political leaders that the "national interest" or the "public interest" requires their cooperation. During World War II, for example, corporations stopped producing consumer goods and mobilized to build ships, tanks, and aircraft.

Increasingly, corporations must be sensitive to the wishes and machinations of certain investors, including institutional investors and corporate raiders. Institutional investors include banks, insurance companies, universities, and other entities with substantial stock portfolios. These institutional investors, more aware and active than ever before, wield power by threatening to sell their stock unless corporate policies change. In the 1980s, corporate raiders, such as Carl Icahn and T. Boone Pickens, became powerful players. Raiders frequently created waves within their target companies and throughout the stock market by letting it be known they intended to take over. In some cases takeover artists resorted to "greenmail" as part of an "unfriendly" takeover attempt: the raiding company offered to sell its stock, in a deal not offered to other stockholders, to the target company. In return for this lucrative buyout, the raider agreed to drop the hostile takeover bid. Some corporations paid a high price to prevent takeovers. To foil James Goldsmith's takeover attempt, Goodyear was forced to sell its energy operations. CBS had to reduce its staff because it had spent so much money fighting Ted Turner's takeover attempt.

Despite pressure from investors and public officials, corporations have considerable autonomy, in large part because they have legal rights that protect them from politicians, bureaucrats, and judges. Government laws and regulations frequently pose obstacles and challenges to corporate officials, but such leaders are usually well equipped (with lawyers, lobbyists, and money) to meet these challenges. Moreover, corporate power can be highly concentrated. A relatively small number of corporations controls a relatively high percentage of certain markets. Highly concentrated industries include aircraft production, heavy electrical equipment, synthetic rubber, metal cans, organic fibers, explosives, tobacco, beet sugar, and flat glass.[16] Moreover, power within corporations tends to be concentrated in the hands of a few individuals, including the company's chief executive officer, chief financial officer, president, and board chairman.

The archetype for sociologist Max Weber's hierarchical model of organization was the government bureaucracy, but the modern corporation comes closer to his ideal type than the modern government bureaucracy. As previously noted, the bureaucracy's chain of command is blurred by the fact that it has multiple sovereigns. In addition, the bureaucracy's political executives must bargain with career executives; they cannot simply issue an order and wait for it to be carried out. Top corporate officials can behave more autocratically if they wish to do so. Private corporations normally operate with a clear chain of command and fixed responsibilities.

Wizards and Whales

There is no such thing as a corporate leader for all seasons because corporations differ in their dependence on sound management, creative experimentation, public favor, and government support. Some corporations require leaders who can play an "insider" game, that is, people who excel at organizational management. Others require leaders who can play an "outsider" game, that is, those who excel at public relations. If demand for a product or service is stable and a company's market share is secure, an insider game may be sufficient. A more volatile situation may require greater reliance on an outsider game.

There are different types of outsider games. In some instances, corporate leaders must win the support of customers; in others, they must curry the favor of government officials. Public utilities do not have to worry a great deal about marketing strategies because the demand for their product is fairly stable; but they must be mindful of their image in the regulatory community, for regulators determine what rates they may charge. In contrast, television stations, protected to some extent by the First Amendment, are subject to rather light-handed government regulation, but they must constantly be concerned about the popularity of their programming, because advertising revenue is directly dependent on market share or ratings.

Corporate leadership styles are highly diverse. Whitney MacMillan, chief executive officer and chairman of the board of Cargill, the largest grain company in the world, maintains a very low profile outside the company. He is, by choice, a rather mysterious figure, a sort of Wizard of Oz—one hears about his great deeds and accomplishments but seldom sees the man in the flesh. As the head of a privately held company, MacMillan is free to refuse requests for press conferences, interviews, and public apologies. Henry Hillman, president of the privately held company that bears his name, cultivates the same leadership style. In a rare interview, Hillman explained why he seldom grants interviews: "A whale is harpooned only when it spouts." [17]

Other corporate executives spout all the time. Lee Iacocca, Chrysler's chairman, personifies the corporate executive as impresario. More visible than any other corporate leader in America, Iacocca routinely takes to the airwaves with a direct message: "If you can find a better buy than Chrysler, buy it!" Iacocca's style is bold, direct, forceful, and flamboyant. It reflects his irrepressible personality and the special challenges he faces inspiring confidence in investors, creditors, and consumers in a company that faced bankruptcy in the late 1970s and near bankruptcy in the early 1990s. Ed Woolard, chairman of the board and chief executive officer of the Du Pont Company, recognizes the need for high visibility and public support in his effort to keep Du Pont profitable. Du Pont, the nation's largest chemical company and one of its largest polluters, is an obvious target of environmentalists. But Woolard, who refers to himself as the company's "chief environmentalist," has been able to blunt some of the criticism by making concessions (agreeing to stop production of chlorofluorocarbons by the year 2000), increasing monitoring efforts to detect leaks and other unplanned environmental hazards from Du Pont facilities, and developing recycling and other technologies that protect the environment. Some of Woolard's plans, however, have raised eyebrows among Du Pont's industrial customers who worry that some of their favorite chemicals (like chlorofluorocarbons used in refrigerators and air conditioners) will be pulled off the market suddenly in an effort to assuage environmentalists. Woolard's success in managing the complex set of forces that surround his business is demonstrated by the corporate bottom line—Du Pont's earnings grew steadily in the 1980s.[18]

Woolard and Iacocca may represent special cases because of their companies' central importance to the American economy and their extensive involvement with the government. Some observers perceive a trend toward low-profile chief executive officers who resist the cult of personality.[19] This seems especially likely now that Wall Street firms have retreated from their high-profile images and large bonuses of the 1980s, and chief executive officers around the country have sought to distance themselves from the high-roller image of savings and loan executives who brought widespread bankruptcy to that industry. It seems, then, that the insider game will become more common as a corporate leadership strategy.

Decision Making

Within corporations many decisions are made by managers, with minimal input from boards of directors; other decisions are made by boards, despite opposition from managers. As a general rule, managers are free to make strategic decisions as long as the bottom line is favorable. When the corporation begins to flounder, board members intervene. In short, corporate boards are most active in times of crisis.

If boards are seldom dominant, they are nevertheless more important than they used to be. Corporate boards were once regarded as little more than rubber stamps; decisions were made by top managers and then were simply ratified by members of the board. The role of the board, it seemed, was to legitimate management decisions and to convince investors that the corporation was in fact being guided, or at least monitored, by a distinguished panel of leading citizens.

Since the early 1980s, this practice has begun to change, not dramatically perhaps, but noticeably. First, boards are now much more diverse demographically. Women and minorities in growing numbers now sit on boards, which means a greater variety of viewpoints and more lively debates on topics such as affirmative action. A lone black person on a corporate board may not be able to win a showdown vote, but, as most boards prefer to operate by consensus, the first response to a protest by a minority board member is likely to be a search for a compromise.

Second, boards have given greater representation to outsiders—bankers, lawyers, and others who do not work for the company. According to one estimate, about 65 percent of corporate directors are outsiders,[20] meaning that managers occupy fewer seats than before. Although many of these outsiders are handpicked by the managers, the potential for dissent is greater than it used to be.

A third trend is to place limits on interlocking directorates in which board members are selected from institutions that have official dealings with the company, such as banks, insurance companies, or law firms. The collapse of Penn Central raised questions about such interlocking directorates because a number of Penn Central board members were bankers and shippers with potential conflicts of interest. A different board might not have saved the hapless Penn Central, but a truly unbiased board might be able to head off disaster for another company in the future.

The significance of these trends is that corporate boards, more than ever before, are in a position to voice vigorous dissent, to challenge management decisions, and to identify the corporation's best interest without regard to personal circumstances. These trends increase the potential leverage of boards over managers. The dissent of the board can be dealt with in a variety of ways, however. In March of 1991 both Chrysler and Sears voted to reduce the size of their boards—moves that appeared to be motivated by a desire to limit dissent. In the case of Chrysler, one of the seats that was eliminated belonged to United Auto Workers chief Owen Bieber; in the Sears case, reducing the board from fifteen to ten members was seen as a way of making it more difficult for dissident shareholder Robert Monks to win election to the board.[21]

Like other institutions important in American politics, corporate boards have found it useful to delegate certain tasks to committees, which then make recommendations to the full board. This practice conserves time and permits some board members to develop enough expertise to challenge managers. Corporate boards have also established audit committees, compensation committees, and nominating committees that exercise growing influence in decision making. Back in the 1970s, for example, RCA's compensation committee, disenchanted with Chairman Robert Sarnoff, recommended that he receive no salary. The board agreed. Sarnoff, correctly perceiving this as an insult, promptly resigned.[22]

To understand the role of corporate boards in corporate decision making, it is useful to imagine a situation in which the U.S. president's cabinet, selected by the president, is vested with the authority to make policy for the federal government, to fire White House aides, and ultimately to fire the president. Such an arrangement would probably encourage the president and his aides to be more mindful of cabinet opinions. Similarly, corporate boards can influence decisions without having to resort to the ultimate weapon of dismissal.

Strategies and Policies

Adaptability

If corporations are to prosper in a competitive environment, they must be able to adapt to changing circumstances and trends. The question is not whether corporations are capable of changing but whether they are capable of changing in time. A business tottering on the edge of bankruptcy is desperate enough to try something drastic; a corporation whose strategic decisions will lead to trouble in five to ten years may not yet perceive the need for a new approach.

In the late 1960s and early 1970s, the Ford Motor Company ignored the handwriting on the wall—the growing popularity of small, economical foreign cars—preferring instead to continue the old, familiar pattern of large cars and large inventories in the United States. Surprised by the OPEC oil embargo of 1973-1974, Ford decided to weather the storm rather than to change course. Company executives proposed a shift to smaller cars, but Henry Ford II rejected such suggestions, dismissing small cars as "little shitboxes." [23] Interestingly, Ford did produce a small car for European and other markets, and by the 1980s the Escort was the company's leading seller. Ford missed other golden opportunities as well; it developed a marvelous rustproofing process in 1958 but moved very slowly to use it. Ford was familiar with the technology for front-wheel drive but was slow to pursue it. Ford had a chance to purchase Honda in the 1970s but declined to do so.

The basic problem at Ford was the unwillingness of top managers to take a long-term perspective. Many other companies suffer from the same affliction. Unable to demonstrate a favorable return on investment in a few years, they routinely reject proposals for risky innovations. An exception is Allen-Bradley, a Milwaukee manufacturer of industrial controls. Heavily reliant on assembly lines, Allen-Bradley introduced a new technique, computer-integrated manufacturing, which permits the manufacture of different versions of a product at mass-production speeds in lots as small as a single unit. In effect, this technique combines the advantages of assembly-line speed and customized production. According to conventional accounting principles, which stress short payback periods, this was an unwise strategic decision. In the beginning, the costs of computer-integrated manufacturing outran the profits. In the long run, however, the process is likely to establish Allen-Bradley as a world leader in industrial controls.

Corporations differ in their inclination and their ability to shift gears quickly. According to economics professors Walter Adams and James Brock, size is a factor—big companies are more conservative and more bureaucratic than small companies.[24] Recently, a firm in Indiana, Nucor Inc., introduced a new steelmaking process (borrowed from Germany) that requires considerably less energy and manpower than more conventional methods. Larger companies acknowledge their interest in the new technology (known as thin-slab casting) but will wait until Nucor proves its commercial viability before investing in it.[25] H. Ross Perot, who attempted to change the policies of General Motors from within, remarked that changing GM's corporate culture was like "teaching an elephant to tap dance." [26] Frustrated, Perot resigned from GM's board and turned to other pursuits.

Competition is another factor. Public utilities, which face limited competition for customers, have been notoriously slow to change. Only strong pressure from state public utility commissions in the 1970s persuaded electric utility companies to build fewer plants and redesign their rate structures to promote energy conservation. In contrast, companies that face tough competition, such those in the computer and electronics industries, have to adapt quickly to changing circumstances.

Symbols and the Corporate Image

A positive corporate image is a tremendous asset, and a negative image is a major liability. A drug company that symbolizes safety and reliability is likely to prosper; if the same company is suddenly seen as careless or dishonest, its sales plummet. Clever company executives appreciate the close connection between symbols and their company's image. They also recognize that symbols may reinforce or undermine company policy.

A corporate symbol may be a building, a press release, a charitable contribution, a logo, an advertisement, a year-end bonus, or an appointment. When U.S. Steel changed its name to USX, the company was sending an unmistakable message to investors that a new era had begun: a steel company was becoming a diversified conglomerate. In the late 1970s Chrysler appointed Douglas Fraser, the head of United Auto Workers, to sit on its board of directors, thus extending an olive branch to workers. The intention was to encourage a new cooperative spirit in labor-management relations as Chrysler attempted to step back from the brink of bankruptcy. (In 1991 the labor seat was removed from the Chrysler board.) IBM has long cultivated the image of a progressive, successful firm that takes good care of its employees.

There is no doubt that corporate executives pay attention to symbols. Often, however, they fail to recognize what kind of symbol they are creating, or they have blind spots about the impact of certain symbols on important constituencies. In 1986, when General Motors announced that it was laying off 29,000 workers and then awarded fat bonuses to top executives, the company projected an image of arrogance and insensitivity. Anticipating this announcement, Perot said, "If in fact, they pay the big bonuses, it would be exactly as though the generals at Valley Forge in our revolution had decided to go out and buy new uniforms for themselves, when the troops were fighting in the snow barefooted." [27]

Another negative symbol is the "golden parachute," which became common during the early 1980s when corporate mergers swept the country. A golden parachute is a contractual clause that offers top corporate executives a generous severance payment if they are fired as part of a successful takeover. The executive simply pulls the rip cord and floats gently to the ground as the old corporation goes up in flames. The stated rationale for golden parachutes is that they discourage managerial resistance to hostile takeovers that will ultimately benefit investors. Harvard University professor Robert Reich said the golden parachute suggests that "the only way shareholders could trust corporate executives not to feather their nests at the shareholders' expense was to provide them a prefeathered nest at the shareholders' expense." [28] By the 1990s many large companies had responded to the concerns expressed by large shareholders about golden parachutes and other takeover defenses by abolishing them and, at the same time, providing new avenues for shareholder input into company decisions. [29]

Two Views of Profitability

All corporations pursue higher profits, but a recurring question is how to balance short-term costs and long-term benefits. Johnson & Johnson decided to recall Tylenol products after several people died after ingesting poisoned capsules in 1982. The recall and subsequent design and production of tamper-proof packaging was very costly. In the long run, however, the decision enhanced Johnson & Johnson's credibility in a market that depends on consumer confidence. Although it lost a hefty share of the painkiller market to its competitors, Johnson & Johnson rebounded to its previous market share within a few years. In 1991, when two people died in the state of Washington from Sudafed capsules laced with cyanide, the maker of the product, the Burroughs Wellcome Company, seemed to take a lesson from Johnson & Johnson because it wasted no time taking Sudafed capsules off the market.

Corporations do not always take enlightened, decisive action in times of emergency, however. In the late 1970s, the Firestone Tire and Rubber Company, whose steel-belted radial tires were prone to blow-outs, tread separations, and other dangerous defects, continued to manufacture and sell these tires to unsuspecting customers despite considerable evidence that the tires were hazardous. When pressed by the National Highway Traffic Safety Administration for performance data, Firestone refused and went to court to prevent the agency from releasing to the press the results of a consumer survey. In October 1978, after months of controversy, Firestone agreed to a massive recall. By that time, however, the company's reputation for safety had been badly damaged by hundreds of accidents resulting in at least thirty-four deaths, and the company had a public image of greed and defiance.[30]

Most people would applaud Johnson & Johnson and condemn Firestone. Confronted by evidence that a product is unsafe, it would seem that a company should act swiftly to withdraw the product or improve it. But the issue is not so clear-cut. When does a product become unsafe? All automobiles are unsafe to some extent and could be made safer—for example, by installing airbags to cushion the impact of a collision. Should companies make their products as safe as they can be? Should companies make some products safer, others cheaper, so that consumers have a choice? If so, why not allow one company to produce a relatively safe product, while another company produces a relatively cheap product? Should consumers be free to place cost above safety? And who should define safety—the companies or the government?

At a minimum, the public might insist that companies be honest about their products' virtues and vices. But does this require that they go out of their way to reveal flaws and problems? That question arose when the Federal Trade Commission (FTC) proposed that used-car dealers be required to inform consumers of any known major defects of cars on their lots. The proposal did not seem particularly onerous, but used-car dealers persuaded Congress to stop the FTC from imposing such a requirement. A similar question arises when health experts recommend that cigarette and alcoholic beverage advertising be banned or significantly restricted. Even more complicated are questions about relative risk. Do certain pesticides and preservatives serve a public health function by controlling or eliminating harmful organisms in food, or are their own toxic qualities more of a risk than a benefit to the average consumer?

After the Board Has Met

Implementation Problems

The implementation of corporate policies is seldom automatic. Just as governments depend on corporate cooperation to implement a policy such as environmental protection, corporations depend on government cooperation to carry out policies such as plant construction. Many businesses have been unable to expand because of antipollution laws that forbid new plants in "nonattainment" areas if a new plant would degrade air quality. Many electric utility companies have been unable to build nuclear power plants because of government disapproval, either by the Nuclear Regulatory Commission (NRC) or by a state agency. Implementation of a corporate policy is often the first step in a long chain of problematic events. At any rate, this is true of public utilities and publicly held industrial corporations.

The implementation of corporate policies is especially tricky in an intergovernmental setting. The Pacific Gas and Electric Company (PG&E), a San Francisco-based public utility company, needed the approval of the NRC and the California Energy Conservation Commission to build a nuclear plant. Although the approval of the NRC was assured, that of the Energy Conservation Commission was not. Citing a California statute banning new nuclear power plants in the state until a safe means of nuclear waste disposal had been found, the Energy Conservation Commission rejected PG&E's request. The decision was subsequently upheld by the U.S. Supreme Court, which ruled that state governments are free to object to new nuclear plants on economic grounds, even when such objections are closely related to safety concerns.[31]

Implementation is also highly problematic for corporations characterized by a high degree of decentralization, strong professionalism, or both. When a newspaper or magazine owner leans too heavily on a reporter or editor, the journalist may resign rather than submit to censorship. When a hospital administrator instructs doctors to cut costs to improve the hospital's financial picture, doctors may cite the Hippocratic oath—and utter a few other oaths as well—as grounds for refusal. Multinational corporations face special challenges in implementing policies across a far-flung empire. Indeed, this was Union Carbide's defense when it tried to explain a poisonous gas leak that killed an estimated 2,000 people in Bhopal, India, in 1984. According to Union Carbide headquarters, its foreign subsidiary failed to conform to company safety policies, with catastrophic results.

Despite these difficulties, there are several reasons why corporate policies are more easily implemented than bureaucratic rules and regulations. First, in the private sector it is easier to fire people who are not performing well than it is in the public sector. Although white-collar corporate employees may take their employers to court if they believe they have been fired without just cause, most of the time corporations can make a convincing case that their actions were not arbitrary, capricious, or reckless. In comparison, government regulations controlling civil service employment include procedures and appeal rights that provide more protection to employees. Second, the private sector has access to considerable financial resources that help to remove obstacles. Corporate lobbyists, or trade association lobbyists representing smaller businesses, directly intervene in the implementation of government decisions. And, of course, corporate and trade association political action committees (PACs) remind politicians that reelection is easier if business interests are on their side. Third, the private sector can use gifted public relations professionals when mass persuasion is necessary. Indeed, the leading media experts in American politics are the advertising wizards of Madison Avenue—guns for hire, whose services are available for the right price. Corporations, like government bureaucracies, face obstacles when they propose controversial policies, but they have more power to remove such obstacles from their path.

In Search of Golden Eggs

To many politicians, corporations are geese that lay golden eggs. This observation is especially true at the state and local levels, where politicians perceive corporations as sources of jobs, taxes, economic development, and prosperity. To convince corporations to settle within their boundaries, state and local politicians offer special subsidies and tax breaks, and, if these overtures are successful, the politicians can take credit for a coup. In the 1980s, Governor Martha Layne Collins took considerable pride in announcing that Toyota would build an assembly plant in Georgetown, Kentucky, and Governor Tommy Thompson expressed elation when computer whiz Steve Chen agreed to build supercomputers in Eau Claire, Wisconsin.

Pioneering corporations offer benefits not just to particular states and communities but to society at large. Consider, for example, Bell Laboratories, the most celebrated industrial laboratory in the United States.

Among its many achievements are the development of coaxial cable transmission and microwave radio relay technology, which have significantly reduced the cost of long-distance communication. In addition, Bell developed the transistor, which laid the groundwork for portable radios, space flight, and computers. From 1925 to 1975 scientists from Bell Labs acquired an astonishing 18,000 patents.[32]

Other companies also have developed technologies whose benefits extend far beyond a single community or state. For example, in 1986 IBM scientists published a paper in which they concluded that superconductors could be made from ceramics without the costs of working at extremely low temperatures. This breakthrough, which sent ripples of excitement throughout the scientific community, holds the promise of substantially reducing the costs of generating electricity.[33]

Many communities owe their revitalization to public-spirited corporate leaders. During the 1950s the Mellon family joined forces with the Democratic "machine" to clean up the air in Pittsburgh; in addition, they spearheaded the Pittsburgh renaissance, which included the construction of picturesque skyscrapers and public parks in the city's Golden Triangle. Following a second renaissance in 1988, Rand McNally hailed Pittsburgh as the most livable city in America.[34] In Minneapolis the Downtown Council, a business coalition, supported an extensive downtown revitalization program in the 1950s, including the building of pedestrian skywalks that protect shoppers from Minnesota's harsh winters. Since then, Minneapolis has been praised for its favorable business climate, progressive government, and cultural amenities. It is no coincidence that a number of leading corporations are headquartered in Pittsburgh and Minneapolis. In general, local owners demonstrate greater community spirit than absentee owners.

Corporations demonstrate a sense of social responsibility by donating money to charity, but they differ dramatically in their generosity. Most corporations give less than 1 percent of their pretax profits to charity.[35] Some give 5 percent, however, which is the maximum tax-deductible contribution allowed by the IRS. Corporate giving can become contagious in cities that foster a strong sense of community and solidarity. In the Twin Cities, for example, sixty-two companies gave 5 percent of their pretax profits to charity in 1981; twenty-one gave 2 percent or more.

Decisions regarding charitable contributions, although they are significant expenditures, pale in comparison to big ticket corporate decisions such as wage settlements, plant modernization, diversification, dividend payouts, and compliance with government regulations. Moreover, these decisions often resemble a zero-sum game in which one party's gain is another's loss. Corporations often must choose between higher profits or higher wages, expansion or environmental protection, higher dividends or a secure future for the company. The natural instinct of all corporations is to pursue higher profits, and the natural instinct of all managers is to pursue better perquisites (company cars, expense accounts, supplemental insurance, club memberships). As a result, the most frequent beneficiaries of corporate decisions are the investors and managers. Employees also benefit, but they are the ones most likely to suffer (wage cuts or lost jobs) in hard times.

Shattered Dreams

Corporate policies can have devastating consequences for workers, taxpayers, and consumers. For example, the steel industry's policies of the 1960s and 1970s eventually resulted in a steep decline in the size of its work force. In 1978 U.S. Steel had 166,800 employees; by 1984 that number had plunged to 88,753.[36] Unemployment is a bitter pill to swallow. Unemployed workers experience self-doubt, guilt, shame, depression, and despair, which often affect their physical and mental health. Alcoholism, child abuse, spouse abuse, and suicide are occasional side effects. In American society, as in many others, a person's self-image is intimately connected to his or her job. This is especially true of men, who have been taught to think of themselves as breadwinners. Moreover, unemployment almost always has serious consequences for a family's economic well-being. Even if another member of the household works during the period of unemployment, that one income may not be sufficient, and finding a new job at comparable pay is often very difficult.

The effects of unemployment are especially harsh in certain communities and certain segments of society. Small towns, long dependent on a particular industry, may have difficulty coping when a company decides to mothball a plant. Restaurants and shops may close their doors forever, and city services may decline as the city's tax revenue drops. A virtual ghost town may result. Black Americans are disproportionately affected by unemployment, and the black community suffers acutely when unemployment increases. In 1983, at the end of a recession, black teenage unemployment reached nearly 50 percent, an alarmingly high level.[37] These conditions are breeding grounds for crime and drug abuse. A society that tolerates high unemployment pays a high price in many ways.

Unemployment need not be tragic if it is temporary and if it leads to a new, better job. In fact, if workers are laid off from relatively unproductive jobs and find more productive ones, society benefits. Many Western countries have retraining programs that facilitate transition from one job to another. Germany, for example, offers every adult up to two years of full-time training or retraining. A number of other countries provide vouchers that workers may use for on-the-job training wherever and in whatever field they wish. In contrast, job training programs in the United States are severely limited in scope and focus. Most private job training is geared to a particular job rather than to acquisition of a broader set of marketable skills. The U.S. government conducts job-training programs, but they are generally restricted to the unskilled, and there are few programs to retrain people with obsolete skills or those who wish to improve their skills. Moreover, government outlays for job training have been declining rather than increasing since the 1970s. For all these reasons, the consequences of unemployment in the United States are worse than they need be.

Bankruptcy is another possible consequence of corporate policies. From a societal point of view, the occasional bankruptcy is not alarming if it is caused by changing market conditions or technological advances in related industries. But the collapse of a pivotal company can be disturbing, especially if the company is part of a complex web of other companies. Society can ill afford the bankruptcy of major companies in industries that are heavily concentrated or that are central to commerce or national security. Even more disastrous is the collapse of an entire industry. When such catastrophes occur, taxpayers are often asked to mop up the mess.

In 1979, Congress agreed to bail out Chrysler, at a cost of $1.2 billion, when bankruptcy seemed imminent; it also came to the rescue following the collapse of Penn Central, creating Conrail and Amtrak to preserve a national rail service. (Conrail was sold in 1987, but Amtrak still is heavily subsidized by the federal government.) But the grand-daddy of federal bailouts occurred in the late 1980s through the early 1990s, following the collapse of the savings and loan industry. Although this debacle had many causes, including shortsighted government deregulatory policy and a recessionary economy, poor investment choices and extravagant spending by savings and loan executives contributed greatly to the problem. The whole mess could end up costing taxpayers nearly $500 billion. From time to time state governments also find it necessary to rescue businesses. In 1985, in order to keep state savings and loan associations from declaring bankruptcy, the government of Ohio was forced to contribute as much as $120 million in state funds.[38] A similar situation occurred in Rhode Island in 1991. The cost of a bailout can be very high indeed.

Taxpayers pay in still another way for corporate mistakes. Many industries, especially defense and aerospace, receive large amounts of their revenue from public funds. More than 85 percent of the budget of the National Aeronautics and Space Administration (NASA) goes to contracts awarded to aerospace industries.[39] When these industries are wasteful and inefficient, the costs ultimately are borne by taxpayers. Although the government is partly to blame for awarding these contracts in the first place and for tolerating huge cost overruns, corporations bear primary responsibility.

If taxpayers pay for some corporate mistakes, consumers pay for others. Consider the case of the Dalkon Shield, an intrauterine birth control device marketed by the A. H. Robins company between 1970 and 1974. The shield was used by approximately 2 million women, and approximately 90,000 of them reported pelvic infections, sterility, or involuntary abortions. The deaths of at least twenty-one women can be traced to use of the device.[40] It is impossible to estimate the costs of this disaster in terms of shattered dreams and shattered lives. These costs are especially hard to bear when one considers evidence that Robins was aware of these dangers months before the product was marketed.

Other companies also have caused consumer health disasters—sometimes wittingly, sometimes unwittingly. Eli Lilly's Oraflex, an arthritis drug, caused an estimated twenty-seven deaths in the United States alone. Ford's Pinto, with its notorious exploding gas tank, resulted in multiple injuries and deaths. Johns Manville's asbestos has caused numerous health-related problems.

Sometimes an entire industry must shoulder the blame for policies that adversely affect consumers. In the late 1970s and early 1980s, insurance companies sharply reduced premiums and agreed to take on poor risks in order to generate revenue to invest. Their aim was to take advantage of temporarily high interest rates. When interest rates declined and numerous claims came due, insurance companies found themselves short of cash, and they again raised their rates. This contributed directly to a liability insurance crisis that continues to the present, and makes it difficult for doctors, municipal governments, and others to secure insurance. In some communities, doctors will not deliver babies because of the high cost of malpractice insurance. Cities have closed public skating rinks and have limited access to public parks because they cannot afford insurance coverage.

Redemption

Corporations do learn from their mistakes. Under new management since the 1980s, Ford Motor Company now makes small cars and cars with front-wheel drive, and it maintains small inventories. By the early 1990s, Wall Street firms such as Shearson Lehman Hutton and Drexel Burnham Lambert had reduced the number and salaries of their brokers, and were shying away from corporate takeover efforts and junk bonds because of the criticisms and losses they had suffered in the late

1980s as a result of spectacular, risky transactions.[41] Firms producing products that are environmentally damaging for reasons ranging from plastic packaging to toxic chemicals have begun to develop recycling and waste management programs in order to stave off criticism by citizens and politicians.

Electric utility companies also have learned from their mistakes, thanks in part to pressure from public utility commissions and citizen groups. After years of overbuilding, they have opted for more creative ways of meeting customer demand, relying on time-of-day rates, seasonal rates, and other rate structures that encourage energy conservation. These policies have paid off for investors. From 1972 to 1987, two-thirds of America's major electric utilities returned to investors more profits on the average with less risk than did the nation's industrial giants.[42] No longer on the ropes, the electric utilities are thriving.

The most successful electric utilities have been those willing to invest resources in problem solving and quality improvement. For example, Florida Power & Light devoted considerable time and effort to a power outage problem falsely attributed to lightning storms. After hiring an ornithologist, the company discovered that many power outages were caused by bird droppings from hawks perched on transmission lines. Following this revelation, the company installed umbrella-like shelters to redirect the droppings away from highly vulnerable pylons and grids. Thanks to these and other initiatives, the company's average outage rate per customer declined from 75.8 minutes in 1983 to 48 minutes in 1988.[43]

If companies learn from their mistakes, they also learn from the successes of risk-taking pioneers; a "diffusion of innovations"[44] often occurs in the private sector. For example, when some newsrooms installed cathode ray tubes for computerized editing and production, other newsrooms did likewise. Computer-aided design/computer-aided manufacturing (CAD/CAM) is now nearly universal. Grocery stores have stamped bar codes on packaged foods to reduce congestion at checkout lines. More and more companies are investigating the advantages of biotechnology. Utility companies have delegated telephone hookup and meter-reading tasks to customers, thereby cutting costs.

In more abstract terms, companies also alter management strategies in response to exhortations from academics and market analysts. U.S. corporations are scrambling to emulate Japanese corporations, with their emphasis on teamwork between management and labor, inventory control, and customer satisfaction.[45] They are also attempting to move toward flexible-system production, as in the case of Allen-Bradley. Although such corporate learning generally has positive results for the company, there is a danger that corporations will respond too quickly to the latest fad. At the moment, corporations seem to be heeding Thomas Peters and Robert Waterman's admonition to stick to their knitting and concentrate on what they do best.[46] Yet this new strategy would be unnecessary if corporations had not earlier responded to another adage: hedge your bets through diversification. Perhaps the best kind of corporate learning is that which recognizes the importance of frequent experimentation. This permits corporations to move in new directions, but one step at a time.

Summary

The distinction between public policy and private policy is a cultural artifact. Most Western democracies regard industrial policy as public policy; in the United States, industrial policy is private, with some governmental supervision. Most Western democracies view rail transportation, steel production, electricity, and telecommunications as public enterprises; in the United States, these are, for the most part, private. Most Western democracies rely on the government to employ a substantial number of people and to retrain employees when necessary; in the United States, the private sector provides most of the employment and training.

To use E. E. Schattschneider's terms, we have "privatized" conflict by removing certain issues from public debate.[47] The privatization of conflict limits participation in the policy-making process, but it does not limit policy effects. As a result, there is a mismatch between the importance of many private decisions, the stakes, the degree of public involvement, and the scope of conflict. Most citizens are bystanders and spectators when these critical decisions are made. Although ordinary people are not completely powerless, their ability to affect corporate decisions is quite limited.

During the 1970s the government intervened more forcefully in the private sector to promote goals such as affirmative action, environmental protection, and consumer protection, which will be discussed in the chapters that follow. It should be noted, however, that government intervention, particularly that of the federal government, has diminished once again as a result of deregulation and privatization. Some see an advantage in these changes because privatizing conflicts reduces the number of issues on which public policy makers must achieve consensus, and thus makes governing less difficult.

The trend toward less government intervention leaves more decisions in the hands of corporate managers and corporate boards. The metaphor "boardroom politics" is used to describe this phenomenon not because boards are more important than managers but because the major decisions are made by a relatively small group of people who are tied in some fashion to the corporation. As for the relative importance of managers and board members, the managers usually dominate the decision-making process until a crisis erupts; then the board intervenes to try to save the day.

In making strategic decisions, officials of publicly held corporations are influenced by investors and their perceived interests. But it is often difficult to discern the course of action that will yield maximum benefits for the corporation and its investors. There is the issue of short-term versus long-term profitability, the need to stay on a par with the competition, and the desire to blunt criticisms from consumers and the government. Privately held corporations have greater flexibility in making decisions, but they have similar difficulty in determining what will produce the most favorable bottom line.

Not surprisingly, corporations have made some spectacular mistakes. Prominent examples include the U.S. auto industry's inability to meet consumer demand for small, fuel-efficient cars until it was too late, and the U.S. steel industry's failure to modernize and alter production techniques in a timely manner. Companies do learn from their mistakes, but they learn slowly. In the meantime, the nation pays a heavy price for their errors.

Employees are the most obvious victims of corporate mistakes; layoffs inflict economic and psychological damage. Moreover, neither the government nor the private sector goes very far to ensure that displaced workers will land on their feet. The U.S. government does little to cushion the blow of unemployment and to prepare workers for new jobs.

Consumers also suffer when corporations make mistakes. Despite the work of government agencies such as the Consumer Product Safety Commission, the Food and Drug Administration, the National Highway Traffic Safety Administration, and the Occupational Safety and Health Administration, companies still produce defective automobiles, tires, birth control devices, drugs, insulating materials, and power plants. Some of this danger is understandable; life has its risks. Yet all too often corporations manufacture products that they know to be unsafe.

Finally, taxpayers are harmed by poor corporate judgment. Cost overruns on government contracts and bailouts of failed corporations or industries are the most obvious examples. The savings and loan debacle has cost taxpayers and the government billions of dollars that could have been devoted to other priorities, mainly because government policy makers and savings and loan executives were intoxicated by the allure of large profits in the 1980s.

Our intention in evaluating boardroom politics is not to be overly harsh. The government bears partial responsibility for many corporate mistakes. In appraising boardroom politics, we must ask not whether it is perfect but whether it is superior or inferior to other political processes, where the scope of conflict is broader. By examining these other political processes, we will be able to make useful comparisons.

Notes

1. Harold Lasswell, *Who Gets What, When, How* (Cleveland: Meridian Books, 1958).

2. Charles E. Lindblom, *Politics and Markets* (New York: Basic Books, 1977), 171-172.

3. E. S. Savas, *Privatization: The Key to Better Government* (Chatham, N.J.: Chatham House, 1987), 131.

4. Eagleton Institute of Politics, Rutgers University, *Alternative Methods for Delivering Public Services in New Jersey* (New Brunswick, N.J.: Rutgers University Press, 1986), 7.

5. Mark Schlesinger, Robert A. Dotwart, and Richard T. Pulice, "Competitive Bidding and States' Purchase of Services: The Case of Mental Health Care in Massachusetts," *Journal of Policy Analysis and Management* (Winter 1986): 245-259.

6. Maggie McComas, "Atop the Fortune 500: A Survey of C.E.O.s," *Fortune*, April 28, 1986, 26-31. The Fortune 500 is a list compiled annually of the 500 publicly held U.S. industrial companies with the largest sales.

7. John Portz, "Politics, Plant Closings, and Public Policy: The Steel Valley Authority in Pittsburgh" (Paper presented at the annual meeting of the Midwest Political Science Association, Chicago, April 9-11, 1987).

8. William Gormley, Jr., *The Effects of Newspaper-Television Cross-Ownership on News Homogeneity* (Chapel Hill, N.C.: Institute for Research in Social Science, 1976), 51.

9. Doron P. Levin, "Chrysler Dividend Cut in Half," *New York Times*, March 8, 1991, D1.

10. Bro Uttal, "Behind the Fall of Steve Jobs," *Fortune*, August 5, 1985, 20-24.

11. Proxy resolutions are proposals introduced by shareholders and voted on by shareholders. If adopted, they become corporate policy.

12. *Munn v. Illinois*, 94 U.S. 113 (1877).

13. Lisa Mesdag, "The 50 Largest Private Industrial Companies," *Fortune*, May 31, 1982, 108-114.

14. Jack Walker, "The Origins and Maintenance of Interest Groups in America," *American Political Science Review* 77 (June 1983): 390-406.

15. Donald Regan, quoted on the "MacNeil/Lehrer News Hour," April 16, 1987.

16. Walter Adams, "Public Policy in a Free Enterprise Economy," in *The Structure of American Industry*, ed. Walter Adams (New York: Macmillan, 1977), 483-516; Robert Sherrill, *Why They Call It Politics*, 5th ed. (San Diego: Harcourt Brace Jovanovich, 1990), 465.

17. See Mesdag, "The 50 Largest," 114.

18. John Holusha, "Ed Woolard Walks Du`Pont's Tightrope," *New York Times*, October 14, 1990, Sec. 3, 1, 6.

19. Steven Prokesch, "Remaking the American CEO," *New York Times*, January 25, 1987, C1.

20. Victor Brudney, "The Independent Director—Heavenly City or Potemkin Village?" *Harvard Law Review* 95 (January 1982): 599.

21. *New York Times*, March 14, 1991, D1, D4.

22. Lee Smith, "The Boardroom Is Becoming a Different Scene," *Fortune*, May 8, 1978, 150-170.

23. David Halberstam, *The Reckoning* (New York: William Morrow, 1986), 462.

24. Walter Adams and James Brock, *The Bigness Complex* (New York: Pantheon Books, 1986).

25. Jonathan P. Hicks, "Making Steel Faster and Cheaper," *New York Times*, February 27, 1991, D7.

26. Eric Gelman, "GM Boots Perot," *Newsweek*, December 15, 1986, 56-58.

27. H. Ross Perot, "Perot to Smith: GM Must Change," *Newsweek*, December 15, 1986, 59-60.

28. Robert Reich, "Enterprise and Double Cross," *Washington Monthly*, January 1987, 17.

29. Leslie Wayne, "Seeking to Stay Out of Proxy Battles," *New York Times*, April 8, 1991, D1, D4.

30. Arthur Louis, "Lessons from the Firestone Fracas," *Fortune*, August 28, 1978, 44-48; Stuart Feldstein, "How Not to React to a Safety Controversy," *Business Week*, November 6, 1978, 65.

31. *Pacific Gas & Electric Co. v. State Energy Resources Conservation and Development Commission*, 461 U.S. 190 (1983).

32. John Brooks, *Telephone* (New York: Harper & Row, 1976), 12-16.

33. Dale Russakoff, "A High-Tech, High-Stakes Race Begins," *Washington Post* national weekly edition, June 15, 1987, 10.

34. Two of the authors of this volume, who grew up in Pittsburgh, heartily agree. The third agrees with Frank Lloyd Wright, who, when asked what should be done about Pittsburgh, thought for a moment and replied, "Abandon it!"

35. William Ouchi, *The M-Form Society* (Reading, Mass.: Addison-Wesley, 1984), 16-31, 192-193.

36. Ralph Nader and William Taylor, *The Big Boys* (New York: Pantheon Books, 1986), 58.

37. *Economic Report of the President* (Washington, D.C.: Government Printing Office, 1991), 331 (Table B-4).

38. Saundra Saperstein, "The S&L Crisis Is Over, but It Won't Go Away," *Washington Post* national weekly edition, September 2, 1985, 33-34.

39. Stuart Diamond, "NASA Wasted Billions, Federal Audits Disclose," *New York Times*, April 23, 1986, A1.

40. Robin Henig, "Behind the Shield of Deception," *Washington Post* national weekly edition, December 2, 1985, 35.

41. Sarah Bartlett, "Steady, Painful Transition to a Humbler Wall Street," *New York Times*, November 22, 1989, A1, D5.

42. "Regulators See Utilities' Return on Stock as Good-news, Bad-news Situation," *Milwaukee Journal*, March 13, 1987, C7.

43. Andrea Gabor, *The Man Who Discovered Quality* (New York: Random House, 1990), 162-187.

44. Jack Walker, "The Diffusion of Innovations in the American States," *American Political Science Review* 63 (September 1969): 880-889.

45. See Gabor, *The Man Who Discovered Quality*.

46. Thomas Peters and Robert Waterman, *In Search of Excellence* (New York: Warner Books, 1982), 292-305.

47. E. E. Schattschneider, *The Semi-Sovereign People* (New York: Holt, Rinehart and Winston, 1960), 1-19.

4   Bureaucratic Politics

The federal government employs 2.8 million civilians. State and local governments account for roughly 13 million additional public employees.[1] Congress, the presidency, and the courts, with their supporting coterie of staff, advisers, and patronage appointees, make up about 2 percent of the federal total, and their institutional counterparts at the state and local levels claim a similarly small share of their public work forces. Most government employees work in executive branch agencies administering programs or providing services to citizens; these workers are referred to as bureaucrats. The American bureaucracy or the "administrative state" is often said to constitute a fourth branch of government.[2]

These bureaucrats work in the Internal Revenue Service (IRS) office in Philadelphia sorting tax returns, entering information into computers, and shipping computer tapes to the IRS Center in West Virginia.[3] They work for the Nuclear Regulatory Commission as field investigators reviewing plant construction plans with engineers from the Texas Power and Light Company and negotiating agreements on contested issues having to do with power plant construction standards. They are highway patrol officers enforcing speed limit laws.

Sometimes bureaucrats have to make very controversial decisions. In 1990, for example, bureaucrats in the Wisconsin Department of Health and Social Services had to decide how to implement a controversial "Learnfare" program aimed at keeping the children of welfare recipients in school. Their decisions determined which welfare recipients would have their Aid to Families with Dependent Children (AFDC) benefits reduced because a child played hookey from school. In some instances, this meant a substantial reduction in benefits.[4]

Central to the political world of bureaucratic agencies are the statutes authorizing their existence and specifying their structure, activities, and budgets. Also central are the relevant legislative committees and citizens whose lives are affected by the particular bureaucracy. Many agencies carry out policies based on broad, vague statutes. The Interstate Commerce Act of 1887, for example, gave the Interstate Commerce Commission (ICC) the mandate to regulate railroad rates to ensure that they were "reasonable and just." The Wagner Act of 1935 created the National Labor Relations Board (NLRB) and instructed it to control "unfair labor practices." [5] Even more detailed statutes, such as environmental or social service laws, give agencies significant discretion in determining how a policy will be implemented. After all, legislators cannot anticipate all the contingencies of policy implementation, and in many cases they do not even know what they want out of policies. This discretionary power is a vital component of bureaucratic politics.

The size, structure, and resources of an agency are also essential to its identity. Large staffs and budgets generally carry a certain measure of power and influence and consume the time of the legislatures that debate how agencies should be organized, to whom they should report, and how much money they should receive. The range of variation in staffing and resources is enormous (see Table 4-1). Figure 4-1 shows the organizational structure of a typical bureaucratic agency.

Contrary to popular belief, bureaucrats do not try to be obstructionist or unpleasant. Indeed, they are very attentive to the concerns and preferences of certain individuals and groups—the occupational or categorical groups they serve, the industries they regulate, and the ideological groups with whom they share an affinity; these private sector groups are often referred to as an agency's "clientele." Bureaucrats are also attentive to legislative committees and high-ranking executive branch officials. Having and maintaining supporting coalitions both within and outside government is often the key to agency strength and survival. To put it more emphatically, bureaucrats want to be liked.

Internal forces are another aspect of bureaucratic politics. Government agencies typically put many knowledgeable and well-trained individuals to work on highly complex problems; these individuals soon acquire additional expertise and develop preferred ways of dealing with such problems. Expert knowledge and standard operating procedures simplify daily decisions and help to protect an agency from outside criticism. In addition, skillful leadership within the bureaucracy is necessary because an agency's success depends in part on its positive relationships with other government elites.

The Low Game

Agenda Content

American bureaucracies have two major functions—regulation and service delivery—and the issues of bureaucratic politics fall into these categories. Virtually every administrative agency was created either to regulate private sector industries or to provide services to citizens, including the monthly cash payments made by the Social Security Administration (SSA) and unemployment insurance programs. Many

*Table 4-1   Outlays and Employees of Federal Departments and
Selected Agencies, 1989*

Agency	Outlays (in billions)	Full-time employees
Agriculture	$ 48.3	109,567
Commerce	2.6	40,150
Defense	317.4	1,051,019
Education	21.6	4,424
Energy	11.4	16,535
Health and Human Services	399.8	117,495
Housing and Urban Development	19.7	13,212
Interior	5.2	71,372
Justice	6.2	76,402
Labor	22.7	18,444
State	3.7	25,491
Transportation	26.6	63,197
Treasury	230.6	154,432
Veterans Affairs	30.0	212,231
Small Business Administration	0.1	4,005
Environmental Protection Agency	4.9	14,088
NASA	11.0	23,054

Source: Office of Management and Budget, *The Budget of the United States, FY 1991*
(Washington, D.C.: Government Printing Office, 1990).

large agencies or departments perform both functions. The distinction
between the two is obvious when we contrast, for example, the regulation of food and drug quality with the provision of food stamps or
medical care. But it is also obvious that all government service delivery
and cash transfer programs must have regulatory components that
identify eligible recipients, outline procedures, and prohibit certain
actions. The distinction between regulatory and service delivery policy
is not hard and fast.

Regulatory policy occupies an important place in American history.
Federal laws passed in the late nineteenth century to regulate railroad
pricing and corporate mergers were a central part of the Populist/Pro-
gressive reaction to the arbitrary practices of big business. These
precedent-setting government interventions into the private sector were
quite controversial. The present scope of government regulation is
enormous, encompassing such areas of private sector activity as advertising, agriculture, air and water pollution, aviation safety, banking,
consumer products, corporate mergers, food and drug quality, hospitals
and medical practice, nuclear energy, radio and television, transportation, and utility pricing. And regulation is still a controversial enter-

Figure 4-1 The Department of Justice

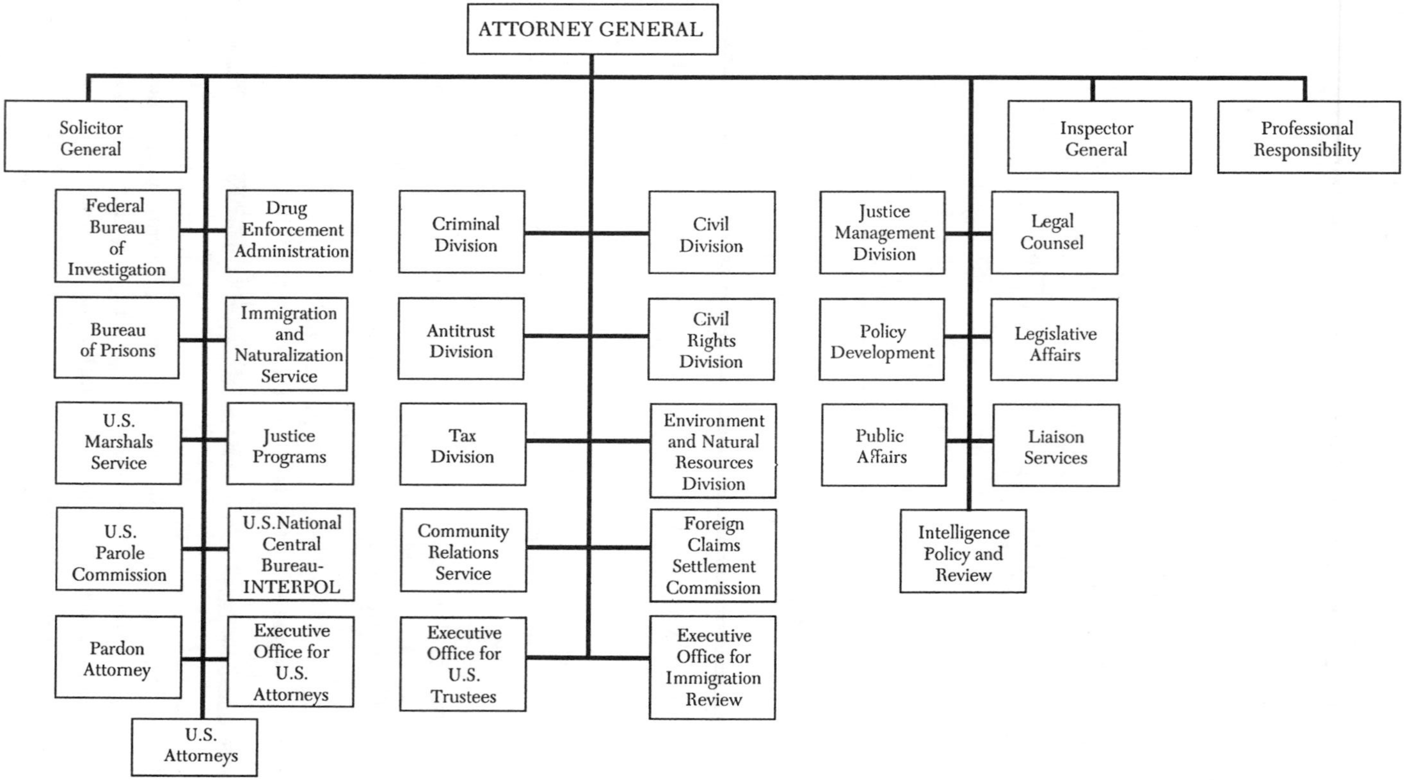

ATTORNEY GENERAL

Professional Responsibility

Inspector General

Legal Counsel

Legislative Affairs

Liaison Services

Justice Management Division

Policy Development

Public Affairs

Intelligence Policy and Review

Civil Division

Civil Rights Division

Environment and Natural Resources Division

Foreign Claims Settlement Commission

Executive Office for Immigration Review

Criminal Division

Antitrust Division

Tax Division

Community Relations Service

Executive Office for U.S. Trustees

Drug Enforcement Administration

Immigration and Naturalization Service

Justice Programs

U.S. National Central Bureau-INTERPOL

Executive Office for U.S. Attorneys

Solicitor General

Federal Bureau of Investigation

Bureau of Prisons

U.S. Marshals Service

U.S. Parole Commission

Pardon Attorney

U.S. Attorneys

Source: Washington Information Directory, 1991-1992 (Washington, D.C.: Congressional Quarterly, 1991), 468.

prise. Regulatory statutes provide aggrieved parties with the right to appeal agency decisions, which means that many of these issues are resolved through formal judicial procedures either within the agency or in the court system. Therefore, two characteristics of regulatory issues are their focus on the actions of private industry and their highly legalistic nature.

Service delivery issues typically involve categorical groups of citizens and public sector organizations—veterans and the Department of Veterans Affairs, welfare recipients and state departments of social services, state and local governments and the Department of Housing and Urban Development. The issues are usually distributive or redistributive in nature. Should education grants received by welfare recipients be counted as income when determining future benefits? Should local in-kind contributions be counted as meeting matching-funds requirements in federal urban development programs? How should garbage pickups be scheduled in different city neighborhoods? The appeals of agency decisions on such matters are likely to be directed at legislators or chief executives, not the courts. Service delivery issues can be contrasted with regulatory issues in that they are confined largely to the public sector and are usually resolved through political rather than legal channels.

Because regulatory policy is aimed at private sector organizations such as businesses and unions, regulatory issues often reflect the concerns of these groups. Bankers are usually the first to react to Federal Home Loan Bank Board rules; and the same is true of radio and television stations and Federal Communications Commission decisions, meat packers and drug companies and decisions of the Food and Drug Administration (FDA), and unions and regulations of the NLRB. The rules promulgated by regulatory agencies and the adjudicative decisions they make also stimulate questions and criticisms from many quarters, however. Citizen groups, legislative committees, other agencies, the media, and ordinary citizens all contribute to the ongoing chorus of commentary about regulatory actions or the need for them. Regulatory issues spring largely from this commentary.

Most service delivery issues originate in much the same way. Services are delivered, and various individuals and groups react. The commentary and subsequent bureaucratic response to it lead to the definition of problems for which solutions must be sought. Like regulatory policy, government-sponsored social service programs in the United States had a slow, halting start, but they are now extensive.[6] The government provides a vast array of cash and in-kind assistance programs to the poor, the elderly, the unemployed, the disabled, the handicapped, veterans, farmers, migrant workers, and many other categories of needy individuals. (In 1987 federal human service spending amounted to roughly $500 billion; state and local spending in the human service category added about $335 billion to the federal total.)[7] Governments at all levels also supply traditional public services such as highway construction and maintenance, water and sewers, electrical power, police and fire protection, and parks and recreational facilities. The programs through which all these services are provided are subject to varying degrees of scrutiny, as are the agencies that administer them; and issues arise among those who are watching and those who are receiving.

Shaping Agendas

Administrative agencies have an almost instinctive reaction when issues are raised about their performance, and that is to try to define them in nonthreatening ways and to process complaints through established channels. If welfare rights advocates are complaining about bureaucratic insensitivity, contradictory and self-defeating regulations, and meager social welfare budgets, the likely response by federal or state agencies will be to define the issues in very specific terms. Should case loads be decreased by a certain percentage? Should day care allowances be increased to $75 from $50 per week? In the regulatory realm, complaints about testing requirements for chemical pesticides, for example, would be whittled down to very specific questions about the number and kinds of tests that have to be completed, the time allowed for test results to be released, and the physical and procedural safeguards that should accompany the use of the chemicals. These are the kinds of questions and issues bureaucratic agencies can deal with effectively. Broad questions about fairness, equity, sensitivity, and the like are usually matters of statutory law and, therefore, have to be decided by legislative and executive authorities.

Bureaucrats normally play what Laurence Lynn calls "the low game." This means that deep within the bureaucracy, issues are narrowly framed and focused. In Lynn's words, "Low games involve the fine-resolution, small-motor processes of government and reflect the concerns of those with operating responsibilities." [8] Thus within the federal Administration for Children and Families the question is not whether to require welfare recipients to work (a high game decision already made by Congress and the president) but rather how to induce state governments to provide the supportive services needed to make "workfare" work.

Despite the operational specificity of bureaucratic agendas, they are by no means unaffected by the "high games" of politicians. Bureaucratic agendas reflect and change with the politics of the administration. We can take as an example the Civil Rights Division of the Justice Department. During the Carter administration the Justice Department actively pursued affirmative action by arguing on behalf of numerical hiring goals for blacks, women, and Hispanics in cases involving public agencies, most notably police and fire departments, that were being sued for discrimination. Its position on affirmative action changed dramatically under the Reagan administration. The Justice Department began entering employment discrimination cases on the other side, arguing against numerical hiring systems that earlier federal efforts had established. In cities like Detroit, Indianapolis, and New Orleans, the department challenged affirmative action plans for police and fire departments that local officials had finally accepted after years of resistance and many rounds of negotiation with federal officials.[9]

The argument put forth here is that the agenda of bureaucratic politics is determined by the interaction of the major "process streams"—problem identification, the formation of policy proposals, and politics—that run through government.[10] Problems are being identified all the time by individuals and groups affected by bureaucratic actions, by legislators, by the media, by agency personnel, and by other levels of government. Problems for which politically and bureaucratically acceptable solutions are available receive attention, and the rest are ignored. Agendas change when these major process streams, particularly the political one, change. Long lists of identified problems and potential solutions for them are continually circulating around legislative, bureaucratic, and academic communities; those that dominate the agendas of bureaucracies at any given time tend to fit best with the prevailing political climate.[11] Because the chief executive is the most powerful agenda setter, an agency like the Office of Management and Budget, which performs the central clearinghouse and oversight functions for the president, plays a major role in determining what does or does not fit with the administration's politics. Internal bureaucratic forces, such as standard procedures, expertise, and control of information, can offer considerable resistance to changing political winds, but they cannot shield an agency's agenda from the effects of political forces generated at the top.

The Cross-Pressured Bureaucracy

It is now widely recognized that bureaucrats live in a highly political world. Politics and administration are inextricably intertwined. In administering programs and enforcing regulations, bureaucrats are making public policy. Even "low game" decisions are laden with policy content. Recognizing this, politicians, interest groups, and judges have stepped up their efforts to control the bureaucracy. As a result, the bureaucracy is more cross-pressured than ever before.[12] Power struggles abound, and the bureaucracy's power resources, so impressive during the days of Lyndon Johnson's Great Society, now seem finite and stretched.

Power

Power in the world of bureaucratic politics comes in a variety of forms. Career bureaucrats, especially professionals and administrators, have power because of what they know and what they do. Their expertise is based in part on access to and control over specialized information that their organizational superiors may not be able to process on their own.[13] Engineers for the Army Corps of Engineers or the National Aeronautics and Space Administration, for example, help to shape the practices and policies of those agencies with their specialized training and knowledge. The same is true, but to a lesser extent, of program analysts and managers in agencies such as the Departments of Labor or Health and Human Services. Clearly, the rarer the expertise, the greater the power that goes with it.[14]

In addition to power based on expertise there is power conferred by authority. The political executives who are placed at the tops of bureaucratic hierarchies have a certain amount of formal authority to impose their will on an agency or a department. Independent regulatory commissioners have the authority, as specified by Congress, to promulgate rules and adjudicate cases involving the industry practices they regulate. Secretaries of state, attorneys general, and local fire chiefs have a great deal of formal authority over the procedures and policies of their organizations. This power is not always as straightforward as it might first appear, however. There are many areas of overlapping jurisdiction and numerous conflicting claims to authority within the administrative state. This is especially true in the intergovernmental arena, where local, state, and federal agencies frequently compete for power over policy.

A third kind of bureaucratic power comes from outside political alliances, affiliations, and connections. Strong agencies usually have strong constituencies, the client groups they serve or other groups that identify with the agency. Reciprocal relationships between bureaucratic organizations and outside interest groups, in which the groups try to protect the agency from hostile citizens or elected officials in exchange for favorable policies, are common at all levels of government. Notable examples include veterans' groups and the Department of Veterans Affairs and farmers' organizations and the U.S. Department of Agriculture (USDA). How a policy option affects client groups is a very important consideration in agency policy making, a consideration that can both guide and constrain action. Courting interest groups is not as easy as it once was, however; the number of groups an agency must be concerned about has proliferated, and they often strongly disagree about policy.[15] For example, the Environmental Protection Agency (EPA) tries to keep environmental groups satisfied without alienating business groups.

Power Struggles

Policy making is a continuous enterprise in most bureaucracies. Line bureaucrats (those in direct contact with clients and problems), investigators, and policy analysts supply a steady stream of policy ideas to legislative staffs for drafting into agency regulations or statutory language. These policy proposals move up through the organizational hierarchy, and high-level officials either accept them or reject them.[16] Top administrators play a pivotal role in the bureaucratic policy-making process because they stand between agency personnel and the central administration and have alliances on both sides. They try to satisfy politicians and career staff by making sure the careerists see some of their ideas put into practice while preventing conflicts with the chief executive's preferences. Central administrative units—budget and policy offices—are now used by nearly all chief executives to review agency regulations and legislative proposals before they go to the legislature, as a further check on policy entrepreneurs or renegades within the bureaucracy.

The most common form of power struggle within an agency occurs between the careerists who have standard routines, turf, and interests to preserve and protect and agency heads with partisan or ideological agendas they seek to promote. Normally, outright conflict is avoided through "mutual accommodation." [17] Agency heads often have considerable substantive knowledge of the policy issues they confront and experience with the organization they direct, and they try, for the most part, not to threaten bureaucratic values. On the other side, careerists are accustomed to seeing leaders come and go—the median term of office for presidential appointees is approximately two years[18]—and are willing to make certain concessions to appease the leadership of the moment.

When internal bargaining and accommodation procedures break down, which occurs most often when a markedly new policy direction is being imposed from above, bureaucratic conflict ensues. This situation is generally unpleasant; conflicts attract outsiders—interest groups, the media, legislators, and chief executives—and their entry fundamentally changes a bureaucratic political struggle. The power, influence, and authority of these outsiders usually overwhelms the bureaucratic combatants and shifts the dispute into the larger political arena. Such a development represents a failure of administrative politics. In this larger arena almost anything can happen; indeed, it is likely that unusual actions will take place: firings, resignations, or dramatic policy changes or reversals. Shifting policy disagreements to this level is very risky, yet it is sometimes seen as necessary by threatened bureaucratic actors.

A typical scenario of bureaucratic conflict occurs when careerists work through interest groups, legislative committees, or the courts to bring to light unwelcome actions or policies of agency heads. A well-publicized example is the controversy over the EPA during Ronald Reagan's first term. Reagan appointed Anne Gorsuch (later Burford) to head the agency, and she and her top staff, who had little knowledge of, or experience with, agency procedures or practices, began making major changes such as new regulations and personnel and budget alterations. Before long, congressional committees, at the prodding of environmental groups and veteran agency employees, began looking into EPA activities. They discovered what appeared to be overt attempts to circumvent environmental statutes.[19] Several resignations resulted, including Burford's, and the president replaced the agency's leadership with a group of experienced EPA administrators headed by William Ruckelshaus.

The discovery of illegalities and improprieties was a major factor in the shake-up at EPA. Rita Lavelle, an EPA official, was convicted of perjury and sentenced to jail for lying to Congress about her role in settling a hazardous waste suit involving her former employer. Bureaucratic fraud, waste, and abuse are salient items in the political world, and they are often what enable outsiders, usually with some inside help, to succeed when they attack an agency.

The normal state of a bureaucratic agency is low-visibility politics, unchallenged authority over a certain policy and program domain, and support from outside groups and legislative committees. Under these circumstances, internal administrative norms, tempered by statutes and the policy preferences of agency heads, determine policy. Bureaucratic conflict disrupts normal procedures and relationships. When an agency's authority to make certain decisions is challenged, control can be lost to outside institutions—the legislature, the chief executive, or the courts. This situation is obviously one that agencies try to avoid.

Leadership

Leadership in bureaucratic politics consists of strategies and tactics for gaining and maintaining a powerful and autonomous role for bureaucratic actors in the policy process. Bureaucratic officials exercise influence over a certain realm of policy in large part because they are able to use organizational tools to mask the extent of their power. Plainly, certain administrative officials are more successful in this endeavor than others. Robert Moses, who planned and saw through to completion much of New York City's present infrastructure of high-ways, bridges, tunnels, and parks, was a strong leader. Another was Admiral Hyman Rickover, who, despite the misgivings of most other Navy leaders, led the Navy into the nuclear era by showing that nuclear reactors could be designed to run submarines. J. Edgar Hoover, who shaped the Federal Bureau of Investigation (FBI) to his own specifica-tions and became powerful enough to challenge presidents, was a leader of almost mythic strength.[20] Analyses of the careers of these and other bureaucratic leaders suggest that leadership in the administrative state has three basic determinants: motivation, context, and personal ability.

Anthony Downs describes five bureaucratic types based on differ-ences in motivation. There are climbers, who are interested only in power, money, and prestige; conservers, who seek "convenience and security" above all else; zealots, who vigorously promote certain ideas and policies and seek power to advance these ideas; advocates, who promote somewhat broader organizational interests and policies and seek power as a way of advancing or elevating their organizational functions; and statesmen, who promote the public interest, and seek power to steer government in a direction that is advantageous to the society as a whole.[21]

The kind of bureaucratic leadership that emerges depends on the political context an agency faces. Young agencies, for example, usually need advocates, and maybe a few zealots, to establish a reputation and power base in policy-making circles. Sargent Shriver's vigorous promo-tion of the Peace Corps in the early 1960s is cited as a classic example of effective advocacy on behalf of a fledgling agency. Admiral Rickover was essentially a nuclear power zealot, and he fought to establish his own organizational domain within the Navy's Bureau of Ships to get his projects under way.

Advocates, but also conservers, can be effective defenders of agencies during periods of budget stringency, a time when more statesmanlike behavior might result in dramatic agency losses. Zealots come to the fore when functional crises hit—when dams break, power plants fail, satellites explode, or reserve stockpiles overflow—because such circum-stances put a premium on ideas and people who are sure of their ideas. Robert Moses, Admiral Rickover, and J. Edgar Hoover were always sure of their ideas, and they rose to prominence during crises—the Great Depression, World War II, and the cold war.

Many effective bureaucratic leaders are entrepreneurs who extend their organizational domain and become more powerful. Moses used his base as president of the Long Island State Park Commission and chair-man of the New York State Council of Parks during the early 1920s to become the head of more than ten city, state, and metropolitan commissions and authorities at the peak of his career in the late 1950s.[22] Entrepreneurs like Moses exhibit the characteristics of advocates and climbers; they aggressively promote their organization and themselves. Bureaucratic imperialism is not always possible or even desirable, however. When the climate of opinion, elite and public, regarding an agency is unfavorable, bureaucratic leaders often try to consolidate rather than extend their authority.[23]

The need for statesmanlike leadership is most evident in mature administrative organizations and during times of national crisis, when it is important to offset the myopic inclinations of advocates and conservers. Hoover was discredited in part because his zealous leadership was no longer appropriate in a mature and established FBI. One of the most serious problems in the administrative state is not having a leadership that is flexible enough to adapt to changing political environments, and one of the major impediments to flexible leadership is that the most consistently rewarded bureaucratic motives—those of advocates, zealots, and conservers—are not particularly conducive to flexible leadership.

Effective administrative leadership also requires individual ability. Studies of bureaucratic organizations have identified a consistent set of attributes, behavioral patterns, and outlooks associated with successful leaders. Leadership in administrative politics demands intelligence, especially the ability to acquire substantive knowledge and to use organizational processes; the will to achieve or succeed; highly developed interpersonal skills; the willingness and ability to listen and learn from others; and the inclination to enjoy organizational and political work and the exercise of power.[24] Leaders are quick to identify the wielders of power and know how to deal with them in various situations. They are capable of thinking creatively, of solving difficult problems, and of resolving internal conflicts. They appreciate the normative and symbolic aspects of their decisions and actions and take seriously their role as teachers and promoters of esprit de corps. They must also know how to make effective use of the media when circumstances require it or when opportunities present themselves.

Like most analysts, we have stressed the role of high-profile political executives as bureaucratic leaders. But civil servants also provide leadership on numerous occasions. Consider, for example, the role of David Edie, a civil servant with the Wisconsin Department of Health and Social Services. Edie, the department's child-care coordinator, became concerned that the department's rules and regulations were limiting the number of licensed family day-care homes by imposing substantial economic costs on tiny, fragile business enterprises. Over a period of three years, he spearheaded a departmental effort to craft a new set of rules that would be more acceptable to providers and that would be easier for the department to enforce. The result was a substantial improvement over the status quo.[25] Without Edie's initiative and perseverance, Wisconsin's day-care rules would probably have remained untouched. It is important to add, however, that Edie's effort ultimately succeeded because he won the tacit support of political executives within his agency and key members of the Wisconsin state legislature.

How Bureaucracies Decide

The literature on political and organizational decision making is emphatic about the tendency of public bureaucracies to make only marginal changes in existing policies in any given round of decision making, a practice known as incrementalism.[26] Administrative decision makers rarely consider problems in their entirety. They restrict themselves to a specialized slice of the problem, react to feedback about the success or failure of current policy by considering a limited number of alternative approaches, and choose options that seem to satisfy all or most of the major interests in their political environment.[27] Past policy decisions serve as the highly valued base for subsequent decisions precisely because of their political character—they represent the best compromise decision makers could devise in the past, and, in the absence of overwhelming evidence to the contrary, there is no reason to believe that the problems or the attendant politics have changed enough to require a radically new approach.

Incremental decision making is in many ways a result of bureaucratic inertia, the adherence to standard operating procedures or professional norms, and internal support for long-standing policies, which has a powerful conservative effect on administrative decisions.[28] The specialized knowledge and information that exists in the middle and lower levels of the bureaucracy is often effectively used to protect internal interests. From his study of information transmission in the military, Morton Halperin identified eleven different ways information can be packaged to influence decisions.[29] Some of them are: report only those facts that support the stand you are taking; structure the reporting so that senior participants will see what you want them to see and not other information; request a study from those who will give you the desired conclusions; advise other participants on what to say; direct the facts toward a desired conclusion if necessary and if you can get away with it.[30] In his study of police and other "street-level" bureaucratic behavior, Michael Lipsky notes that police often exaggerate the danger connected with their jobs to reduce the likelihood that superiors will impose sanctions on those who take certain "threat-reducing" actions—in other words, tough treatment of suspected criminals.[31]

The link between bureaucratic politics and incrementalism does not entirely eliminate the importance of rational or analytic factors in bureaucratic decision making. The so-called rational model of decision making would have administrators look at problems comprehensively and employ certain analytic techniques to evaluate policy options with precision. Rational decision making can be distinguished from incremental/political decision making in that a wider range of alternatives for achieving policy objectives can be considered (nonincremental options are not ruled out automatically) and because decision makers search for solutions that provide the most benefits at the lowest cost rather than for solutions that satisfy as many interests as possible.[32] Rational decision makers use techniques like cost-benefit analysis in identifying the best solutions to policy problems.

The Army Corps of Engineers was probably the first government agency to make consistent use of cost-benefit analysis in determining the best water projects to undertake and in justifying the projects to Congress. For example, a proposal to build a dam on a particular river to create a lake would be evaluated by listing all the costs and benefits of the project and then attaching dollar values to them. The costs would include items such as the value of the land that would be flooded, the cost of relocating families whose homes would be destroyed, the value of lost recreational opportunities, and the cost of construction. The benefits would include new hydroelectric power, irrigation water for farmers, new recreational opportunities, and reduced damage from floods.[33]

Market prices are commonly used in assigning dollar amounts to costs and benefits. Where no market values apply, as with questions regarding the preservation of natural habitats or the psychological and social turmoil associated with destroying communities, imagination and creativity must be put to use. The basic rule is that projects whose benefits are larger than their costs should be pursued, and future costs and benefits have to be discounted to their present value to make this determination. When there are many potential projects from which to choose and there is a limited amount of money that can be spent, as is the case in any real-world setting, the projects offering the largest net benefits, often expressed by benefit-to-cost ratios, are preferred.[34] As this brief discussion of cost-benefit analysis illustrates, the technique provides decision makers with fairly clear-cut choices. But many assumptions—that market prices accurately reflect the social value of different outcomes, for example—and a good deal of guesswork, especially in projecting future costs and benefits, go into the final calculations.

The problem with rational approaches to decision making is that most administrators find them difficult to use because of the cognitive demands they impose, such as evaluating long lists of alternatives and sorting through highly technical analyses, and because of the economic pressure caused by the amount of staff time needed to complete all the analytic chores. Moreover, the rational approaches are often politically irrelevant—legislators are usually more interested in how popular programs are with constituents than in their cost-benefit ratios. Because rational/analytic decision-making processes do not necessarily give preference to existing policies, and are therefore capable of producing nonincremental results, however, they have gained a certain political appeal among those who seek to make dramatic changes in administrative policy and practices. Jimmy Carter tried to make executive agencies more efficient by insisting that they employ a new, nonincremental budgeting procedure known as zero-based budgeting,[35] and Ronald Reagan pursued regulatory reform by creating a White House unit that subjected all new regulations proposed by executive agencies to cost-benefit tests.

Overall, the influence that analytic procedures have on administrative decisions varies according to the nature of the problem and the dispositions of decision makers. Highly technical matters invite analytic solutions, but most of the questions administrators confront are too political to be answered wholly, or even primarily, by analysis. Among bureaucratic officials there are many who dislike and distrust analysis, but a growing number are comfortable with it.[36] Many see mastery of policy planning and analytic activities as a path to greater power and influence in decision-making circles because analysis has become an accepted part of the process by which most organizational decisions are made. Unless the interests associated with policy decisions have numbers to back up their views, they operate at a disadvantage.

Rules and Regulations

Bureaucratic policies come in a number of different forms. First, there are written rules and regulations that have wide applicability and carry the force of law. Second, there are adjudicatory decisions that settle, through quasi-judicial procedures, disputes between antagonistic parties, usually an agency and a business accused of violating an administrative rule or regulation. Third, there are guidelines, policy statements, and advisory opinions that convey to interested parties an agency's thinking or intentions about various matters, but do not have the full legal force of formal rules and regulations. Fourth, there are informal means of settling disputes that do not entail full adjudication. Finally, there are the actions that line bureaucrats take that define the meaning of regulatory or service-delivery policy in practice.

Administrative agencies have developed a mountain of rules and regulations that specify the meaning of legislative statutes. These are published in the *Federal Register* and the *Code of Federal Regulations* and in comparable documents in the states and localities. The adoption of such rules and regulations at the federal level takes place in accordance with procedures spelled out in the Administrative Procedure Act of 1946 (APA); similar statutes exist in most states. When an agency wants to develop rules to enforce provisions of statutes, which Congress has authorized agencies to do, the APA requires that (1) a public notice be entered in the *Federal Register* specifying the time, place, and nature of the rule-making proceedings; (2) interested parties be given the opportunity to submit written, and in some cases oral, arguments and facts relevant to the rule; and (3) the statutory basis and purpose of the rule be indicated. After rules are promulgated, thirty days' notice is required before they take effect.[37] These procedures, known as informal rule making, are designed to give everyone a chance to participate in this essentially legislative activity.

The APA rule-making procedures can be much more formal and cumbersome when a statute requires rule making "on the record after a formal hearing." Under such circumstances agencies must conduct proceedings that resemble trials; witnesses present testimony and submit data or other evidence, there are opportunities for cross-examination of witnesses, and interested parties are prohibited from contacting agency officials during the proceedings. After the hearings, time is set aside for further evidence to be submitted, and agency officials must go over the entire record and carefully document their reasons for issuing a rule. Such hearings often last for weeks or even months. Although agencies are seldom enthusiastic about this degree of formality, they may use this procedure even when they are not required by statute to do so, as a means to blunt criticism of the rules and to bolster their position with the courts, which see adherence to formal procedures as one of the justifications for allowing agencies to exercise rule-making power. Reliance on rules and formal rule-making procedures by agencies increased during the 1970s and 1980s.

Administrative adjudication has a narrower focus than rule making. When there is a disagreement between a company and a union about labor standards, or between the Social Security Administration and a recipient about eligibility for certain benefits, or between a utility company and the NRC about a plant safety issue, a settlement can be reached through adjudication. The procedures are similar to those in a court of law—formal notifications to appear are given to all parties, public records are kept, only certain kinds of evidence are admissible, and each party gets a chance to cross-examine adverse witnesses.[38]

To conduct these proceedings, the bureaucracy employs specially trained personnel, called administrative law judges, who bring with them impartiality and legal and substantive knowledge.[39] The judges interpret administrative law as it applies to the particular case and either issue "orders" (in other words, make a decision) or submit recommendations for a decision to commissioners or chief administrators. In virtually every case, appeals to federal courts are guaranteed. Adjudicated decisions provide a clear indication of agency policies with regard to the specific issues raised in particular cases, but, unlike rules and regulations, they do not establish policy that can be applied with confidence to similar cases.

Bureaucratic agencies also make policy statements and issue advisory opinions (courts refrain from issuing them), but these pronouncements, usually made informally, are not as authoritative as rules and regulations. Statements and advisory opinions enable an agency to tell individuals or companies how it intends to react to certain actions or conditions, or what that agency's operating policy is, with the understanding that such statements do not bind the agency and are subject to full review by the courts, which regard such guidelines as less deserving of deference than formal rules or adjudicatory decisions. An example of a policy statement is a 1990 Internal Revenue Service announcement that cash rebates for energy-saving equipment shall be considered taxable.[40] Businesses of all sorts seek advisory opinions from agencies like the Federal Trade Commission, the Securities and Exchange Commission, the Labor Department, and the EPA on matters ranging from whether certain employees are subject to provisions of the Fair Labor Standards Act to whether certain air pollution devices will satisfy Clean Air Act requirements.

Advisory opinions often are issued to head off litigation. In fact, most of the disputes about policy enforcement that could lead to litigation or to formal adjudication are resolved through informal agreements between agency personnel and the other parties involved. For example, the Labor Department and a company agree that an outside arbiter should meet with company employees to discuss their grievances, or a utility company promises the NRC that it will make certain changes in plant safety procedures. These informal agreements are another attempt to cope with reality because agencies cannot possibly use formal adjudication to resolve all the disagreements they encounter about matters of fact and policy application.

The day-to-day actions taken by bureaucratic officials in their efforts to administer statutory law represent a final large piece of the policy picture. As incredible as it may seem, despite the thousands and thousands of pages of administrative rules and regulations, many real-life situations are still ambiguous, and on-the-spot bureaucratic discretion is needed. Street-level bureaucrats, such as police officers and welfare case workers, are continually faced with the need to make judgments in ambiguous situations—when to make arrests for certain crimes, when to waive certain evidentiary requirements for benefits or special assistance.[41] Although the use of such discretion may seem inevitable, many argue that the police and others who engage in selective enforcement should establish more rules and follow them in more situations.[42] Policy that is determined through direct action or informal agreement tends to be unsystematic and inconsistent; but there are limits to what can be specified and, in certain circumstances, there are advantages to be gained for the agency and its clients from acting informally.

Symbolism

At first glance bureaucratic politics would not seem to provide fertile ground for symbolism. After all, it is the bureaucracy that has to translate the often ambiguous and symbolic statutes enacted by legislatures into concrete rules and activities. Bureaucrats cannot fudge the details; they have to make decisions about who gets what, where, and how. When an individual is granted public assistance or a firm is fined for polluting a river, that means the administrative state has acted in a tangible, substantive manner. Rules, regulations, and adjudicative decisions allocate benefits, specify administrative procedures, and prescribe certain public sector or private sector behaviors; none of these would seem to be a symbolic exercise. Furthermore, most administrative officials do not conceive of their activity as symbolic. They see themselves as executing the will of the legislature—defining problems, designing solutions, and evaluating the effectiveness of past actions.

A number of scholars who have written about bureaucracy have emphasized its symbolic aspects, however. At one extreme, some argue that the administrative state exists largely to carry out symbolic functions.[43] Regulatory policy is said to provide reassurance to the citizens that certain decisions (concerning transportation and utility pricing, for example) are being made with regard for their interests, even though the results of the decisions may not benefit them. Regulatory policy also serves notice to elite interests, the regulated industries, that punitive steps may be taken if they engage in excessively selfish behavior, even though such steps are rarely taken. For social welfare agencies the symbolism argument is that their administrative policies are designed to indicate to the lower classes that they are not entitled to government assistance, even though many of them are, while suggesting to the middle class that assistance is available to anyone who really needs it, even though it is not, and finally to reassure the upper classes that traditional values of individualism and self-reliance are not being abandoned.[44] The thrust of such arguments is that administrative policies, either purposefully or unwittingly, are designed not to solve problems, but to appease or legitimate certain interests and to provide an institutional forum in which recognized interests can compete for influence over policy.

One can find symbolism in other administrative behaviors. Federal and state commissions may hold hearings to obtain citizen input or to grant agenda status to issues raised by grass-roots groups, but then continue to formulate policies in accordance with bureaucratic or industry preferences, thereby revealing the purely symbolic nature of their public actions.[45] Highway patrol officers send a symbolic message when they allow motorists to exceed the speed limit by ten miles per hour. Social workers also send symbolic messages if they keep welfare clients waiting in their outer office for long periods of time. Whether bureaucratic officials recognize it in their actions or not, symbolism is an unavoidable aspect of policy implementation and enforcement.

Change

Bureaucracies depend on continuity. Most agencies prefer to build up a solid base of effective policies and then work carefully and patiently to extend that base as they confront new problems. This way of working is the incrementalism described in the previous section. Administrative agencies are capable of change and innovation, however; this observation applies not only to young agencies, where one might expect some novelty, but also to older, established agencies. Politics, not incrementalism, is the constant in bureaucratic life. When political developments convince bureaucratic leaders that change and innovation are necessary, they can bring them about.

During the 1970s significant changes took place in administrative policies, especially in the area of regulation. These changes can be traced to the growing consumer and environmental movements that brought together previously unorganized interests to exert pressure at all levels of government.[46] Regulatory agencies and policies, which were notorious for favoring the industries being regulated, were a primary target of consumer and environmental groups. Over time these reformers were able to achieve an impressive number of victories over the regulatory dragons. Ralph Nader's breakthroughs on automobile safety regulations helped to pave the way for many other reform efforts.[47] State public utility commissions all over the country began eliminating reduced rates for high-volume industrial users after citizen groups armed with the analyses of economists argued convincingly that such pricing schemes discouraged conservation, caused unnecessary strain on generating facilities, and penalized homeowners and the poor. The solutions they proposed—peak-load and marginal cost pricing and lifeline rates—were widely adopted.[48] New leadership and supportive political environments also led to the reinvigoration of the FTC as a protector of consumers in the early 1970s and even to a major change to a more environmentally sensitive philosophy within the Army Corps of Engineers.[49] New forces were pushing their way into the political environments of government agencies and were stimulating policy change.

Because not all of the changes sought by reform groups become policy, it is important to identify the circumstances that favor change in administrative policies. Political strength is one factor; consumer and environmental groups were solidly grounded in the middle class, and some of the issues they raised had widespread appeal. Movements with this kind of constituency base can strike effectively where politicians feel it most—at the voting booth. Many elected officials at the local, state, and national levels quickly became sympathetic to some of the demands coming from consumer and environmental groups.

Elected officials appoint bureaucratic officials, so the changes in the political landscape during the 1970s soon had effects inside the bureaucracy as consumerists and environmentalists went to work at a growing number of agencies. William Gormley's study of public utility commissions emphasized the role of agency staffs and what he called "proxy advocates" in bringing about changes in utility pricing policies.[50] Proxy advocates are public officials, such as attorneys general, and members of consumer councils who work on behalf of the citizenry, focusing on a wide range of policies in various decision-making settings. Gormley found that the combination of sympathetic and knowledgeable staff and dedicated proxy advocates was a potent source of policy innovation and change.

It is also necessary to consider the distributional effects of policy changes. In most of the cases mentioned here, earlier policies provided substantial benefits to a few (the industry) with the cost being widely distributed among the many. When the many became organized and began to feel strongly about the benefits to be gained from policy change, they found many elected officials who sympathized with their arguments for such change. Where the advantages of policy change are less obvious from a political standpoint, in a situation in which costs and benefits are borne by antagonistic groups of similar size and strength, one would not expect politicians to be inclined to make policy changes.[51]

Finally, political developments influence policy. The energy crisis in the 1970s made conservation a popular, compelling cause, and environmentalists used it to great advantage, especially in areas such as utility pricing and natural resource policy. The near meltdown at Three Mile Island, which shook up the NRC, led to major changes in policy and outlook among nuclear power regulators.

Change and innovation are sometimes short-lived. The recent history of the FTC is instructive. As was mentioned, the FTC was an important part of the proconsumer shift in federal policy during the 1970s. With a supportive Senate Commerce Committee headed by Warren Magnuson, D-Wash., in the early 1970s, new personnel, strong statutory backing, and, after Carter's election, Michael Pertschuk, a forceful consumer advocate, as its chairman, the FTC set out to make capitalism fair and safe for the American people. Between 1976 and 1980 it took on the American Bar Association, the insurance industry, the sponsors of children's advertising on television, used-car dealers, and funeral home directors, but it lost as many of these battles as it won. Congress voided a number of the FTC's major rulings and imposed a host of restrictions on it beginning in 1977. Sentiment in the House and Senate Commerce committees had shifted noticeably back to industry, and the FTC fought an uphill battle for change until Pertschuk was replaced by James Miller, a Reagan conservative.[52] Under Janet Steiger, President Bush's choice as chairperson, the FTC has pursued a more moderate course.

Winners and Losers

It is commonly alleged that regulatory policies primarily benefit the regulated industries, and that social service policies primarily benefit the bureaucrats who administer them. These rather cynical observations can serve as a useful starting point for a discussion of who benefits from administrative politics.

In the regulatory realm the so-called capture theory is often put forward.[53] The basic argument is that over time, regulated industries come to dominate regulatory agencies. This capture takes place because the fervor for reform, usually stimulated by callous industry behavior, results in the creation of a regulatory entity. It quickly becomes apparent, however, that the expertise, interest, and dependable political support the regulatory agency needs to sustain itself reside mainly in the regulated industry. As time passes, a symbiotic relationship—the movement of personnel back and forth and shared interest in each other's priorities and policies—develops between the two, and the capture process is well under way. This analysis has been applied fairly convincingly to the ICC and the railroads, the Federal Power Commission (FPC) and the natural gas industry, the Civil Aeronautics Board and the airlines, and several other pairs.[54] According to economist George Stigler, industries come to see regulation as a benefit, mainly because most forms of regulation restrict entry into regulated markets, thereby reducing competition.[55]

There is no doubt that the capture concept is apt for a number of different regulatory situations past and present, but it is also true that not all regulatory agencies are captured, that captured agencies do not necessarily stay captured, and that some regulatory legislation is intended to promote and protect industry. There are also important differences in regulatory realms that need to be taken into account. The capture theory was typically applied to regulatory agencies that focused on a single industry or on a limited number of companies and to situations in which regulatory objectives were primarily economic. Many current regulatory agencies oversee more than one industry and have social objectives, such as environmental protection, health and safety in the workplace, and civil rights. The multifaceted political environments these agencies face make any simple influence model implausible. One would expect these agencies to pursue various objectives—serving the public, accommodating industry, ensuring their own survival—with the emphasis given to each changing over time in accordance with external and internal pressures.

Gormley's differentiation of regulatory policies according to complexity and conflict provides a useful framework for sorting out expectations about beneficiaries.[56] Regulations that are not terribly complex, such as seatbelt rules, procedures to cut off service by public utilities for nonpayment of bills, or smoking bans in public facilities, give various groups some say in policy because unusual expertise is not required to exert influence. If citizen advocacy groups are active and skillful, there is a good chance that the public will benefit from the policies or at least that some conception of the public interest will be considered in policy making. If public advocacy groups are not present, self-interested groups will dominate. When policies are technically complex (for example, the use of genetically altered material, securities fraud, or banking regulations), a proxy advocate is usually needed to secure policies beneficial to the public. In such cases the specialized expertise and political muscle needed for an effective challenge to objectionable industry behavior may not be available except in a government agency.

The argument linking bureaucrats and social service policies is similar in some ways to the capture theory. Concern about poverty in the 1960s brought into being some hastily designed programs that were not nearly strong enough to solve the problem, but they did create a certain number of jobs for those interested in administering social services. Some alleged that black community organizers were the primary beneficiaries of many War on Poverty programs because community groups were enlisted to implement programs, and known minority leaders were hired to administer them. The actual subsidies and services provided by the programs were said to be too meager or too difficult to obtain for the truly needy to benefit, and unnecessary or even harmful for many of those who did receive them.[57]

The systematic research that has been done on social service programs does not completely refute the arguments just presented, but it suggests that they are simplistic and misleading. Food stamps have helped to reduce malnutrition among America's poor; Medicaid has allowed many poor people to receive medical treatment previously unavailable to them; job-training programs have helped people find jobs; and Head Start and Upward Bound have enabled many minority students to complete high school and college.[58] It is also true, however, that Medicaid has resulted in expensive and in some cases unnecessary treatment, that some of those who benefited most from job-training programs were not especially disadvantaged, and that the largest welfare programs—Aid to Families with Dependent Children, food stamps, Medicaid, and housing subsidies—do not encourage self-sufficiency or reward industry and entrepreneurship. A more accurate appraisal of the beneficiaries of social service programs, therefore, would be that recipients of services as well as bureaucrats benefit from the programs, but there is clearly a need for ongoing programmatic reform.

Distinctions among service delivery programs should also be noted. The War on Poverty programs are often referred to as "social welfare" programs. As the term suggests, these programs aim to improve the lives and aspirations of poor and disadvantaged citizens. But many American social service programs are not aimed at the poor; they have a middle-class clientele. Veterans' benefits and farm subsidies are prime examples, as are Social Security and Medicare. Another category of service programs—highways, mass transportation, water and sewer construction projects—benefits the public as a whole, as well as contractors and their employees. Overall, more money is spent on these nontargeted, middle-class programs than on programs designed to help the poor. In fiscal year 1990 means-tested human services programs, such as Medicaid, food stamps, and AFDC, amounted to $96.6 billion. In contrast, non-means-tested human services programs, such as Social Security and Medicare, amounted to $351.6 billion.[59]

Protected Beaches, Unprotected Workers

We begin this examination of policy consequences with brief descriptions of two programs and then discuss how they illustrate the common patterns and outcomes of bureaucratic implementation and impact. To reflect the variety of implementation settings, one of the examples is a state regulatory policy carried out by a commission; the other is a federal program implemented through an intergovernmental service delivery network.

California Coastal Commissions

The Pacific Ocean is one of California's greatest natural resources, and the policy for land use in coastal areas is of great interest to its citizens. Until the 1970s city and county zoning boards governed the coastal areas within their jurisdictions, which in most cases meant that conservation had a lower priority than development. As the environmental movement took hold in California, activists began to call for state control of the coastal zones. After the state legislature failed to pass regulatory legislation in 1970, 1971, and 1972, an initiative effort was undertaken, and Proposition 20, the Coastal Initiative, was enacted by the voters in November 1972.[60]

The initiative called for the creation of a state coastal commission and six regional commissions, which had the exclusive right to review and approve all forms of development within 1,000 yards of the shore. The regional commissions had an equal mix of local officials and public representatives appointed by the governor and the legislature, and the state commission comprised representatives from each of the six regional commissions with six public members.[61] The idea was neither to ignore local interests nor to allow them to dominate. Staff for the commissions was guaranteed by a $5 million appropriation that was part of the initiative.

The commissions' mandate was fairly clear: "preserve, protect, and, where possible, restore the resources of the coastal zone," and this environmental tone was not compromised by language invoking economic considerations.[62] The initiative set forth strict timetables for making decisions regarding the granting of development permits, and it called for advance publicity of, and public participation in, commission hearings and decisions. All major development projects required a two-thirds approval of the regional commissions, and all important regional commission decisions could be appealed to the state commission and from there to the state superior court. In short, the commissions were responsible for protecting the coastline from construction projects that would produce deleterious environmental, recreational, or scenic effects.

Although they dealt mainly with insignificant cases, the commissions were generally tough on environmental issues in the more important cases. The record shows that in well over 50 percent of the cases involving statutory issues, such as improving public access to beaches, enhancing scenic resources, or protecting wildlife habitats, the commissions either denied the permit or imposed significant new conditions. Some philosophical variation among them was reflected in their decisions; the South Coast Commission in San Diego was the most permissive, and the North Central Commission in San Francisco was the most restrictive. The state commission was definitely restrictive in its rulings, denying permits or imposing conditions on 75 percent of the cases it heard in which statutory issues were raised.[63] Few of its decisions were overturned in court.[64]

Because the commissions reviewed projects that had already been approved by local governments and other state agencies, their decisions to deny construction permits or to impose additional requirements on contractors had very real impact. Not surprisingly, denials of proposed projects sometimes created a furor among developers, construction unions, and some local governments. A frequently imposed requirement in Southern California was that land be set aside for public access to the beach. But the commissions could not require anyone to develop and maintain such pathways; they could only hope, usually to no avail, that local governments or another state agency would do so. Not all of the requirements imposed by the commissions, therefore, had the desired effect. Commission decisions almost completely halted construction on or near wetlands areas, which had been disappearing at an alarming rate before the initiative was passed. This shutdown was probably the most notable short-term impact of commission actions. Another anticipated, but nevertheless problematic, impact of the initiative and its implementation was a rise in housing costs, estimated at $4,000 on the average for houses in the coastal zone and $1,000 for those in the areas bordering it.[65]

The state and regional commissions' staffs also solicited a great deal of expert advice on methods of preserving coastal resources and in 1975 completed the Comprehensive Coastal Plan, as required by the initiative. The plan was used to formulate the 1976 California Coastal Act. This legislation provided for a permanent state coastal regulating body and called for some state acquisition of environmentally sensitive coastal lands, a power the earlier commissions had lacked. The approval process for development projects was altered significantly, however, to give local government more control and to incorporate economic considerations into the decision-making process. The change resulted from political pressure on legislators by unhappy developers.

Public Service Employment Programs and the Labor Department

One of the clearest policy differences between Jimmy Carter and Gerald Ford during the 1976 presidential race was that Carter promised to spend money to combat unemployment if he were elected. Carter pushed Congress to appropriate about $20 billion for jobs in 1977. More than half of this money went to implement the Comprehensive Employment and Training Act (CETA), and most of the CETA money went into its public service employment (PSE) programs. These programs provided state and local governments and nonprofit agencies with money to hire full-time employees, who, it was hoped, would gain the training and work experience necessary to qualify for regular jobs. The number of people holding PSE jobs stood at around 300,000 in June 1977, but would jump to 725,000 in just nine months. The Department of Labor, in conjunction with 450 agencies of the state and local governments, known as prime sponsors, were responsible for implementing the jobs initiative.[66]

The normal difficulties of such a rapid expansion were compounded because the supplemental public service employment money carried a number of new restrictions on participant eligibility and program design. Some state and local governments had begun to practice what is known as substitution. Through questionable layoffs and rehirings on CETA payrolls, or the transfer to CETA of openings created by attrition, the state and local governments were using PSE funds, but were not creating new jobs for the unemployed. Concern over substitution led to the stricture that new money was to be used only for special projects lasting no longer than a year. The Department of Labor strongly encouraged prime sponsors to funnel a large portion of their new PSE money to nonprofit groups, which were less prone to indulge in substitution. New eligibility requirements increased the duration of unemployment necessary to qualify for PSE jobs from fifteen days to fifteen weeks.

Early in 1977, at the prodding of the new administration, the Labor Department sent prime sponsors a series of urgent directives instructing them to perform various tasks, such as assessing community needs and assembling pools of eligible applicants, that would lead to a smooth and effective expansion. In May, however, at about the time the appropriation was passed, the department again changed a number of definitions and directives concerning projects and eligibility, thereby making earlier plans meaningless. As a result, the preparation process fell apart, and the department emphasized an easier priority: the prime sponsors were to hire as many people as quickly as they could.

And hire people they did. About 450,000 new PSE jobs were created in the nine-month period. In some localities the job creation and hiring process was conducted in a carnival-like atmosphere. Organizations of every conceivable variety submitted project proposals and received funding. Although there was some order and rationality with regard to proposal review in most prime sponsorships, little direction or long-term purpose was reflected in the decisions. The principal motivation was to get people on board quickly and to spend the money in accordance with Labor Department timetables.

The results, not surprisingly, included the creation of many projects of questionable value, the enrollment of many ineligible participants (about 20 percent of the total), and the neglect of other aspects of CETA, such as job-training and youth programs. Perhaps most damaging of all was the growing suspicion among citizens and the press about the wisdom of using public funds in this way. A *Reader's Digest* article that included descriptions of "nude body sculpting workshops" and "body drumming classes" operating under CETA auspices touched a raw nerve in Congress and throughout the CETA establishment.[67]

By 1978 the fraud, waste, and abuse in CETA programs had become the overriding issue in unemployment policy. Congress enacted a major reauthorization of the law, which carried an unambiguous message for the Department of Labor: Find and stamp out the abuse. The department quickly imposed a series of new record-keeping requirements and liability sanctions on the prime sponsors, and then sent people into the field to investigate and audit prime sponsor operations. When the results were tallied, the department estimated the illegal expenditure rate in CETA programs to be only 0.5 percent.[68] Congressional critics were not convinced by this finding and chided the department for not looking harder for abuses.

At the prime sponsor level, staff resources shifted toward ensuring regulatory compliance—documenting the legality of expenditures—and away from program operations. The Labor Department was now reviewing all aspects of prime sponsor operations and handing out harsh criticisms and punishments, forcing some localities to pay back illegally spent funds. Administering PSE programs became so burdensome and unpleasant that few administrative or elected officials wanted them. Less than two years after the 1978 reauthorization, Congress eliminated PSE programs, which, during their ten years of operation (1971-1981), had spent $20 billion.

Implementation

These two examples illustrate how statutory language contributes to successful or unsuccessful implementation. When the objectives of a policy are stated without ambiguity, administrators can design regulations and settle disputes in ways that further those objectives. California's Proposition 20 had clear environmental objectives, and the state coastal commission steadfastly pursued these goals. In the case of CETA's public service jobs, some objectives were in conflict—hire people quickly, but find those most in need—and the Department of Labor gave the prime sponsors inconsistent signals about priorities. This inconsistency led to confusion at the state and local levels.

Successful implementation also depends on whether the agency is capable of executing the duties assigned to it. Does it have knowledgeable staff and enough people and money? California's Proposition 20 included a staffing appropriation that allowed the commissions to hire top-notch people without having to approach the legislature for funds. The commissions' staffs achieved most of the major objectives of the initiative. The Department of Labor did not add to its operations and liaison personnel during the massive expansion of PSE in 1977, and this certainly contributed to sloppy implementation. At the prime sponsor level, the differences in the staff capability were quite apparent to field researchers and were seen as one of the main reasons for uneven performance.[69]

Staff capability alone does not ensure successful implementation; attitude and leadership also count. The ideal combination is a capable staff, philosophically committed to the goals of the program, and effective leaders. In California, the commissions were solidly behind the goals of the coastal initiative, and Mel Lane, the chairman of the state commission, provided strong, competent leadership.[70] The CETA situation was quite different. Few within the Labor Department were committed to public service employment, and nothing that would qualify as outstanding leadership came from the department during the 1977 expansion. Skillful leadership did exist in many prime sponsorships, however, and its presence was the most reliable predictor of effective implementation.

Effective communication is also necessary for implementation, particularly when more than one level of government is involved. During the CETA period, the Labor Department issued massive planning documents to state and local prime sponsors in conjunction with changes in policy. Prime sponsor staffs were often overwhelmed by the volume of communications flowing from the department, and their reaction was to ignore most of it.

Administrative agencies are frequently restricted in their enforcement capacity. To fully protect California's coast the commissions would have needed the power to force the cooperation of other state and local agencies and the money and authority to buy wetland habitats and construct the beach pathways. They did not have such power. The CETA program suffered from a different problem. Stricter accountability and more aggressive enforcement led to considerable unhappiness at state and local levels, for elected officials objected to Labor Department auditors breathing down their necks. The burden of implementation eventually led to the refusal of state and local elected officials to defend the program when it was on the congressional chopping block, and their silence certainly contributed to its demise.

Impact

The California Coastal Initiative had a fairly clear antidevelopment impact—a slowdown in construction in the coastal area and a halt to development in wetland areas. Not surprisingly, these substantive results also had political effects. Construction and development interests were not at all shy about expressing their unhappiness with the commissions' policies in 1975 and 1976 when new coastal legislation was being formulated in Sacramento.[71] The new law reflected the tug-of-war between environmental interests and the construction industry by providing for the completion of pathways to the beach and the protection of wetlands, but also by returning to local governments primary responsibility for approving most construction projects in the coastal zone. It is common for programs that produce noticeable effects to also stimulate political opposition.

Public service employment provides an excellent example of why many social services are controversial: their impacts are difficult to document or demonstrate and are subject to various interpretations. The desired results were a reduction in unemployment, additional public services for communities, and assistance for economically disadvantaged people. This attractive combination of benefits ensured the program's popularity among legislators in the 1970s, but there were always good reasons for questioning whether these benefits were actually realized.

For the goal of reducing unemployment, the main difficulty arose from the practice of substitution, which, to the extent it took place, nullified the effects of PSE. Policy analysts disagreed on the most accurate way to measure the phenomenon; substitution estimates ranged from 15 percent of PSE jobs to 90 percent.[72] If all the PSE positions had been newly created jobs, every 500,000 jobs would have represented a 0.5 percent reduction in the unemployment rate. An educated guess is that roughly 25 percent of the PSE jobs were substituted jobs. Because the cost of a 500,000-job program was more than $4 billion, the program lost about $1 billion through substitution.

Evaluating public service was equally complicated, ambiguous, and controversial. Many questioned the wisdom of having public service employees working on arts projects, on the numerous cleanup campaigns started around the country, or in many of the social service agencies that secured CETA funding. Most of the studies pronounced the bulk of PSE projects worthwhile, but this did little to deter critics.[73]

The typical PSE participant was found to be a white male of prime working age with a high school education who was not receiving welfare. This discovery cast doubt on the claim that the program was serving the neediest. The point is underscored when program participants are compared with the population eligible for PSE. The participant group includes a substantially smaller percentage of high school dropouts and welfare recipients.[74] The program helped many needy people get on their feet, but its benefits were disproportionately enjoyed by the less disadvantaged among the unemployed.

Learning

It seems reasonable to expect bureaucratic agencies to learn from their experiences and to incorporate that learning into their implementation policies and practices. Most people would regard this process as central to effective administration. It is also understood, however, that many bureaucratic actors are creatures of habit and others are tuned in mainly to political messages; therefore, internal and external factors sometimes limit an agency's openness to new ideas and responsiveness to new developments.

The California Coastal Commission is a classic case of an agency ready and able to learn. The combination of a young, committed staff and a clear mandate to undertake a comprehensive analysis of coastal issues was ideal for bureaucratic learning. The initiative also protected the commission from legislative interference while it developed the coastal plan, and this protection reduced some of the political pressures, especially from development interests. The coastal plan incorporated the principal lessons the coastal commission experience had provided, and many of these lessons found their way into the 1976 coastal legislation.

The CETA public service employment case was different in nearly every respect. The staff of the Employment and Training Administration of the Department of Labor was not particularly young, committed, capable, well funded, or well led; the agency suffered from high turnover among its top officials. One might conclude that the department learned from the PSE expansion that strict regulatory compliance was necessary to make CETA programs effective, but in fact Congress more or less forced this posture on the department, with dubious consequences. The Labor Department inhabited a world in which politics was intrusive and volatile, and department officials learned to react quickly to changing political winds. But it is not at all clear that these reactions included much learning about effective program administration or policy design.

Overall, several observations about learning in bureaucratic politics seem warranted. First, an openness to new personnel, new ideas, and new approaches is critical in enabling agencies to learn. Second, leadership and learning go hand in hand. Without encouragement and guidance from high-level administrative officials, bureaucrats are unlikely to learn constructive lessons from their experience because they may have difficulty seeing the big picture; top officials should have it in plain sight. Third, the political context must be considered. Agencies with a solid base of political support and a reputation for competent administration among policy makers have the time to learn from their mistakes. Agencies that are subject to constant attention and frequent criticism from elected officials tend to become so paranoid that learning is virtually impossible.

Summary

The Constitution has very little to say about the administrative state. The president is given primary authority over the executive branch, and therefore the bureaucracy, but Congress has the power to create, abolish, organize, and reorganize executive agencies. Congress also can specify authority relationships between the administrative entities it creates and the other branches of government. Any bureaucratic agency can be rendered powerless by Congress, and most of them can be severely crippled, if not paralyzed, by the president or the courts. For bureaucratic agencies, the exercise of power is mostly a matter of having the backing and support of interest groups and other branches of government that have the political influence or constitutional authority they lack.

This support is by no means automatic. Chief executives frequently try to reshape agencies whose policies they oppose. When an attack of this sort occurs, career bureaucrats may fight back by using sympathetic interest groups, the legislature, and the courts to help them protect their domain. If the assault comes from the legislature, a different coalition must be assembled. Agencies can sometimes compete effectively in the high-stakes, high-visibility arenas of politics by playing one branch of government off against another. This skill is part of what has enabled the bureaucracy to become a fourth institutional force in American government.

Clearly more important than their ability to resist incursions from other institutions is the fact that administrative agencies generally remain outside the political limelight. Their influence over policy is greatest when other institutional powers are not watching too closely. Because their policy-making power is derivative, it is always subject to review and alteration: legislatures can abolish agency rules, adjudicative decisions can be overturned by the courts, and administrative regulations can be changed in the offices of chief executives. But these kinds of checks are used sparingly; the normal environment of bureaucratic agencies permits them to exercise considerable power over public policy precisely because the other branches want the bureaucracy to make the tough unpopular decisions. The bureaucracy is one of the places in government where "the rubber meets the road."

Notes

1. Bureau of the Census, *Statistical Abstract of the United States: 1986* (Washington, D.C.: Government Printing Office, 1986), 294, 322.

2. Emmette S. Redford, *Democracy in the Administrative State* (New York: Oxford University Press, 1969).

3. Kathy Sawyer, "The Mess at IRS," *Washington Post* national weekly edition, November 11, 1985, 6.

4. "Wisconsin Will Revise 'Learnfare' Program," *Washington Post*, August 18, 1990, 5.

5. For more on the ICC see Marver Bernstein, *Regulating Business by Independent Commission* (Princeton, N.J.: Princeton University Press, 1955); on the NLRB see Benjamin J. Taylor and Fred Whitney, *Labor Relations Law*, 4th ed. (Englewood Cliffs, N.J.: Prentice-Hall, 1983).

6. See Harrell R. Rodgers, Jr., *The Cost of Human Neglect* (Armonk, N.Y.: M. E. Sharpe, 1982), chaps. 3 and 4.

7. Bureau of the Census, *Statistical Abstract of the United States: 1990* (Washington, D.C.: Government Printing Office, 1990), 350.

8. Laurence Lynn, *Managing Public Policy* (Boston: Little, Brown, 1987), 64.

9. See Philip Shenon, "U.S. Acts to Stop Quotas in Hiring It Backed in the Past," *New York Times*, April 30, 1985, A1, A29; and John L. Palmer and Isabel V. Sawhill, eds., *The Reagan Record* (Cambridge, Mass.: Ballinger, 1984), 204-208.

10. John W. Kingdon, *Agendas, Alternatives, and Public Policy* (Boston: Little, Brown, 1984), 92.

11. Ibid., chap. 6.

12. For an extensive discussion of this trend and its implications, see William T. Gormley, Jr., *Taming the Bureaucracy: Muscles, Prayers, and Other Strategies* (Princeton, N.J.: Princeton University Press, 1989).

13. Francis E. Rourke, *Bureaucracy, Politics, and Public Policy*, 3d ed. (Boston: Little, Brown, 1984), chap. 3.

14. Ibid., chap. 4.

15. See Lance de-Haven Smith and Carl E. Van Horn, "Subgovernment Conflict in Public Policy," *Policy Studies Journal* 12 (Summer 1984): 627-642.

16. See Robert S. Gilmour, "Policy Formulation in the Executive Branch: Central Legislative Clearance," in *Cases on Public Policy-Making*, ed. James E. Anderson (New York: Praeger, 1976), 80-96.

17. Charles E. Lindblom, *The Intelligence of Democracy* (New York: Free Press, 1965).

18. See James Fesler and Donald Kettl, *The Politics of the Administrative Process* (Chatham, Mass.: Chatham House, 1991), 153.

19. See Norman J. Vig and Michael E. Kraft, eds., *Environmental Policies in the 1980s* (Washington, D.C.: CQ Press, 1984), chaps. 5, 7, 8, 17; and Palmer and Sawhill, *The Reagan Record*, 146-151.

20. See Eugene Lewis, *Public Entrepreneurship* (Bloomington: Indiana University Press, 1980).

21. Anthony Downs, *Inside Bureaucracy* (Boston: Little, Brown, 1967), 88-89.

22. Lewis, *Public Entrepreneurship*, 214-215.

23. Rourke, *Bureaucracy, Politics, and Public Policy*, 118-119.

24. Laurence Lynn, *Managing Public Policy* (Boston: Little, Brown, 1987), 119-125.

25. William T. Gormley, Jr. *Family Day Care Regulation in Wisconsin: The Bureaucracy Heals Itself* (Madison, Wis.: La Follette Institute of Public Affairs, University of Wisconsin, 1990).

26. See Herbert A. Simon, *Administrative Behavior: A Study of Decision-Making Processes in Administrative Organizations* (New York: Macmillan, 1957); James G. March and Herbert A. Simon, *Organizations* (New York: John Wiley, 1964); Richard M. Cyert and James G. March, *A Behavioral Theory of the Firm* (Englewood Cliffs, N.J.: Prentice-Hall, 1963); Aaron Wildavsky, *The Politics of the Budgetary Process*, 3d ed. (Boston: Little, Brown, 1979); and Charles E. Lindblom, "The Science of Muddling Through," *Public Administration Review* 19 (Spring 1959): 79-88.

27. Lindblom, "The Science of Muddling Through," 79-88.

28. Rourke, *Bureaucracy, Politics, and Public Policy*, 29-35.

29. Morton H. Halperin, "Shaping the Flow of Information," in *Bureaucratic Power in National Politics*, 3d ed., ed. Francis E. Rourke (Boston: Little, Brown, 1978), 102-115.

30. Ibid., 102-110.

31. Michael Lipsky, "Toward a Theory of Street-Level Bureaucracy," in *Bureaucratic Power in National Politics*, 135-157.

32. For a modern version of the rational perspective, see Charles J. Hitch, *Decision-Making for Defense* (Berkeley: University of California Press, 1965); or E. S. Quade, *Analysis for Public Decisions* (New York: Elsevier, 1975).

33. A more complete discussion of this example can be found in B. Guy Peters, *American Public Policy: Promise and Performance*, 2d ed. (Chatham, N.J.: Chatham House, 1986), 297-309.

34. For an excellent discussion of the principles and techniques of cost-benefit analysis, see Edith Stokey and Richard Zeckhauser, *A Primer for Policy Analysis* (New York: W. W. Norton, 1978), chaps. 9 and 10.

35. The basic idea of zero-based budgeting is to offer decision makers information in a form that allows them to make choices based on effectiveness, rather than on past funding levels. First, agencies are divided into "decision units," which should correspond to the program-operating entities within the agency. Each decision unit prepares "decision packages" that indicate which programs and activities that unit would continue at higher or lower funding levels. The packages then move up the agency hierarchy and are used to establish priorities at each level until an overall agency budget request is assembled. The process is supposed to identify the programs that work best so that they can be continued or expanded, and those that are not working well can be cut back or eliminated. For a full discussion, see Fred A. Kramer, ed., *Contemporary Approaches to Public Budgeting* (Cambridge, Mass.: Winthrop,

1979), chap. 4.

36. Lynn, *Managing Public Policy*, 187.

37. See Kenneth Culp Davis, *Administrative Law of the Seventies*, supplementing Davis's *Administrative Law Treatise* (Rochester, N.Y.: Lawyers Co-Operative Publishing, 1976), 170; and A. Lee Fritschler, *Smoking and Politics*, 3d ed. (Englewood Cliffs, N.J.: Prentice-Hall, 1983), 79.

38. See Davis, *Administrative Law of the Seventies*, chap. 8.

39. See Fritschler, *Smoking and Politics*, 93-98.

40. Thomas Lippman, "Utility Rebates for Energy-Saving Equipment Deemed Taxable," *Washington Post*, November 25, 1990, 3.

41. Lipsky, "Toward a Theory of Street-Level Bureaucracy."

42. See Davis, *Administrative Law of the Seventies*, chap. 4.

43. See Murray Edelman, *The Symbolic Uses of Politics* (Urbana: University of Illinois Press, 1964), chap. 3.

44. See Frances Fox Piven and Richard A. Cloward, *Regulating the Poor* (New York: Vintage Books, 1971); or Piven and Cloward, *Poor People's Movements* (New York: Vintage Books, 1979).

45. William T. Gormley, Jr., Joan Hoadley, and Charles Williams, "Potential Responsiveness in the Bureaucracy: Views of Public Utility Regulation," *American Political Science Review* (September 1983): 704-717; and William T. Gormley, Jr., *The Politics of Public Utility Regulation* (Pittsburgh: University of Pittsburgh Press, 1983), 113-130.

46. See Andrew S. McFarland, *Public Interest Lobbies* (Washington, D.C.: American Enterprise Institute, 1976); or Jeffrey M. Berry, *Lobbying for the People* (Princeton, N.J.: Princeton University Press, 1977).

47. See Mark V. Nadel, *The Politics of Consumer Protection* (Indianapolis: Bobbs-Merrill, 1971); and Kenneth J. Meier, *Regulation* (New York: St. Martin's Press, 1985), 96-97.

48. Gormley, *The Politics of Public Utility Regulation;* and Douglas D. Anderson, "State Regulation of Electric Utilities," in *The Politics of Regulation,* ed. James Q. Wilson (New York: Basic Books, 1980), 3-41.

49. See Meier, *Regulation*, 106-113, on the FTC; and Daniel A. Mazmanian and Jeanne Nienaber, *Can Organizations Change? Environmental Protection, Citizen Participation, and the Corps of Engineers* (Washington, D.C.: Brookings Institution, 1979), on the Army Corps of Engineers.

50. Gormley, *The Politics of Public Utility Regulation*, 152-177.

51. See *The Politics of Regulation*, chap. 10.

52. See Meier, *Regulation*, 106-113; and Michael Pertschuk, *Revolt Against Regulation* (Berkeley: University of California Press, 1982).

53. See Bernstein, *Regulating Business by Independent Commission;* Theodore J. Lowi, *The End of Liberalism*, 2d ed. (New York: W. W. Norton, 1979); Grant McConnell, *Private Power and American Democracy* (New York: Alfred A. Knopf, 1966); and George Stigler, "The Theory of Economic Regulation," *Bell Journal of Economic and Management Sciences* (Spring 1971): 3-21.

54. See Bernstein, *Regulating Business by Independent Commission;* Bradley Behrman, "The Civil Aeronautics Board," in *The Politics of Regulation*, 57-120; and David Howard Davis, *Energy Politics*, 3d ed. (New York: St. Martin's Press, 1982), 130-165.

55. Stigler, "The Theory of Economic Regulation."

56. Gormley, *The Politics of Public Utility Regulation*, 152-159.

57. For evaluations of American social welfare programs by authors with

contrasting ideological perspectives, see Piven and Cloward, *Regulating the Poor;* and Charles Murray, *Losing Ground: American Social Policy, 1950-1980* (New York: Basic Books, 1984).

58. See Robert H. Haveman, ed., *A Decade of Federal Antipoverty Programs* (New York: Academic Press, 1977); John E. Schwarz, *America's Hidden Success* (New York: W. W. Norton, 1983); Karen Davis and Kathy Schoen, *Health and the War on Poverty* (Washington, D.C.: Brookings Institution, 1978); and Robert Taggart, *A Fisherman's Guide: An Assessment of Training and Remediation Strategies* (Kalamazoo, Mich.: W. E. Upjohn Institute for Employment Research, 1981). For a recent evaluation of Head Start, see Valerie Lee et al., "Are Head Start Effects Sustained?" *Child Development,* 61, no. 2 (April 1990): 495-507.

59. House Ways and Means Committee, *1990 Green Book* (Washington, D.C.: Government Printing Office, 1990), 1388.

60. Our discussion of the California Coastal Commissions is based on Daniel Mazmanian and Paul Sabatier, *Implementation and Public Policy* (Glenview, Ill.: Scott, Foresman, 1983), 218-265.

61. Ibid., 224.

62. Ibid.

63. Ibid., 233.

64. Ibid., 227.

65. Ibid., 246.

66. This discussion of public service employment is based on Donald C. Baumer and Carl E. Van Horn, *The Politics of Unemployment* (Washington, D.C.: CQ Press, 1985), chaps. 4-5.

67. Ralph Kinney Bennett, "CETA: The $11 Billion Boondoggle," *Reader's Digest,* August 8, 1978, 72-76.

68. Baumer and Van Horn, *The Politics of Unemployment,* 133.

69. See Randall B. Ripley et al., *The Implementation of CETA in Ohio,* Employment and Training Administration, U.S. Department of Labor, R&D monograph no. 44 (Washington, D.C.: Government Printing Office, 1977); and Ripley et al., *CETA Prime Sponsor Management Decisions,* Employment and Training Administration, U.S. Department of Labor, R&D monograph no. 56 (Washington, D.C.: Government Printing Office, 1978).

70. Mazmanian and Sabatier, *Implementation and Public Policy,* 229.

71. Ibid., 250.

72. For estimates of substitution, see Alan Fechter, *Public Employment Programs* (Washington, D.C.: American Enterprise Institute, 1975); National Planning Association, *An Evaluation of the Economic Impact Project of the Public Employment Program* (Washington, D.C.: National Planning Association, 1974); George Johnson and James D. Tomola, "The Fiscal Substitution Effects of Alternative Approaches to Public Service Employment," *Journal of Human Resources* 12 (Winter 1977): 3-26; and Richard Nathan, Robert Cook, and V. Lane Rawlins and Associates, *Public Service Employment: A Field Evaluation* (Washington, D.C.: Brookings Institution, 1981).

73. See William Mirengoff and Associates, *CETA: An Assessment of Public Service Employment Programs* (Washington, D.C.: National Academy of Sciences, 1980); or Nathan et al., *Public Service Employment.*

74. Baumer and Van Horn, *The Politics of Unemployment,* 116.

5　Cloakroom Politics

Much of American politics and policy making takes place in the cloakrooms, committee rooms, and chambers of city councils, state legislatures, and the U.S. Congress. Legislative institutions are often perplexing and frustrating to members and ordinary citizens alike. Describing and assessing the way legislatures operate is a little like retelling the story of the blind men who try to say what an elephant is by describing what they can feel. The impression one gets depends on where one is standing.

Legislatures are highly democratic, open institutions that are also responsive to narrow, specialized interest groups. Legislatures are powerful actors in the policy process, but they delegate responsibility for many significant decisions to other political institutions. Legislatures are the most responsive political institutions and in some ways the least responsible. To many observers, legislative policy making is both appealing *and* appalling.

Compared with most other domains of politics, cloakroom politics is perhaps the most visible, democratic, chaotic, and human. Only chief executives command more public attention; only living room politics is more democratic. Legislatures embody a fundamental urge in the American experience—to have a place where the conflicts of public life are debated, deliberated, and decided in full view.

Legislatures are a focal point for the inside players. Government administrators, lobbyists, citizen activists, and journalists have easy access to the legislative chambers and committee rooms and offices. Legislators do not dominate the policy process, but they insinuate themselves into all aspects of public policy. They raise important issues, allocate public goods and services, and influence public and private behavior even when they delegate decisions to others.

Although Americans approve of what Alexis de Tocqueville called "this ceaseless agitation" [1] of legislatures, citizens often are frustrated by the chaos of legislative life. Legislatures reflect not only democratic impulses, but also the interests of the powerful. Sometimes legislatures courageously tackle the tough issues of the day; at other times they seem to cower before the challenges that face them. Sometimes legislative actions make the situation worse; when legislatures do nothing, things sometimes get better. Legislatures mirror the conflicts that exist in American society. Consensus is achieved slowly, and it can evaporate quickly.

The Crowded Agenda

The scope of cloakroom politics is incredibly broad. It includes economic affairs, environmental protection, defense and foreign policy, health, education, and welfare issues. Every year members of legislatures cast hundreds of votes on public laws and resolutions. Countless issues receive attention from committees, subcommittees, and individual members. The scope of cloakroom politics is illustrated by the issues considered during the 102d Congress (1991-1992). Table 5-1 is an incomplete list, but it conveys the breadth of Congress's responsibilities and public policy interests. As American legislatures go, Congress is not unusual in having a far-reaching policy agenda. State legislatures also have extremely varied agendas. During a recent session, the California legislature held hearings and passed legislation covering topics as diverse as urban economic development, insurance reform, child care, health services for senior citizens, and hazardous waste policies.

One might at first conclude that legislatures, their committees, and their members consider practically everything imaginable. Open and democratic as they are, however, legislatures do not respond to everyone who knocks on their doors. Legislatures are collections of many smaller organizations—the offices of the senators and representatives and legislative committees. Most issues are handled first by subcommittees and committees, especially in the U.S. Congress, and are never considered by legislators other than committee members. Committees and subcommittees have wide latitude to conduct hearings on, investigate, and review legislation within their jurisdictions. With input from party leaders, committees are then able to formulate bills (major and minor) that go to the floor for action by the entire chamber. Most floor votes are simple yes or no choices on measures structured for the members by committee and party leaders.

Most legislative activity is debate and discussion rather than lawmaking, and legislatures can influence policy without making laws. Legislatures often engage in protracted considerations of issues without making decisions because, unlike other institutions, they are important democratic and political forums—where symbolism can be just as important as substance. A great deal of time and energy is spent raising issues, seeking publicity, educating the public, helping political supporters, and embarrassing opponents.

Table 5-1   Some Issues Considered in the 102d Congress, 1991-1992

AGRICULTURE: reauthorization of the Federal Insecticide, Fungicide, and Rodenticide Act

BANKING: overhaul of commercial banking regulations, recapitalizing the Federal Deposit Insurance Corporation, salvaging savings and loan associations

DEFENSE: provision of benefits for combat veterans, modernization of weapons and aircraft, completion of arms control treaties

ECONOMIC AFFAIRS: implementation of new budget resolution, levying of new taxes, paying for the Persian Gulf War

ENERGY/ENVIRONMENT: oil production in the Alaskan wilderness, reauthorization of Resource and Conservation Recovery Act, fuel efficiency standards

FOREIGN POLICY: military aid to El Salvador, U.S.-Israeli relations, regulating intelligence activities, internal divisions in the Soviet Union, China's trade status

GOVERNMENT OPERATIONS: campaign finance reform, congressional pay and honoraria and ethics, term limitations

HEALTH, EDUCATION, WELFARE: child welfare, anti-tobacco legislation, family medical leave, reauthorization of Higher Education Act and Job Training Partnership Act

HOUSING/COMMUNITY DEVELOPMENT: setting funding levels for new and old federal housing and community development programs (authorizing legislation was overhauled in 1991)

LAW ENFORCEMENT/JUDICIARY: reconsideration of job discrimination bill (Civil Rights Act of 1990), gun control, vertical price fixing

SCIENCE/TECHNOLOGY: cable television regulations, restrictions on regional telephone companies, reallocating the government radio wave spectrum

TRADE: General Agreement on Tariffs and Trade (GATT) negotiations, textile import restrictions, trade agreements with Mexico and the Soviet Union

TRANSPORTATION: reauthorization of federal highway, bridge, and mass transit programs

---

Source: Congressional Quarterly Weekly Report, January 19, 1991.

If a problem is not already on the institution's agenda, it is difficult to get it there. One scholar noted that the bulk of Congress's time is consumed considering matters that recur each year.[2] The struggles to get a vote on the floor of the House or Senate are often intense because the time these institutions can spend in collective deliberation is scarce and there are many claimants to it. Often sponsors have to wait several years after committees have finished work on a bill to get it on the floor. Legislatures frequently must revisit past policy actions or deal with unfinished business from previous Congresses. Many of the issues listed in Table 5-1 are bills that were passed by Congress five, ten, or even forty years ago, but in a different form.

Another large chunk of legislatures' limited time is consumed by crises. A war in the Middle East, a space shuttle disaster, famine in Africa, arms for hostages, bank failures, stock manipulation on Wall Street, an oil spill, scandals, and other problems command the immediate attention of elected representatives. In some cases their response is quick legislative action. But in other cases they do a lot of talking about whether and how to respond, while looking to the chief executive for direction. When Iraq invaded Kuwait, Congress waited several months before taking votes on resolutions to either give or withhold authorization for the president to use military force against Iraq.

Many features of cloakroom politics keep the legislature doors open to a broad range of views; power is dispersed, and there are many ways to gain access to the institution's agenda. Legislatures respond to the concerns of members and of a wide range of outsiders, including presidents and governors, executive agencies, interest groups, and individual citizens, but the response is not always the same in kind or degree. In general the attention of a single representative may be easily gained, but not that of an institution.

Members

The issue agendas of individual legislators are strongly influenced by the concerns of citizens and organizations from their districts. Dealing with constituency problems consumes much of the time of members and their personal staffs. Representatives use their influence to speed up approval of grants for sewer projects, obtain funds for the building of agricultural research laboratories, obtain tax breaks for a steel mill, or fight for more financial aid for students. Collectively, the concerns of constituents play a strong part in shaping the policy activity of legislatures. A study of the Minnesota and Kentucky legislatures found that about one-third of the legislators considered casework to be their most important function, and about half of them spent between 25 percent and 50 percent of their time performing casework-related chores.[3]

When legislators stand for reelection every two, four, or six years, they must account, however loosely, for their action or inaction on important matters. Voters and journalists, who shape evaluations of legislators, like to ask, "What have you done for us lately?" Despite the fact that nine members of Congress in ten who seek reelection win their contests, most "run scared" even in districts that appear safe for the incumbents. Indeed, one reason so many seats are safe is that members work so hard at reelection.[4] The uncanny ability of Democratic incumbents to secure reelection led President Bush in 1991 to endorse a constitutional amendment to limit the number of terms members of Congress can serve.

Some legislators develop reputations as "policy entrepreneurs" because they exhibit a keen interest in advancing a cause, an idea, or a new program. That interest, combined with ambition, makes them very influential. As they seek legislative accomplishments or perhaps higher office, they push new items onto committee or subcommittee agendas. They respond quickly to national and international events and mass media reports. Policy entrepreneurs do not necessarily want to expand government spending programs. For example, Senator Phil Gramm, R-Texas, who led the charge for reductions in federal spending in the early 1980s, is no less an entrepreneur than Senator Edward Kennedy, D-Mass., a longtime advocate of expanded education, child-care, and public health insurance programs.

Legislators also use their committee and subcommittee positions to focus attention on scandals or government mismanagement and fraud. Investigations throw light on the members as well as the issues. A typical congressional probe was launched in early 1987 after a New York–bound Amtrak train traveling faster than 130 miles an hour rammed a Conrail freight engine. Sixteen people were killed, more than 150 people were injured, and train service between Washington, D.C., and New York City was disrupted for days.

Under existing law, the Federal Railway Administration (FRA) and the National Transportation Safety Board (NTSB) began investigating the accident. Within days, they determined that Conrail engineers had ignored signals on the track and had taped shut a whistle that would have warned them to stop. Safety officials also disclosed blood and urine tests that suggested the Conrail crew might have been physically and mentally impaired by the use of marijuana.

Before the administrative investigations were complete, Senator Frank Lautenberg, D-N.J., chairman of a Senate transportation subcommittee, called a hearing on the causes of the accident. Before television cameras and representatives of the print media, the chairman and his colleagues grilled witnesses from the railroads, members of the unions representing the engineers, and officials of the safety agencies. Assuming the role of judge and jury, Republican Senator Alfonse D'Amato of New York concluded that drug abuse by the crew caused the accident and demanded random tests of all train operators. (Such tests were later ordered by President Reagan and the order was upheld by the Supreme Court.) Little dramas like this train accident investigation occur dozens of times each year and help to set Congress's agenda, while enabling members to increase their visibility back home.

The agendas of legislators are shaped not only by constituency pressures, but also by pressures from outside groups. Executive branch agencies and interest groups generally focus their concerns on the committees and subcommittees that develop the policies and programs which most directly affect them. Indeed, many of the issues considered by legislative committees originate in administrative agencies. Although committee chairs and other influential committee members exercise a great deal of independent power, they are responsive to concerns expressed by the executive branch.

Outside interest groups influence legislators because these groups supply the milk and honey of politics—money and grateful voters. Running for office costs a great deal of money; Senate campaigns run to millions of dollars. The quest for campaign funds compels legislators at least to listen to the concerns of their contributors. Organizations with money employ several methods to get the attention of subcommittees and committees. They hire lobbyists to monitor legislation, meet with members and staff, and pay legislators to speak at group meetings. Organizations that cannot deliver money or votes have a much tougher time gaining attention.[5]

The Institution

Issues that dominate the attention of the entire legislature are broad societal concerns and issues advanced by presidents, governors, or legislative leaders. Take the issue of air pollution, for example. In 1990 both President Bush and Senate Majority Leader George Mitchell announced that new clean air legislation was their top legislative priority. Congress had tried unsuccessfully over a thirteen-year period to revise the Clean Air Act, but with both Mitchell and Bush pushing for action Republicans and Democrats were able to agree on compromise legislation. Despite considerable opposition from both affected industries and environmental groups, the 1990 revision of the Clean Air Act passed both houses of Congress and was signed by the president.

The mere mention of a policy initiative by the president or a governor stimulates legislative activity and may yield new laws. Just after taking office, Governor Lowell Weicker of Connecticut threw the legislature, and most of the citizens, into a flurry of debate by proposing a new set of tax laws that included the state's first-ever income tax. Instantly, the Weicker tax proposals leaped to the top of the Connecticut legislature's agenda.

Legislatures listen to outsiders, especially chief executives, but the entrepreneurial instincts of members and committees also bring new ideas to the agenda that chief executives would prefer to ignore. Between 1986 and 1988, Congress made sweeping changes in national immigration policy, passed a massive highway building and rehabilitation program, revised the Clean Water Act, and imposed economic sanctions on the South African government. None of these policies was promoted by President Reagan; some he actively opposed.

Legislative leaders occasionally can turn the spotlight on policy issues even when they do not percolate up from committee and subcommittee power centers. For example, new antidrug legislation appropriating nearly $2 billion was adopted in late 1986, yet the traditional sources of policy proposals (committees, executive agencies, major interest groups) were not advocating major legislation at the year's beginning. Why did this happen so swiftly? Two well-known athletes—a college basketball star and a professional football player—died of cocaine overdoses, and President Reagan (with his wife, Nancy) made a televised appeal for a "national crusade" against drugs. Despite the absence of reliable statistics showing an increase in drug use, opinion polls revealed increasing public anxiety about drug abuse among young people, especially the use of crack cocaine. The *New York Times* reported: "Antidrug bills that have lingered in committees for months or years are now passing out 'in minutes.'... Cost doesn't seem to be an object now." [6]

A similar situation occurred in the spring of 1991, when members of Congress could not wait to pass legislation granting new or expanded benefits to past and future veterans of military conflicts despite the looming presence of the largest budget deficit in history. They began by passing a long-delayed bill to provide compensation to Vietnam War veterans suffering from the effects of exposure to the herbicide Agent Orange. They went on to pass new educational, small business, home loan, and medical care benefits for participants in the Persian Gulf War.[7]

Legislative staff members are another fertile source of policy proposals. Congress employs an army of professional analysts, lawyers, and political advisers—a personal and committee staff numbering more than 18,000.[8] Another 10,000 work for support agencies, including the Congressional Research Service (CRS), the General Accounting Office (GAO), the Congressional Budget Office (CBO), and the Office of Technology Assessment (OTA). These agencies provide general and specific research assistance to legislative members and committees, conduct studies either on their own initiative on in response to requests by members or committees, and review and investigate the actions of executive agencies. State legislatures used to rely almost entirely on centralized staffs (offices of legislative councils and reference bureaus) that served entire chambers, but have now "congressionalized" by greatly expanding the number of staff personnel and assigning them to work for committees, legislative parties, and individual members. Nationally there are about 20,000 full-time state legislative staffers.[9]

Entrepreneurial Politics

Although legislatures can engage in policy debates and focus public attention on social and economic problems, it is much harder for them to take decisive action. When legislators want to make policy, they must deal, bargain, and compromise in order to develop the several majorities required to enact legislation. This majority-building enterprise is difficult and complicated, in large part because cloakroom politics is molded by the complex contemporary political and economic environment. Legislatures do not function in hermetically sealed chambers; deliberation and debate within them reflects societal differences about public problems and solutions.

Suppose someone asked for an explanation of why a landmark tax law was passed in 1986 but not in 1980 or 1990. We might begin by outlining the basic features of the political landscape in 1986. The presidency and the U.S. Senate were controlled by Republicans, the House of Representatives was controlled by Democrats. With public opinion polls revealing widespread displeasure with the tax system's complexity and favoritism and tax experts agreeing that it was unfair and inefficient, a popular president advocated a major overhaul. Democrats were loath to bear any blame for blocking reform because their 1984 presidential nominee, Walter Mondale, had promised a tax increase and had lost in all but one state. Indeed, Ways and Means Chairman Dan Rostenkowski, D-Ill., came forward to play a major role in the passage of the Tax Reform Act. Seeking desperately to retain control of the Senate, the Republicans needed a tax bill before the 1986 election.[10]

Painting tax reform politics in such broad brush strokes, however, conceals important nuances. To get a bill through, committee chairs, legislative leaders, and the president were obliged to satisfy the parochial demands of dozens of legislators and interest groups. Passage was threatened by the potential defection of House Republicans. As noted in the following excerpt from the *Washington Post*, the bill's fortunes were determined in part by the doling out of favors.

> President Reagan may have wanted to talk taxes when he invited Rep. Steven Gunderson to the Oval Office last week, but the young Republican from Wisconsin wanted to talk cows. . . . By the time the session was over, both men had what they wanted: Gunderson knew Reagan would sign the farm bill sought by his rural district; Reagan knew that Gunderson would vote for the tax-overhaul legislation in the House. . . . Says Gunderson, "I

think that's a sensible way for adults to do business." And that's the way business was done up and down the Republican and Democratic aisles of the House.[11]

Similar politics molds hundreds of bills that do not make headlines. In the cloakrooms of every capitol, politics is characterized by fragmented power, bargaining and compromise, deadlines, and legislative and executive leadership.

Fragmented Power

No one controls or commands legislatures. At times it seems that there are 535 leaders on Capitol Hill and no followers. House and Senate elected leaders retain their positions only as long as the members support them. Unlike bureaucracies where there is a hierarchy of authority, legislatures are collections of independent contractors. No one tells a member how to run a committee or how to vote. Environmental Protection Agency regulations governing auto emission standards are issued by the administrator who may seek advice from staff, industry, and the public, but the final decision on many matters rests with the administrator. When Congress writes laws governing air pollution, 535 members have some say in the outcome.

Legislatures are not without organization. Committees and subcommittees are the heart and soul of legislative policy making. Writing about Congress in 1885, political scientist (later president) Woodrow Wilson referred to its committees as "little legislatures." [12] What Wilson observed then is no less true today. Committees are powerful vehicles for policy deliberation and action. In fact, a legislature's ability to shape public policy is vastly expanded by the division of labor and development of expertise made possible by the committee and subcommittee system.

Congress is divided into hundreds of little legislatures. In 1990 the House had 22 major legislative committees and 138 subcommittees; the Senate had 16 committees and 86 subcommittees. Because subcommittees are chaired by members of the majority party, more than half of the Democrats in the House chaired a subcommittee. Each majority party senator chaired at least one subcommittee and sometimes two.[13] The subcommittees of the Senate Labor and Human Resources Committee and the House Agriculture Committee are listed in Table 5-2.

In fact, power is so widely dispersed in legislatures that the media and the public have trouble keeping track of the star players in each legislative ball game. Even powerful groups, such as the House Ways and Means Committee, which handles such matters as taxation, trade policy, Social Security, and health programs, are practically invisible to the public. Most committees and subcommittees are even more obscure. Few people outside Washington, D.C., know that the House Appropriations

Table 5-2   Subcommittees of Two Congressional Committees

Senate Committee on Labor and Human Resources

Aging
Children, Family, Drugs, and Alcoholism
Disability Policy
Education, Arts, and Humanities
Employment and Productivity
Labor

House Committee on Agriculture

Conservation, Credit, and Rural Development
Cotton, Rice, and Sugar
Department Operations, Research, and Foreign Agriculture
Domestic Marketing, Consumer Relations, and Nutrition
Forests, Family Farms, and Energy
Livestock, Dairy, and Poultry
Peanuts and Tobacco
Wheat, Soybeans, and Feed Grains

Source: Congressional Quarterly Weekly Report, (Special Report), May 4, 1991, 25, 34-35.

Subcommittee on Labor, Health and Human Services, Education, and Related Agencies appropriates more than one-third of the entire federal budget. Fewer still have heard of the Subcommittee on Surface Transportation or the Subcommittee on Commerce, Consumer Protection, and Competitiveness, let alone have the foggiest idea about what they do.

The policy issues handled by each subcommittee give rise to "issue networks" that include members of Congress and their staffs, executive agencies, interest groups, journalists, and academics. Many important policy decisions that go unnoticed by the public are made within this subcommittee-centered power structure. The fragmented system satisfies legislators because it permits more of them to exercise power. Interest groups are pleased because they gain access and attention to their concerns. If the fishing industry is feeling threatened by environmental regulations, the Subcommittee on Fisheries (of the House Committee on Merchant Marine and Fisheries), whose members are from coastal areas, can provide representatives of this group with an opportunity to press their case in a public forum. Executive agencies also recognize some benefit from the convenience and familiarity of dealing with a limited number of legislators who are knowledgeable about a particular agency's programs and policies.

Subcommittees also create power bases for promoting innovative policies. The chairman and subcommittee chairmen of the House Energy and Commerce Committee, for example, have used their platforms to launch investigations and formulate sweeping changes in health policy, environmental protection, and telecommunications. According to Chairman John Dingell, D-Mich., the jurisdiction of the committee is "anything that walks and anything that thinks about walking." [14]

One of the House Energy and Commerce Committee's most effective issue entrepreneurs is Henry Waxman of California, chairman of the Health and Environment Subcommittee, who has been fighting with Dingell (who represents Detroit and the auto industry) over environmental policy for many years. Waxman is a long-standing proponent of acid rain legislation and tough auto emission standards. In 1982 he successfully staved off Dingell's move to relax the emission standards of the Clean Air Act, and in 1990 he was finally able to get acid rain provisions included in the act. He has also sponsored a number of health initiatives over the years, including an AIDS prevention and treatment bill in 1988, and a measure that would place strict limitations on the promotion, distribution, and sale of cigarettes that he pushed through his subcommittee in 1990.

Bargaining and Compromise

Because power is widely dispersed, bargaining and compromise are central to legislative politics. Fragmentation enhances the power of members and subcommittee leaders, but it makes reaching consensus more difficult; a few determined individuals can stall the process. Legislatures may fail to make progress on important policy issues for months or even years. At times, the legislative process moves at a snail's pace. Yet when agreement is reached and the deals are struck, legislatures can move with blinding speed.[15]

A majority of legislators must support a bill repeatedly before it reaches a chief executive's desk for signature. Majorities must be obtained in subcommittees and committees, and in the entire House and Senate. If there are disagreements between the House and Senate—and there usually are—a temporary conference committee is appointed to iron out the differences and then seek yet another majority in each chamber.

Deference to the legislative handiwork of committees can simplify the majority-building process. Until the late 1960s, members approved most of the committee proposals that came to the floor, making few or no amendments. By the mid 1970s, however, floor debates had changed dramatically; members insisted on introducing large numbers of amendments after committee bills reached the floor. In the Senate, the loose rules governing floor debates gave (and still give) the new breed of policy-active senators ample opportunity to amend legislation and engage in a variety of delaying tactics on the floor.[16] By the mid-1980s, floor-amending activity had produced so much frustration in the House that the leadership, working through the Rules Committee, took action to place significant new restrictions on the making of floor amendments.[17]

Although members of Congress often take cues from party leaders and the president, majorities assembled to pass one law may not stick together for the next battle. As new issues arise, majorities must be put together at all stages of the legislative process—one vote at a time. Building coalitions is painstaking work that often resembles Monty Hall's "Let's Make a Deal." David Stockman, Reagan's first budget director, called the task of pulling coalitions together in Congress the "politics of giving."

> An actual majority for any specific bill had to be reconstructed from scratch every time. It had to be cobbled out of the patchwork of raw, parochial deals that set off a political billiard game of counter-reactions and corresponding demands. The last ten or twenty percent of the votes needed for a majority in both houses had to be bought, period.[18]

If presidents and governors prefer "wholesale" politics—sweeping, popular ideas—legislators prefer "retail" politics—rewards for their district or state. A House leadership aide put it simply: "No matter how members ask the question it always comes down to one issue—how will it affect me?"[19] Crafting laws requires many different types of agreements. Deals may involve one member agreeing to vote yes on a bill with the understanding that the favor will be returned. Or legislation may include a higher appropriation, lower taxes, or favorable treatment for an industry in a member's district as the price for a positive vote.

Some observers regard the horse-trading, compromise, and vote swapping that characterize the legislative process as distinctly unsavory. These critics believe German Chancellor Otto von Bismarck was correct in saying "Politics is like sausage. Neither should be viewed in the making." But the nature of representative democratic institutions makes it unlikely, and even undesirable, for them to behave otherwise. To fashion laws in an open democratic institution, a broad consensus must be achieved and sustained. "Good" policy benefits, or at least does not harm, the people and interests represented by elected officials.

Deadlines

This underlying dynamic helps explain why the members of legislatures often procrastinate until the last possible moment before reaching a decision. Just before adjournment or an election, legislatures often rush through hundreds of bills. For example, the 101st Congress waited until October of 1990 (just before adjourning for midterm elections) to pass most of the important bills—the 1990 farm bill, the Clean Air Act, new housing programs, child-care legislation, an omnibus crime bill, Head Start reauthorization, immigration reform, and budget legislation—that it would successfully enact into law.

Why does a legislature facing a deadline act like a football team executing a two-minute drill—quickly and efficiently moving the ball down the field for a touchdown, when at first they seemed unable to move it two feet? Why does a legislature not always act as if the deadline is fast approaching? Action is postponed primarily because everyone waits until the end to get the best deal. Knowing that decisions on major legislative initiatives and tax and spending bills may not be made until the eleventh hour encourages everyone to hold off their commitments.

Legislators also delay action in the hope that unfavorable political conditions will improve. Perhaps public opposition to a controversial policy will soften; maybe the governor will take a different position; perhaps the next election will bring more like-minded individuals to the legislature. Without deadlines, legislatures find it difficult to make decisions. The end of a fiscal year, the expiration of a law's authorization, an impending election, or adjournment forces legislatures to act, whether they are ready or not.

Leadership

Fragmented power and the need for compromise increase the importance of leadership in putting things together. Legislative leaders assemble coalitions and set priorities for the institution.[20] But leaders derive their power from the members and often must defer to their wishes to keep their support. The positions that legislative leaders take on policy issues are heavily influenced by the views of other legislators in their party.

According to Randall Ripley, a perceptive student of American politics, congressional leaders perform five policy-related tasks:

1. Help determine who sits on the most powerful committees
2. Help decide when legislative business will come to the floor of the House and Senate
3. Help organize votes on the floor of the House and Senate by contacting—whipping—members to attend and vote
4. Communicate leadership preferences and collect information on member needs and preferences
5. Serve as focal points for contact with the White House and the press.[21]

A leader's most important power is the ability to persuade his or her colleagues to follow.

Majority and minority leaders exercise more influence on procedural matters—when a bill is considered or how an issue is framed for a vote—than they do on the substance of legislation, its policy objectives and strategies.[22] Leaders often package issues so that fellow party members can cast votes that help them satisfy their constituents or interest groups. When Robert Dole, R-Kan., was Senate majority leader in 1985, he arranged for Republican senators seeking reelection to introduce budget amendments restoring proposed cuts in popular programs in their states. Senators from urban states called for increases in urban development grants and mass transit aid. Senators from tobacco-growing states asked for decreases in the cigarette tax. Senators from agricultural states demanded higher price supports, and so on. The value of such techniques has been magnified by television coverage of House and Senate proceedings.

Members are most likely to play follow-the-leader when it advances their electoral goals. But members have an ironclad excuse for ignoring a leader's requests: "I can't vote with you because it could cost me reelection." Even the leaders themselves sometimes resort to this defense. House Majority Leader Jim Wright, D-Texas, opposed his party's tax reform bill in 1986 because it was not sufficiently generous to the Texas oil and gas industry. Wright did not suffer for his defection; he was elected Speaker of the House a few months later.

Congressional leaders are the essential glue for holding coalitions together, but until the late 1980s they did not show much inclination to advance their own legislative agendas. By 1987, Democrats in the House were sufficiently frustrated by six years of Ronald Reagan's presidency to want stronger congressional leadership. And Jim Wright was eager to lead. Using a three-pronged strategy that included generous provision of services to members to aid in coalition building, the structuring of choices to serve the policy ends of the House leadership, and the expansion of leadership organizations and circles to include as many members as possible (the strategy of inclusion), Wright, Majority Leader (now Speaker) Tom Foley, and then Whip Tony Coelho were able to establish an agenda (clean water legislation, aid for the homeless, a trade bill, catastrophic health insurance, welfare reform, and tax increases) and move it through the chamber.[23]

In the 101st Congress (1989-1990), Senate Majority Leader George Mitchell employed some of the same strategies to achieve similar ends. Working through the Democratic Policy Committee and the Senate Democratic Conference, Mitchell was able to establish a legislative agenda and gain Senate approval for many of the items on it. One clear indication of the presence of stronger Democratic congressional leadership in the 101st Congress was the ability of Senator Mitchell and Speaker Foley to confront President Bush on the budget and get him not only to agree to new taxes (reversing his principal campaign pledge), but to accept a tax package that the Democrats developed.[24]

Leaders in state legislatures have generally been more influential than congressional leaders in the last thirty years. Presiding officers in state legislatures often appoint the members and chairs of standing committees, decide which committee will consider legislation, determine when bills will be "posted" for a vote, and closely oversee deliberations on the floor of the chamber. They may also promote substantive programs and persuade standing committees to implement them. Alan Rosenthal, a leading authority on state legislatures, has written: "On some issues . . . leaders are inclined to play a prominent role. On revenue policy, the shots are likely to be called by legislative leaders. In the field of education . . . leaders in over half of the states play a significant role." Even in the states, however, Rosenthal concluded, "Aggressive policy leadership is probably the exception rather than the rule." [25]

Ironically, leadership within the legislature may be more difficult to achieve than leadership from chief executives. Presidents and governors can go directly to interest groups and to the public upon whom legislators depend for support. As a result, chief executives are often the most effective "legislative leaders." They not only set the legislative agendas, but also formulate policies and then push them through to final adoption. "Whatever the precise sources of policy formulation," Rosenthal observed, "the processes by which proposals make the agenda, receive serious consideration, and get adopted may depend considerably on executive leadership." [26]

Although divided government very significantly diminishes the possibilities for legislative leadership by chief executives, presidents and governors have political powers that are unavailable to members of Congress and state legislatures (see Chapter 6). Chief among them is the ability to be heard above the clamor of voices. As Representative David Obey, D-Wis., said, "The President has the only megaphone in Washington." [27]

Rites of Passage

The characteristics of cloakroom politics profoundly influence what legislatures do. What does this mixture of individual needs, fragmented power, compromise, and leadership produce in the way of public policies?

Symbols over Substance

Symbol often triumphs over substance in cloakroom politics. Much legislative activity involves talk, not action. Hearings are held, bills are introduced, speeches are delivered, but no legislation passes. Significant policy results are often hard to achieve because they may require legislatures to wield the coercive power of government (to regulate public or private behavior, or to impose taxes), and unpopular action of this type can cost members their jobs. A popular alternative to decisive action is symbolic policy. An example of an almost purely symbolic legislative policy was a proposal to change the lyrics of the state song of Virginia that the legislature debated in 1991. The state song, "Carry Me Back to Old Virginia," included references to "darkey" and "massa," which most blacks, including Governor Douglas Wilder, found offensive. The plan to replace these offensive words, however, encountered opposition from those fond of the original, and gave the legislature something to talk about.[28]

Sometimes primarily symbolic laws are passed to reassure politically aroused groups.[29] Without offering tangible benefits, the legislature addresses the concerns of aggrieved parties with policy pronouncements that mollify them. Disadvantaged groups, such as the unemployed and the poor, seldom have sufficient political clout to hold elected officials accountable.[30]

Legislatures often adopt policies that are long on goals but short on the means for carrying them out. Such policies may strike only a glancing blow at the problem. The gulf between rhetoric and reality is frequently exposed by the difference between the authorizing language and the actual appropriations bills. Authorizations set out the objectives and strategies for ameliorating a problem; appropriations bills supply money for programs and benefits to people. The Head Start Program, which provides preschool education and other support to low-income children, is a rarity among domestic social service programs in that it is popular among both Democrats and Republicans. In 1990 the reauthorization of Head Start received a good deal of attention, and ambitious funding levels were prescribed in the new legislation ($2.4 billion in FY 1991, rising to $7.7 billion in FY 1994). Nevertheless, the actual FY 1991 appropriation for Head Start was only $1.95 billion.[31]

Actions taken for symbolic reasons may still have important consequences. Public concern over the degradation of the environment was met with the National Environmental Policy Act of 1970, which announced the government's intention to protect the environment. Although it began as a symbol, this act became an important policy instrument because it requires federal agencies to prepare environmental impact statements. Working through the courts, environmental activists use this requirement to block projects whose effects are perceived as detrimental to the environment.

Incremental Change

The drawn-out policy process and fragmented power often yield only minor policy changes. When legislatures finally act, problems typically are addressed in small, manageable steps—modest departures from past practice. The stabilizing forces holding back substantial change are very powerful indeed. Agendas are crowded with proposals; only a few receive serious attention. Legislators opposing change have abundant opportunities to veto or water down proposals.

Policy issues are rarely considered comprehensively. Legislatures slice up broad policy areas into many parts so that a large number of members serving on committees and subcommittees can participate. Rather than structure a governmentwide policy on health care, for example, Congress divides health-related issues into discrete programs. Fear of the unknown also inhibits rapid and radical change. In contrast to business persons, who tend to be risk takers, legislators tend to be risk avoiders. When they vote for a law, they want to be certain that it will not make things worse. Under these circumstances they choose to tinker with solutions, through trial and error, rather than to embrace innovative approaches that have the potential of disastrous consequences. Reconsiderations are practically guaranteed; most laws have a three- to five-year life span, so a legislature can look at the issue again and change its mind.

Future policy directions often are molded by past decisions. Legislators find that the compromises reached by their predecessors serve as useful guides. Because lawmakers want to avoid controversy and conflict during a drawn-out process, they find it politically feasible and prudent to seek modest changes in current policy. Opposition is less likely when changes in the status quo are minor and nonthreatening to other vested interests.

Congressional policy making with regard to the annual budget demonstrates incrementalism at work. Congress usually makes minor adjustments from year to year. Major departures, such as the substantial increase in defense spending during the 1980s, are rare; they take place only if accompanied by strong presidential leadership. The budget under consideration usually equals last year's budget, plus or minus a small percentage.[32] Battles occur over what seem like inches of territory to the outside observer. Will spending increase by 2 percent or 3 percent? Will formulas governing grant-in-aid programs benefit smaller or larger cities? Should support prices for corn fall by five cents? The competition is fierce, but the public rarely understands what, if anything, is at stake. To insiders, these battles are important because they are, quite literally, the principal policy issues before the legislature.

Pork-Barrel Policies

Legislators want to deliver benefits, sometimes known as pork-barrel programs, to people, businesses, and communities in their states and districts. The desire to parcel out "particularized benefits" produces what are called distributive policies.[33] Members of Congress are not the only ones who want to participate in the politics of giving and credit claiming; ample supplies of pork are available to many state legislators. In North Carolina, appropriations that are not needed for the state budget or for major legislation are dubbed "special entries" and are divided equally between the chambers, and then within the chambers, so that every member gets a piece. In 1985, for example, each representative received $50,000 and each senator received $100,000 for district projects.[34]

Pork-barrel politics was evident when Congress overrode President Reagan's veto and enacted the Water Quality Act of 1987, which was loaded with special projects for more than 400 congressional districts and every state in the nation. James Weaver, a maverick Democratic representative from Oregon, tried in vain to eliminate questionable projects. He proposed cutting Oregon's Elk Creek Dam, deemed costly and unnecessary by the Army Corps of Engineers and the GAO, but Representative Robert Smith, R-Ore., objected. "We should deal with this project as the member representing the area desires," he said.[35] The Elk Creek Dam survived.

Organized interests benefit from this system of handing out government largess. The economically disadvantaged and politically unorganized usually lose when their interests conflict with those of more powerful groups. For example, in the early 1980s President Reagan convinced Congress to drop public jobs programs for the long-term unemployed and the poor. But Congress refused to terminate the Economic Development Administration (EDA)—even though it was a program characterized by the president's budget director David Stockman as a "boondoggle" and "demonstrably useless." The difference? The EDA distributes low-interest loans and other forms of assistance to businesses and construction companies in 80 percent of the country. Public service job holders did not have a political action committee; the construction industry did.[36]

Innovation

Occasionally, public policy undergoes radical change. Landmark laws may increase government involvement in matters previously left to the private sector, such as health insurance for the elderly. The Social Security Act of 1935, which guaranteed government support for senior citizens, the Civil Rights Act of 1964, which forbade discrimination against minorities and other groups, and the tax and spending cuts enacted in 1981 represent fundamental innovations in public policy.

From time to time, conditions arise that foster innovation by legislatures. According to political scientist Charles Jones, significant policy shifts may occur when a well-organized and vocal group of citizens unites and demands government action, or when policy makers achieve a temporary consensus on unprecedented proposals.[37] Strong political leadership, often from the president or governor, and economic and political conditions that make the need for change apparent are also powerful agents of policy innovation. President Lyndon Johnson was able to turn his strong electoral showing in 1964 into a mandate for liberal change, and he then drew on his experience as a legislative leader to push Congress to enact his Great Society programs. Governor Madeleine Kunin managed to navigate a minefield of competing interests to get a precedent-setting land-use planning law enacted by the Vermont legislature in 1988. Senator Edmund Muskie, D-Maine (1959-1980), galvanized the environmental movement in promoting passage of the Clean Air Act of 1970 and other environmental laws.

Events, political conditions, and the state of the economy all affect the degree of innovation. When federal budget deficits are high, opportunities for more federal spending are severely restricted, but other innovations, such as deregulation and privatization of public services, become more likely. Conversely, when federal revenues exceed projected expenditures, as was the case in the mid-1960s, new programs are born. President Johnson's Great Society promised both guns (for the war in Vietnam) and butter (domestic spending programs). And when state governments realized a revenue bonanza in the late 1980s, major reforms in education and economic development strategies were quickly initiated. Overriding concern about crime, especially murder, prompted the Maryland legislature to pass a hand-gun control bill in 1988 and the California legislature to pass similar legislation in 1989. With help from Governor William Schaefer, the Maryland gun control law survived a referendum, despite a massive public persuasion effort by the National Rifle Association.

Significant policy breakthroughs inevitably create problems, but once new government initiatives are established, the fundamental questions are less frequently discussed. Instead legislators try to fix and refine—to "rationalize" breakthrough policies. Political scientist Lawrence Brown makes a useful distinction: breakthrough policies are highly partisan, ideological, contentious, and visible; rationalizing policies are less partisan and contentious and concern relatively fewer citizens or interest groups. Debates about how to rationalize breakthrough policies gener-

ally revolve around proposed incremental changes that reflect perceptions of what has worked and what has not, rather than ideological
preferences.[38] Still, some breakthrough policies never seem to take hold.

The history of federal programs dealing with unemployment provides examples of breakthrough policies that became accepted and
some that did not.[39] During President Franklin Roosevelt's administration, a major breakthrough in unemployment policy occurred when the
government provided assistance to the jobless through unemployment
insurance and job creation programs. Since then, the unemployment
insurance program has been modified dozens of times—increasing or
decreasing benefit payments, expanding categories of program recipients—but it has never been seriously threatened with elimination. It is
the largest and most durable government program for helping the
unemployed; between 1974 and 1988, the expenditures averaged
roughly $14 billion annually.[40]

In contrast, federal job creation programs have been alternately
embraced and rejected by U.S. politicians over the years. The Depression era public works programs vanished during World War II when
unemployment declined. During the 1970s, federal jobs programs averaged more than $3 billion in expenditures annually, and had employed
more than 700,000 people by 1978. In 1981 the jobs programs were
completely eliminated, for politicians had become convinced of the
need to trim the federal budget. Two years later, public employment
made a brief reappearance when unemployment exceeded 10 percent,
but then faded from view again.

Gridlock

When legislatures deal with extremely controversial policies, the
policy process sometimes gets stuck in a gridlock of opposing viewpoints
and power plays. Representative David Price, D-N.C., has observed:
"Congress is often difficult to mobilize, particularly on high-conflict
issues of broad scope." [41] Legislatures have ground to a halt over civil
rights policy, aid to education, environmental policy, and other issues in
the past, but the continuing budget crisis of the 1980s and early 1990s
has repeatedly deadlocked Congress and has severely curtailed its ability to act. Congressional budget scholar Allen Schick points out that
"Congress now has difficulty legislating because the role demanded of
it by economic conditions is not congruent with the type of legislation
encouraged by its organizations and behavior." [42]

After President Reagan's breakthrough budget policies of 1981 (tax
and domestic spending cuts with increased defense spending), Congress
debated deficit reduction strategies for the remainder of his first term
without taking strong action. By 1985 the budget deficit had swollen to

$200 billion. The deficit deadlock stemmed not so much from disagreements over whether the problem was serious, as from dispute over which course of action to pursue. Most Democrats favored tax increases and lower defense spending. Most Republicans preferred no tax increases and less domestic spending. No matter which party prevailed, meaningful deficit reduction required one or more unpleasant policy actions—hiking taxes or slashing popular programs.

While Congress groped for answers, the deficit problem worsened, and the options became fewer and more painful. Reluctant to adopt sufficient program cuts and tax increases, the president and Congress decided to borrow huge sums of money. By the end of 1985, the public debt had risen above $1.8 trillion—more than double what it was at the beginning of 1981. This spectacular growth in the nation's debt brought about an even more spectacular growth in interest payments to service the debt—from $53 billion in 1980 to approximately $130 billion in 1985.[43] (By 1990 the national debt had risen to more than $3 trillion, and annual interest payments were more than $180 billion.)[44]

The gridlock was eventually finessed in 1985 when Congress passed the Gramm-Rudman-Hollings (GRH) Deficit Reduction Act—named after its sponsors, senators from Texas, New Hampshire, and South Carolina, respectively. The act mandated reductions in federal deficit spending that would achieve a balanced budget by fiscal year 1991. Unlike previous budget-balancing resolutions, it empowered the president to make automatic, across-the-board spending cuts should Congress fail to reach specified reductions by the beginning of each fiscal year. Social Security benefits, existing contracts for defense and other projects, programs for poor people, and interest on the national debt were excluded. House Budget Committee counsel Wendell Belew said, "It's a kind of mutual assured destruction theory of fiscal policy. What they're doing is creating a kind of artificial crisis . . . an action-forcing mechanism."[45]

Shortly after GRH's enactment, the U.S. Supreme Court ruled that portions of it were unconstitutional. In 1987 the law was modified to remove the provisions that the Court had objected to, establish a new annual timetable for budget legislation, and set forth a new deficit reduction schedule (a balanced budget is due in FY 1993). In GRH's early days, deficit reduction targets were met by resorting to one-time gimmicks, accounting tricks, and sales of government assets. But the 500-point stock market meltdown in 1987 forced Congress to swallow the strong medicine of tax increases and cuts in real spending that yielded more than $33 billion in deficit reductions in FY 1988. Still, deficits ran higher than expected in FY 1989 ($153 billion) and FY 1990 ($220 billion), and with an FY 1991 deficit target of $64 billion,

Congress and President Bush locked horns over the budget in 1990.[46] The budget agreement that resulted did away with deficit targets for entitlement programs in favor of a "pay-as-you-go" system of budgeting (all new spending provisions must be offset by cuts in other programs or by revenue increases), but the FY 1991 deficit reached a new high of over $300 billion. Thus, despite some apparent breakthrough agreements on the budget in recent years, policy gridlock continues because neither Congress nor the president is willing or able to take truly decisive action.

Shaky Ground Rules, Unreliable Watchdogs

Legislative lawmaking is often a blunt instrument for addressing public problems. The surgical precision with which courts and the executive branch can sometimes perform is rarely evident. Broad, vague, and sometimes contradictory policies are a direct by-product of the need to reconcile competing claims and preferences. Consequently, many public laws contain ambiguous statements that a majority of the legislature can endorse. The task of translating aspirations into programs and services is delegated to government administrators, other levels of government, courts, private businesses, and citizens. Indeed, the more controversial the policy, the more likely that legislatures will ask others to make the tough choices.[47]

When legislators delegate hard decisions to others, they can garner political rewards while shifting the wrath of aggrieved parties elsewhere. Delegating authority also gives legislators leeway to blame federal agencies or other levels of government for failing to fulfill legislative intent and to take credit for correcting faults by conducting oversight hearings and investigations and by undertaking constituent casework.[48]

The most common form of policy delegation occurs when Congress or a state legislature defines a problem in legislation and then mandates federal or state agencies to solve it. Recognizing and defining a problem are important, but the responsibility for deciding precisely how to cope with it is likely to be much more difficult. Consider the problem of hazardous waste management. State legislatures around the country have required the construction of safe facilities for the storage and disposal of dangerous wastes generated by chemical plants. The choice of where to locate facilities is up to state environmental protection agencies or special commissions, and their siting decisions have frequently outraged citizens leading to threats of civil disobedience and violence, lawsuits, and eventually to passage of legislation to block implementation of the decisions.

Legislators also impose difficult policy tasks on individuals and businesses. Affirmative action hiring policies are carried out by private organizations that decide whether to follow the letter and spirit of the law or to ignore it. Responsibility for enforcing immigration laws rests with private employers who must verify an individual's citizenship or permit to work in the United States. Failure to do so can result in a substantial fine. Often the courts must rule on whether congressional intent has been followed by private firms.

Congress frequently hands complicated problems to state and local governments, and state legislatures pass tough issues on to local governments. Legislatures also mandate changes in policies and programs at other levels of government without providing adequate resources and then hold them accountable, which is particularly irksome for those on the receiving end. Congress has ordered state and local governments to upgrade the education of young children, reform their welfare systems, enhance air and water quality, and improve highway safety, but many state and local officials believe that the funds appropriated for these purposes are insufficient to permit the realization of policy goals and expectations.

The nature of cloakroom politics influences not only laws and policy objectives but also the results. Even when legislatures delegate authority, they establish the ground rules for who gets what, when, and how from government. Legislatures are often the final arbiters of how much government spends on important societal goals and how money will be raised to pay for those commitments. Few individuals, institutions, and organizations are untouched by legislative action or inaction.

Policy Implementation

Laws are seldom written with potential implementation problems in mind. Because it is so difficult to reconcile competing interests, legislators expect administrative agencies and others to figure out how to put laws into effect. In fact, excessive legislative goals are often regarded as an effective method to achieve change. The authors of the Clean Air Act of 1970 were proud of their achievement, even though it quickly became obvious that the law's air quality standards would not be met.[49] They reasoned that setting high standards would stimulate the auto industry to work harder to reduce pollution. In fact, the method worked; the deterioration of air quality decreased, and there have been some significant improvements.

Nevertheless, a disregard for potential implementation difficulties can reduce the likelihood of achieving positive results. Public laws are sometimes endorsed without legislators ever carefully defining the problems the laws are supposed to address. Policy entrepreneurs who perceive a need for government programs may not be sure how to translate their aspirations into workable laws. The know-how to "solve" problems like minority youth unemployment or drug use may not yet be available, but legislators seize opportunities to advance innovative policies concerning these issues when they arise.

Legislators tend to be concerned about the distribution of program benefits provided by law and about the efficient application of administrative regulations. Generally, they assume that programs or policies will be helpful to people if implemented properly—even though this view may be highly inaccurate. For example, a member of the House Education and Labor Committee may believe that spending more money on education is an end in itself. The committee member's basic goal is to get more money out to teachers and schoolchildren, not to determine the ultimate results of education programs, because such results will not show up for years and will be difficult to gauge definitively. This perspective on policy impacts not only influences lawmaking; it also has consequences for the distribution of benefits in society.

Government benefits come in many different forms: tax breaks for companies; grants to fund social service programs or to build bridges; regulations that protect domestic industries from foreign competition; and income-support payments for the unemployed, poor, and retired. Underlying all tax and expenditure decisions, regulations, and policies is the struggle over who benefits and who does not. In general, legislative policy tends to favor the haves over the have-nots, the organized over the unorganized, and the middle class over the lower class because the poor and unorganized have great difficulty making a case for themselves to legislators who view most decisions through electoral lenses.

When government programs try to serve poor Americans exclusively, they often have difficulty surviving. From the Resettlement Program of the 1930s, which aimed to increase black land ownership in the South, to the public service employment programs of the 1970s, which over time acquired very restrictive eligibility standards that excluded all but the long-term unemployed and the poor, programs that help only the poor have been vulnerable to attack. Charges of mismanagement or corruption make headlines and lead legislators to withdraw support. Effective lawmaking depends upon finding the delicate balance of benefits that holds the majority together long enough for passage, and does not fall apart when negative claims about program implementation are aired.

Ignoring implementation issues when laws are crafted may erode respect for government. To get laws enacted, legislators (and chief executives) may exaggerate not only the problem but also the potential effectiveness of the remedy under consideration. Then, if the problem fails to go away, the public and many legislators may falsely conclude that it cannot be remedied with government programs or that the policy approach was misguided. Repeated rounds of hyperbole and rising expectations followed by disappointment and condemnation undermine public support for governmental solutions.

Policy Impacts

Sometimes laws are written so as to have clear and immediate impacts. This usually occurs after several earlier legislative attempts to solve a problem have failed, and the problem and a solution become well defined. The Voting Rights Act of 1965 is a good example. Previous civil rights laws (1957, 1960, 1964) had attempted to solve the problem of low black voter registration in counties in the Deep South by encouraging citizens who had been intimidated or otherwise discouraged by local registration officials to go to federal courts with their grievances. This approach resulted in only marginal increases in black voter registration, and by 1965 Congress was ready for more decisive action. This time it simply declared that any county where black registration was below 50 percent was suspect, and that federal officials would be sent to all such counties to make sure black citizens could register without interference. Black voter registration in the seven states of the Deep South covered by the law increased by more than 1 million between 1964 and 1972, an increase to 57 percent from 29 percent of eligible black voters. Effective implementation of the law depended on federal officials and the courts, but congressional initiative was critical to making progress.[50]

Still, legislatures are probably more notable for their delays or failures to act than for their willingness to grapple with difficult problems. And legislative inaction can have serious consequences. The problems created by harmful chemicals in the nation's water supply and by worldwide air pollution can be traced to careless and unregulated industry practices. Strong federal regulations were not legislated until the 1970s, and decades of neglect meant slow progress in enhancing environmental quality. The failure of state legislatures to take strong action against drunk drivers until the mid-1980s probably resulted in thousands of unnecessary deaths. Congress's inability to curtail the federal deficit during the 1980s imposes a heavy burden of debt on future generations of Americans.

Oversight and Learning

As elected representatives grope for solutions to difficult problems, such as cleaning up toxic waste dumps, or ameliorating poverty, or curbing the AIDS epidemic, they often approve politically appealing but poorly designed policies. Legislators typically do not concern themselves with the details of program administration unless bureaucrats and private citizens run into trouble and people start complaining. But political institutions can and do learn from experience. Feeble and misguided attempts can be reshaped through trial and error. After several attempts, Congress successfully revised and strengthened education programs for disadvantaged youngsters. It took more than a decade, but compensatory education programs now have clearly defined objectives and programs better suited to achieve them.[51]

Legislators form their impressions of program performance from what they hear from constituents and interest groups, from reports in the news media, from testimony at hearings, and from evaluations conducted by government agencies and others. Over time, members acquire pictures of success or failure that become the basis for intervening in program administration and for major legislative reforms.[52]

Objective evaluations of how programs work are difficult to achieve and expensive to conduct, and their results are sometimes distrusted by legislators. Many systematic studies do not yield unequivocal answers because it may not be possible to establish cause-and-effect relationships for government programs or policies. Suppose, for example, that we needed to determine whether the multibillion dollar food stamp program improves the nutrition and health of the eligible population. We would have to monitor the health and eating habits of people before and after they received aid, track similar groups of people who did not receive it, and compare the results.

But when evaluations provide clear evidence that a program works or does not work, the data are quite persuasive. For example, the Reagan administration could not persuade Congress to eliminate employment and training programs for the disadvantaged that are run by the Job Corps because strong evidence, gathered through systematic evaluations, indicated that the program worked.

Indeed, Congress has paid increasing attention to oversight in recent years for a number of reasons. First, declining resources due to chronic deficits have severely constricted the possibilities for creating new programs, and committees and subcommittees have therefore devoted more of their attention to overseeing the programs that are in place. Second, conflict and competition between Republican presidents and Democratic congressional majorities have raised the stakes in oversight. In some cases, Congress has suspected the executive branch of not implementing programs in good faith; in other cases, Democrats have fought hard to defend programs the White House has targeted for cuts or elimination. Third, the staff resources—personal, committee, GAO, OTA, and CRS—available to members for oversight activities have greatly increased. The GAO alone produces more than 1,000 reports (most of which are responses to congressional requests for information) and its representatives testify at more than 200 hearings per year.[53]

Thus Congress today has both the capability and an incentive to conduct more oversight. Between 1971 and 1983, the number of days during the year that congressional committees devoted to oversight activities increased from 146 to 587, and the percentage of committee time spent on oversight increased from 8 to 25.[54] One member of Congress explained the changed attitude toward oversight as follows: "In the 1960s . . . you had to go back to your district and say, 'I passed Joe Zilch a piece of handicapped elephant legislation.'. . . Well, that's not where the returns are now. The political returns are from oversight." [55]

Increased interest in oversight does not necessarily translate into systematic, comprehensive, or even rational oversight activity. In making up their minds about programs, legislators use whatever information they can get. The problem is that unsystematic and anecdotal information is often more available and influential than careful systematic evaluations. Impressions about policy success or failure enter the policy process through many channels. Senior citizens write members of Congress to complain about exorbitant fees for routine visits to the doctor, or CBS's "60 Minutes" exposes fraud in contracts for highway construction, or the *Washington Post* reports alarming increases in airline safety violations. A legislative staffer in Arizona described the impact of a carefully selected anecdote.[56] During a hearing on licensing procedures for beauticians, a woman with bright orange (originally brown) hair complained about the incompetence of unlicensed practitioners. Her vivid portrayal convinced lawmakers to strengthen state requirements and monitoring efforts. Such evidence may be inconclusive or unrepresentative, but it exerts a powerful influence on a legislator's judgments about government programs.

Legislative oversight of public policies can be harmful, especially if the legislators reach inaccurate conclusions. The resulting criticism heaped on administrators can be demoralizing and, more important, dealing with it may distract them from essential tasks. Since members of Congress and of state legislatures engage in oversight activities with an eye to possible electoral payoffs, it should come as no surprise that such activities are greeted by experienced administrators with a mixture of alarm and cynicism.

When the policy process is competitive and diverse points of view are fully expressed, legislatures may be able to learn from their mistakes. For example, careful scrutiny of environmental laws has been ensured by continuing public health fears and the high degree of controversy surrounding proposed solutions. The Superfund Toxic Waste Cleanup

Law passed in late 1980 turned out to be anything but super. By 1987, hundreds of millions of dollars later, only about 30 of the nation's 950 toxic waste dumps had been cleaned up, according to the EPA. Intense oversight efforts by members of Congress, focused on toxic dumps in their districts, led to passage of a much stronger cleanup law in 1986.

There is an interesting paradox in legislative politics and policy. Widespread consensus is usually required to implement innovative policies, but some amount of disagreement and conflict is necessary to refine them. Too much consensus in the policy environment either supports the status quo—however effective or ineffective it may be—or fosters gigantic expansions in government power and spending that have little chance of achieving success.[57] When conflict and disagreement are too severe, efforts to revise policy may deadlock. Institutional learning is most likely when partisans and interest groups advance diverse policy remedies for the problems of program implementation.

Summary

No major government activity can be undertaken without the consent of legislatures, whether federal or state. No money can be borrowed or spent and no taxes can be levied unless the elected representatives willingly consent to the request of the president or a governor. No executive agency or top administrator can function for long without legislative support. The ground rules for the distribution of public goods, services, and regulations are established by legislatures, which may attempt to influence program implementation at any time.

Congress and the state legislatures are responsive to the changing mood of public opinion and to the views expressed by constituents, interest groups, and chief executives. But the desire of legislators to serve the public and curry favor with potential voters and supporters creates problems. Legislative institutions are subject to fads and whims and tend to respond to the loudest, most persistent demands. Legislators can be manipulated by outsiders who can stir up public support for a position or raise campaign contributions. Groups that are already powerful tend to get what they want, or at least avoid harmful legislative action.

The desire to be responsive and democratic also shapes the organization and practices of American legislatures. The dispersal of power across committees and subcommittees creates opportunities for legislators to influence public policy and gain the gratitude of potential supporters who will help to keep them in office. But because they are fragmented and operate by consensus and compromise, legislatures find it difficult to speak with a clear and consistent voice when making public policy. The need to accommodate diverse political interests often produces confusing public policies or no policy at all. Legislatures sometimes are unable to look ahead or to address controversial issues decisively.

Legislative indecision and timidity reflect deep cleavages and uncertainty in society. Legislatures have no trouble moving swiftly to clean up the environment, crack down on drug dealers, or raise the legal drinking age, if there is a strong and clear public demand for action. In recent years, conflict with the president has led Congress to try to set the nation's agenda and provide policy leadership, but this is an unusual posture for American legislatures to assume. The greatest strength of legislatures lies in acting as a forum where state and national controversies are debated in public. Legislatures are at their best when they educate the public, provide an outlet for the expression of diverse viewpoints, and forge consensus on new directions for public policy.

Notes

1. As quoted by Charles O. Jones in *The United States Congress: People, Place, and Policy* (Homewood, Ill.: Dorsey Press, 1982), 13.

2. Jack L. Walker, "Setting the Agenda in the U.S. Senate: A Theory of Problem Selection," *British Journal of Political Science* 7 (1977): 423-445.

3. See Richard C. Elling, "The Utility of State Legislative Casework as a Means of Oversight," in *Legislative Studies Quarterly* 4 (August 1979): 353-379.

4. Thomas Mann, *Unsafe at Any Margin* (Washington, D.C.: American Enterprise Institute, 1978).

5. On the relationship between congressional committees and campaign contributions, see Richard L. Hall and Frank W. Wayman, "Buying Time: Moneyed Interests and the Mobilization of Bias in Congressional Committees," *American Political Science Review* 84 (September 1990): 797-820.

6. Joel Brinkley, "Competing for the Last Word on Drug Abuse," *New York Times,* August 7, 1986, A10.

7. Robert Pear, "Congress Rushes to Pass Benefits for Gulf Veterans," *New York Times,* February 19, 1991, A12.

8. Norman Ornstein, Thomas E. Mann, and Michael J. Malbin, *Vital Statistics on Congress, 1989-1990* (Washington, D.C.: CQ Press, 1990), 130.

9. See Alan Rosenthal, *Governors and Legislatures: Contending Powers* (Washington, D.C.: CQ Press, 1990), 39-66.

10. See David R. Beam, Timothy J. Conlon, and Margaret T. Wrightson, "Solving the Riddle of Tax Reform: Party Competition and the Politics of Ideas," *Political Science Quarterly* 105 (Summer 1990): 193-217.

11. Dale Russakoff, "Deals Are Struck, Hands Are Held—and the Tax Bill Sneaks By," *Washington Post* national weekly edition, December 30, 1985, 10.

12. Woodrow Wilson, *Congressional Government* (New York: Meridian Books, 1956).

13. Randall B. Ripley, *Congress: Process and Policy,* 4th ed. (New York: W. W. Norton, 1988), chap. 5.

14. Interview with authors, Washington, D.C., November 19, 1984.

15. John F. Hoadley, "Easy Riders: Gramm-Rudman-Hollings and the Legislative Fast Track," *PS* (Winter 1986): 30-36.

16. See Barbara Sinclair, *The Transformation of the Senate* (Baltimore: Johns Hopkins University Press, 1989), 111-138.

17. See Steven S. Smith, *Call to Order: Floor Politics in the House and Senate* (Washington, D.C.: Brookings Institution, 1990).

18. David Stockman, *The Triumph of Politics* (New York: Harper & Row, 1986), 250-251.

19. Interview with authors, Washington, D.C., December 10, 1984.

20. Legislative leaders in this sense are individuals elected by their respective party memberships. In Congress the leadership is the Speaker of the House, the majority and minority leaders, assistant leaders (sometimes called party whips), and the party caucus officers in the House and Senate.

21. Ripley, *Congress*, 210-212.

22. Barbara Sinclair, *Majority Party Leadership in the U.S. House* (Baltimore: Johns Hopkins University Press, 1983); and Randall B. Ripley, *Majority Party Leadership in Congress* (Boston: Little, Brown, 1969).

23. See Barbara Sinclair, "House Majority Party Leadership in the Late 1980s," in *Congress Reconsidered*, 4th ed., ed. Lawrence C. Dodd and Bruce I. Oppenheimer (Washington, D.C.: CQ Press, 1989), 307-329; and John Barry, *Ambition and Power* (New York: Penguin Books, 1989).

24. See Donald C. Baumer, "Senate Democratic Leadership in the 101st Congress," in *The Atomistic Congress: An Interpretation of Congressional Change,* ed. Ronald M. Peters and Allen D. Hertzke (Armonk, N.Y.: M. E. Sharpe, 1991).

25. Alan Rosenthal, *Legislative Life* (New York: Harper & Row, 1981), 167-168.

26. Ibid., 266.

27. Interview with authors, Washington, D.C., May 29, 1985.

28. Donald P. Baker, "Old Va. Song May Finally Get New Lyrics," *Washington Post,* January 26, 1991, B1.

29. Murray Edelman, *The Symbolic Uses of Politics* (Urbana: University of Illinois Press, 1964).

30. Randall B. Ripley and Grace Franklin, *Congress, the Bureaucracy, and Public Policy,* 5th ed. (Pacific Grove, Calif.: Brooks/Cole, 1991).

31. See *Congressional Quarterly Weekly Report,* November 3, 1990, 3702.

32. Aaron Wildavsky, *The Politics of the Budgetary Process,* 3d ed. (Boston: Little, Brown, 1979).

33. David Mayhew, *Congress: The Electoral Connection* (New Haven, Conn.: Yale University Press, 1974); and Theodore Lowi, *The End of Liberalism,* 2d ed. (New York: W. W. Norton, 1979).

34. Alan Rosenthal, "The Legislative Institution: Transformed and at Risk," in Carl E. Van Horn, ed., *The State of the States* (Washington, D.C.: CQ Press, 1989), 90.

35. Cass Peterson, "Despite Gramm-Rudman Diet, The House Still Likes Its Pork," *Washington Post* national weekly edition, November 25, 1985, 13.

36. Stockman, *The Triumph of Politics,* 209.

37. Charles O. Jones, "Speculative Augmentation in Federal Air Pollution Policy-Making," *Journal of Politics* 36 (May 1974): 438-464.

38. Lawrence Brown, *New Policies, New Politics: Government's Response*

to Government's Growth (Washington, D.C.: Brookings Institution, 1983).

39. The following discussion of job-training and employment programs is drawn from Donald C. Baumer and Carl E. Van Horn, The Politics of Unemployment (Washington, D.C.: CQ Press, 1985).

40. Figures for 1974-1983 spending are from Baumer and Van Horn, The Politics of Unemployment, 26; figures for 1984-1988 spending are from Bureau of the Census, Statistical Abstract of the United States: 1990 (Washington, D.C.: Government Printing Office, 1990), 352 (Table 578).

41. David E. Price, "Congressional Committees in the Policy Process," in Congress Reconsidered, 3d ed., ed. Lawrence C. Dodd and Bruce I. Oppenheimer (Washington, D.C.: CQ Press, 1985), 211-222.

42. Allen Schick, "The Distributive Congress," in Making Economic Policy in Congress, ed. Allen Schick (Washington, D.C.: American Enterprise Institute, 1983), 258.

43. U.S. Congress, Joint Economic Committee, Annual Report on the Economy, 99th Cong., 1st sess., May 15, 1985, 47-49.

44. Economic Report of the President (Washington, D.C.: Government Printing Office, 1991), 375-377 (Tables B-76 and B-77).

45. Jonathan Rauch and Richard E. Cohen, "Budget Frustration Boiling Over," National Journal, October 12, 1985, 2138.

46. Economic Report of the President, 1991, 375 (Table B-76). Figures on deficit reduction and Gramm-Rudman-Hollings target are from John Cranford, Budgeting for America, 2d ed. (Washington, D.C.: CQ Press, 1989), 1.

47. Lowi, The End of Liberalism.

48. Morris Fiorina, Congress: Keystone of the Washington Establishment (New Haven, Conn.: Yale University Press, 1977), chaps. 7 and 8.

49. Charles O. Jones, Clean Air: The Policies and Politics of Pollution Control (Pittsburgh: University of Pittsburgh Press, 1975).

50. Charles S. Bullock III and Charles V. Lamb, Implementation of Civil Rights Policy (Monterey, Calif.: Brooks/Cole, 1984), 20-54.

51. Michael Kirst and Richard Jung, "The Utility of a Longitudinal Approach in Assessing Implementation: A Thirteen-Year View of Title I, ESEA," in Studying Implementation, ed. Walter Williams (Chatham, N.J.: Chatham House, 1982), 119-148.

52. Baumer and Van Horn, The Politics of Unemployment, 53.

53. Martin Tolchin, "Critique of Reagan Years from Unlikely Source," New York Times, December 27, 1988; and Frederick Mosher, The General Accounting Office (Boulder, Colo.: Westview Press, 1979), 178.

54. Joel D. Aberbach, Keeping a Watchful Eye (Washington, D.C.: Brookings Institution, 1990), 35.

55. Ibid., 47.

56. Telephone interview with authors, June 1, 1987.

57. Jones, "Speculative Augmentation."

6   Chief Executive Politics

Americans have always preferred politics with a personal touch, making heroes and villains out of public figures and evaluating politicians on the basis of human qualities such as integrity, leadership ability, and physical attractiveness. It is rare for the American public to be mobilized by ideological debate or to be interested for very long in institutional deliberations and actions. Political interest typically focuses on individuals, and in most cases this means chief executives—presidents, governors, and mayors. Chief executives are the most visible, and in many ways the most important, actors in American government.

The prominence of chief executives in American politics today is commonly attributed to the media. The modern media, especially television, find that covering powerful individuals in government is much more appealing and manageable than following developments in legislative, judicial, or bureaucratic institutions. The visibility of chief executives contributes to the public perception that politics and government are principally about what they do.

But media attention is only part of the reason that American politics centers on chief executives. The system of governance set up by the federal and state constitutions also helps to explain the phenomenon. The United States is notable in the world for the number of independent, elected chief executives in government. Presidents have a nearly exclusive claim to a national electoral constituency and, unlike the prime ministers in parliamentary governments, they are independent of the national legislature. Governors and "strong" mayors have a somewhat less distinctive electoral position, but they are also independent of the legislatures in their jurisdictions and the national government.[1] Chief executive-centered politics is not simply a cultural oddity encouraged by media that seek above all else to sell more cornflakes; rather, it reflects in many ways the intentions of constitution writers at the national and state levels.

The term "chief executive politics," as used here, does not encompass the full range of policy-making activity of American chief executives, but includes only those aspects that are most exclusively attributable to these public officials. What will be explored are the more visible and important positions taken, decisions made, and policies whose enactment is secured by chief executives—the public record by which they are judged. These records have two main components: decisions made by chief executives during crises and policy initiatives or innovations sponsored by chief executives. Chief executives are also involved in a great many routine policy actions, most of which are covered in the chapter on bureaucratic politics.[2]

Rulers of the Agenda

Chief executives dominate the agenda-setting process in the United States. More often than not they are able to transform policy ideas from items of discussion among a few to items of discussion among the many. Because they have the public's attention, they force other politicians to pay attention to the matters they think are important. This gives them a tremendous advantage over any rivals in defining the issues for the public and, ultimately, for other politicians. In short, chief executives typically set the terms of debate about political issues at the national, state, and local levels. This is not to say that chief executives are always, or even usually, successful in securing enactment of the policies they prefer. Indeed, it must be understood that chief executives are more impressive in the issue creation and agenda-setting process than in policy formulation and adoption.[3]

Modern presidents are expected to be opinion leaders. Their unique relationship with the national electorate gives them a certain flexibility in choosing issues and policies that other national policy makers do not have. Woodrow Wilson championed the League of Nations, Franklin Roosevelt pushed the New Deal, Lyndon Johnson began the Great Society, Richard Nixon made a breakthrough with China, Ronald Reagan launched an antigovernment crusade, and George Bush forged a new relationship with the Soviet Union. Chief executive politics encompasses the entire spectrum of policy types, including distributive, redistributive, regulatory, social and moral, intergovernmental, intragovernmental, economic, foreign, defense, and national security.

Chief executives dominate certain issue domains more than others. At the national level, presidents traditionally have dictated American foreign and military policy. This power has enabled them to shape public opinion about America's proper role in the world; indeed, recent presidents have regarded the international scene as a vast set of "opportunities" for improving their popularity at home, especially around election time. Nixon was an adept exploiter of these international opportunities, presenting the SALT I agreement and Henry Kissinger's pledge that "peace was at hand" in Vietnam as he faced reelection in 1972, and taking trips to the Middle East and the Soviet Union as the Watergate scandal heated up.[4]

International crises and foreign and military policy adventures also have caused big problems for presidents. Since the Vietnam War, negative responses by the national media, Congress, and the public have become a more common reaction to statements presidents have made and actions they have taken in the international arena. Jimmy Carter's and Ronald Reagan's presidencies were damaged by festering foreign policy problems (the Carter administration's handling of the hostage crisis in Iran and the Soviet invasion of Afghanistan, and the Reagan administration's trading of arms for hostages with Iran and support of Nicaraguan contras). George Bush's management of the war in the Persian Gulf created opportunities to demonstrate his leadership in wartime, but also tested his skill in bringing stability to the troubled Middle East. International affairs continue to offer opportunities for presidents to mold public opinion, but there are limits to the public's inclination to believe what presidents say about the world and America's place in it.

Within their respective jurisdictions most governors and many mayors take the lead on issues and policies. As is true of presidents, the combination of the media attention and their formal powers makes them substantially more visible and influential than other state and local politicians. The public and other policy makers look to them for new ideas and new proposals, and they have a flexibility in articulating policy concerns and proposing remedies that elected officials with narrower constituencies do not share. In his successful race for the governorship of Arkansas, Governor Bill Clinton made welfare reform and education central issues and convinced the legislature to enact sweeping reforms. Governor Rudy Perpich of Minnesota devoted his administration to job creation and economic development. New Jersey Governor Jim Florio has focused the efforts of his administration on property tax reform and the improvement of education in urban communities. California Governor Pete Wilson has vowed to reduce the size of state government in the 1990s.[5]

Issue Choice and Definition

Although chief executives have a good deal of freedom to choose their issues, there are limits to this freedom. Occasionally, an issue in the form of a crisis is thrust upon the chief executive. Iraq's invasion of Kuwait was a crisis that demanded an immediate, and then prolonged, presidential response. Stability in the Middle East and the world's oil supply were threatened and a policy needed to be formulated at once. Governor Pete Wilson of California immediately confronted a serious drought, requiring sharp reductions in the water supply to residents, farmers, and commercial users. The Supreme Court's decision in *Webster v. Reproductive Health Services* (1989) placed immediate demands on governors to reassess their positions on the state role in regulating abortions.

Not all crises are as compelling as the examples just cited, but chief executives have considerable latitude in labeling an event a crisis or a noncrisis. Reagan often portrayed the presence of the Sandinista government in Nicaragua as a national security crisis to convince Congress to aid the contras. Many regard the destruction of the rain forests in South America and the increase in world temperatures as a crisis demanding immediate and forceful responses from the president, but George Bush has refused to apply the crisis label to the problem or to behave accordingly. In part, crises exist in the eyes of the beholders, and presidents are able to open or close those eyes.

Table 6-1 shows some of the relationships between issues, stages in the agenda-setting process, and chief executive discretion or range of choice. The table shows that crisis situations tend to involve problems that are very difficult for chief executives to ignore, but they usually give chief executives a good deal of flexibility in defining the problem for other policy makers and the public and in choosing a response. For issues that chief executives choose to promote, what happens at the different agenda-setting stages follows the opposite pattern. Chief executives have a wide range of choice in the selection of problems to address and they have a strong position from which to define these problems; but their ability to craft innovative responses is limited because they must take into account the preferences of the many other actors in the policy-making process, most of whom defer to chief executives during crises.

Available evidence suggests that governors and mayors may have somewhat less discretion than presidents in choosing issues to emphasize. For these politicians there are certain perennial issues, reflecting the basic services that state and local governments provide—education, streets and highways, law enforcement and prisons, and social services—and these issues are nearly always addressed by leading candidates and officeholders.[6]

Taxes frequently dominate all other issues, sometimes to the point of ensuring the end of the political careers of incumbents who have raised taxes and giving other candidates no real choice about how to position themselves.[7] Caught between the constitutional requirement to balance budgets and the cutback of federal grants to states, many governors have been forced to raise taxes—an action that has ended many political careers. In the 1990 election, for example, 6 of 23 governors who stood

Table 6-1 *Issues, Agendas, and Chief Executive Discretion*

		Agenda stage	
	Problem/issue	Problem definition	Specification of policy alternatives
CRISIS SITUATIONS	American hostages seized in Iran	Moslem extremism American weakness Russian meddling	diplomacy military action international sanctions
	Inmates riot at a state prison	prisoners take hostages and threaten lives prison conditions cause violent responses lax security creates crisis	address prisoners' demands negotiation use of force
Level of chief executive discretion	low	moderate	moderate/high
NONCRISIS SITUATIONS	tax reform	high tax rates for middle class low tax rates for the wealthy corporate give-aways	change tax rates eliminate deductions increase corporate taxes
	education reform	declining literacy in society low pay for teachers teacher union resistance to innovation	improve educational facilities adopt performance-based pay system increase teacher salaries across the board
Level of chief executive discretion	moderate/high	moderate	moderate/low

for reelection were defeated. In almost all instances voter anger over tax increases brought about incumbent defeats. And several governors, including Madeleine Kunin in Vermont, Michael Dukakis in Massachusetts, and William O'Neill in Connecticut, chose not to seek reelection in part because they had backed tax increases to balance state budgets.[8]

Decisions made in Washington command the attention of many state and local officials because intergovernmental grants-in-aid represent about 11 percent of state and local revenue. Domestic spending cuts begun during the first Reagan term and continued during the Bush presidency have forced many states to assess their budget priorities as they have had to decide whether and how to replace lost federal funds. In short, the leading issues for states and localities often are "givens" that represent long-standing or pressing problems.

Presidents and other chief executives are rarely, if ever, whimsical or freewheeling in their choices about what issues to emphasize; too much is at stake for decisions to be made haphazardly. Presidential scholar Paul Light stated, "All presidential decisions are purposive. Presidents select issues on the basis of their goals."[9] He listed the principal goals as reelection, historical achievement, and good policy.[10]

Most chief executives want to be reelected and therefore choose issues they think will help them garner votes. In general, they believe their positions on issues matter—indeed, that their own success or failure can hinge on issue stances and policy pledges.[11] This belief does not mean that chief executives are always aggressive in taking positions on a wide range of issues. It means that most perceive a need to address some important issues and to act in a way consistent with what they have said, even if vigorous follow-up is lacking. With all the media hype and money that go into contemporary campaigns, chief executives with reelection in mind are likely to be listening to their political advisers, media consultants, and public opinion pollsters as much as to their policy specialists.

Policy agendas are often formed around issues that are evocative and remedies that are thought to be popular, rather than based on a serious effort to diagnose what is wrong and to find viable solutions. For example, recently most governors and presidents have taken strong stands in favor of tougher criminal penalties for drug use, including the death penalty for so-called drug kingpins. In taking on drug users and drug pushers, chief executives are clearly addressing a popular cause with a popular remedy that will likely fall considerably short of actually ameliorating the problem.

Not all chief executives are concerned with reelection. In fact, some of them—presidents in their second term, governors who have reached the legal limit of their tenure in office, or others who decide they do not wish to run again—do not have to think about it at all. For most presidents, governors, and mayors, elections are a means to some larger and more substantive end, such as initiating good public policies, not an end in themselves. Chief executives want to leave a favorable historical legacy, and most of them recognize that sponsoring noteworthy and effective public policies is the best way to achieve this goal. The goals of historical recognition and good policies typically blend into one effort. Fortunate chief executives have knowledgeable advisers with ideas that are worthy of consideration. Chief executives who succeed in getting these ideas translated into policy are recognized and remembered.

Sometimes chief executives use their positions to promote particular ideologies, and ideological expression cannot be neatly subsumed under the categories of reelection, historical recognition, or good public policy. Chief executives emphasize certain issues that have strong ideological content, even though some of them are not particularly popular, as part of a larger effort to build, maintain, or repudiate a dominant ideological coalition. Lyndon Johnson, who had not been a strong supporter of civil rights policies, became in the mid-1960s a champion of programs for poor and minority citizens in an effort to defend and expand the liberal Democratic ideology (and political coalition) that his predecessor, John Kennedy, had begun to build. Reagan led an effort to destroy this coalition and replace it with one built around conservative causes. He attacked all of the most ideologically loaded policy legacies of the Kennedy/Johnson era—such as public school busing, affirmative action, social welfare programs, reduced military spending, prohibitions on school prayer, and intrusive regulations.[12]

In every administration there is tension among those who are concerned about issues that contribute to short-term popularity, those who seek to promote ideological principles, and those who are interested in establishing policies of long-term effectiveness. Achieving a balance between these forces is one of a chief executive's main tasks, and some are better at it than others. Franklin Roosevelt offered ideas that brought not only electoral success but also historical recognition for his policy accomplishments and his ideological leadership.

Chief executives, particularly presidents, are rarely at the cutting edge of new issues or policy ideas. In a strict sense, they do not initiate agenda issues or lead the way to innovative approaches to problems. The real initiators are likely to be political activists, interest groups, researchers, or even legislative staffers or bureaucrats.[13] Most new issues and policy ideas have humble beginnings as the number of people interested in them is small. Some of these ideas, however, attract the attention of more visible spokespersons, become widely discussed, and eventually attract coalitions of supporters.[14] At any given time there are streams of acknowledged problems and potential solutions—policy proposals—flowing around and through policy-making institutions.[15] Chief executives and their policy advisers pick out those that fit with their philosophy and direction and promote them.

Obviously, many considerations figure in choosing issues, among them the political costs associated with certain ideas and the fit between the new ideas and the other positions taken by a chief executive.[16] Political parties add another voice to be heard in the process of selecting issues. Every four years the parties' platforms give various groups and advocates the opportunity to debate policy ideas, thereby helping chief executives determine those that have broad support.[17] Typically, chief executive policy leadership does not consist of a flash of inspiration and a headlong rush to legislative action; most often it consists of a set of cautious, purposive decisions made by chief executives and their advisers after surveying the ideas and proposals circulating among the politically active and aware.

Chief executives' agendas frequently follow a predictable pattern dictated by their economic and political environments. For example, in times of economic recession, governors and presidents invariably emphasize government support for public works projects and the importance of helping private sector firms expand. When the economy is strong, the attention of chief executives is likely to shift to quality of life issues, such as educational opportunity or environmental protection. Governors and presidents just taking office are likely to promote bolder ideas and plans for "cleaning up" the mess of the previous administration—especially if it was left by a different political party. Chief executives seeking reelection are more likely to cling to mainstream proposals and to highlight recent accomplishments.

Neglected Matters

Compared with other American policy makers, chief executives raise an exceptionally wide variety of issues. As tribunes of the people they are free to discuss just about any policy question they wish. Still, there is no doubt that certain kinds of issues are systematically neglected or excluded from their policy agendas; the spectrum of chief executive politics may be wide, but it is far from unlimited. With two major parties each striving to assemble majority coalitions, there is an undeniably centrist bias to American politics. Like the parties, and usually as leaders of them, chief executives need majorities to support them. Therefore, they aim most of their political pitches at the largest sector of the electorate. Because most Americans belong to the middle class, U.S. politics tends to revolve around issues that most directly affect the middle class. A serious socialist agenda is consequently irrelevant, and few, if any, conservative leaders seriously challenge the New Deal reforms. Although it may be difficult to pin down, there is a kind of majority consensus that defines the acceptable range of political discourse in the United States, and successful chief executives remain within this range.[18]

Generalizations such as the one just offered are deliberately imprecise and can be easily misinterpreted. Our emphasis on middle-class/centrist politics does not mean that minorities and the poor are neglected altogether. The political history of black Americans—neglect by the white majority for many years, followed by selective attention as their political significance was recognized—confirms the basic thrust of the claim about the forces that dominate agendas, but also demonstrates that the trends can change. Significant events, media attention, and effective advocacy coalitions can turn a neglected issue into a salient issue in a fairly short time. By the same token, an issue may remain submerged indefinitely if no one with political muscle chooses to promote it.

The collapse of the savings and loan industry in the 1980s and the subsequent government-sponsored bailout is perhaps the best illustration of an issue that was long ignored and with great cost to the American public. The deregulated savings and loan industry of the 1980s compiled a stunning record of "greed, mismanagement, fraud, and lax government regulation," yet nothing was done to address the problem systematically until Congress passed a savings and loan cleanup law in August of 1989. But by then, the federal government and the public were faced with the biggest bailout in U.S. history. The federal government is expected to spend $50 billion in the first three years of the bailout and perhaps as much as $500 billion for the whole program.[19]

There are no absolutes in the issue creation process. Societies change, sometimes rapidly, and policy ideas that seemed outlandish at one time can become serious agenda items at another. Economic, technological, and environmental developments are not the only causes of these societal changes; human beings may be the agents of social and political change. Chief executives can and do change the nature of political discourse by daring to explore new directions.

The Power to Persuade

The presence or absence of crisis conditions is of overarching significance in explaining the politics associated with chief executive policy making. During crises normal politics is suspended, and the power to decide comes to rest with chief executives and those they choose to advise them. Policy is determined in a centralized, hierarchical manner.

This is one of those matters about which there is nearly universal consensus among legislators and other policy makers. Presidents are expected to lead during times of crisis, and other political elites recognize that presidents need room to maneuver if they are to do this effectively. With this unilateral power goes the responsibility for the decisions that are made. Crises test a chief executive's leadership and decision-making ability in an arena where the stakes are very high.

From the time that Saddam Hussein's armies invaded Kuwait on August 2, 1990, to the cease-fire on February 27, 1991, President Bush was firmly in charge of U.S. policy and strategic actions. With little or no input from Congress, the president initially ordered the deployment of 240,000 troops to Saudi Arabia. That task completed, he expanded the American commitment by another 200,000. He forged a worldwide coalition against Iraq and committed the United States to spending at least an additional $13 billion on war preparations. Not until five months later, when it was clear that the president was about to end the policy of economic sanctions and embark on a war to rid Kuwait of Iraqi troops, was Congress invited to pass a resolution endorsing the president's actions. Throughout the entire Persian Gulf War, it was clear that Congress was no more than a sideline player.[20]

In noncrisis situations chief executives have to employ different political skills. Their ability to act unilaterally is greatly diminished, and their most important asset becomes the capacity to persuade others that their policy ideas deserve consideration and action. One aspect of this political skill is working with advisers and executive officials to put together an attractive program of policies. The other is selling the program to the legislature or the bureaucracy. In general, the government apparatus is stacked against chief executives who seek to innovate. There are many competing power centers that can frustrate the designs of chief executives if they are ignored or dealt with improperly. To be successful in normal politics, chief executives have to demonstrate the ability to be a leader among equals.

The Persian Gulf crisis stands in sharp contrast to President Reagan's tax reform effort in 1986. Reagan and his economic advisers, intrigued by the prospect of offering the American public even lower tax rates (they had already been cut in 1981), made tax reform the top domestic policy objective of his second term. If successful, this tax cut would make history. But history also taught that tax policy was one of the most, if not the most, prized congressional prerogative. Both the House Ways and Means Committee and the Senate Finance Committee would have strong views about the nature of any tax reform. Moreover, special interests save some of their biggest political guns for battles over tax policy, and their power and influence would somehow have to be nullified if meaningful tax reform was to be implemented. In short, many powerful people were unwilling to defer to the president on this matter, and he had to fight, bargain, cajole, and broadcast appeals to the public over an extended period of time to get a tax reform bill signed into law. The package that finally emerged, after two years of negotiation and compromise, differed in several significant respects from the one that Reagan originally had proposed. One of the distinctive features of normal politics is that no one gets exactly what he or she wants.

Tools of the Trade

Richard Neustadt's enormously influential book, *Presidential Power*, provides a useful framework for understanding how chief executives exercise power.[21] Neustadt points out that executive power in American government is both protected and restricted by the Constitution. Presidents have a great deal of authority over the implementation of laws passed by Congress and over foreign affairs and military matters, but their domestic policy-making authority is limited. Certain presidents, however—Franklin Roosevelt was always uppermost in Neustadt's mind—have exerted tremendous influence over both foreign and domestic policy.

This observation leads to one of Neustadt's major points: executive power is largely potential. Actual power depends on the ability of chief executives to leverage their formal powers and to stretch their influence over as many aspects of government as possible. Success implies that chief executives have convinced other government actors that going along with the plans and policies of the chief executive is in their best interest. Because this kind of governing entails extensive bargaining, Neustadt's primary and best-known conclusion is that presidential power lies mainly in the ability to persuade.

Political scientist Alan Rosenthal elaborates on Neustadt's observation, pointing to the various tools that governors have at their disposal to practice the art of persuasion. They include several important powers, such as the powers of initiation, rejection, provision, publicity, and popularity.[22]

The line-item veto is an especially useful weapon that governors can use in political battles. Whereas the Constitution does not afford the president the authority to strike out individual sections of bills, governors in most states can veto parts of bills that offend them or even revise sentences to make them more to their liking. If the legislatures try to graft unrelated language onto a bill or attempt to insert projects to benefit particular legislative districts, governors can strike whatever they want from the bill without rejecting the entire law. For example, Governor Tommy Thompson of Wisconsin exercised nearly 300 partial vetoes between 1987 and 1989, yet the Democratic-controlled legislature could not muster enough votes to override any of them.[23]

The governorships in most states have evolved in a way that closely parallels the evolution of the presidency; the once largely ceremonial offices are now the engines of state politics. But the formal powers of governors are constrained in many important ways, which makes bargaining skills even more necessary. Governors may face tougher persuasive tasks than presidents because in most states certain cabinet officers are elected by the voters, not appointed by the governor. It is not unusual for these officials to be political rivals or opponents of the governor. In either case, their political independence is a virtual certainty. Big-city mayors face a similar situation in that major bureaucratic officials are either elected by the citizens or selected by boards or commissions; therefore, the mayors may have a difficult time persuading these officials to support their policies. Governors and mayors operate in smaller arenas than presidents, which reduces somewhat the number of powerful political actors with whom they must contend. But they do not have as much formal authority over their executive branches as presidents.[24]

Chief executive power is clearly elastic. Chief executives with similar or identical formal powers exert widely varying degrees of influence within their governments. Part of this variation can be attributed to political or economic factors, such as the presence or absence of crises, which affect the degree of centralized leadership. There can be no doubt, however, that the aspirations and abilities of chief executives also influence how much power they wield. Mario Cuomo of New York and Bill Clinton of Arkansas have exerted more influence on the national political scene than their recent predecessors, in part because they harbored ambitions to influence national politics and policy. At the national level, President Carter's inability to gain control of the political process during his administration, despite the presence of solid Democratic majorities in both houses of Congress, reveals him to have been considerably less adept at the power game than Lyndon Johnson or Ronald Reagan.

Comparisons between the most recent presidents and those whose served in the 1940s, 1950s, or 1960s should leave the student of contemporary politics somewhat uneasy. Political conditions have changed, and these changes have affected the way chief executives exercise power. Probably the most important changes have been in the number of active participants in the political process and the relationship between politicians and their constituents.

In the days of Franklin Roosevelt and Dwight Eisenhower, there were a limited number of truly powerful interest groups, and like-minded groups often worked together so that deals could be struck with the leaders who represented broad segments of society, such as business, labor, and agriculture. Party leaders exercised a great deal of influence over their ranks, which simplified presidential negotiations with Congress. There were some strong and independent executive branch officials and military leaders who had to be taken into account, but as Neustadt has emphasized, one man with sound management ability, good interpersonal skills, a knowledge of politics, and a clear sense of direction could hold the various pieces of government together throughout the bargaining process.

By the 1970s many presidential scholars had begun to doubt whether anyone could do what Roosevelt had done.[25] The increasing number and variety of interest groups, the staunch independence of elected officials, the accompanying erosion of party cohesion, and the persistent institutional conflict and competition seemed to produce an unmanageable pluralism. It was and is unmanageable if the chief executive uses traditional bargaining strategies. Bush, like Reagan and Carter, encountered tremendous resistance to his policy initiatives from the many power centers of the national government. Reagan demonstrated that power can be amassed in a significant new way. He did not rely on bargaining with political elites; instead he took his message directly to the people, using his weekly radio broadcasts and speeches on television to persuade them to pressure political officials to endorse his initiatives. The mass media emerged as the most potent weapon in a president's arsenal, and Reagan, the "great communicator," used it to his advantage. In the mass media age it may not matter very much whether political power brokers admire a chief executive's political acumen, as long as they have sufficient respect for, or fear of, the chief executive's ability to arouse the public through direct appeals.[26]

Increased use of direct appeals to the public as a way of enhancing chief executive power is well suited to contemporary political reality, just as bargaining was an appropriate strategy to pursue in the political environment of the 1950s. The independence of other elected officials comes from their certainty that they have established, and can maintain, a favorable image with voters. These relationships hinge more and more on money and the use of advanced communication technology. To the extent that chief executives can break into these relationships, the independence of other political actors is threatened. Legislators pay close attention to constituent opinions, and chief executives who use the media effectively can influence these opinions.[27] When this kind of influence occurs, or when politicians think it is occurring, resistance to a chief executive's policy preferences dissipates, and persuasive power has been exercised.

Tax reform again provides a good illustration. Shortly after his reelection, President Reagan set out to sell the idea of tax reform directly to the public. In 1985 he spoke on behalf of tax reform wherever and whenever he had a chance. The issue has natural political appeal, but the barriers to meaningful tax reform from political elites were legendary. Political action committee contributions to the most influential members of the House Ways and Means and Senate Finance committees were, and still are, very generous, which only begins to suggest the difficulties associated with overhauling the tax code.[28] Nevertheless, the chairman of the Ways and Means Committee, Dan Rostenkowski, D-Ill., gave tax reform a push by reporting a bill out of his committee. In addition to trying to influence the content of any tax reform package that Congress might approve, Rostenkowski was interested in denying Reagan the opportunity to pillory the Democrats during the 1986 election season for killing tax reform. To be sure, traditional bargaining was also at work—Rostenkowski and Treasury Secretary James Baker spent time together on Capitol Hill and on local golf courses—but everyone close to the process acknowledged the effectiveness of Reagan's appeals to the public. The interests that had the most to lose from tax reform were too strong to be overcome by pluralist bargaining. The only way to break their hold on legislators was to send a message through the constituents.

The ability to persuade is still the major determinant of chief executive power. Political persuasion is a multifaceted enterprise, however; it can be accomplished through traditional political bargaining among self-interested parties, through momentum-building appeals to the public, or by some combination of the two. When opportunities for "going public" are plentiful, as they are in contemporary national politics, one should expect extensive use of this tactic by telegenic politicians.[29] But bargaining and other customary political skills will continue to dominate when direct appeals to voters are difficult, when chief executives lack media appeal, or when there is a manageable number of ranking participants in the policy process. In most circumstances, chief executives must find the right mix of wholesale (public) and retail (private) politics to achieve their objectives.

Leaders and Followers

Most of those who have written on the subject seem to agree that the acquisition of power is the sine qua non of executive leadership.[30] Without power, leadership is virtually impossible. The fragmented nature of American government at all levels makes coherent action difficult; therefore, the essence of chief executive leadership is providing government with a direction or purpose. Implied in this conception of leadership is change. Leaders need to produce tangible results, and typically these take the form of identifiable changes in government organization or policy.[31] Planned changes that are effective and long-lasting and decisive action in crises are the hallmarks of effective leadership.

The essential ingredients of chief executive leadership are both personal and institutional. Judgments about personality or character are highly subjective; therefore, it is difficult to generalize, but personality seems more important than ever in the age of media politics. James David Barber, who has made a career of studying the role of personality in politics, points out that some chief executives derive positive feelings, such as satisfaction, exhilaration, and joy, from their political activity, while others experience mostly negative feelings, such as paranoia, resentment, and sadness.[32] Exhibiting some sort of positive disposition is part of effective leadership. Advisers, subordinates, and even rivals and opponents are at their best when they are driven by a forceful and inspiring personality.

The institutional side of executive leadership is concerned with the selection of advisers, analysts, political operatives, public relations specialists, and the others who are part of an administration. Most chief executives are able to surround themselves with a sizable cadre of loyalists, and their success at channeling the energies and skills of these individuals on behalf of their objectives is critical in determining their ultimate effectiveness as political leaders. Once the appointees are in place, the chief executives make the most critical choices: whose advice to take and when. And their range of options is quite large. They can rely on many advisers or a few; they can make frequent or little use of cabinet officials, outside specialists, or members of their personal staff; or they can establish hierarchical, competitive, or collegial relationships among their advisers. There are no proven formulas for success, but the experiences of several presidents provide useful insights into this aspect of chief executive politics.

Having many close and able advisers who represent various perspectives is widely regarded as a prudent practice, although relatively few presidents have followed it. Franklin Roosevelt and John Kennedy usually get the highest marks on this score. Nixon's complete reliance on three or four advisers during his second term is regarded as a reason for his downfall and should serve as a warning to other presidents of the dangers of inaccessibility.[33] Despite the Nixon precedent, concerns about leaks of politically sensitive information to the press and the natural unpleasantness associated with hearing unfavorable reports about the administration limited the openness of the Ford, Carter, Reagan, and Bush presidencies.

President Bush, by all accounts, arranged his White House staff hierarchically with Chief of Staff John Sununu at the top. He also placed trusted friends and allies in three important cabinet posts: Jim Baker as secretary of state, Nicholas Brady as secretary of the treasury, and Richard Cheney as secretary of defense.

Governors have very different needs than presidents and organize their staffs accordingly. The average governor has 48 staff members; governors of small states like Wyoming have only 8 staff members, whereas New York's governor has more than 200.[34] Nearly all governors employ political advisers, legislative liaisons, bureaucratic liaisons, press secretaries or public relations specialists, legal advisers, and budget experts.[35] The use of teams of agency officials and political advisers to develop policy initiatives is common. Most governors regard selling their policy ideas to the legislature as one of their most difficult tasks, a true test of their leadership ability.[36] Mayors also need this kind of assistance. Bureaucratic liaisons, often called chief administrative officers, help mayors handle challenges from independent-minded bureaucratic agencies.[37] Depending on the extent of their appointment power and resources, mayors may also employ political advisers, press secretaries, and budget specialists.

Facts and Politics

Making a distinction between decision making in crisis situations and that in normal, noncrisis situations helps simplify the enormous variation in the way presidents, governors, and mayors go about carrying out their responsibilities. At one end of the spectrum are visible and threatening crises in which the number of participants is small, advice consists mainly of substantive information and analysis, and chief executive decisions are authoritative. At the other end are controversies over domestic initiatives in which the number of active participants is large, political advice and calculations are usually more important than analytical information, and chief executives and legislatures battle with one another over the ultimate outcomes. The power of chief executives is obviously greatest during crises, but some aspects of these situations are dangerous in that they create political risks, and unpleasant because difficult choices must be made, when many would rather avoid them. Presidents and governors often try to achieve greater control over policy making by defining problems in crisis terms and then demanding that legislatures comply with their suggestions. For example, many governors argued that their state's schools were performing so poorly that rapid and substantial change was required to remedy the situation. They called special legislative sessions and introduced far-reaching reforms. By taking this approach, they hoped to put additional pressure on the legislature and on interest groups to act swiftly and in accordance with the governors' objectives.

The chief executive sets the basic outline of policy action in campaign promises and other statements. Translating these ideas into concrete policy proposals is the job of advisers and policy development groups. The personal involvement of chief executives in the formulation process varies with their personalities and abilities. Some try to master most of the details, whereas others content themselves with sketching the big picture; some are rigid and doctrinaire, and others are flexible and accommodating. Reagan and Carter offer illustrative contrasts. Carter impressed other politicians with his command of the details of policy options, but he could never chart a clear course with the policies he promoted. Reagan's knowledge of policy was quite general, in some cases mostly anecdotal, but many of his pronouncements inspired successful and significant policy actions that reflected the conservative philosophy he championed.

In times of crisis chief executives have the power to make policy with little or no approval of parties outside their administration. For noncrisis policy initiatives the path from policy idea to governmental accomplishments can be tortuously long. Once a preferred approach has been devised, chief executives and their staffs turn their attention to eliminating the many barriers to enactment. The outcome of this effort is determined largely by their ability to persuade others to follow their lead. If those with a stake in a decision can be herded into a few identifiable groups and agree to be bound by the bargains their leaders strike, policy change is likely. Unless competing interests are brought together, initiatives get shredded in the fragmented governmental machinery.

Chief executives have an array of persuasive devices that can be deployed on behalf of their initiatives—the invocation of party loyalty, direct appeals to the public, the dispensation of special favors, the making of political trades and promises, the real or threatened use of a veto—and these strategies are commonly used in this high-stakes arena of power and politics.

The enactment of the nation's toughest laws governing the purchase and ownership of assault weapons in New Jersey is a case of strong gubernatorial leadership against entrenched opponents. During his campaign for the New Jersey statehouse, Jim Florio announced that if elected he would seek a ban on the sale and ownership of the assault weapons often used by drug dealers in 'street fighting against police officers. Within a month of his inauguration, he called upon the legislature to pass a tough ban on assault weapons. With the public opinion polls showing overwhelming public support, he pushed for action and lined up backing from gun control and law enforcement organizations.

The National Rifle Association, sportsmen's organizations, and hunting groups quickly organized to stop or water down the Florio proposal. Knowing that public support would not be forthcoming, they focused their fire on legislators and the governor. Thousands of letters poured into legislators' offices. District phone lines were jammed with calls from irate gun owners. Most effective were the weekend visits made by anti-gun control advocates to legislators at their homes and local offices to engage in face-to-face lobbying. A week before the vote, more than 5,000 gun enthusiasts rallied in the state capital and cheered as their leaders denounced Governor Florio and warned legislators that they would pay a price at the polls if they supported the ban on assault weapons. On the day of the vote, hundreds of NRA members chanted threatening slogans in the courtyard outside the legislative chambers while their leaders tracked individual legislators and reminded them of the consequences of voting against the NRA.

As the vote neared, the staff in the governor's office became fearful that the NRA tactics were working. Several Democrats were threatening to vote against the governor's plan. Wavering or uncommitted legislators were brought to the "front office" (the governor's office in Trenton) and reminded that they would need the governor's support for future measures. Others were promised favorable actions on jobs or other pending legislative initiatives. The ban finally passed both senate and assembly, with no votes to spare. Governor Florio had succeeded in the art of persuasion, but not without putting maximum pressure on some of his supporters. As one senior New Jersey legislator described the experience, "I never want to be put through that kind of vote again. I am not cut out for suicide missions." [38]

The Buck Stops Here

Harry Truman, in characterizing his presidency, was fond of saying that "the buck stops here." Indeed, chief executives are involved in a staggering list of issues because the ultimate authority to carry out governmental policy nearly always rests with them. It is helpful to think of this vast range of issues as falling into three categories: (1) international and intergovernmental policies and actions; (2) economic and budgetary policies; and (3) domestic "quality of life" policies.[39]

As the international economy becomes more extensively interwoven, states and cities are having more frequent direct dealings with foreign nations. But foreign policy is still reserved mainly for presidents. Modern presidents usually make foreign policy their highest priority because they have more power to determine policy in this area and they cannot ignore international crises. Economic and budgetary policies come next, for these presidents recognize that perceptions about the success or failure of their administrations hinge on the state of the economy. Domestic policies tend to come last because breakthroughs in this area are so difficult to achieve.[40]

For governors and mayors, budgetary and domestic policy matters dominate. Budgets are particularly important; they represent the ultimate expression of the chief executive's priorities and are a principal means of exercising control over the legislature, the courts, and the bureaucracy.[41] Budget preparation affords chief executives at the state and local levels the opportunity to assert their preferences on nearly every aspect of policy—from the cost of college tuition to the cost of a bus ride. Budget decisions may be especially difficult for them because, unlike the federal government, they are typically unable to borrow money when revenues fall short of government needs. Instead they must cut programs, raise revenues, or both to get through tough times. Due to shortfalls in projected revenues during 1990, for example, twenty-six states increased revenues and twenty states reduced government spending to avoid year-end deficits.[42]

For more than a decade, budget decisions have overshadowed all others at the national level as Congress has scrambled to cope with huge deficits. Washington insiders speak of the "budget driving the policy process," by which they mean that substantive policy questions are subordinated to budgetary considerations, such as not exceeding the spending levels specified in budget resolutions, when new programs are authorized or, more commonly, when old programs are reauthorized.

Slogans and Symbols

Presidents, governors, and mayors inhabit worlds filled with symbolism. Aside from the many ceremonial functions associated with these offices, symbolic rhetoric is used to build consensus on matters of general principle or for specific policies. For example, President Reagan continually invoked certain themes and slogans in relation to his policies. Tax cuts and regulatory reform were ways of "getting government off the backs of the people"; large military budgets and new weapon systems helped to "make America strong"; and aid to Nicaraguan "freedom fighters" kept communists away from U.S. borders. When the policies of a chief executive are announced, they are often described in highly symbolic terms, typically portraying the chief executive as being above parochial politics and working in the larger interest of the nation, state, or city.

Political scientist Jeff Fishel has studied the relationship between presidential rhetoric and policy actions in great detail and has compiled some interesting data (see Table 6-2).[43] For the most part these data

Table 6-2 Presidential Promises, Action, and Policy

	Kennedy (1960)[a]	Johnson (1964)[a]	Nixon (1968)[a]	Carter (1976)[a]	Reagan (1980)[a]
Number of identifiable campaign promises[b]	133	63	153	186	108
Percentage of campaign promises calling for concrete action[c]	64	60	64	67	36
Percentage of campaign promises for which full or partial executive action was taken[d]	67	63	60	65	43
Percentage of congressional dependent promises for which executive action was taken and which were enacted[e]	53	62	34	41	44

Sources: The categories first appeared in Gerald Pomper, *Elections in America* (New York: Dodd, Mead, 1968); data for Johnson and Nixon compiled by Fred I. Grogan in "Candidates Promises and Performances, 1964-1972" (Paper presented at the 1977 meeting of the Midwest Political Science Association); the rest of the data presented by Jeff Fishel in *Presidents and Promises* (Washington, D.C.: CQ Press, 1985), 33, 39, 42.

[a] Year in which promises were made.

[b] The figures for Johnson and Nixon include some foreign policy promises (14 for Johnson, 36 for Nixon). All the others include domestic policy promises only.

[c] Fishel uses four categories of campaign promises: pledges of continuity, expression of goals and concerns, pledges of action, and detailed pledges. The latter two comprise this category.

[d] Fishel uses seven categories of executive action: proposals that were fully or partially comparable to promises, token action, contradictory action, no action, mixed action, and indeterminate. Categories one and two are collapsed here for these low percentages.

[e] The total from which these percentages were calculated is slightly lower than the number of promises because some promises were not dependent on congressional actions (for example, orders and unclassifiable promises).

support the conventional wisdom about the inclinations of recent presidents to use rhetoric and action. Kennedy made many promises and followed up on most of them, but had some trouble with Congress. Johnson's 1964 campaign was high on rhetoric and very low on specific promises, but he was exceptionally effective in getting what he wanted from Congress. Nixon had trouble with the Democratic-controlled Congresses with which he had to work. Carter made more specific promises and took action on a higher percentage of them than his predecessors, but he never managed to gain control of Congress. Reagan stands out for making only a few specific policy pledges and for neglecting most of them; his overall record with Congress was mediocre, although his success rate in 1981-1982 was quite high. Bush has been faulted for having little or no domestic policy agenda. He pushed for a capital gains tax, but the Democratic-controlled Congress rejected his proposal. Bush talked about being an environmentalist and an education president but has offered few proposals for Congress to consider.

Nonrhetorical symbols also contribute to the leadership mystique of chief executives. By jogging, going fishing, and driving powerboats in the Atlantic Ocean, George Bush has sought to reenforce the image of a vigorous man who is strong enough to handle the job and who shares the average American's love of recreation and sports. Former governor Bob Graham of Florida built his popularity as a man of the people by periodically spending "work days"—he left the governor's mansion to work as a truck driver or a teacher for a day.[44] Projecting a compelling image can be crucial to effective political leadership.

It is not uncommon for political observers to complain that certain chief executive policies are merely symbolic. This charge has often been leveled against policies in such areas as civil rights, welfare, environmental protection, and foreign policy, where rhetoric usually exceeds action by a large margin. The civil rights statutes of 1957 and 1960 and executive orders dating back to 1950 did little to reduce the various forms of discrimination at which they were directed. Eventually, however, they led to stronger and more effective statutes—the Civil Rights Act of 1964 and the Voting Rights Act of 1965 and executive orders in 1965 and 1969—that produced significant changes in black employment and voting.[45] Given the nature of American policy making, initial steps that are high on symbolism and low on substance are often necessary to pave the way for policies that produce real change.

Symbolism also plays a major role in crisis decision making. The conduct of the Persian Gulf War was, in effect, a series of carefully orchestrated symbols. Before launching a war against Iraq, President Bush visited the troops at Thanksgiving, consulted with world leaders at the White House, and summoned congressional leaders to his office for private briefings. The purpose of all this was to demonstrate that the president was carefully and deliberately weighing the options before risking American lives.

These examples point up how difficult it is to make definitive judgments about symbolism and substance, particularly with regard to the high-visibility policies of chief executive politics. Chief executives sponsor policies for both symbolic and substantive reasons; the balance between the two is probably best judged after the results of such policies have surfaced and been analyzed.

Opportunities for Innovation

The conservative inclinations of American government are likely to be embodied in chief executive policies. Nevertheless, the elective institutions of American government can make innovative decisions, and when they do, it is almost always chief executives who provide the driving force. Presidential scholar James Ceaser pointed out that "presidents have an important role to play in covering the struggle of self-interest [that pervades American politics] with a veneer of poetry and calling at certain moments for sacrifice for the common good." [46]

A crisis creates an opportunity for a chief executive to pursue innovative policies. Wars permit all sorts of unusual measures—industry seizures, rationing, strict wage and price controls, and plans for world government. The Great Depression brought forth the New Deal programs and the beginning of the welfare state. It is difficult to overstate the significance of agencies like the Rural Electrification Administration (REA) or the Tennessee Valley Authority (TVA) for the millions of rural Americans who lived in primitive conditions until the New Deal brought them electrical power, or of minimum wage and labor relations laws for the millions of blue-collar workers of that era. Policies that produce changes of such magnitude have long-standing political force and enshrine the leaders who sponsored them. They also encourage other chief executives to aspire to similar accomplishments.

It would be a mistake, however, to equate crises and innovation in American politics. One of the most significant revelations of a crisis like the depression is that centralized policy action is possible when the president can count on support in Congress. President Johnson supervised a Democratic majority with a broad consensus on the need to alleviate poverty, and they worked together to create innovative policies. But over the last forty years, the presidency has more often than not been in the hands of the Republican party and the Congress has been under the control of the Democrats. Such divided government frequently leads to gridlock or compromise, but seldom to rapid policy innovation.

In recent years, conditions favoring change in governmental programs have existed more frequently in state capitals as governors and legislatures of the same party have tackled such difficult problems as education and welfare reform, environmental problems, and economic development. Welfare reform is an especially good example of state leadership eventually pushing the federal government to act. Since the 1950s, federal policy makers have bemoaned the dismal performance of welfare programs but failed to effect significant change. Then, in the 1980s, governors as diverse as Michael Dukakis in Massachusetts and George Deukmejian in California forged a new consensus. Put simply, welfare programs had to be redefined; entitlements that encouraged dependency became education and employment programs that foster independence. By the end of the decade, more than thirty states had adopted welfare reform programs and Congress had enacted legislation to implement reforms already undertaken in most states.[47]

Working majorities do not simply appear out of the blue. They come about because popular chief executives make an effort to assemble them. Policies and politics are inseparable: Innovative policies are most often the product of an evolutionary process that includes an awareness among politicians of widespread public concern about certain problems, the selection of popular solutions, and the use of persuasive techniques to build a policy majority among legislators. Chief executives can easily stumble in any of these steps, but they can also succeed; their successes are policies that produce change.

Benefits for Whom?

Chief executives are fond of claiming that their policies benefit all members of society. In a sense this is true. To the extent that macroeconomic policies contribute to overall economic growth, there are widely shared gains. When threats to national security are effectively rebuffed, everyone benefits. When bureaucracies are reorganized to function more efficiently or law enforcement is improved to reduce crime, the whole society is said to be better off. Analysis easily uncovers variations in the benefits different population segments or geographical areas realize from policies, however. And, not surprisingly, these variations have political roots.

Like most elected officials, chief executives pursue policies that benefit their main constituents. This support of constituent interests is not always a matter of narrow partisanship or cynicism about doing what is best for the collectivity. For most chief executives there is a natural merging, over time, of their views about what is best for society and their preference for policies that disproportionately benefit their supporters. New Deal Democrats, for example, tended to view the world in terms of the struggle of workers and other ordinary citizens to use government to curb the abuses of big business. The policies of Franklin Roosevelt and Harry Truman were aimed primarily at helping white male workers, who became the core of the Democratic party as the quality of their lives improved during the 1940s and 1950s. In the early 1960s, John Kennedy presided over an increasingly fragile Democratic majority coalition that needed the votes not only of blue-collar whites but also of blacks to control national elections.[48] This need led to the serious pursuit of civil rights policies and programs to aid the poor, but always with an eye to not alienating white, middle-class Democrats. Since the 1960s black Americans have been the most cohesive Democratic voting bloc.[49] Reagan's antigovernment policies were aimed at pleasing the middle and upper classes from which the Republican party draws its strength. Bush's program to lower capital gains taxes and to assert a more sensitive environmental policy was designed to hold on to hard-core Republican supporters and to expand the base to include younger Americans, who tend to be more concerned about protecting the environment.

The meshing of chief executive policies and constituent preferences is never by any means complete. The policy universe is too crowded and complicated for chief executives always to help their friends and hurt their enemies. Carter lost the support of organized labor because he did not push minimum wage and national health insurance legislation hard enough to suit union leaders.[50] Senate Majority Leader John Engler ousted incumbent governor Jim Blanchard of Michigan in his bid for a third term in 1990. Blanchard had alienated many supporters and senior citizens when he implied that Lieutenant Governor Martha Griffiths was too old to join him for a third term in the statehouse. Republican governor Kay Orr of Nebraska lost her bid for reelection to Democrat Benjamin Nelson in 1990. With revenues falling and costs soaring, Orr had been forced to renege on her campaign pledge and to call for tax increases.[51]

It is not uncommon for chief executives to contradict one of their publicly stated positions rather than to pursue policies that displease important voting blocs. For much of his public career, George Bush supported a woman's right to choose an abortion, but he shifted positions 180 degrees in order to fit comfortably on the Republican ticket in 1980. By 1988, when he sought the presidency on his own, Bush had become an ardent advocate of restrictions on abortion. Reagan often changed his mind at politically opportune moments, making adept adjustments in his positions on Social Security, farm subsidies, public works programs, and import restrictions. A most striking example of a chief executive who adjusted to a changing constituency is Governor George Wallace of Alabama. The leading symbol of southern racism in the 1960s, Wallace successfully courted Alabama's black voters in his 1982 gubernatorial bid. Ironically, political leaders sometimes have to follow changes in the political wind in order to stay in charge.

Promise and Performance

Chief executive policies are born of grand promises and often generate great expectations about societal change. Invariably the results fall short of what was promised, but what is accomplished may be quite significant nonetheless. The true results of chief executive policies are realized over an extended period of time as programs and procedures become institutionalized and policies are modified. Studying the consequences of such policies reveals many examples that confirm the essentially political nature of the implementation process and underscore how difficult it is to make precise judgments about the impacts of public policies.

In 1967 Lyndon Johnson came up with an idea for helping the poor with one of their most pressing problems, the lack of decent, affordable housing. The deplorable conditions in many cities had led to rioting, and no one seemed to know how to improve matters. Johnson remembered that the federal government owned land in most cities and could more or less give the land to builders who would construct low-cost housing. With federal help the cities could build "new towns in-town." [52] Johnson brought together the relevant agency heads and a program was launched. Four years later the program had produced almost no new housing in the seven cities chosen to demonstrate its viability. Why?

The problems encountered during the implementation of the new towns program are familiar to experienced observers of public policy: local political opposition; inadequate federal resources, incentives, and guidance; poor communication between federal and local implementers; and a faulty program design.[53] What struck Johnson as a great idea made a number of community groups irate, left local elected officials cold, and kept bureaucrats confused. The more general lesson is that pluralism and federalism make chief executive initiatives in domestic policy areas such as urban redevelopment extremely difficult to implement. Many well-intentioned programs have floundered because of the difficulties associated with getting bureaucratic agencies, elected officials, and citizen groups to cooperate.

Implementation problems are by no means limited to domestic policies; they also occur in foreign policy, even during crises. The most common difficulties are the same as in the domestic area: presidential intentions may be poorly communicated; implementers lack the resources necessary to carry out directives; and implementers sometimes resist doing what they are told.[54] The State Department and the military are notorious for their adherence to standard procedures—perhaps the most common form of bureaucratic resistance to orders from above (see Chapter 4). At critical times during the Cuban missile crisis of 1962, President Kennedy ordered the Navy to move its blockade closer to Cuba and not to act belligerently toward the first few Soviet ships it encountered after the quarantine had been declared. Evidence indicates that the Navy did not move its quarantine line as the president ordered, and a long argument ensued between Secretary of Defense Robert McNamara and Navy Admiral George Anderson about how intercepted Soviet ships would be treated. It ended with Anderson waving the *Manual of Navy Regulations* at McNamara and remarking, "Now Mr. Secretary, if you and your Deputy will go back to your offices, the Navy will run the blockade."[55] The Navy's reluctance to depart from standard operating procedures in the midst of this type of crisis shows that even when the president is directly involved, and the need for effective action is obvious, implementation is by no means automatic.

The existence of problems should not obscure the fact that some policies are effectively implemented with little apparent difficulty. Social Security, for example, is mainly a matter of eligibility determination and the issuance of checks, and the government seems to be capable of executing these tasks quite well. Similarly, even a major change like the 1986 tax reform can be implemented without too much difficulty because it mostly requires that the Internal Revenue Service make a series of fairly specific changes in the tax code, which is something that agency is experienced at doing.

The chances of encountering major problems during the implementation of chief executive policies are largely dependent upon: (1) the amount of societal or organizational change the policy seeks to generate; (2) the complexity of the implementation process—how many different bureaucratic agencies and elected officials are involved; and (3) the level of consensus among the principal implementation actors about the desirability and feasibility of making planned changes.

Policies that seek to bring about fundamental change are difficult to implement successfully because they call for widespread modification in behavior, and the government usually has only limited resources for encouraging it. The degree of difficulty associated with implementing policies of fundamental change is also affected by the complexity of the implementation process and the level of consensus among the implementers. A major innovation such as tax reform, carried out by a simple organizational network in which those involved understand and support programmatic goals, has a good chance of succeeding. Complex implementation arrangements and competing priorities among implementers are almost certain to distort the original goals of innovative policies such as education or welfare reform.

For policies aimed at producing limited change the expectations are quite different. In general, such policies are likely to be implemented with reasonable effectiveness. They can be derailed by a cumbersome implementation process or fundamental disagreement among implementers, however. Johnson's new towns program was not dramatically new in what it sought to accomplish, but the organizational network required to implement it was complex and clumsy, and the consensus among implementation actors was decidedly narrow. These two factors accounted for the program's minimal success.

Intended and Unintended Consequences

Ambitious and innovative programs often have effects that can be clearly identified only many years after they are implemented. In an interesting and revealing study, political scientist Lester Salamon examined the effects of a New Deal program thirty years after it had been terminated. The Resettlement Program of 1934 authorized the federal government to purchase nearly 2 million acres of land in 200 different locations and to supervise specially designed agricultural or industrial communities that would make use of the land.[56] A common way of implementing the agricultural program was for the government to break large plantations up into family-size parcels and sell them under lenient terms to tenant farmers, regardless of their race. Because black land ownership in the South was uncommon, and black poverty was pervasive, this program, although small in scale, represented a "bold experiment in social reform."[57] Not surprisingly, the program had many critics, primarily white southern legislators, and it was killed in 1943, nine years after it began. The fact that it was terminated led to the general view that the program had been a failure. Salamon's analysis of the program's impacts in 1973, however, documented a solid record of land retention by the black families it had assisted. These families had moved out of poverty into the middle class. They now owned cars, television sets, and refrigerators. Their children had obtained white-collar jobs, and as a group they were active in political and community organizations and promoted causes. The effects, which Salamon called "sleepers," took many years to emerge in a discernible form.[58]

Head Start, a product of Johnson's War on Poverty, did not seem an unqualified success in its first major evaluation, which was conducted in 1969, four years after the program's inception; but more recent studies have documented long-term positive effects for the participants and funding was substantially increased in the 1990s.[59] Much the same pattern of delayed impacts has held for other major social welfare programs like job training, food stamps, and Medicaid.[60]

The main problem with sleeper effects is that they do nothing to relieve the pressure chief executives feel to produce visible, short-term results from the policies they sponsor. Because of this, chief executives favor programs that have more immediate payoffs. Policies that cannot survive by demonstrating quick positive results must maintain a certain level of political popularity during the time it takes for definitive impacts to emerge.

Chief executive policies often produce unintended results, and these, like latent or sleeper effects, must be considered if the full impact of a policy is to be accurately assessed. The iron curtain was an unanticipated result of Truman's effort, known as the Marshall Plan, to rebuild the economies of Western Europe after World War II. Kennedy's determination to land a man on the moon by 1970 resulted in many technological breakthroughs that have had a tremendous influence on the commercial electronics industry and the way of life in the United States. Acid rain in New England and Canada is widely believed to be caused in part by coal burned in the Midwest, a practice furthered by the Carter administration's energy program, which sought, through subsidies for coal conversion, to reduce the industrial use of crude oil and natural gas. The precarious state of the U.S. airline industry in the early 1990s is due in large part to deregulation initiatives in the late 1970s that were intended to strengthen the industry. It should be clear that chief executives do not always get the results they expect from the policies they sponsor.

Even more basic than the uncertainties introduced by time and unanticipated results is the problem of establishing cause-and-effect relationships between policies and outcomes. This is particularly true of chief executive policies because they are often aimed at making significant changes in society, but such changes almost always have complex causes. The Reagan administration's monetary and fiscal policies—the tax cut and stricter control of the money supply—are frequently credited with reducing inflation during the 1980s. Increasing foreign competition in certain core industries and lower energy costs may have had as much to do with keeping prices down as did government policy, however. State reforms of education have been praised, but linking changes in teaching techniques, approaches to discipline, or working conditions in the schools with student aptitude and achievement test scores is a notoriously complex task.[61]

Foreign policies and subsequent developments are also difficult to connect. How much did the allegedly "soft" foreign policy of the Carter administration have to do with the Soviet invasion of Afghanistan? How much did the more belligerent Reagan foreign policy affect the willingness of the Soviet Union to sign meaningful arms control agreements? It should be emphasized that politicians show little reluctance to assert that positive cause-and-effect relationships exist between policies they support and favorable outcomes and that the opposite is true of policies they oppose.

Some chief executive policies and results have fairly straightforward relationships. It is possible to determine the amount of money elderly recipients receive from Social Security and then to measure the impact of such payments on poverty, defined as a monetary threshold, among the elderly.[62] Decisions about the size, accessibility, and location of state highways have undeniable impacts, such as changes in population, property values, and commercial sales. Precise, carefully defined relationships can be established between certain policies and their impacts, but many chief executive policies are so broad that the results and their causes are unclear.

The Management Puzzle

Organizational management and policy administration are core responsibilities of chief executives. But because of the pressures and incentives to take the lead in setting the policy agenda and pushing for the enactment of policies, few chief executives have the time or the inclination to oversee the implementation of the policies they have championed. Therefore, most of the institutional learning that results from the implementation of chief executive policies takes place in bureaucracies or specialized legislative committees. At this point chief executive politics gives way to bureaucratic or legislative politics.

Efforts to reorganize the executive branch are perhaps the most common form of chief executive activity that reflects institutional learning. Bureaucratic resistance to chief executive initiatives has been recognized as a problem at least since the turn of the century. Franklin Roosevelt, Truman, Nixon, and Carter all sponsored executive branch reorganizations aimed at establishing more rational bureaucratic structures and enhancing central control. The results usually fell short of expectations, mainly because Congress and the interest groups that were tied to the existing subgovernmental networks effectively opposed the changes these presidents sought.[63] In state government, reorganizations have been common. Since 1965, half of the state governments have undergone comprehensive reorganizations and nearly all states have reorganized at least part of their government operations.[64] The goals of these reforms are basically the same as those of federal reforms: establishing clear chains of command and making public service delivery more economical and responsive to central control.

Through the Civil Service Reform Act of 1978, President Carter tried to shake up the bureaucracy, starting with individual employees. The act provided incentives for high-ranking civil servants to take on special tasks at the request of the president or cabinet officer, and it made the hiring, firing, and transfer of civil servants somewhat easier. Many governors have also pushed for higher standards in the hiring and retention of government employees, the inclusion of more jobs in civil service or merit systems, and the improvement of in-service training.[65]

Chief executives are not reluctant to get involved with implementation problems if questionable results become public concerns. In fact, chief executives who sponsor policy innovations that are adopted—either their own or those inherited from their immediate predecessor—are likely to assign a high priority to certain matters of program delivery. A common reaction to implementation problems is to propose program reform. Many of the War on Poverty programs were designed to avoid reliance on entrenched federal and state bureaucracies and to restrict state discretion because the policy formulators in the Kennedy and Johnson administrations doubted the commitment of those bureaucratic and political officials to the programs' goals. Not surprisingly, these policies generated their own implementation problems, such as duplication of service, lack of coordination among related programs, and state and local political resistance, which Republican presidents Nixon, Reagan, and Bush used to justify proposals for a "new federalism." The result of new federalism reforms is a modified intergovernmental program delivery system, fewer separate programs, and a larger state role in implementation decisions.

Summary

Chief executive politics commands the attention of almost every American. More than any other politicians, chief executives define and articulate the leading issues of the day and propose policy solutions. Much of what they say and do is covered by the media and becomes the focus of discussion among citizens. Their visibility and their formal powers give chief executives enormous political influence.

Their political strength is clearly evident in their ability to define issues and set agendas. The concerns they choose to address become issues for the entire political community. They can force others to pay attention to their priorities and accept their definitions of issues. Their domination of the political agenda gives them a tremendous advantage in policy development.

Many chief executive proposals fail to gain the approval needed to become policy, which diminishes the political strength of the leaders who offer them. Chief executive power and policy effectiveness, therefore, depend for their success on the ability of the individuals who occupy high office to convince the public and other political elites. When the quality of chief executives' leadership is widely questioned, their political muscles atrophy. The ability of chief executives to overcome the many hurdles that confront them on the path to policy change may justifiably earn them legendary reputations.

All chief executives have long lists of important policy proposals they hope to have enacted. If they are successful, the public has a tangible basis for evaluating chief executive performance. Concrete policy accomplishments are a valuable form of political currency. Established politicians display a strong allegiance to the status quo, but the values of the public are continually changing. Chief executives, taking advantage of their unique relationship with the public, frequently have acted as agents for change in American politics.

All the time and energy chief executives devote to voicing public concerns and securing adoption of new policies naturally limits the attention they can devote to matters of administration and policy implementation. Still, because new policies tend to breed implementation problems, issues of program design and delivery frequently command the interest and concern of chief executives.

When crises occur, nearly every aspect of chief executive politics changes. Media and public attention become a hindrance rather than an asset, and other political actors become much more cooperative and deferential. The power to act usually belongs unambiguously to chief executives, but the repercussions of ill-advised action can be severe. Effective crisis management is how many chief executives build their reputations as effective leaders.

Notes

1. Most governors have formal powers that are similar to those of presidents. They serve four-year terms and can run for reelection at least once. They can appoint high-ranking state officials, although on this point there is a good deal of variation as state legislatures share this power and some state officials are elected. Governors have considerable control over the budget process and have a veto over legislative actions, in some cases a line-item veto. Strong, as opposed to weak, mayors are those who have formal powers much like those of presidents and governors. The characteristics of a strong mayoralty are: terms longer than two years, the power to appoint heads of executive departments, veto power over city council actions, and a large role in the budget process. Most major cities have a strong mayor-council form of government. For more details, see Thad C. Beyle, "Governors," in Virginia Gray, Herbert Jacob, and Kenneth

Vines, *Politics in the American States*, 3d ed. (Boston: Little, Brown, 1983), 193-203; Larry Sabato, *Goodbye to Good-Time Charlie*, 2d ed. (Washington, D.C.: CQ Press, 1983); and Robert C. Lineberry and Ira Sharkansky, *Urban Politics and Public Policy*, 3d ed. (New York: Harper & Row, 1978), 161-169.

2. In describing the president's agenda, Paul Light categorizes executive branch proposals in the same way as the Office of Management and Budget, separating those that are in accordance with the president's program and that have been mentioned in a State of the Union address. This scheme is an appropriate way to distinguish the issues and policies that we regard as proper to chief executive politics from those that are more appropriately viewed as part of administrative politics. See Paul C. Light, "Presidents as Domestic Policy Makers," in *Rethinking the Presidency*, ed. Thomas E. Cronin (Boston: Little, Brown, 1982), 351-370.

3. See John Kingdon, *Agendas, Alternatives, and Public Policies* (Boston: Little, Brown, 1984), 26.

4. James K. Oliver, "Presidents as National Security Policy Makers," in *Rethinking the Presidency*, 396-397.

5. Alan Rosenthal, *Governors and Legislatures* (Washington, D.C.: CQ Press), 96-98.

6. See Beyle, "Governors," 211.

7. See Sabato, *Goodbye to Good-Time Charlie*, 105-110, 115-116.

8. Dick Kirschten, "Targets of Discontent," *National Journal*, November 10, 1990, 2736-2742.

9. Light, "Presidents as Domestic Policy Makers," 361.

10. Ibid., 362-364.

11. Jeff Fishel, *Presidents and Promises* (Washington, D.C.: CQ Press, 1985).

12. Stephen Skowronek discusses the intellectual/ideological and practical aspects of several efforts to build and then reform national government in *Building a New American State: The Expansion of National Administrative Capacity, 1877-1920* (New York: Cambridge University Press, 1982).

13. See Thomas Cronin, "On the Separation of Brain and State: Implications for the President," in *Modern Presidents and the Presidency*, ed. Marc Landy (Lexington, Mass.: Lexington Books, 1985), 54.

14. Ibid., 54-58.

15. Kingdon, *Agendas, Alternatives, and Public Policies*.

16. Light, "Presidents as Domestic Policy Makers," 365.

17. Fishel, *Presidents and Promises*, 26.

18. For a discussion of bias in presidential agendas, see ibid., 20-22. For more general treatments of this subject, see E. E. Schattschneider, *The Semi-Sovereign People* (New York: Holt, Rinehart and Winston, 1960; rev. ed. 1975); Peter Bachrach and Morton S. Baratz, *Power and Poverty: Theory and Practice* (New York: Oxford University Press, 1970); and Steven Lukes, *Power* (London: Macmillan, 1974).

19. Paul Starobin, "Going Overboard," *National Journal*, April 21, 1990, 940-946.

20. Christopher Madison, "Sideline Players," *National Journal*, December 15, 1990, 3024-3026.

21. Richard E. Neustadt, *Presidential Power: The Politics of Leadership from FDR to Carter* (New York: John Wiley, 1980).

22. Rosenthal, *Governors and Legislatures*, 35ff.

23. Ibid., 10.

24. See Duane Lockard, *The Politics of State and Local Government*, 3d ed. (New York: Macmillan, 1983), chaps. 7 and 8.

25. See Bert A. Rockman, *The Leadership Question* (New York: Praeger, 1984).

26. This argument is presented more fully by Samuel Kernell in *Going Public* (Washington, D.C.: CQ Press, 1986).

27. Ibid., chap. 6.

28. See Elizabeth Drew, *Money and Politics* (New York: Macmillan, 1983), 67-76.

29. Kernell, *Going Public*.

30. See Rockman, *The Leadership Question;* James MacGregor Burns, *Leadership* (New York: Harper & Row, 1978); and Neustadt, *Presidential Power*.

31. Rockman, *The Leadership Question*, chap. 2.

32. See James David Barber, *The Presidential Character*, 2d ed. (Englewood Cliffs, N.J.: Prentice-Hall, 1977).

33. Arthur M. Schlesinger, Jr., *The Imperial Presidency* (Boston: Houghton Mifflin, 1973).

34. Thad Beyle, "From Governor to Governors," in *The State of the States*, ed. Carl E. Van Horn (Washington, D.C.: CQ Press, 1989), 36.

35. Coleman B. Ransone, Jr., *The American Governorship* (Westport, Conn.: Greenwood Press, 1982), 109-111.

36. Ibid., 114.

37. Lockard, *The Politics of State and Local Government*, 242.

38. Personal interview with author, March 1990.

39. These categories are a slightly modified version of those used by Thomas Cronin in *The State of the Presidency*, 2d ed. (Boston: Little, Brown, 1980), 145-153.

40. Ibid.

41. Beyle, "From Governor to Governors," 37.

42. Marcia Howard, *Fiscal Survey of the States, September 1990* (Washington, D.C.: National Governors' Association, 1990).

43. Fishel, *Presidents and Promises*, 30-45.

44. Rosenthal, *Governors and Legislatures*, 25.

45. See Harrell R. Rodgers, Jr., and Charles S. Bullock III, *Law and Social Change* (New York: McGraw-Hill, 1972), chaps. 2 and 5; and Phyllis Wallace, "A Decade of Policy Developments in Equal Opportunities in Employment and Housing," in *A Decade of Federal Antipoverty Programs*, ed. Robert H. Haveman (New York: Academic Press, 1977).

46. James C. Ceaser, "The Rhetorical Presidency Revisited," in *Modern Presidents and the Presidency*, 33.

47. Carl E. Van Horn, "The Quiet Revolution," in *The State of the States*, 7-9.

48. See Frances Fox Piven and Richard A. Cloward, *Regulating the Poor* (New York: Vintage Books, 1971).

49. For specific figures on black voting for Democratic presidential candidates, see Herbert B. Asher, *Presidential Elections and American Politics*, 3d ed. (Homewood, Ill.: Dorsey Press, 1984).

50. See Fishel, *Presidents and Promises*, 93.

51. Kirschten, "Targets of Discontent," 2736-2742.

52. Martha Derthick, *New Towns In-Town* (Washington, D.C.: Urban Institute Press, 1972).

53. Ibid., 82-102.

54. Morton H. Halperin, "Implementing Presidential Foreign Policy Decisions: Limitations and Resistance," in *Cases in Public Policy Making*, ed. James E. Anderson (New York: Praeger, 1976), 208-236.

55. Graham T. Allison, *Essence of Decision* (Boston: Little, Brown, 1971), 132.

56. Lester M. Salamon, "Follow-ups, Letdowns, and Sleepers: The Time Dimension in Policy Evaluation," in *Public Policy Making in a Federal System*, ed. Charles O. Jones and Robert D. Thomas (Beverly Hills, Calif.: Sage, 1976), 257-283.

57. Ibid., 267.

58. Ibid., 263.

59. The original Head Start evaluation was done by Westinghouse Learning Corporation and Ohio University, see *The Impact of Head Start: An Evaluation of the Effects of Head Start on Children's Cognitive and Affective Development*, Report to the Office of Economic Opportunity, July 12, 1969. For subsequent research, see Irving Lazar, *Summary: The Persistence of Preschool Effects*, Community Service Laboratory, New York State College of Human Ecology at Cornell University, October 1977. For a bibliographic summary, see Ada Jo Mann, *A Review of Head Start Research Since 1969* (Washington, D.C.: George Washington University, 1978).

60. On the impact of federal job-training programs, see Robert Taggart, *A Fisherman's Guide: An Assessment of Training and Remediation Strategies* (Kalamazoo, Mich.: W. E. Upjohn Institute for Employment Research, 1981). For a summary, see Michael Borus, "Assessing the Impact of Training Programs," in *Employing the Disadvantaged*, ed. Eli Ginzburg (New York: Basic Books, 1980). On the impact of food stamps, see U.S. Senate, Subcommittee on Nutrition, Committee on Agriculture, Nutrition, and Forestry, *Hunger in America: Ten Years Later*, 96th Cong. 1st sess., 1979; also Congressional Budget Office, *The Food Stamp Program: Income or Food Supplementation?* (Washington, D.C.: Government Printing Office, 1977). On Medicare and Medicaid see Karen Davis and Cathy Schoen, *Health and the War on Poverty: A Ten-Year Appraisal* (Washington, D.C.: Brookings Institution, 1978).

61. See Egon G. Guba, "The Failure of Educational Evaluation," in *Evaluating Action Programs*, ed. Carol H. Weiss (Boston: Allyn & Bacon, 1972), 250-266; or James S. Coleman, "Problems of Conceptualization and Measurement in Studying Policy Impacts," in *Public Policy Evaluation*, ed. Kenneth M. Dolbeare (Beverly Hills, Calif.: Sage, 1975), 19-40.

62. For an excellent example, see Laurence E. Lynn, Jr., "A Decade of Policy Developments in the Income Maintenance System," in *A Decade of Federal Antipoverty Programs*, 55-117.

63. For a discussion of presidential reorganization efforts, see Erwin E. Hargrove and Michael Nelson, *Presidents, Politics, and Policy* (New York: Alfred A. Knopf, 1984), 249-265.

64. Beyle, "From Governor to Governors," 38.

65. Thad L. Beyle, ed., *State Government: CQ's Guide to Current Issues and Activities, 1985-1986* (Washington, D.C.: CQ Press, 1985), 119.

7 Courtroom Politics

It is sometimes said that courts implement policies made by other branches of government. But for a number of issues—abortion, capital punishment, search and seizure, school prayer, and school desegregation—the opposite is true: the courts make policy, and other political institutions respond to their lead. When politicians are silent or ambiguous, judicial action cannot be described as policy implementation; there may be no policy to implement until the courts act. For a wide variety of other issues, such as the environment, welfare, and communications, the courts, although their powers are somewhat circumscribed, have considerable discretion. Judges do more than resolve disputes in accordance with the law. Through their decisions, they create law every bit as much as legislators do.

The policy-making role of U.S. courts arouses considerable controversy because it is unique. In Great Britain judges are more accurately described as technicians than as policy makers. With a few exceptions, their role is to dot *i*'s and cross *t*'s.[1] U.S. courts are more powerful than other courts in the Western world, and their power is growing. Law professor Donald Horowitz observed "The courts have tended to move from the byways onto the highways of policy making."[2] Although from time to time politicians object to the growing power of the courts, the main force driving judicial policy making is the abdication of responsibility by elected officials.

Many courts make policy, including federal courts and state courts. As the highest federal court, the U.S. Supreme Court is the ultimate arbiter of legal controversies. The Supreme Court's preeminence should not be construed to mean that other courts play a minor role, however. In fact, the Supreme Court decides only about 150 cases each year. In contrast, the other courts combined handle millions of cases annually, and many of these cases have far-reaching policy implications.

Cases and Controversies

The issues confronted by courts are rich and diverse. Many of them, classified as private law, involve disputes between private parties. This category comprises contracts (Is an agreement legally binding?); property (Has property been illegally damaged or confiscated?); and torts (Have people or property been directly harmed?). In public law cases, government officials are parties to a legal dispute. Under this category are questions of constitutional law (Are decisions by government officials constitutional?); statutory law (What is legislative intent?); and administrative law (Are administrative decisions constitutional, legal, and consistent with past decisions?).

These categories overlap in many ways (see Figure 7-1). Antitrust actions by government officials often have public and private components. For example, government officials function as prosecutors in a case, but the charge is that one company has engaged in anticompetitive behavior against another. Torts become public when a private party sues a government official or an agency for malfeasance or nonfeasance. Overlaps within categories are even more common. In many administrative law cases, the key is legislative intent; in many constitutional law cases, the constitutionality of a statute is questioned; in both instances, statutory law is involved.

Because the concern here is public policy, the focus is on public law cases, which have broader implications for society than do private law cases. If one person sues a neighbor over a barking dog, the world does not anxiously await a verdict. If an administrative agency proposes a change in welfare eligibility rules, the verdict may affect many thousands of people. Examples from administrative law and constitutional law are cited to illustrate differences in judicial behavior. Although administrative law occasionally overlaps with constitutional law, each more often overlaps with statutory law. In administrative and constitutional law, questions of statutory interpretation are seldom far from view. A review of the dynamics of administrative and constitutional law inevitably touches on statutory interpretation.

Constitutional Law

Constitutional law raises questions about civil liberties, states' rights, interstate commerce, and other protections guaranteed by the U.S. Constitution or the constitutions of the states. The questions are enormously varied. Under what circumstances is evidence gathered by police admissible in a criminal proceeding? Under what circumstances may state governments provide financial assistance to parochial schools? What conditions may states impose on abortions? Should states be free to execute persons found guilty of murder? When must an individual's right to privacy yield to freedom of the press? When must freedom of the press yield to an individual's right to a fair trial? May insurance companies charge male drivers higher rates than female drivers? May

Figure 7-1 Branches of Law

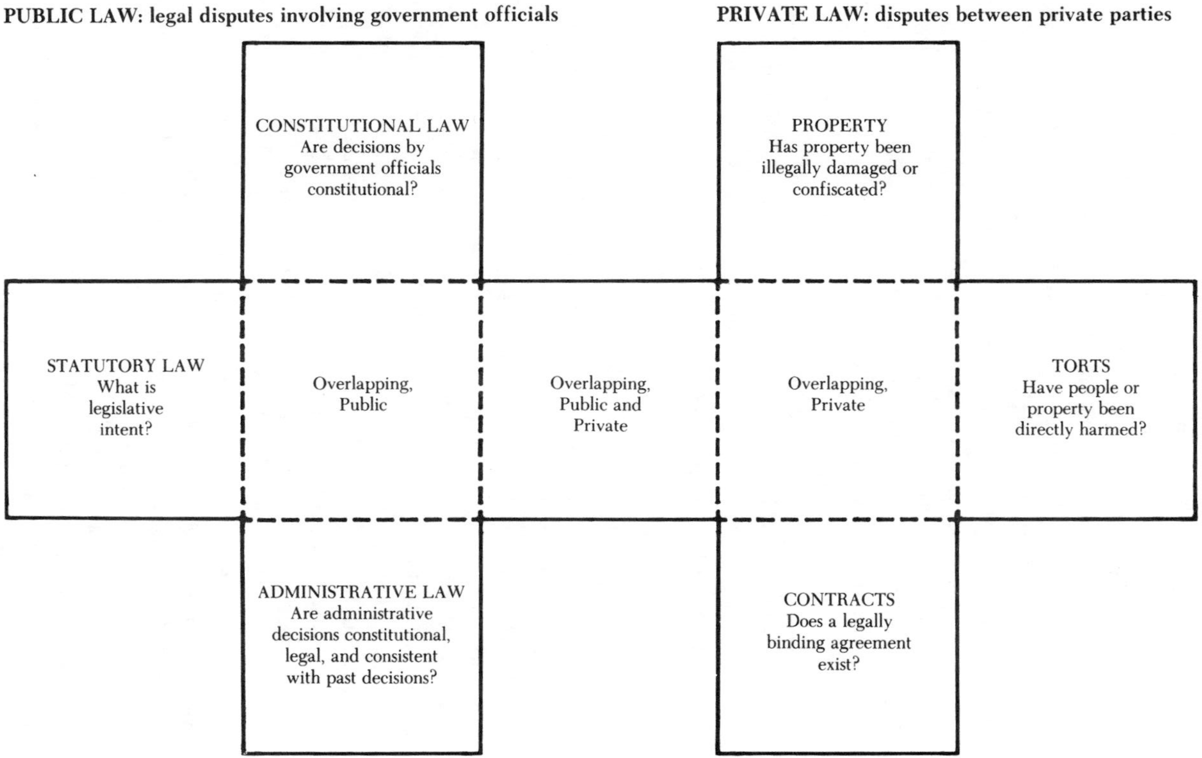

PUBLIC LAW: legal disputes involving government officials

PRIVATE LAW: disputes between private parties

CONSTITUTIONAL LAW
Are decisions by government officials constitutional?

STATUTORY LAW
What is legislative intent?

ADMINISTRATIVE LAW
Are administrative decisions constitutional, legal, and consistent with past decisions?

Overlapping, Public

Overlapping, Public and Private

PROPERTY
Has property been illegally damaged or confiscated?

CONTRACTS
Does a legally binding agreement exist?

Overlapping, Private

TORTS
Have people or property been directly harmed?

employers specify the sex of applicants in want ads?

As these questions illustrate, constitutional law concerns some of the most vexing dilemmas facing society. These issues of social policy are difficult, not because they are technically complex (although some are) but because they pit one right against another—a woman's freedom of choice versus the rights of an unborn fetus, a criminal's right to a fair trial versus a newspaper's right to freedom of the press, and so forth. Obviously, the stakes are high, and some interests will be adversely affected, whatever the court decides. Constitutional law is characterized by a high degree of conflict, salience, and manifest costs.

Some courts are especially likely to handle constitutional law cases. The U.S. Supreme Court deals almost exclusively with such cases, which explains the tendency among laypersons to equate judicial review with constitutional interpretation. State supreme courts also deal with constitutional issues much of the time. But the overwhelming majority of lower court decisions, at the state and federal levels, do not pertain to constitutional issues. These cases almost always concern private law, statutory law, or administrative law.

Administrative Law

Administrative law cases focus on the behavior of administrative agencies—their interpretation of statutes and their application of administrative rules, regulations, and procedures. Should automobile manufacturers be required to install airbags? Should a dam be built if it poses a threat to an endangered species? When are utility rates unjustly discriminatory? When does a nuclear power plant pose an unacceptable health risk to the public? May a hospital deny service to a poor person without forfeiting federal tax breaks? May an interstate highway be built through a public park? May a newspaper own a television station or a radio station in the same city? What criteria should be applied to the location of a halfway house? These questions require courts to consider whether an administrative agency has acted in accordance with legislative standards and with provisions of the federal Administrative Procedure Act of 1946 or its state-level counterparts. These laws spell out the procedures that agencies must follow in different situations and the criteria for judicial review.

Administrative law cases are enormously complex. Federal courts have evaluated the adequacy of statistical experiments on foam insulation, the health effects of benzene and lead, and the capacity of the auto industry for technological breakthroughs. In passing judgment on public utility commissions, state courts must decide whether depreciation rates have been properly calculated, whether the utility's rate base should include plants under construction, and whether a given rate of return allows the utility to compete for capital. One judge, exasperated by such complexities, decided to narrow the focus of the case to a single issue, rate of return.[3] Otherwise, he argued, the court's task would be hopeless, and the case interminable.

Administrative law cases are decided initially by administrative agencies. If they are appealed, many administrative agency decisions at the federal level may go directly to the circuit courts of appeals, bypassing federal district courts. Some circuit court decisions on administrative law are appealed to the U.S. Supreme Court, but most never go that far. For all intents and purposes, circuit courts are final arbiters of many administrative decisions. Among circuit courts, the D.C. Circuit Court of Appeals, in particular, handles a higher percentage of administrative law cases than do other circuit courts.[4] It has sometimes been called the second most powerful court in the land. On questions of administrative law, it is, in practice, the most powerful. At the state level, administrative law cases are handled by intermediate appeals courts and further appealed to state supreme courts.

Neglected Issues

Courts seldom address issues in two important policy domains: foreign policy (responses to international crises or the use of armed forces abroad) and macroeconomic policy (taxing and spending decisions). The failure of courts to address these issues is due more to self-restraint than to a lack of plaintiffs. Many taxpayers would love to take Uncle Sam to court, if only they were permitted to do so. Although the courts have lowered barriers to standing—the right to sue—by consumer advocates and environmentalists, they have refused to facilitate taxpayer suits.[5] Taxpayers often wind up in court as defendants, with the Internal Revenue Service or its state counterpart as plaintiff, but they seldom appear as plaintiffs in taxation cases.

On the rare occasions when the courts address questions of macroeconomic policy, they normally defer to elected officials, especially when elected officials are in agreement. When Congress granted President Richard Nixon the authority to impose wage and price controls in 1970, a special federal district court panel upheld the statute as a constitutional delegation of power to the president.[6] Similarly, the U.S. Supreme Court has upheld congressional delegations of authority to the president in foreign affairs.[7] Justice William H. Rehnquist wrote in *Dames & Moore v. Regan* (1981), "Presidential action taken pursuant to specific congressional authorization is supported by strongest presumptions and widest latitude of judicial interpretation, and the burden of persuasion rests heavily upon anyone who might attack it." In plain English, even the Supreme Court is reluctant to second-guess politicians in foreign policy.

Selection of Cases

Unlike other public policy makers, judges can address only those issues that come before them. Although courts are alike in their inability to initiate cases, they differ in their freedom to ignore them. As a general rule, supreme courts have more discretion than other courts. Federal district courts and circuit courts of appeals are supposed to hear all cases within their jurisdiction that come before them.[8] The agenda of the U.S. Supreme Court is largely discretionary. With the exception of a few kinds of cases, which seldom arise,[9] the Supreme Court may decline to hear cases. Even the Court's mandatory agenda is less mandatory than it seems to be. The Court may use devices such as the summary decision or a denial of leave to file to evade the requirement that certain cases be heard.

A similar pattern prevails at the state level, although state supreme courts differ in their discretion. In some states, the supreme court must hear appeals from trial courts; in others, the supreme court is free to choose only "significant" cases if it wishes. The variations can be explained by the existence in some states, but not others, of intermediate appeals courts. In general, supreme courts have more discretion over their caseload in states with such courts. The assumption is that one appeal from a trial court decision should be available to all parties, but that two may be excessive.

Judicial Coalitions

It is sometimes said that the courts are more independent than other institutions of government. This is true in one sense but not another; judges are remarkably independent of politicians, but they are not independent of politics. Indeed, partisan politics is a significant factor in judicial recruitment and judicial behavior. Once appointed to office, federal judges are independent of the politicians who put them on the bench. Although federal judges may be impeached by the House and convicted by the Senate for "high crimes and misdemeanors," this cumbersome machinery has been used successfully only five times in U.S. history. State judges are also independent of politicians, but not always of the electorate. In thirty-six states, judges may be removed from office by the voters through regular elections or through retention elections in which the judge runs unopposed but may be unseated by a vote of no confidence. Unpopular judges are unseated from time to time (Rose Bird, the former chief justice of the California Supreme Court, for example), but the overwhelming majority of judges who must face the voters are reelected.

Judges are not immune from partisan politics. Most federal judges belong to the party of the president who appointed them, and the same is true of state judges and the governors who appointed them. Furthermore, judges remain remarkably faithful to their party while in office. Although this loyalty may vary from issue to issue, party identification is the single best predictor of judicial voting behavior.

Diffuse Power

Many textbooks on American government portray the court system as a pyramid, with the U.S. Supreme Court at the apex. This image conveys a false impression, implying a hierarchical route that in reality very few cases follow. Most lower court decisions are never reviewed by higher courts. The majority of federal district court decisions are not appealed to the circuit courts; the majority of circuit court decisions are never appealed to the U.S. Supreme Court; and most circuit court decisions appealed to the Supreme Court are not accepted for review. The situation at the state level is much the same.

State supreme court decisions are usually final. Although decisions raising constitutional questions may be appealed to the U.S. Supreme Court, the Court hears no more than fifty such cases in any given year. Even if the Court reverses the state supreme court and returns the case for further proceedings, the state supreme court may reiterate its basic conclusion, while modifying some of the specifics. Although state and federal court systems intersect, they are more independent than is commonly supposed (see Figure 7-2).

When a higher court declines to review a lower court decision, that does not necessarily imply approval. Rather, it may mean that although the higher court would have decided the case differently, it cannot say that the lower court made a mistake. It may mean that the higher court is not prepared to address a certain legal issue, or it may mean that the higher court has too many other cases to hear.

All cases are not created equal, and the more important cases tend to be heard in the higher courts. Nevertheless, many critical decisions have been made by federal district court judges. For example, Judge Arthur Garrity desegregated Boston's public schools; Judge Frank Johnson, Jr., reformed Alabama's prisons and mental hospitals, and Judge Harold Greene ordered the divestiture of AT&T. These cases illustrate the degree to which judicial power is dispersed throughout the United States.

Leadership Styles and Strategies

When a federal district court judge issues a decision, he or she acts alone. Higher courts are characterized by collective decision making. Intermediate appeals court decisions usually are made by three-judge panels, and supreme court decisions are made by all the members.

Figure 7-2   The Structure of the Judicial System

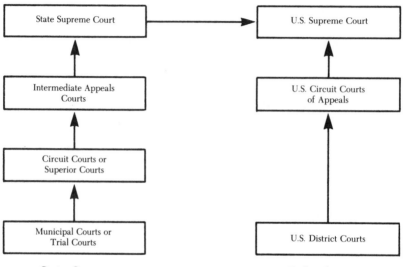

Coalition building is essential in such courts. Before a case is decided and the opinion written, a majority of judges must agree on the outcome and on the reasoning behind it. This consensus requires leadership—a mysterious but not altogether incomprehensible quality.

Within the courts there are three forms of leadership: political, institutional, and intellectual. Political leaders are those who can build coalitions, and the task of political leadership often falls on the shoulders of the judge assigned to write the opinion. To satisfy other members of the court, the opinion writer inserts new phrases and deletes others, with the goal of securing as many votes as possible in support of a coherent opinion. The opinion writer also seeks to discourage dissenting opinions, which convey judicial fragmentation. Centrists or "swing voters" are strategically situated to exercise political leadership because they hold the balance of power, especially when a court is ideologically divided, as was the Burger Court and as is the Rehnquist Court.

Institutional leaders are those who defend the courts against various external threats and who attempt to develop the courts as institutions. When Chief Justice Charles Evans Hughes denounced President Franklin Roosevelt's attempt to "pack" the Supreme Court, he was exercising institutional leadership.[10] Chief Justice Warren Burger led the battle to add judges to the federal bench and for more discretion in case selection, which he thought would protect the Supreme Court from "overload." Various state judges also have exercised institutional leadership when they fought to modernize the courts, to reorganize the judiciary, or to reform judicial selection procedures.

Intellectual leaders are those who influence their colleagues—and subsequent generations—through the force of their reasoning and the power of their ideas. Harlan Stone's argument that "discrete and insular minorities" warrant special protection under the Constitution—an argument buried in a footnote in the 1938 case *United States v. Carolene Products*—provided the rationale for broad interpretations of the Fourteenth Amendment by subsequent courts. Hugo Black's strong views on civil liberties provided the intellectual underpinnings for many of the decisions of the Warren Court. Judges on other courts have also exercised intellectual leadership. Judge Harold Leventhal of the D.C. Circuit Court of Appeals articulated the "hard look" doctrine of administrative law, which justifies careful judicial scrutiny of the reasoning behind administrative decisions. His colleague, David Bazelon, is credited with (or blamed for) the view that the mentally ill have a right to treatment under the Constitution. The reverberations from these ideas continue.

Although courts are less hierarchical than other government institutions, the chief justice or chief judge has certain powers. The chief justice of the U.S. Supreme Court presides at Court conferences and is the first to speak. If the chief justice votes with the majority, he (or she) assigns the opinion to a particular justice. Because the reasoning behind a decision often has a longer lasting impact than the decision, chief justices exercise power even when they choose not to write. The chief judges of other federal courts are more constrained. The chief judge of a federal district court assigns cases to other judges, but randomly. The chief judge of a federal circuit court of appeals assigns the opinion when the court sits en banc, or all together, provided he or she is in the majority. Most circuit court of appeals cases are decided by three-judge panels, however, and the cases are assigned randomly.

At the state level, there appears to be considerable variation in the leadership potential of chief judges. In states where supreme court judges are elected, partisan conflict often is intense enough to thwart attempts at leadership. In states where supreme court judges are appointed, the opposite is true.[11] At the local level, chief judges have the authority to assign cases.[12] Because the chief judge of local courts is usually selected by peers, he or she must be careful not to offend sensitive colleagues.

Decision Making

If leadership is a variable that adds an element of surprise to the judicial process—the "wild card" in the judicial deck—there are four more predictable elements of judicial decision making. They are law, evidence, party identification, and judicial philosophy.

Law. In resolving constitutional disputes, judges get a good deal of guidance from the constitution itself, whether federal or state. A constitution is not a legal cookbook, but neither is it a Rorschach test. Perhaps it is best to say that a constitution establishes a set of presumptions or burdens of proof. The U.S. Constitution does not define phrases such as freedom of the press, freedom of speech, or freedom of religion, but these phrases are laden with meaning from years of precedents, prior decisions that command respect. Although precedents are seldom determinative, they serve as guideposts to judges as they wrestle with difficult problems. In general, courts pay more attention to their own precedents and to those of higher courts than to the precedents of other courts.

Constitutions have less relevance for administrative law because most administrative law cases do not raise constitutional questions. Precedents are scarcer in administrative law; the administrative state is only about fifty years old, and higher courts offer less guidance on administrative law than on constitutional law. As judges evaluate administrative law cases, their guides are the federal APA and state administrative procedure acts. If administrative procedures are informal, the courts ask whether the agency acted "arbitrarily and capriciously." If administrative procedures are relatively formal, the courts ask whether the agency's decision is based on "substantial evidence" in the record. The latter is a more exacting form of judicial review. Agencies face a higher burden of proof as formality increases.

Evidence. Whether a case concerns constitutional law or administrative law, courts base their decisions on evidence submitted by litigants. For the most part, evidence consists of historical facts, such as who did what to whom. Courts also look at social facts, the probable consequences of decisions. Courts have been guided by empirical research on the effects of segregation on blacks (*Brown v. Board of Education*, 1954), the effects of teacher experience on pupil performance (*Hobson v. Hansen*, 1967, 1968), and the effects of judicial procedures on the rehabilitation of juvenile offenders (*In re Gault*, 1967).

Some litigants have a distinct advantage in presenting evidence. In particular, the "haves," who tend to be repeat players who know how to use the court system, usually are better at the game than the "have-nots," who tend to be one-shot participants.[13] This gap has narrowed as a result of court decisions granting certain have-nots the right to counsel in criminal cases (*Gideon v. Wainwright*, 1963) and the creation of legal aid societies, which represent the poor in civil cases. Public interest groups draw on their experience and resources in representing the disadvantaged or the public in court. The National Association for the Advancement of Colored People (NAACP) has filed numerous school desegregation suits, and the American Civil Liberties Union (ACLU) many First Amendment suits. Environmentalists have been represented in court by the Natural Resources Defense Council, the Environmental Defense Fund, the Sierra Club, and other groups. These public interest groups have won a wide variety of cases securing protection of wilderness areas and wetlands and enforcement of antipollution laws. In some instances the federal government has reimbursed them for the costs of successful lawsuits—a practice known as "intervenor funding."

Party identification. Few judges would cite party identification as a factor in their decisions. Indeed, many judges would take umbrage at the implication that partisanship enters into judicial decision making. Nevertheless, it is well established that Democratic judges and Republican judges decide certain kinds of cases differently. Democratic state supreme court judges are much more liberal in deciding worker's compensation cases than are their Republican counterparts,[14] and they are more supportive of the claims of criminal defendants, the disadvantaged, and individuals alleging deprivations of civil liberties.[15]

This pattern holds at all levels of the federal judiciary: Democratic judges tend to be more liberal and Republican judges more conservative.[16] Therefore, it is a matter of some consequence whether a Democrat or a Republican sits in the White House. Federal district court judges appointed by President Ronald Reagan have acquitted criminal defendants only 14 percent of the time; the record is 52 percent for President Jimmy Carter's appointees.[17]

A president's ideology also matters, especially in the appointment of Supreme Court nominees. Despite Reagan's failure to place staunch conservatives Robert Bork and Douglas Ginsburg on the Supreme Court, he was successful in appointing one staunch conservative— Associate Justice Antonin Scalia—and two moderate conservatives— Associate Justices Sandra Day O'Connor and Anthony Kennedy—to the nation's highest court. He also designated the most conservative member of the Court, William Rehnquist, as chief justice.

In appointing David Souter of New Hampshire to the Supreme Court, President Bush selected a safe and apparently nondoctrinaire nominee rather than a true-blue conservative. In part, this may have been a reaction to the disastrous Bork nomination, which embarrassed the White House and did no good for the conservative cause. In his other appointments to the federal bench, however, Bush has selected conservatives who are tough on crime and who see themselves as strict constructionists.[18]

Judicial philosophy. Judges differ in the extent to which they allow their personal values to decide the outcome of a case. Felix Frankfurter, who professed to be an unswerving civil libertarian, dissented against Warren Court decisions protecting individuals against the government. Frankfurter believed the courts should defer to other branches of government under most circumstances. Oliver Wendell Holmes took a similar view. As he saw it, judges should uphold laws even though they epitomize economic mistakes or futile experiments.[19] This point of view is sometimes referred to as the doctrine of judicial restraint. Other judges have been much more willing to overturn statutes. William Douglas and Hugo Black, staunch civil libertarians, routinely voted to void statutes that diminished First Amendment liberties. Black and Douglas were also judicial activists who believed that the courts should not defer to other branches of government, especially when First Amendment rights are at stake. In constitutional law a critical question for judges is whether to override the legislative branch; in administrative law, they must decide whether to overrule administrative agencies. During the 1970s the Supreme Court was more likely than ever before to overturn state and local laws as well as acts of Congress.[20] The U.S. Circuit Courts of Appeals were more likely to overturn administrative agencies.[21] Since then, evidence suggests that the pendulum is swinging back. Swings of the pendulum are seldom equal, however. Although the courts in the late 1980s are perhaps less activist than they were in the 1970s, they are far more activist than at the beginning of the twentieth century.

New Wine in Old Bottles

Judges, like other policy makers, are attentive to appearances, but judges are less likely than other public officials to substitute symbolic action for substantive action. Very few court decisions are purely symbolic. Unlike other public officials, judges do not avoid difficult problems or unpopular solutions. Instead, they confront many of society's most vexing problems, and, having done so, they then rely on symbols to legitimate their decisions.

Two norms confirm judicial attentiveness to symbols. First, judges seek to avoid public feuding, viewed as unseemly and detrimental to the image of the courts. In contrast, public feuding is a popular legislative sport. Second, judges try to convey the impression of an unbroken line of precedents, dating back to the Founding Fathers, whereas politicians are forever talking about new ideas, new deals, and new American revolutions. Judges care about two symbols: unity and continuity.

Unity and Continuity

The school desegregation rulings of the Warren Court demonstrate the commitment to unity. Since the decision in *Brown v. Board of Education* (1954), the Court has struggled to maintain the appearance of unity on this extraordinarily divisive issue. During the Warren years, the justices were remarkably successful. Despite deep divisions, they managed to issue a series of unanimous decisions, which sent an important message to recalcitrant school boards, especially in the South: Desegregation is the law of the land.[22]

School desegregation cases also demonstrate the commitment to continuity. The *Brown* decision reversed *Plessy v. Ferguson* (1896), a ruling that upheld the constitutionality of segregated facilities and services. In reversing *Plessy* as untenable in a modern age, the Court cited a wide variety of precedents that supported a broad interpretation of the Fourteenth Amendment. In subsequent cases the federal courts have portrayed court-ordered busing as a logical outgrowth of *Brown* and the Fourteenth Amendment. Politicians serve old wine in new bottles, but judges prefer to serve new wine in old bottles. This modest deception legitimates policy making by public officials who, according to a narrow reading of the Constitution, are not supposed to be making public policy.

Innovative Decisions

The commitment of courts to continuity may be good for the Republic, but it obscures the extent to which judges are innovators in American politics. It also conveys a false impression that judicial policies differ only incrementally from earlier policies. Although most court decisions, like most decisions of other political institutions, are incremental, a remarkably high percentage of decisions made by the highest courts are innovative, especially when the issues are divisive and the decisions will have far-reaching effects.

It is widely acknowledged that the Warren Court was innovative. Its decisions on school desegregation, criminal justice, school prayer, and other matters transformed the Bill of Rights into a blueprint for economic and political equality. Other Warren Court decisions, on less visible topics, were equally revolutionary. For example, in *New York Times v. Sullivan* (1964) the Warren Court ruled that public figures must demonstrate actual malice to win a libel suit against a newspaper. This decision, which overruled 175 years of settled legal practice, virtually immunized the press against libel suits.[23]

Scholars are beginning to recognize that the Burger Court was also

remarkably innovative.[24] *In Furman v. Georgia* (1972) the Burger
Court found existing capital punishment statutes unconstitutional,
which triggered changes in these statutes throughout the country. In
Roe v. Wade (1973) the Burger Court established different ground rules
for abortion during the three trimesters of pregnancy and ruled that a
woman's right to privacy, although not absolute, is a constitutionally
protected right. The Burger Court was also innovative in a wide variety
of other areas, such as commercial free speech, sex discrimination,
procedural due process, and freedom of the press.

A number of state supreme courts have also blazed new trails in
public law. The New Jersey Supreme Court outlawed the use of the
property tax as the sole basis for local school financing, established a
right-to-die procedure for permanently comatose patients, and held
hosts liable for drunk-driving accidents if they knowingly served alcohol
to an intoxicated person. In *Southern Burlington County NAACP v.
Township of Mt. Laurel* (1975), a landmark decision, the New Jersey
Supreme Court ruled "exclusionary zoning" unconstitutional. The court
said that local governments have an affirmative duty to provide housing
opportunities for lower-class persons, even if they do not already live in
the community. If applied to zoning ordinances in other states, this
decision would truly revolutionize residential patterns and practices.

A number of state supreme courts have taken the lead in civil
liberties questions. Eleven states now bar school-financing formulas
based exclusively on local property taxes, despite a U.S. Supreme Court
ruling that such formulas are compatible with the U.S. Constitution
(*San Antonio Independent School District v. Rodriguez*, 1973). State
supreme courts in Alaska, California, Massachusetts, Michigan, New
York, and Pennsylvania have gone beyond the U.S. Supreme Court in
protecting the rights of criminal defendants.[25] The Supreme Judicial
Court of Massachusetts ruled in 1985 that the standard for obtaining a
search warrant is higher under the state constitution, which "provides
more substantive protection to criminal defendants" than the U.S.
Constitution. In the same year the Alaska Supreme Court said that the
state constitutional guarantee against unreasonable searches and seizures is broader than the Fourth Amendment to the U.S. Constitution,
even though the wording is almost identical.

State supreme courts can go beyond the U.S. Supreme Court because
the federal court sets a floor, not a ceiling, on constitutional rights. If
state supreme courts find that state constitutions provide stronger protection than the U.S. Constitution, they are free to follow the state
constitution, provided their conclusion is based primarily on state law
(*Michigan v. Long*, 1983). According to one estimate, from 1970
through 1985 state courts handed down 300 published opinions declar-

ing U.S. Supreme Court guarantees of civil liberties to be insufficient.[26]

State court procedures have also shown innovation. For example, state courts have been pioneers in allowing electronic and photographic media coverage of court proceedings, including criminal proceedings.[27] In 1990, 45 states allowed television, radio, and photographic coverage of certain judicial proceedings. Many observers believe that state courts have managed to promote freedom of the press without inhibiting constitutional rights to a fair trial.[28] Indeed, even the U.S. Supreme Court has conceded that television coverage of a criminal proceeding does not automatically violate a defendant's constitutional right to a fair trial (*Chandler v. Florida,* 1981). Although federal courts have traditionally barred cameras from the courtroom, federal judges recently approved the use of cameras in several federal courts on an experimental basis.[29]

Minorities as Beneficiaries

Students who take courses in constitutional law and administrative law must wonder whether their professors are talking about the same judicial system. Constitutional law students see the courts as liberal; administrative law students see them as conservative. Constitutional law students see the courts as champions of the underprivileged; administrative law students see them as protectors of special interests. These impressions are not without foundation: the fact is that constitutional law and administrative law benefit different groups in society.

The argument may be summarized as follows: (1) courts adopt policies favorable to minorities, despite opposition to such policies; (2) in constitutional law, the courts adopt policies that benefit disadvantaged minorities such as blacks, the handicapped, and the mentally ill; and (3) in administrative law, the courts adopt policies that benefit advantaged minorities—for example, utility companies, insurance companies, and transportation companies.

Constitutional Law

Because the U.S. Supreme Court is preeminent in matters of constitutional law, scholars interested in assessing the beneficiaries of constitutional law decisions have focused on this court. Most recent studies of the Court find considerable support for disadvantaged minorities in its decisions.[30] Of the twenty-eight cases in which the Court overturned a congressional statute between 1958 and 1974, twenty-seven upheld minority rights, as guaranteed by the Bill of Rights or the Fourteenth Amendment.[31] The principal beneficiaries in these cases were blacks and other disadvantaged minorities.

Some scholars assert that these studies give too much weight to the Warren Court (1954-1969), whose strong commitment to civil liberties is universally acknowledged. Political scientist Robert Dahl found that most Supreme Court decisions overturning congressional statutes through 1957 actually harmed minorities.[32] According to Dahl, the Court reinforces majoritarian decisions made by Congress. In 1985 law professor Geoffrey Stone noted that 85 percent of the Court's "noneasy" (not unanimous) civil liberties decisions during the 1983-1984 term were decided against minority rights.[33] In his view, the Burger Court launched a new era of "aggressive majoritarianism." But the Burger Court's reputation as majoritarian in a conservative era can be traced directly to its criminal procedure decisions. In this area the Burger Court was more sensitive to public safety than to minority rights. In *Michigan v. Long* (1983), for example, the Burger Court upheld protective searches of the passenger compartment of a car if police have a reasonable belief that the suspect is dangerous. In *New York v. Quarles* (1984) the Burger Court ruled that the police may postpone the reading of a defendant's *Miranda* warnings until they have investigated a potential threat to public safety. The Court also upheld vehicle searches by border patrol officials, provided that circumstances are suspicious and that intrusions on privacy are limited (*United States v. Brignoni-Ponce*, 1975; *United States v. Cortez*, 1981). Despite these decisions, a fair appraisal of the Burger Court's entire record, not just its criminal procedure rulings or the decisions of a single term, must acknowledge a general pattern of support for minority rights.

Even the Rehnquist Court, widely expected to be conservative, has handed down a number of decisions favoring minorities. It voted to extend the reach of the Voting Rights Act (*City of Pleasant Grove v. United States*, 1987) and to allow special job protections for pregnant workers (*California Federal Savings and Loan Assn. v. Guerra*, 1987). On affirmative action the Court ruled in *United States v. Paradise* (1987) that a judge may order agencies to use promotion quotas temporarily when there is a history of "egregious" racial bias. In *Johnson v. Santa Clara County* (1987) the Court ruled that employers may give special preferences to women in hiring and promotion decisions even if no prior discrimination existed. In *Metro Broadcasting v. FCC* (1990) the Court upheld two FCC programs aimed at encouraging minority ownership of broadcast licenses. And in *University of Pennsylvania v. EEOC* (1990) the Court held that universities accused of discrimination in tenure decisions must make relevant personnel files available to federal investigators.

To be sure, decisions unfavorable to minorities can also be cited. In *Wards Cove Packing Co. v. Atonio* (1989), the Court made it more difficult for minorities to win employment discrimination cases. And in *Richmond v. Croson* (1986), the Court overturned a rigid racial quota in awarding public contracts in Richmond, Virginia. This decision cast a pall over long-standing minority preferences in local government contracts. *Richmond v. Croson* can be construed as a decision against quotas, especially rigid quotas, however, and not a decision against affirmative action. Overall, the Rehnquist Court, like other recent Supreme Courts, has been relatively sympathetic to minority rights on constitutional issues outside the criminal justice area.

Although less is known about other courts, a study of federal district court decisions on education policy confirms a strong tendency for judicial support of disadvantaged minorities. A study of sixty-five education policy decisions between 1970 and 1977, sixty-four of which concerned constitutional issues, found that minority plaintiffs were successful 71 percent of the time.[34] Plaintiffs in these cases included blacks, Hispanics, native Americans, aliens, women, the handicapped, the poor, the elderly, and nonconformists such as long-haired students. These findings are especially interesting because the authors deliberately excluded school desegregation cases from their sample. Their findings do not simply reiterate the well-known conclusion that school desegregation cases have been decided in favor of minorities.

What accounts for the relatively strong support of courts for disadvantaged minorities in constitutional law cases? In particular, what caused the noticeable shift in the disposition of the courts that began in the mid-1950s? One possibility is that judges are more liberal than they used to be, and this liberalism may be attributed to changes in judicial selection practices at the state and federal levels. Consultation with bar associations prior to appointment to the bench may have encouraged the selection of judges who share the bar's commitment to civil liberties, and the appointment of more women and blacks may have further sensitized courts to minority rights.

Changes outside the courtroom—in the political and legal culture—probably explain more than changes inside the judiciary. The U.S. Constitution and the state constitutions provide a formidable arsenal of legal weapons to minorities who are willing and able to use them. Until the 1950s minorities were aggrieved but not aroused, victimized but not mobilized. Since then public interest groups have emerged to champion minority rights in the courts and in other forums. These groups—the NAACP, the ACLU, and NOW (National Organization for Women)—have fought successfully to extend the frontiers of the First, Fourth, Fifth, and Fourteenth amendments. As a result of their efforts, the Constitution has become the functional equivalent of the Statue of Liberty—a beacon to the weak and the oppressed. Whatever the intentions of the Founding Fathers, the language of the Constitution, in its modern interpretation, offers considerable hope to the disadvantaged.

Administrative Law

The most common result of judicial review of administrative agency actions, either at the state or federal level, is for the court to sustain the agency.[35] This result confirms law professor Marc Galanter's argument that repeat players have the advantage in civil litigation.[36] The government is the quintessential repeat player. It has greater expertise, fewer start-up costs, greater bargaining credibility, and a greater stake in shaping rules of the game than other litigants, especially the one-shot litigant. It is not surprising that the government wins most of its cases.

Nevertheless, a substantial minority of administrative decisions reviewed by the courts are reversed or remanded, which means sent back to the agency for reconsideration. According to a study of state supreme court reviews of administrative agencies' decisions, nearly 44 percent of the court decisions did not fully support the agency.[37] Even the more deferential U.S. Supreme Court reverses 30 percent of federal agency decisions.[38]

The willingness of the U.S. Supreme Court to reverse a federal agency decision depends on many factors, including the ideology of the sitting justices. According to one recent study, the Warren Court and the Burger Court were equally likely to sustain federal agency decisions but they handled liberal and conservative decisions differently. For example, conservative decisions by social regulatory agencies were sustained 63.4 percent of the time by the Warren Court, 81.7 percent of the time by the Burger Court. As expected, liberal decisions by the same agencies were sustained more often by the Warren Court than by the Burger Court. And liberal justices were more likely to sustain liberal decisions.[39]

Who benefits when the courts reverse the decision of an administrative agency? The answer depends on who the plaintiff is and what issue is under consideration.[40] When the courts reverse a social welfare agency decision, the plaintiff is almost certain to be an individual claimant—a welfare recipient or a disabled worker, for example. Typically, the beneficiaries are members of a disadvantaged minority, and the losers are the citizens, in their role as taxpayers. When the courts reverse a regulatory agency decision, the plaintiff is almost certain to be a business such as an insurance company or a utility company. Normally, the beneficiaries here are members of an advantaged minority, whereas the losers are citizens, in their capacity as consumers.

If this pattern looks fairly symmetrical, it seems less so when one realizes that disappointed individuals are far less likely to challenge an

adverse administrative action in court than are disappointed corporations. Only 8 percent of all final Social Security Administration decisions go to court, and only one-third of these result in the restoration of
benefits for the claimant.[41] In contrast, about 40 percent of state public
utility commission decisions in major rate cases are appealed to the
courts.[42] The most frequent appellants are business groups, usually
utilities, and the most frequent winners, when the public utility commission is overruled, are also business groups, again usually utilities.

These figures highlight an important difference between the "bias"
of the judicial system and the "bias" of individual judges. There is no
reason to believe that judges are biased in favor of business groups. If
they were, one would expect the courts to be noticeably tougher on
regulatory agencies, whose decisions are challenged by business groups,
than on social welfare agencies, whose decisions are challenged by
disadvantaged minorities. This does not appear to be the case.[43] The
system is biased, however, in that certain claims are more likely than
others to be adjudicated. It is not absolutely clear that business groups
use the courts more effectively than other groups, although that may be
true. But it is clear that business groups use the courts more often than
other groups. For this reason, tough judicial scrutiny of administrative
agencies tends to benefit business groups.

The principal exception to these general rules is in the area of
environmental policy. Environmental statutes encourage citizen participation in administrative and judicial proceedings, and the courts generally have granted standing to these litigants. A wide variety of environmental groups have taken the government and industry to court.
Indeed, the most frequent plaintiffs in federal district court cases
concerning environmental disputes are environmental groups.[44] Moreover, in many instances, environmental litigants are well funded, experienced, and persistent.

Who wins environmental cases in court? In one respect, the familiar
pattern holds: the government is most likely to win. In another respect,
however, a new pattern emerges: when the government loses a case,
business groups are not necessarily winners. Rather, environmental
groups are as likely to win these disputes as are industry groups.[45] This
pattern, well-documented during the 1970s, persisted through the
1980s. As judicial scholar Lettie Wenner has noted, "Industry ended the
1980s with lower [success] scores than did its environmental opponents,
despite the increased number of Reagan judges."[46] These findings
suggest that a well-organized majority can neutralize the advantages of
the business community in court, if legislators adopt stringent statutes
and if the courts are liberal in giving groups standing. Both conditions
have been met in environmental policy. As a result, environmental

litigation differs from litigation in other regulatory policy arenas, where the regulated industries win most often.

Constitutional Law versus Administrative Law

If administrative law appears more fragmented and chaotic in its policies than constitutional law, appearances are not deceiving. Constitutions in the United States explicitly protect disadvantaged minorities. These minorities are identified with some precision in various constitutional amendments. Administrative procedure acts are more neutral. They seek to protect affected parties from arbitrary and capricious behavior by the bureaucracy, but they do not specify which parties are to receive protection. At the time of passage, the federal APA was expected to benefit business groups in particular, and it often has done precisely that. But the emergence of broad-based public interest groups, which have secured standing, has transformed the APA into an instrument for protecting well-organized groups generally, whether they represent an advantaged minority or the majority of citizens.

Another important difference between constitutional law and administrative law is that the Supreme Court sets more precedents in the former than in the latter. The Court, with limited time, has chosen to focus on constitutional law, which gives a certain coherence to constitutional law. In contrast, administrative law is largely the province of other courts, especially state supreme courts and federal circuit courts of appeals, and they frequently disagree. Moreover, administrative agencies sometimes announce that they will not follow administrative law precedents set by lower courts when they conflict with the directives of the agency head.[47] This remarkable doctrine, which has no legal basis, limits the ability of lower courts to set precedent and makes administrative law less coherent than constitutional law. This practice also illustrates another point: A court decision is only the beginning of a lengthy process with consequences that may be either narrower or broader than anticipated.

The Long Road to Justice

Confusion and Reluctance

Judges depend on other public officials to implement their policies. Implementers include bureaucrats such as regulators, police officers, and social workers; legislative bodies such as Congress, state legislatures, and city councils; quasi-legislative bodies such as school boards and zoning boards; and other judges—lower courts are expected to implement the policies of higher courts. The implementation of judicial policies, like the implementation of other policies, is not without problems, which may include unclear standards, poor communication, inadequate resources, and hostility.[48]

Unclear standards. Judicial policies are sometimes vague, contradictory, or variable. This is particularly true of appellate court opinions, which must accommodate the views and sensibilities of more than one judge. As noted earlier, the judge assigned the task of writing an opinion for an appellate court often finds it necessary to yield to a colleague on an important point. A first draft that is crisp, blunt, and direct may end up a patchwork of compromises. The Supreme Court's decision in *Swann v. Charlotte-Mecklenburg Board of Education* (1971) illustrates this phenomenon. Divided but anxious to issue a unanimous opinion on school busing, the Court (1) endorsed busing as a permissible remedy but warned against busing small children; (2) established a presumption against one-race schools but declined to prohibit them; and (3) allowed lower courts to correct for residential segregation patterns but only if caused by school board decisions. Reflecting on *Swann*, a federal judge observed, "There is a lot of conflicting language here. . . . It's almost as if there were two sets of views laid side by side." [49]

An ambiguous opinion is only one of several sources of confusion. Even a clear opinion, decided by a close vote, sends conflicting signals. Astute court watchers know that a 5 to 4 decision against including evidence in a criminal case may yield to a 5 to 4 decision the other way in a subsequent case. A flurry of concurring and dissenting opinions attached to Supreme Court decisions also generates confusion. Although such opinions make it easier for judges to write their memoirs, they make it more difficult to implement judicial policies.

Poor communication. People responsible for implementation are sometimes unfamiliar with the specifics of important court decisions—especially street-level bureaucrats, who do not make a habit of reading court opinions over their morning coffee. Following *Miranda v. Arizona* (1966), police officers did not clearly understand what was required of them.[50] After *Mapp v. Ohio* (1961), in which the Court ruled that evidence obtained in violation of the Fourth Amendment could not be used in state trials, police officers could not be absolutely certain under what circumstances evidence was inadmissible in court.[51] Following *Goss v. Lopez* (1975), in which the Court ruled that students who were suspended have the right to due process, schoolteachers had a "muddled" understanding of the procedures to be followed in school discipline cases.[52]

Some blame can be laid on the mass media, which are notoriously negligent in their coverage of court decisions, except that of major U.S. Supreme Court decisions. When the Pennsylvania Supreme Court announced that public utilities are not constitutionally entitled to rates high enough to guarantee their financial viability—a decision hailed by one observer as an "extremely important" victory for ratepayers—the *Pittsburgh Press* covered the news in a brief notice on page fourteen. When a U.S. Circuit Court of Appeals overturned a lower court decision concerning comparable worth, the *Press* covered the story on page eight, despite the assertion that "the ruling could set standards for similar disputes across the country." Such limited coverage of important court decisions is quite common, and public ignorance of court rulings is, therefore, hardly surprising.

Inadequate resources. Many court orders explicitly or implicitly require the expenditure of additional funds for public purposes. School boards may have to purchase buses, hire drivers, and obtain more insurance if the courts require school busing as an antidote to racial segregation. When the courts require back pay for victims of employment discrimination by the government, agencies must somehow obtain the funds to carry out the order. When the courts require state bureaucracies to upgrade the services to the mentally ill and the mentally retarded, the states need to spend more money on psychiatrists, custodians, and physical facilities.

Lacking the power of the purse, the courts depend on legislative bodies to allocate the funds to implement court orders. But politicians have their own priorities, and minority rights are seldom high on their agendas. When Judge Frank Johnson ordered improvements in the quality of Alabama's prisons, Governor George Wallace accused him of trying to turn the state's prisons into Holiday Inns. Eventually, the Alabama legislature increased appropriations to the state's prisons but not by enough to comply with the judge's directives.

Hostile attitudes. Judges are widely respected in American society, but their views do not automatically command deference. People charged with implementation often question the wisdom of judicial decisions, especially on matters of social policy. Many school board members strongly disapprove of busing; many teachers fervently believe in school prayer. Many police officers object to court decisions that limit their ability to put criminals behind bars. Where such hostility is present, resistance may develop.

If hostility runs deep enough, the implementers may not comply. The members of the Boston School Committee, all of whom were white, refused to draw up a desegregation plan demanded by Judge Arthur Garrity, who then took over the school system. Outright noncompliance is rare, but evasion is not at all uncommon. For example, as a response to tough evidentiary requirements in *Mapp*, some police officers resorted to perjury.[53] The public sometimes refuses to comply by taking evasive action. Many whites responded to court-ordered busing by sending their children to private schools or by moving to the suburbs.

It is clear that the implementation of judicial policies cannot be taken for granted, but we should distinguish between short-term and long-term implementation problems. Short-term problems are often formidable, but they do not necessarily doom judicial policies to failure. Most court orders are eventually implemented, and there are several reasons why this is so.

First, a single case may be ambiguous, but several interrelated cases enable the courts to establish a pattern of decisions that can guide implementers. Blockbuster opinions, such as *Brown*, *Miranda*, or *Mapp*, usually are followed by a series of interpretive opinions that reduce confusion. This clarification is strongest when the courts are reasonably consistent, as they have been in libel cases. Even when the courts are less consistent, as they have been in criminal cases, additional decisions usually clarify more than they obscure. Precedents are often deflected but seldom overturned. The norm of *stare decisis*, meaning deference to precedent, encourages courts to render reasonably consistent opinions over time, especially in matters of constitutional law, where the brooding presence of the U.S. Supreme Court ensures a modicum of consistency.

Second, knowledge of court orders travels slowly at first but eventually trickles down to the bureaucrats responsible for day-to-day implementation. Indeed, the mass media deserve some of the credit for this. For example, anyone who has watched a police drama on television knows about *Miranda* rights and their importance. Ironically, citizens and street-level bureaucrats may have been enlightened about court decisions more by the entertainment programming of television than by the news reports of newspapers.

Third, institutions can deal with resource shortfalls in various ways, if given sufficient time. The deinstitutionalization of mentally ill and retarded residents was a quick way of coping with court requirements for improved care. Administrative reorganization and the hiring of more skilled personnel is another strategy. The Army Corps of Engineers responded to court orders to prepare environmental impact statements by establishing environmental units in their district offices and by hiring personnel with the necessary training.[54]

Fourth, courts can go quite far in requiring spending to remedy a problem. For example, in *Missouri v. Jenkins* (1990) the U.S. Supreme Court upheld a lower court ruling requiring expenditures by the state of Missouri and the Kansas City school district to remedy school segregation. The Court even upheld the lower court's decision to mandate a tax increase, although the Supreme Court stressed that the tax hike must be approved by local authorities. Thus judges have found ways to get around their limited control over the public purse strings.

Finally, attitudes change over time. Police officers may not be enthusiastic about *Miranda* requirements, but they have learned to live with them. School boards may not be happy about busing, but they also have adapted. Immediately following an important court ruling, the disappointed parties assume the end of civilization. But when the world does not come to an end, acceptance often follows. Perhaps the most striking illustration of this is the sharp change in the attitudes of whites toward school desegregation. In the late 1950s, 83 percent of southern whites objected to sending their children to a school that was half black; by 1981, only 27 percent objected.[55] For years, scholars have debated whether "stateways" can change "folkways." Although there are limits to what courts can accomplish, it appears that they have influenced attitudes on some basic issues.

Real Solutions and Solutions as Problems

Many scholars are reluctant to ascribe so much influence to the courts, instead seeing the policy impact of the courts as rather limited.[56] Political science professor Lawrence Baum wrote, "In reality, the Court's impact on society is severely constrained by the context in which its policies operate."[57] At first glance, this conclusion appears reasonable, given the implementation problems mentioned earlier. But most studies of the policy impacts of court decisions focus exclusively on short-term effects. If we look at long-term effects, we see the power of the courts.

One of the most conspicuous successes of the courts is the effort to promote racial justice. In education, voting rights, employment, and housing, the courts have breathed life into constitutional requirements for due process of law and have helped to ensure equal opportunity for racial minorities, especially blacks. This has not happened overnight. For a full decade after *Brown*, southern schools remained separate and unequal. In the mid-1960s, however, the picture began to change. By the 1972-1973 school year, 91 percent of black students in the South were going to school with whites.[58] Progress in northern schools, although slower, has also been noticeable.[59]

Court decisions on voting rights have produced results more quickly, in part because all three branches of government moved aggressively on this issue. The Voting Rights Act of 1965 was followed one year later by an 8 to 1 Supreme Court decision affirming the act in full (*South Carolina v. Katzenbach*, 1966). Over the next two years, the Justice Department sent federal examiners to some southern voting districts and appointed poll watchers in others. The effects were dramatic. From 1964 to 1968, black voter registration rates in the South jumped from 38 percent to

62 percent.[60] Increased registration led to higher black voter turnout and to the election of black local officials, which in turn generated increases in public employment and other public services for blacks.[61]

The courts have been less aggressive in promoting equal opportunity in housing, partly because of the tradition of judicial deference to local zoning boards and city councils.[62] Several state supreme courts have invalidated exclusionary zoning practices as violations of state constitutions, however. The desegregation of housing, like the desegregation of the public schools, is likely to proceed slowly. Eventually, the elimination of exclusionary zoning practices should result in some affordable housing for racial minorities even in affluent white suburbs.

Court decisions in administrative law have also had significant impact, especially in communications and environmental policy and in standards for institutional care. For years, station WLBT-TV in Jackson, Mississippi, fanned the flames of racial discontent in its editorials against integration and its acceptance of ads paid for by a local racist group. When well-known blacks were featured on network newscasts, the general manager would sometimes show a "Sorry, Cable Trouble" sign until the segment ended. A church-related citizen group, the Office of Communication of the United Church of Christ, opposed in court the renewal of the station's license on the grounds that the station had violated the Federal Communications Commission's fairness doctrine.[63] In two important decisions, *United Church of Christ v. FCC* (1966) and *United Church of Christ v. FCC* (1969), the U.S. Court of Appeals, D.C. Circuit, agreed with the church and ordered the FCC to grant the license to someone else. The immediate consequences for Jackson television viewers were that the license was awarded to another company, which promptly hired a black general manager, assigned a black anchor to read the evening news, and improved the quantity and quality of news and public affairs programming.[64] The long-term consequences were even more significant. Using these cases as precedents, citizen groups intervened in administrative and judicial proceedings on behalf of television consumers, and in many cases, they secured important concessions. In addition, these cases helped to establish standing for aggrieved consumers in other issue areas.

Court decisions on environmental impact statements have also generated far-reaching changes. The National Environmental Policy Act of 1969 (NEPA) requires administrative agencies to file an environmental impact statement for "major federal projects with a significant environmental effect," and the federal courts interpret the words "major" and "significant" rather liberally. When in doubt, they require the agency to prepare an environmental impact statement. The repercussions have been widespread. The Army Corps of Engineers, long known for its "edifice complex," began to look at nonstructural alternatives to dams and dredging projects.[65] The courts' interpretations of NEPA also sensitized other agencies to environmental impacts.

The consequences of judicial efforts at institutional reform have been equally profound. In 1973 a federal district court ordered the closing of Willowbrook, a New York facility for the mentally retarded, where conditions were shown to be unsanitary, unsafe, and inhumane. The immediate effects of judicial intervention were disappointing. The state's Department of Mental Health at first refused to yield client records and failed to submit progress reports on time, as required by the court. Between 1976 and 1979, however, the state bureaucracy opened 100 group homes for 1,000 Willowbrook residents. Community placement was achieved without lowering property values or destroying neighborhoods. Audits revealed that group homes were properly administered and, more important, that the lives of the residents had improved. At first, the group homes resembled "puppet shows." Choreographed to behave as more intelligent people would, residents played parts they did not understand. Eventually, the puppets became animated, as they learned how to make decisions concerning choices of food and clothing.[66] Such choices, which most people take for granted, marked a major breakthrough and signaled a significant improvement in their quality of life.

These examples demonstrate the capacity of the courts to effect changes that are in the public interest, especially over time. Many court decisions produce tangible results that benefit disadvantaged minorities or the public. A problem with court decisions, however, is that they are not easily contained. They have spillover effects never imagined by judicial decision makers. Many of these unintended consequences are undesirable. At best, they detract from judicial policies; at worst, they undermine them.

The *Mapp* decision, extending the exclusionary rule to local police departments, appears to have resulted in greater reliance on plea bargaining in cases where evidence may have been obtained through questionable methods.[67] The *Goss* decision, requiring a hearing before suspension from school, discouraged teachers from disciplining disruptive students.[68] *Gault*, which established formal procedures for trying juveniles accused of a crime, made it difficult for juvenile court judges to counsel and advise informally, as they had done, in cases where no crime had been committed.[69]

The unintended consequences of school desegregation and environmental policy decisions have been especially troublesome. In many cities court-ordered busing prompted whites to abandon inner-city public schools and to place their children in private schools or move to the suburbs. When Judge Garrity took over Boston's public schools in 1974, 61 percent of the pupils were white; when he terminated his involvement in 1985, only 27 percent were white.[70] In those eleven years, numerous white parents, feeling abandoned by the courts, decided to abandon Boston's public schools.

Court decisions on air pollution have also been a mixed blessing. The courts imposed tough standards for the design of new industrial plants, for example, by requiring the "prevention of significant deterioration" in air quality in wilderness areas and polluted cities. In enforcement cases, however, the courts relaxed the standards for existing plants, such as utilities, steel mills, and smelters. In effect, the courts have frozen existing technologies and facilities and discouraged the building of modern plants. According to some observers, this unintended consequence has increased the costs of achieving clean air.[71]

In environmental policy, as in school desegregation, the courts have accomplished what they intended to accomplish. School segregation and air pollution have declined appreciably, and the courts deserve much of the credit. The country paid a high price for these gains, however— probably higher than necessary. Nor is this surprising. Judges are not very good at calculating costs, and they are not particularly inclined to do so. Judges think in terms of rights and duties rather than economic analysis. In contrast to politicians, judges have no need to hide the costs of their actions or to think much about them. There is, in short, an irony here. In courtroom politics, costs are often manifest, but irrelevant. The costs of judicial decisions, although unintended, are not always unforeseen, but judges maintain that they are not responsible for the adverse consequences of their actions.

The Paradoxical Decree

Although they are less sensitive to costs than other public officials, judges are more sensitive than is commonly supposed to the consequences of their actions. Judges recognize the limitations of a single court order and, because they see the potential for implementation problems, judges sometimes are unwilling to entrust the delicate tasks of implementation to the bureaucracy. In certain cases, judges have assumed responsibility for carrying out their own orders, becoming, in effect, managers and administrators.

Nowhere is this more evident than in the behavior of federal district court judges who have coped with school busing and institutional reform cases. These judges have not issued orders and hoped for the best. Rather, they have upgraded the court's capacity to receive feedback, to learn from it, and to correct errors. The principal mechanism for this judicial role is the court decree, which judges use to fashion relief in an ad hoc manner and on a continuous basis.[72] The modern decree is a paradox. It is at once extremely specific as to the affected parties and extremely fluid, giving the judge wide latitude. It contains detailed instructions and calls for a continuing dialogue, progress reports, and midcourse corrections. All of these characteristics reduce implementation problems and narrow the gap between intended and actual policy impacts.

One characteristic of the decree is its specificity. When Judge Garrity issued his first order concerning Boston's schools, he specified not only the racial balance to be achieved but also the geographic boundaries of new school districts. Garrity became, in effect, the superintendent of the Boston school system. He assigned pupils, hired staff and administrators, closed or upgraded schools, and acted on spending requests. He justified these controls on the grounds that it was necessary to prevent sabotage by the Boston School Committee, which had openly resisted the court's efforts to desegregate the public schools.

Judges have been equally specific in institutional reform cases. Judge Johnson took over Alabama's prisons and mental health facilities, issuing detailed requirements for nutrition, personal hygiene, recreational opportunities, educational programs, and staffing ratios.[73] Judge Orrin Judd took control of Willowbrook, ordering outdoor exercise for the residents five times a week, a ratio of one attendant for every nine residents, and the repair of all the home's toilets.[74]

A second characteristic of the decree is its continuity. In contrast to the standard pattern, a judge does not simply issue a single decision. The decree is the first step in a long, interactive process. The judge meets frequently with parties to the case and listens to their grievances, receives progress reports, dispenses criticism and praise, and issues new orders. Judge Garrity issued 415 school desegregation orders from 1974 to 1985. Although this probably qualifies him for the *Guinness Book of World Records*, other judges have also issued numerous court orders.

A third characteristic of the decree is its fluidity. In anticipation of unexpected developments, judges retain the option of modifying their initial order. To assist them, they often appoint special masters. The use of masters is not new, but it has grown, especially in school desegregation cases. Garrity appointed four masters and two experts; the masters held hearings and proposed a plan, which Garrity modified and incorporated into his second decree.[75]

Instead of masters, some judges appoint monitoring committees. The committee's task is to inform the judge as implementation problems arise. Johnson established monitoring committees, called human rights committees, for each of Alabama's major mental institutions. Among other tasks, these committees were authorized to inspect institutional records, to interview patients and staff, and to consult with independent specialists.

Monitoring committees were seldom greeted with open arms by the bureaucrats whose performance they were to investigate. In Alabama the director of one mental health facility barred his staff from talking with representatives of the monitoring committee without his permission. Johnson intervened to overturn that policy, but problems persisted. The monitoring committee in the *Willowbrook* case also ruffled a few feathers by its relentless insistence on community placement. Eventually, the Willowbrook monitoring committee was abolished by the New York state legislature, which grew weary of its criticisms.

Judges are fallible, and their decrees are seldom perfect. Judge Garrity unnecessarily polarized the races by pairing Roxbury, the heart of the black ghetto, with South Boston, the citadel of white resistance to busing. A more judicious solution might have been to pair South Boston with nearby Dorchester or to intersperse South Boston and Roxbury students throughout the city. Judge Johnson undermined his credibility by insisting that all Alabama prison cells be sixty square feet. No Alabama prison cell met this specification, which lent credence to Governor Wallace's charge that Johnson was insensitive to the costs of prison reform. Johnson later modified his order on prison cell size, and other judges have done the same.

At its best, the modern decree is an error-correction device that works two ways. First, it enables the judge to identify and correct errors made by government officials, who may not share the court's commitment to a particular policy goal. Second, it enables the judge to correct errors made by the court when it goes too far. The judicial decree, therefore, represents a milestone in judicial policy making. It is the court's way of saying that judicial activism and judicial responsibility go hand in hand. If judges are going to make public policy on controversial issues, they cannot simply render a decision and walk away. Although the decree does not guarantee that the courts will be alert to implementation problems, it does provide ample opportunity for judicial oversight.

Summary

The failures of other branches of government and the litigious character of U.S. society go a long way to explain the courts' prominence in making public policy. Although courts avoid macroeconomic policy and foreign policy disputes, they directly address other issues, which are characterized by a high degree of conflict and manifest costs. Issues addressed by the courts are also marked by a high level of technical complexity, a high level of moral complexity, or both. They are among the most vexing problems society faces.

In reaching decisions on these issues, judges are guided by factors that transcend politics—law, evidence, and judicial philosophy. But judicial decision making is also political. Judges are usually affiliated with a political party, and their voting behavior reflects party affiliation. Internal politicking, especially on supreme courts where several judges must agree on the wording of an opinion, gives judges the opportunity for leadership. In the courts, as elsewhere, political leadership can make the difference between arriving at a tough policy and a weak one, between formulating a clear policy and a vague one.

Many court decisions are at first diluted by unclear standards, poor communication, inadequate resources, and hostile attitudes. Over time, however, most are successfully implemented and have the impact they were intended to have. Unfortunately, they often have unintended consequences, some of which may be attributed to judicial insensitivity to consequences. But even if judges wish to take consequences into account, they cannot foresee every result.

Courts have changed in many ways. More women and blacks sit on the bench, lending more judicial support to minority rights in constitutional law disputes. More public interest groups litigate in court, which results in occasional triumphs for environmental and consumer interests. Finally, the choice between judicial activism and judicial restraint has been resolved largely in favor of judicial activism. The courts are more likely to overturn statutes and administrative agency decisions and more likely to prescribe specific ground rules and remedies.

Activism and liberalism are not one and the same. In constitutional law, activism runs in a liberal direction; in administrative law, activism runs in a conservative direction. Criminal justice and environmental protection are exceptions to these general rules. In criminal justice, judicial enthusiasm for defendant rights waxes and wanes; in environmental protection, the courts support environmentalists on standards, business groups on enforcement. Whatever the policy tilt of the courts, the fact remains that judges are making policy.

Notes

1. Martin Shapiro, *Courts: A Comparative and Political Analysis* (Chicago: University of Chicago Press, 1981), 105-124; and Richard Posner, *The Federal Courts: Crisis and Reform* (Cambridge, Mass.: Harvard University Press, 1985).

2. Donald Horowitz, *The Courts and Social Policy* (Washington, D.C.: Brookings Institution, 1977), 9.

3. Richard Neely, *How Courts Govern America* (New Haven, Conn.: Yale University Press, 1981), 212.

4. J. Woodford Howard, Jr., *Courts of Appeals in the Federal Judicial System: A Study of the 2nd, 5th, and D.C. Circuits* (Princeton, N.J.: Princeton University Press, 1981), 25-33.

5. See *United States v. Richardson*, 418 U.S. 166 (1974); and *Valley Forge Christian College v. Americans United for Separation of Church and State*, 454 U.S. 464 (1982).

6. *Amalgamated Meat Cutters v. Connally*, 337 F. Supp. 737 (1971).

7. *United States v. Curtiss-Wright Export Corp.*, 299 U.S. 304 (1936); and *Dames & Moore v. Regan*, 453 U.S. 654 (1981).

8. Federal judges are not entirely powerless in these matters. District court judges can—and do—encourage parties to settle a case without going to trial. Also, judges may refuse to hear a case on the grounds that a party lacks standing, that the issue is not ripe, or for other reasons.

9. The U.S. Supreme Court is required to hear the following kinds of cases: (1) disputes between states; (2) cases in which a federal court has held an act of Congress unconstitutional, if the federal government is a party, and cases in which a state supreme court has held an act of Congress unconstitutional; (3) cases in which a state court has upheld a state law against a claim that it conflicts with the Constitution or federal law; (4) cases in which a federal court has overturned a state law on grounds that it conflicts with the Constitution or federal law; and (5) decisions of special three-judge federal district courts.

10. Hughes denounced Roosevelt's plan in a calm but forceful letter to Senator Burton Wheeler. The letter is credited with weakening congressional support for the court-packing plan.

11. Henry Glick, *Supreme Courts in State Politics* (New York: Basic Books, 1971).

12. Herbert Jacob, *Urban Justice: Law and Order in American Cities* (Englewood Cliffs, N.J.: Prentice-Hall, 1973).

13. Marc Galanter, "Why the 'Haves' Come Out Ahead: Speculations on the Limits of Legal Change," *Law and Society Review* 9 (Fall 1974): 95-160.

14. Glendon Schubert, *Quantitative Analysis of Judicial Behavior* (Glencoe, Ill.: Free Press, 1959); S. Sidney Ulmer, "The Political Party Variable in the Michigan Supreme Court," in *Judicial Behavior*, ed. Glendon Schubert (Chicago: Rand McNally, 1964), 279-286; and Malcolm Feeley, "Another Look at the 'Party Variable' in Judicial Decision-Making: An Analysis of the Michigan Supreme Court," *Polity* 4 (Fall 1971): 91-104.

15. Philip Dubois, *From Ballot to Bench: Judicial Elections and the Quest for Accountability* (Austin: University of Texas Press, 1980), 231.

16. C. Neal Tate, "Personal Attribute Models of the Voting Behavior of U.S. Supreme Court Justices: Liberalism in Civil Liberties and Economics Decisions, 1946-1978," *American Political Science Review* 75 (June 1981): 355-367; Sheldon Goldman, "Voting Behavior on the U.S. Court of Appeals Revisited," *American Political Science Review* 69 (June 1975): 491-506; and Robert Carp and C. K. Rowland, *Policymaking and Politics in the Federal District Courts* (Knoxville: University of Tennessee Press, 1983).

17. David Whitman, "Reagan's Conservative Judges Are Singing a Different Tune Now," *Washington Post* national weekly edition, August 24, 1987, 23.

18. Ruth Marcus, "Bush Quietly Fosters Conservative Trend in Courts," *Washington Post*, February 18, 1991, 1.

19. Bernard Schwartz, *Super Chief: Earl Warren and the Supreme Court* (New York: New York University Press, 1983), 40-44.

20. Lawrence Baum, *The Supreme Court* (Washington, D.C.: CQ Press, 1981), 156-162.

21. Martin Shapiro, "On Predicting the Future of Administrative Law," *Regulation* 6 (May-June 1982): 18-25; and R. Shep Melnick, *Regulation and the Courts: The Case of the Clean Air Act* (Washington, D.C.: Brookings Institution, 1983).

22. Much of the credit for the unanimous decisions goes to Earl Warren, a remarkably adroit political leader. Warren's handling of the *Brown v. Board of Education* decision is a good case in point. When Warren took over as chief justice, the *Brown* case had already been argued, and the Court was prepared to vote 5-4 in favor of desegregation. In a clever ploy, Warren suggested that the justices postpone the vote. Instead, Warren led a freewheeling discussion that ultimately revealed some common ground on which they could agree. The process was not easy. Three separate conferences and numerous private conversations between Warren and individual justices were required before Warren's efforts were successful. In 1954 the Supreme Court issued a unanimous opinion in a case that is doubtlessly one of the most important in U.S. history. See Schwartz, *Super Chief*, 72-127.

23. Archibald Cox, *The Role of the Supreme Court in American Government* (New York: Oxford University Press, 1976), 38-39.

24. Vincent Blasi, "The Rootless Activism of the Burger Court," in *The Burger Court: The Counter-Revolution That Wasn't*, ed. Vincent Blasi (New Haven, Conn.: Yale University Press, 1983), 198-217.

25. A. E. (Dick) Howard, "State Courts and Constitutional Rights in the Days of the Burger Court," *Virginia Law Review* 62 (June 1976): 873-944; Mary Porter, "State Supreme Courts and the Legacy of the Warren Court: Some Old Inquiries for a New Situation," in *State Supreme Courts: Policymakers in the Federal System*, ed. Mary Porter and G. Alan Tarr (Westport, Conn.: Greenwood Press, 1982), 3-21; and Robert Pear, "State Courts Surpass U.S. Bench in Cases on Rights of Individuals," *New York Times*, May 4, 1986, A1.

26. Pear, "State Courts Surpass U.S. Bench."

27. Charlotte Carter, *Media in the Courts* (Williamsburg, Va.: National Center for State Courts, 1981).

28. Norman Davis, "Television in Our Courts: The Proven Advantages, the Unproven Dangers," *Judicature* 64 (August 1980): 85-92.

29. Saundra Torry, "Federal Courts to Experiment with Televised Civil Trials," *Washington Post*, September 13, 1990, 2.

30. Jonathan Casper, "The Supreme Court and National Policy Making," *American Political Science Review* 70 (March 1976): 50-63; Baum, *The Supreme Court*; and Harold Spaeth, "Burger Court Review of State Court Civil Liberties Decisions," *Judicature* 68 (February-March 1985): 285-291.

31. Casper, "The Supreme Court and National Policy Making."

32. Robert Dahl, "Decision-Making in a Democracy: The Supreme Court as a National Policy-Maker," *Journal of Public Law* 6 (Fall 1957): 279-295.

33. Geoffrey Stone, "Individual Rights and Majoritarianism: The Supreme Court in Transition" (Washington, D.C.: Cato Institute, 1985), monograph.

34. Michael Rebell and Arthur Block, *Educational Policy Making and the Courts: An Empirical Study of Judicial Activism* (Chicago: University of Chicago Press, 1982), 36.

35. Martin Shapiro, *The Supreme Court and Administrative Agencies* (New York: Free Press, 1968); Jerry Mashaw, Charles Goetz, Frank Goodman, Warren Schwartz, and Paul Verkuil, *Social Security Hearings and Appeals* (Lexington, Mass.: D. C. Heath, 1978), 125-150; Craig Wanner, "The Public Ordering of Private Relations, Part Two: Winning Civil Court Cases," *Law and Society Review* 9 (Winter 1975): 293-306; and Stephen Frank, "The Oversight of Administrative Agencies by State Supreme Courts: Some Macro Findings," *Administrative Law Review* 32 (Summer 1980): 477-499.

36. Galanter, "Why the 'Haves' Come Out Ahead."

37. Frank, "The Oversight of Administrative Agencies."

38. Reginald Sheehan, "Administrative Agencies and the Court: A Reexamination of the Impact of Agency Type on Decisional Outcomes," *Western Political Quarterly* 43 (December 1990): 875-886.

39. Ibid.

40. It also depends on the court. For example, the D.C. Circuit Court of Appeals, during the 1970s, was much more supportive of environmental protection than other circuit courts of appeals. See Lettie Wenner, *The Environmental Decade in Court* (Bloomington: Indiana University Press, 1982), 35-63.

41. Mashaw et al., *Social Security Hearings and Appeals*, 125-150.

42. William T. Gormley, Jr., *The Politics of Public Utility Regulation* (Pittsburgh: University of Pittsburgh Press, 1983), 94.

43. Frank, "The Oversight of Administrative Agencies."

44. The gap has narrowed as industry plaintiffs have become more common. Also, industry groups are more likely than environmental groups to file appeals in appeals courts. See Wenner, *The Environmental Decade in Court*, 35-63.

45. Ibid., 94.

46. Lettie Wenner, "Environmental Policy in the Courts," in Norman Vig and Michael Kraft, eds., *Environmental Policy in the 1990s* (Washington, D.C.: CQ Press, 1990), 202.

47. According to Mashaw, this is the practice of the Social Security Administration, the National Labor Relations Board, and the Internal Revenue Service, as well as other agencies. See Jerry Mashaw, *Bureaucratic Justice* (New Haven, Conn.: Yale University Press, 1983), 186. The SSA's refusal to follow precedents set by lower federal courts aroused considerable controversy during the Reagan years, when the agency cut financial awards to disabled workers. There is no evidence that this policy of selective adherence to precedent (or nonacquiescence) is changing, however.

48. Donald Van Meter and Carl Van Horn, "The Policy Implementation Process: A Conceptual Framework," *Administration and Society* 6 (February 1975): 445-488; Carl Van Horn, *Policy Implementation in the Federal System* (Lexington, Mass.: D. C. Heath, 1979); and George Edwards III, *Implementing Public Policy* (Washington, D.C.: CQ Press, 1980).

49. Bob Woodward and Scott Armstrong, *The Brethren: Inside the Supreme Court* (New York: Simon & Schuster, 1979), 112.

50. Neal Milner, *The Court and Local Law Enforcement: The Impact of Miranda* (Beverly Hills, Calif.: Sage, 1971), 225.

51. Horowitz, *The Courts and Social Policy*, 226.

52. Henry Lufler, "The Supreme Court Goes to School: *Goss v. Lopez* and Student Suspensions" (Ph.D. diss., University of Wisconsin, 1982).

53. Horowitz, *The Courts and Social Policy*, 234.

54. Daniel Mazmanian and Jeanne Nienaber, *Can Organizations Change?* (Washington, D.C.: Brookings Institution, 1979), 37-60.

55. Jennifer Hochschild, *The New American Dilemma: Liberal Democracy and School Desegregation* (New Haven, Conn.: Yale University Press, 1984), 180.

56. Kenneth Dolbeare and Phillip Hammond, *The School Prayer Decisions: From Court Policy to Local Practice* (Chicago: University of Chicago Press, 1971); Milner, *The Court and Local Law Enforcement;* Baum, *The Supreme Court;* and Charles Johnson and Bradley Canon, *Judicial Policies: Implementation and Impact* (Washington, D.C.: CQ Press, 1984).

57. Baum, *The Supreme Court,* 211.

58. Ibid., 187.

59. Charles Bullock III, "Equal Education Opportunity," in *Implementation of Civil Rights Policy,* ed. Charles Bullock III and Charles Lamb (Monterey, Calif.: Brooks/Cole, 1984), 68-69.

60. Richard Scher and James Button, "Voting Rights Act: Implementation and Impact," in *Implementation of Civil Rights Policy,* 40.

61. Albert Karnig and Susan Welch, *Black Representation and Urban Policy* (Chicago: University of Chicago Press, 1980); and Peter Eisinger, "Black Employment in Municipal Jobs: The Impact of Black Political Power," *American Political Science Review* 76 (June 1982): 380-392.

62. Michael Danielson, *The Politics of Exclusion* (New York: Columbia University Press, 1976).

63. The fairness doctrine, abolished by the Federal Communications Commission in 1987, required broadcasters to devote a reasonable amount of time to the discussion of issues of public importance. When covering such issues, broadcasters did not need to provide equal time to all points of view, but their coverage had to be balanced and fair.

64. Fred Friendly, *The Good Guys, the Bad Guys, and the First Amendment* (New York: Random House, 1975), 89-102.

65. Mazmanian and Nienaber, *Can Organizations Change?*

66. David Rothman and Sheila Rothman, *The Willowbrook Wars* (New York: Harper & Row, 1984).

67. Horowitz, *The Courts and Social Policy.*

68. Lufler, "The Supreme Court Goes to School."

69. Horowitz, *The Courts and Social Policy.*

70. Matthew Wald, "After Years of Turmoil, Judge Is Yielding Job of Integrating Boston Schools," *New York Times,* August 22, 1985, A16.

71. Melnick, *Regulation and the Courts.*

72. Colin Diver, "The Judge as Political Powerbroker: Superintending Structural Change in Public Institutions," *Virginia Law Review* 65 (February 1979): 43-106; and Abram Chayes, "Public Law Litigation and the Burger Court," *Harvard Law Review* 96 (November 1982): 4-60.

73. Tinsley Yarbrough, "The Judge as Manager: The Case of Judge Frank Johnson," *Journal of Policy Analysis and Management* 1 (Spring 1982): 386-400.

74. Rothman and Rothman, *The Willowbrook Wars.*

75. J. Anthony Lukas, *Common Ground* (New York: Alfred A. Knopf, 1985).

8 Living Room Politics

The United States is a representative democracy. American grade school children are taught that government and public policy are based on the consent of the governed. President Abraham Lincoln said that American government is "of the people, by the people, and for the people," and every national leader before and after him has cited the "will of the people" to justify particular courses of action.

Debates about the proper role of citizens in guiding public policy date back to the founding of the nation. James Madison and other authors of the Constitution were strong advocates of democracy, but they did not believe that elected representatives should slavishly follow mass opinion in determining public policy. Many of the Founders feared that the public could be unstable, tyrannical, and even dangerous to liberal democracy.[1] They believed that periodic elections give citizens sufficient safeguards against elected representatives who serve them poorly. Between elections, leaders should govern as they see fit. This concept of democracy was perhaps best summed up by the British political philosopher and statesman Edmund Burke. In a treatise on representative democracy, Burke said: "Your representative owes you, not his industry only, but his judgment; and he betrays instead of serving you if he sacrifices it to your opinion."[2]

The fact that thousands of elected officials must face the voters every so often keeps many citizens involved in government at the most basic level. But for the most part, public policy is not made and implemented by the *public*. Instead, elected officials, bureaucrats, judges, and corporate leaders determine public policies. They are attentive to, not ruled by, the concerns of the public—a point underscored throughout this book. Yet, people's opinions influence the course of public affairs and occasionally, when aroused, people do play a central role in politics. This chapter on living room politics explores how public opinion, the mass media, and public officials interact in the making of public policy choices between elections.

Public opinion is a potent weapon of democracy, but it is not something one can visit, like a building, or read, like a book. There are many publics, many opinions, and many voices in American society.

Public opinions are defined and channeled into the policy process by groups such as the media, public officials, and citizen activists.[3] Elected officials gauge public opinion by scrutinizing public opinion polls and television and newspaper reports and by talking with interest group representatives, friends and coworkers, and perhaps the local gas station attendant.

The mass media—television, radio, and newspapers—are the principal vehicles through which public opinions are expressed and manipulated.[4] Policy makers, the press, and interest groups attempt to shape the view of reality that is presented to the people. Journalists influence the public's understanding of politics and public policy and then inform public officials about what the "public" thinks. Perhaps most important, the media frame political and policy discussions, telling people what issues are important and who favors each position. When the media or public officials succeed in defining the parameters of the policy debate, they are exercising what E. E. Schattschneider called "the supreme instrument of political power." [5]

The public does not make policy directly, but citizens *can* be more than just an audience watching contests between political elites. Citizens can choose among policy options that affect their states and communities. Through ballot initiatives and referenda—devices of direct democracy available to citizens in most states—voters can force state legislators to write new laws or to eliminate old ones. Citizens who are angered by government decisions or frustrated by inaction can go beyond passive forms of democratic participation and organize grassroots political movements to attempt to achieve their objectives.

Bystanders and Activists

Public opinions are involved in virtually everything that government institutions do, yet most citizens are typically little more than bystanders.[6] The public policy enterprise occurs in the background of their lives: they hear noise, but they seldom listen. A much smaller "attentive public," probably no more than one American in ten, closely follows public affairs. They read newspapers carefully, write letters, and call elected officials; they have opinions and they express them. On rare occasions, the bystanders are drawn into the fray. When large segments of the public become concerned about issues, their preferences can become a powerful force.

Top-Down Public Opinion

Contrary to the civics book notion that the public will drives elected officials to carry out the public's wishes, political elites usually decide what public opinion is, what it means, and whether to use it or ignore it. This does not mean that public opinions are unimportant, only that they are defined by public officials. In this view, public opinions should be thought of as ammunition used by political elites to support their point of view and to advance policy positions.

The creation, interpretation, and use of public sentiment by public officials, the media, and interest groups in the policy process has been called "top-down public opinion." [7] Political elites "construct" a notion of what the "public" wants by listening to a variety of individuals and to reports on public sentiment.[8] According to political scientist V. O. Key, Jr., public opinion is "private opinions which government finds it prudent to heed." [9]

Policy formulation and implementation occur within the boundaries of political culture established by public opinion. The nation's political culture comprises "the enduring beliefs, values and behaviors that organize social communication and make common interpretations of life experience possible." [10] According to political scientist Robert Weissberg, "Virtually all the alternatives . . . considered [during policy debates] will be at least tolerable . . . by the vast majority. Thus although the precise preferences of 50 percent plus one may not be satisfied by the policy outcome, the losers would not regard the results as completely unacceptable." [11]

Under these circumstances, the public's greatest power is as a deterrent. Just as massive nuclear arsenals presumably deter the United States and the Soviet Union from starting a nuclear war, public opinions constrain what government institutions can accomplish or even propose. A "law of anticipated consequences" usually checks public officials, preventing them from implementing policies that offend fundamental values in the political culture. Elected officials know that if the public is ignored or offended, it can be mobilized by political opponents who urge voters to "throw the rascals out."

Political elites also wield interpretations of public sentiment in day-to-day struggles for power and policy advantage. Legislators and chief executives cite public support as the rationale for policy innovation, such as tough new laws against criminals. Governors and legislators also use public opinion as a shield against modification of existing policies, such as tax rates. Even when reliable and up-to-date public opinion polls are available, each side in a policy debate will claim public support.

Chief executives are especially dependent on the mobilization of public support for their positions; they must maintain the perception that the majority stands with them. Scholar Richard Neustadt argues that the principal power of the presidency is the "power to persuade." [12] Legislators try to read the tea leaves of public opinion to see how well the president or governor is doing before deciding whether to lend their support. If the public seems to favor the president's or a governor's policies, legislators may be reluctant to criticize.

Following the successful completion of the Persian Gulf War, President Bush's popularity reached record highs. Members of Congress were understandably reluctant to criticize him in the months immediately following the war. They did not want to be perceived as standing in the way of a popular president. Accomplishing legislative and policy results requires more than high standing in the public opinion polls. Nevertheless, being popular with the public is a great position from which to launch new initiatives.

Most politicians work very hard to build and maintain public support for their policy agenda. Governor Richard Celeste of Ohio (1983-1990) effectively practiced the art of communicating directly to the public to promote his policy agenda. With a staff of nineteen, including radio and television specialists, Celeste used the mass media and public events to build support for his education reform agenda, to fight a proposal to repeal tax increases he proposed, and to mute criticism of his handling of a savings and loan crisis in Ohio. State government funds and political contributions paid for satellite hookups for radio call-in shows, teleconferences with business leaders, and Phil Donahue-style television programs, known as "School Talk with Richard Celeste," broadcast over the state's public television stations. Although Celeste was not always successful, his skillful use of mass communications helped build popular support and made it tough for legislators to oppose his policies.[13]

Conversely, when a politician's popularity dips, legislative support may erode quickly. The following excerpt from the *New York Times* is instructive:

> Democratic senators and representatives used to cringe when President Reagan made one of his televised appeals for public support on a budget or tax issue before Congress. They knew that the telephone calls and letters would pour in and that they would have to explain over and over again why they were not giving a popular President their wholehearted support. But the Democratic cringing became gloating last week as Mr. Reagan's latest appeal ... was met by widespread ... and even startling indifference. The public indifference to President Reagan's entreaties emboldened Democrats to press ahead with their own policy initiatives and to treat the President as "a kindly old relative that you don't have to pay much attention to," according to Senator James Sasser of Tennessee.[14]

Bottom-Up Public Opinion

The public is not always passive. Large segments of the public, marginally interested or even disinterested in politics, may be awakened gradually.[15] Salient issues, such as war, civil rights, morality, public health, or economic hardship, can stir the passions of ordinary citizens. When this happens, public opinions may exert significant pressure on political institutions and public officials from the bottom up. Citizens' concerns are most commonly expressed through elections or indirect plebiscites—public opinion polls. But bottom-up public opinion is felt more directly. Some people may abandon their bystander status and vote on policy issues or even become active participants.

Referenda and Initiatives

Citizens can select policies and structure government institutions by means of referenda and initiatives. There are no provisions in the U.S. Constitution for national referenda or initiatives, but thirty-seven state constitutions authorize referenda that give citizens a voice on measures approved by state legislatures. Typically, referenda allow citizens to vote yes or no on amendments to state constitutions, on state capital spending projects, such as highways or new prisons, or even on major state laws, such as environmental protection and health care programs.

Initiatives—provided for in twenty-one state constitutions—give citizens the right to petition public officials to place issues on the ballot for approval or disapproval, without waiting for the state legislature to act.[16] Before questions are put before the voters, a significant number of state residents must sign petitions, usually 5 percent to 10 percent of the number voting in the last statewide election. If the qualified initiative receives majority support, the legislature is expected to enact a law embodying the purpose of the initiative. Initiatives have been employed on a wide variety of policy questions, including tax and spending issues, public morality, business regulation, and U.S. foreign and defense policy.

Giving the public a vote on policies has a long tradition in American politics. Referenda were first used in 1778 when Massachusetts voters approved the state's first constitution. The initiative grew in importance during the late nineteenth and twentieth centuries as the Progressive political reform movement swept the country west of the Mississippi River. The influential Progressive reformer Robert M. La Follette summarized the rationale for referenda and initiatives:

> For years the American people have been engaged in a terrific struggle with the allied forces of organized wealth and political corruption. . . . The people must have in reserve new weapons for every emergency if they are to regain and preserve control of their governments. Through the initiative and referenda, people in an emergency can absolutely control. The initiative and referenda make it possible for them to demand a direct vote and repeal bad laws which have been enacted or to enact by direct vote good measures which their representatives refuse to consider.[17]

Since 1976 these instruments of "direct democracy" have been used with increasing frequency. The number of state ballot initiatives doubled between that year and 1986.[18] In the 1980s, more than 200 public propositions appeared on state ballots, and one in four was an initiative.[19] In 1990, there were 236 ballot questions in 43 states, including 67 proposals initiated by citizens. This was the largest number of ballot questions since 1914.[20] In recent years, voters weighed important, complex, and controversial proposals, such as:

—establishing a state sales tax in Oregon, which failed
—imposing stringent regulations on the production and disposal of toxic chemicals into California's water supply, which passed
—reducing acid rain in Massachusetts, which passed
—adopting an equal rights for women amendment to the state constitution in Vermont, which failed
—imposing limitations on the number of terms that legislators can serve in California, which passed
—prohibiting the use of state funds to fund abortions in Rhode Island, which failed
—reinstituting criminal penalties for possession of small quantities of marijuana in Alaska, which passed
—establishing a state holiday to honor Dr. Martin Luther King, Jr., in Arizona, which failed

Grass-Roots Politics

Many citizens engage directly and vigorously in the political life of their communities, states, and nation. The New England town meeting, the governing body in hundreds of small communities, invites every citizen to have a say in the making of public policy. Grass-roots political movements have sprung up to demand reform—sometimes with striking success, and at other times with stunning failure. For decades prior to the Civil War, for example, abolitionists sought the end of slavery. In the middle of the nineteenth century, suffragettes began to press for the right to vote for women, which was granted by ratification of the Nineteenth Amendment to the Constitution in 1920. Agrarian populists and labor unionists at the turn of the century demanded economic justice for low-income Americans.

Since World War II, American politics has witnessed strong public movements to secure civil rights for blacks, to stop the war in Southeast Asia, to clean up the nation's air and water, to end the deployment of nuclear weapons, to crack down on drunk drivers, to curb utility rate hikes, and to stop abortions. Each of these political movements emerged outside of conventional political arenas, was sparked by unelected leaders, and was characterized by large, vocal, and active participation by citizens who previously may have played little or no role in politics.[21]

What makes citizens stop relying on the voting booth and march in the streets? What makes people switch from watchers to central players? Grass-roots movements spring up when citizens become impatient with the pace of decision making, frustrated by the unwillingness of public officials to address their concerns, or angered by laws that infringe on basic rights or fundamental interests. When public opinion is "carried through from conversation to action [it] almost always carries with it a sense of outrage or injustice. At this point it is no longer opinion at all ... but rather a state of emotional shock ... a feeling of deprivation." [22]

Citizens frequently are drawn into political conflicts when they believe their health, safety, or property is threatened by government policies. The issue could be a proposed nuclear power plant, a school desegregation order, or a new condominium development that alarms people sufficiently to spur them to act. Under these conditions, a small group of citizens, who normally eschew politics, can be motivated to attend meetings, join protest marches, contribute money, and become political animals. Intense local opposition to public policy decisions has come to be known as the "Not in My Back Yard" or NIMBY syndrome. Public opinion is expressed from the bottom up when communities mobilize to protect their vital interests.

Citizens, Politicians, and Journalists

Living room politics consists of the interaction of political leaders, who want to control and manipulate public opinion; citizens, who want to bring about changes in government policy; and the media, which serve as conduits of important political information about the public. On rare occasions citizens join together to fight the White House, the capitol, or city hall, but even "spontaneous" outbursts of public concern are unlikely to occur or succeed without the drumbeat of newspaper and television coverage and strong political leadership.

The instruments of mass communication—television, radio, newspapers, and magazines—are the most important weapons in the battle for public opinion. Whether public opinions influence policies from the top down or citizens agitate from the bottom up, the mass media are involved. The media not only keep the attentive public informed, but also prominently feature stories that may eventually stir the normally apathetic mass of citizens.

Public officials and citizens can communicate face to face,

but probably not on a regular basis. The media have become the principal intermediaries and therefore exercise enormous power.[23] The media influence people's perception of what is important, frame the terms of debate on many questions, and magnify the voice of a few political figures. From time to time, the media switch from an information "channel" to an information "source" to promote particular policy concerns. When network news programs focused intensely on the Persian Gulf War for more than six weeks, their coverage was not just a conduit of facts and opinions, but a source of information with powerful consequences for the conduct of American foreign policy.

Living room politics, like all politics, is dominated by political elites, rather than by the public or even by journalists. Journalists usually take their cues about policy issues from public officials. News organizations are not neutral, but the media seldom create policy debates on their own. Media criticism of U.S. policy in the Persian Gulf, for example, evaporated when the air and ground war against Iraq began and when public officials on Capitol Hill muted their criticisms.

Policy makers use the press and television to build public support for their policy preferences. They depend on the media for feedback about policy initiatives and programs. But what officials read in the press and see on television is not an independent measure of public concern. Media critic Leon Sigal observed: "Listening to the news for the sound of public opinion, officials hear echoes of their own voices. Looking for pictures of the world outside, they see reflections of their own images."[24] What elected officials regard as public opinion is often derived from what other political actors say, rather than from systematic evidence gathered through reliable public opinion polls.

Citizen activists are also adept at using the media to pursue living room politics. They have learned that when one is losing a political battle, one "expands the scope of conflict" and tries to draw in members of the "audience who might support your cause."[25] The process goes something like this. A group is upset about an issue such as high state taxes. The group members collect signatures on petitions, hold press conferences, march to the state capitol, release public opinion polls, make speeches, appear at editorial board meetings, give interviews to newspapers, and appear on public affairs programs. If they are skillful, diligent, and a little lucky, they can garner millions of dollars' worth of publicity. The press and television give more exposure to their issue; the public becomes more aware and more interested; support builds; the media report that public support is building. Eventually, policy makers, sensing a groundswell of public concern, respond by cutting taxes.

Bringing Issues to the Living Room

The media magnify issues and promote them to the top of the agenda by their choice of what to highlight in the limited space and time available. The media may not tell people what to think, but they tell people what to think about.[26] The nation's leading newspapers—the *New York Times* and the *Washington Post*—can each present only about ten stories on the front page; the network news shows have time for only fifteen to twenty stories in their half-hour shows.[27] Because most citizens have no personal contact with the political process, it is not surprising that they are dependent on the media for interpretations of the world around them.

Elected officials gravitate to issues that are salient to the public: Reports in the media tell them and the public what is important.[28] Elected officials know that issues so identified by the media are likely to become priorities for the public.[29] In this way, the media enhance the importance of the issues they cover and diminish the political significance of the problems they ignore.[30] The same is true of individuals; presidents and governors receive by far the greatest attention from television. This attention gives them considerably more power than other political actors to set agendas, frame policy debates, and influence public sentiment. Conversely, ordinary citizens, even if they represent a widely held view, have trouble gaining access to the public airwaves and to newspaper columns.

Media surveillance of the political process helps keep issues on the agenda, especially if a president or governor addresses a policy question.[31] Once Ronald Reagan raised the issue of tax reform, Congress found it difficult not to act on it because of the number of articles and television stories chronicling every twist and turn of the legislative process. Public opinion polls revealed that most people were indifferent to the tax reform bills moving through Congress. Given the conflict generated by tax legislation, many members would have been happier if the law had died a quiet death. But the media spotlight made it all but impossible to avoid. Speaker Thomas P. (Tip) O'Neill, Jr., said, "I have to have a bill, the Democratic party has to have a bill. . . . If we don't we'll be clobbered over the head by the President of the United States."[32]

The public's agenda is not set in a single stroke; rather, it is built in a cycle of activity that elevates issues that are initially of interest to a few to issues that concern a broader public. The process through which the media, the government, and the citizenry influence one another has been labeled "agenda building" by scholars Gladys Lang and Kurt Lang.[33] Intense media attention to issues such as tax reform or the Watergate break-in, or to the struggles between Congress and the president over the federal budget transforms intramural squabbles into public controversies. A press secretary to a member of Congress has described agenda building on Capitol Hill:

> If I leak a story . . . in the *New York Times* on asbestos and the name Y is attached, what happens is an immediate phenomenal reaction. The calls come cascading in, and the name Y and asbestos in schools are intertwined. Suddenly, he's nationally known because of asbestos compensation and asbestos in schools. Then other members are calling Y asking about the report, asking for more information. . . . Then he can introduce a bill. He kicks the tail of the administration and gets lots of cosponsors who go out and get [media] hits themselves.[34]

The conventions of newspaper reporting and television news influence the kinds of issues brought to the public's attention and the way they are dealt with by public officials.[35] Extreme viewpoints are often highlighted because provocative statements and actions make more interesting reading and better television. Complicated issues—international trade, the savings and loan crisis, health care costs, for example—that are hard to explain and impossible to depict with pictures are frequently eschewed in favor of events that can be filmed, such as families salvaging their belongings after a flood, or a videotape of police beating a suspect during an arrest. News reports often convey a heightened sense of alarm about policy problems. Issues are personalized and dramatized, and a crisis atmosphere is created. In many cases, however, the "crisis is a function of publicity."[36] Public officials then feel compelled to take some action in order to ward off more negative stories.

The media's power to create a mood of urgency and demands for action was reflected in the sudden emergence and disappearance of public concern about famine in Africa.[37] Despite urgent pleas from West African countries, U.S. aid to the region actually declined between 1981 and 1983. Then, for an entire week in October 1984, NBC news televised shocking and gruesome film footage of starvation, suffering, and death on the parched deserts of Ethiopia. The network reported that 6 million people were suffering from starvation and that 500,000 would die within a year. A torrent of mass media stories poured forth during the next month. The dramatic and sustained coverage provoked strong public reactions, elicited millions of dollars in private contributions, and resulted in a huge increase in federal aid to the drought-stricken nations. All this attention, however, did not begin to solve the real problems, and within two years, the issue had disappeared from the media, American living rooms, and Congress's agenda. Starvation and death in West Africa continued.

Issues ignored by the media seldom generate the sustained attention of elected officials and ranking administrative officials. Consider the case of highway traffic fatalities. In the United States, more than 45,000 people die in motor vehicle accidents every year. They are the leading cause of accidental death of Americans under the age of 74. Car accidents cause 38 percent of all fatalities and 75 percent of the accidental deaths of young Americans—those 15 to 24 years of age. Yet because motor vehicle deaths are so commonplace, they are seldom covered by the national media.[38]

Contrast media reporting on motor vehicle deaths with the media's reaction to deaths caused by airplane accidents. Air traffic accidents typically result in fewer than 500 deaths per year, but they receive enormous attention in the national press. If the media reported cumulative statistics on automobile accidents and their causes each day or week, they would focus public attention and political debate on finding methods to reduce them. Without media attention, this yearly loss of thousands of American lives is all but ignored by senior officials of federal and state governments.

Framing the Issue

Newspaper editors and television producers simplify complex issues, place them in common frames of reference, and explain new policies with familiar terms.[39] When the media organizations report an event, a speech, or a policy proposal, they not only describe it but also give the public a context within which to interpret it. "The way the press frames an issue is as important as whether or not it is covered at all. If the press characterizes a policy option one way early on in the decision-making process, it is very difficult for officials to turn that image around to their preferred perspective," according to media analyst Martin Linsky.[40]

Because the media's descriptions of a problem often influence public perceptions, they may narrow the options available to public administrators. A policy debate can be labeled a "partisan squabble" or a matter of "urgent public concern." A governor's speech can be characterized as a "fight for his (or her) political life" or a routine report to the public. If dangerous polychlorinated biphenyls (PCBs) are discovered in a local warehouse, news stories suggesting that the public's health is gravely threatened can provoke panic, forcing public officials to react to an emergency that may not exist.

The media's portrayal of Saddam Hussein illustrates how time and historical context can lead the media to change their tune. When Saddam was an ally of the United States during the Iran-Iraq war, his mistreatment of Iraqi citizens was overlooked. But after Saddam's forces invaded Kuwait, newspapers and television news accounts likened his cold-blooded actions to the second coming of Adolf Hitler. By building up the image of a madman determined to destroy civilization, the media helped build support for the Persian Gulf War and for President Bush's policies. Similarly, the media's concentration on the limited extent of U.S. casualties and the near absence of reports on the deaths of Iraqi civilians and soldiers helped convince Americans that the Persian Gulf War was not only just, but one without much cost.

The Myth of the Neutral Media

Just as public officials claim they are not trying to manipulate the press, journalists perpetrate the myth that they are merely reporting what they see. Walter Cronkite, the former CBS news anchorman, closed his nightly broadcast by saying, "That's the way it is," implying that he was merely letting people know what had happened that day. In fact, the media are not neutral observers of the passing scene; there is a difference between the news and the truth.[41] Newspapers, television networks, and local stations shape the news and thus influence public officials and public opinion.

Bureaucratic routines, organizational politics, competition, and economics distort the view mass media organizations present to the public. What reporters think is probably less important than how they work. "News is thus less a sampling of what is happening in the world than a selection of what officials think—or want the press to report—is happening."[42] Reporters generally have little knowledge of what the mass audience thinks and pay much more attention to colleagues and superiors in their organization. Journalists and television crews position themselves where they decide news will be "made," and, in so doing, they make news.

Journalists and news organizations also can become active participants in the policy process. Newspaper investigations of problems in a local police department or fraud in defense contracting practically force public officials to address the problems. Media organizations commission public opinion polls, then report findings that may alter public policy. Reporters from the Cable News Network (CNN) have, at times, become important participants in the making of American foreign policy. When the Chinese government violently suppressed student protesters occupying Tiananmen Square in 1989, for example, CNN accounts of the event horrified the American public and helped move U.S. policy further in the direction away from supporting the repressive regime. During the Persian Gulf War, CNN reporters provided the most extensive accounts of civilian casualties in Iraq—a practice that led one U.S. senator to charge that CNN was sympathizing with the enemy.

Although they are less important than bureaucratic conditions that drive news reporting, the personal biases of journalists and media managers cannot be overlooked. Media watcher Herbert Gans pointed out that most journalists have a reformist/progressive attitude toward government.[43] They are deeply suspicious of government policy makers and the ability of political institutions to solve problems. These views lead to predictable, formulaic stories about incompetence, fraud, waste, and abuse. Stories about effective programs or the achievements of dedicated civil servants are scoffed at as "not newsworthy." In the shorthand of reporters, "Good news, bad story; bad news, good story."

Real Opinions, Soft Opinions, and Nonopinions

A sizable industry is devoted to surveying the public's thoughts on every subject from baseball players' salaries to the morality of public figures. All the major television networks, newspapers, and news magazines regularly commission public opinion polls or report public attitudes toward political officials, government institutions, and policy issues. Are the concerns measured in public opinion polls what people are really thinking about or merely pale imitations of preferences expressed by public officials through the media? Are Americans like the hapless couple depicted in the cartoon who tell a poll taker, "We don't have any opinions today. Our television is busted." ?

When people have little or no personal experience or stake in the outcome of a policy debate, public attitudes are likely to reflect views expressed by public officials and reported in the media. For people to hold real opinions, the issue must be important to them and they must have information on which to base a conclusion. On many policy questions, people have either no opinion or what might be called "soft" opinions, which may change rapidly in response to events or new information. When the public holds real opinions—about issues that touch basic values, or arouse strong preferences or fears—news reporters and public officials are far less persuasive. The public is also less malleable when the policy remedies under debate are controversial.

Opinion polls suggest that many Americans are deeply troubled about abortion and drug abuse, but the polls show differences in their responses. The vast majority agree that drug abuse should be curtailed quickly and by whatever means necessary, even if certain constitutional protections for citizens must be bent to enforce the laws. The public is easily riled to righteous indignation about crack cocaine dealers and the devastating effects of drug abuse on people's lives. In short, although few people favor drug abuse, the intensity of feelings about the drug issue can be influenced by the efforts of public officials and news organizations.

Abortion is another matter. People believe that abortion is an important issue, but they are deeply divided about the proper course for public policy to take. Some believe that abortions constitute the taking of a human life and should be outlawed. Others believe that a woman has an absolute right to determine whether to complete a pregnancy and that government should not interfere in this intensely private decision. News organizations do not attempt to shape people's attitudes about outlawing or guaranteeing abortions, perhaps because taking either position will cost them public support.

When large segments of the public have direct personal experience with a problem, pollsters are more likely to measure genuine concerns than to reveal media-manipulated sentiment. Public anxiety about unemployment is a good example. During the early 1980s, millions of American workers were unemployed, and millions more had jobless relatives or friends.[44]

Pollsters tap genuine concerns when they quiz people about problems affecting their health and the well-being of their families. Public fears about the Acquired Immune Deficiency Syndrome (AIDS) are palpable. As early as 1985, only a few years after the disease was discovered, pollsters found that 97 percent of the American people knew of the AIDS epidemic and 70 percent regarded AIDS as a direct threat to their health. More than half said the government was not doing enough to halt the disease; only 2 percent felt government spending was too high.[45] By way of comparison, in that same poll, only 44 percent knew that the U.S. House of Representatives was controlled by the Democratic party, which has been the case since 1955.

When pollsters and journalists venture into subjects that are unfamiliar to the public, they often discover, and then communicate, soft opinions or nonopinions to policy makers. Out of politeness or fear of appearing ignorant, people will answer questions about policy issues, even when they have no knowledge or opinions. When this happens, public officials and journalists are more likely to draw false conclusions about what the public really wants. Public opinion jells only when the issue becomes sufficiently important for people to pay attention to it. Until then, public moods can swing widely.

On many public issues Americans hold ambiguous and contradictory opinions, and on such issues public officials are free to interpret what the sentiment is. One might suppose that on important perennial issues such as taxes, spending, and the budget deficit, the public would hold rational views. Yet most polls show that the public wants *lower* taxes, *more* spending, and a *balanced* budget, too. People are unwilling to accept the logic that all three cannot be done simultaneously. For example, an October 1989 poll found that 59 percent of the Americans surveyed were opposed to the general proposition that taxes should be raised to help meet the nation's needs. Yet, when asked whether they supported tax increases to deal with such problems as health care and the war on drugs, to increase retirement benefits and improve public schools, more than three-quarters of the respondents favored higher taxes.[46] Elected officials and pollsters, therefore, are free to argue over what the polls mean, but they cannot ignore them. Even inconsistent and confusing public attitudes establish the options.

Polls and pollsters affect the understanding and impact of public opinion simply by asking certain questions and phrasing them in certain ways. When pollsters asked respondents whether President Reagan was "lying or not" about whether he directed his staff illegally to sell arms to Iran so that his operatives could in turn help equip an anticommunist revolutionary army in Nicaragua, they were implying that he might be a liar. When pollsters ask for opinions on various "crises"—drugs, energy, crime, drunk driving, garbage—and report the results, they may be magnifying concerns that exist primarily in the minds of pollsters, journalists, and public officials. When people were asked during the 1988 presidential campaign whether it is important to know if presidential candidates have committed adultery, pollsters and journalists were implying that personal moral conduct is an important criterion for judging potential presidents.

Despite their limitations, public opinion polls perform valuable functions in democracies. They are the only mechanism, outside of elections, through which the concerns of the ordinary citizen are expressed to political elites. The results of public opinion polls are often more representative of public sentiment than elections because voter turnout, even for presidential elections, is only slightly more than 50 percent. Polls can put issues on the public agenda that go beyond the wish lists of special interest groups. And finally, polls provide some feedback about public satisfaction with the direction and performance of government.

The Conduct of Direct Democracy

The two most direct methods by which citizens select policy options are initiatives and referenda. Most initiative and referenda campaigns rely on volunteers, but some have become costly public relations efforts requiring millions of dollars for television advertising.[47] Supporters and opponents spent $70 million in a fight to roll back California's insurance premiums in 1988; another $59 million was spent on other propositions. In contrast, $40 million was spent on state legislative campaigns in that year.[48] Initiatives that would have required deposits on bottles in Montana, Arizona, and California were defeated as a result of heavy spending by out-of-state beverage interests. Ninety-seven percent of the funds used to successfully oppose an antismoking initiative in California were contributed by out-of-state tobacco firms.[49]

Initiative and referenda campaigns have spawned an industry that collects signatures and mounts public awareness advertising campaigns. These services are available for hire, but they are expensive, and only groups with money can afford them. The Florida Medical Association organized an initiative drive to impose ceilings on financial awards in negligence suits. The doctors dished out $3 million in fees for canvassers who went door to door in "friendly" neighborhoods seeking signatures to place the question on the ballot. The canvassers assured citizens that passing the initiative would reduce medical costs, but they did not mention that their ability to sue for damages would be curtailed. The Florida Supreme Court refused to qualify the issue for the ballot because of the misleading campaign.[50] Reacting to tactics that undermine the democratic nature of the process, Colorado, Massachusetts, and Nebraska now prohibit paid solicitors in initiative and referenda campaigns.

Governors, state legislators, and others aspiring to elected office are using ballot questions to gain political visibility and attain policy objectives. In several states, legislative and gubernatorial candidates are backing ballot initiatives, hoping that their support will bring sympathetic voters to the polls on election day. As David Magleby, a leading student of the initiative process, pointed out, elected officials see referenda and initiatives as another tool in their political arsenal. If they win, initiatives allow legislators and governors to bypass the lengthy, arduous, and chancy legislative process. Even if they lose, politicians can gain political visibility through free media time.[51]

The line between show business and politics has been blurred in the controversy surrounding some ballot initiatives in California. A complex and far-reaching environmental initiative, known as Big Green, went down to defeat in 1990. But it attracted dozens of well-known show business personalities, including Gregory Peck, Jane Fonda, Chevy Chase, and Cybill Shepherd. The supporters of Proposition 128 produced a thirty-minute television commercial with fifteen celebrities, which accompanied a fast-paced program that resembled an MTV video.[52]

Not all initiatives and referenda are endorsed by big business and statewide political candidates; many feature household names as supporters or opponents. In fact, questions about civil rights and moral issues are often raised by grass-roots organizations whose volunteers collect signatures and operate on shoestring budgets. Large corporations are not interested in spending their money or risking their credibility on campaigns about the regulation of pornography, funding for abortions, or civil rights for disabled Americans.

Battles over the insertion of equal rights amendments (ERAs)—amendments that would guarantee equal rights or equal protection under the law to women—in state constitutions are an example of low-cost, door-to-door campaigns waged with intensity by citizen organizations. Since 1973 twelve states have voted on ERA referenda. Voters have approved them in five states and rejected them in seven. No state ERA has passed since Massachusetts amended its constitution in 1976. Typically, the pro-ERA forces have included state chapters of the National Organization for Women, the League of Women Voters, and labor organizations with large numbers of women. The anti-ERA coalition has encompassed the Eagle Forum, founded by Phyllis Schlafly; the Daughters of the American Revolution (DAR); the Federation of Women's Clubs; and assorted conservative organizations. The costs of ERA ballot fights have been considerably less than the costs of statewide campaigns on issues in which business and industry have been involved. Pro- and anti-ERA groups spent a combined total of $60,000 in Florida and $68,000 in Massachusetts, for example.[53]

Popular Leaders

Elected officials, media elites, and large corporations play central roles in living room politics. Public officials and private business leaders attempt to manipulate public opinion to suit their specific purposes. Journalists and pollsters shape public opinion in policy debates. The public, however, does not follow only elected officials and media personalities. In fact, many leaders of initiative and referenda drives and grass-roots citizen campaigns come from the ranks of ordinary citizens. These individuals, who have the power to persuade, have transformed national, state, and local politics by mobilizing citizens to take political action.

With regard to state ballot questions, the name Howard Jarvis is associated with Proposition 13, one of the most influential citizen campaigns in recent times. This tax and spending initiative, which was approved overwhelmingly by California voters in 1978, launched a drive to cut taxes and spending in many other states. Jarvis became so identified with government tax reform and spending limitations that subsequent California initiative campaigns have revolved around positive and negative campaign ads about Jarvis himself, rather than about the policy choices.[54]

Less well known, but more typical of the citizen activist, is Ray Phillips, an octogenarian who, with his volunteers, led a tax reduction movement known as Oregon Taxpayers United. Phillips describes his motivation:

I like being a rabble rouser. If the legislature did what it was supposed to do, we would not have to be out collecting signatures. The legislators spend too much time listening to lobbyists and not enough time listening to the people. Taxpayers don't control taxes anymore. That's what our measure would do—give power back to the people.[55]

Important grass-roots political movements have been led by individuals who emerged from nonpolitical roles into the limelight and became identified with their cause. Dr. Martin Luther King, Jr., a charismatic preacher, developed a large, loyal following as he organized demonstrations, marches, and other efforts to secure the full rights of citizenship for black Americans. Ralph Nader, a shy, ascetic lawyer, raised the consciousness of the American consumer and helped secure passage of new consumer protection laws. His nationwide network of state and local organizations continues to monitor industry production and use of dangerous products. Phyllis Schlafly, a self-described housewife, energized a large conservative movement in dozens of states to prevent passage of the ERA.

The Power of Public Opinion

Living room politics has been the catalyst for significant and startling changes in government policies. Public opinions—whether they originated at the top or at the bottom, played a critical role in forcing a president from office, halting the growth of nuclear power, cracking down on drunk drivers, slowing the growth of government spending, and limiting the number of terms that state legislators may serve. Citizens exert a powerful policy influence in the voting booth, on the streets of America, and perhaps most significantly, in the minds of elected and appointed leaders.

Public Opinion and the Media

Shifts in public support for government policies, often stimulated by media coverage, have brought about important changes. Extensive television coverage of the civil rights marches in the South during the 1960s exposed racism and the use of excessive force against peaceful individuals protesting racial discrimination.[56] Television scenes of the Vietnam War, showing bloody battles and the destruction of a country, crystallized public opposition to America's involvement.[57] Coverage of the nuclear accidents at Three Mile Island and Chernobyl undermined public support for nuclear power and halted the construction of nuclear power plants.[58] Extensive coverage of the violence and deaths caused by drug use influenced public opinion and brought about more stringent criminal penalties for drug users and suppliers.

The power of public opinion—and the role media organizations and political elites play in shaping it—was evident during the Watergate scandal.[59] Despite the efforts of the Democratic presidential candidate, George McGovern, to make an issue of the Republican-financed break-in at Democratic party headquarters at the Watergate complex during the 1972 campaign, President Richard Nixon was reelected with one of the largest votes in American history. A few months later, public support for Nixon fell precipitously. The House Judiciary Committee approved articles of impeachment, but the president resigned before the Senate began hearing the case. How did this tidal change in public attention and support occur?

The president lost the battle for public opinion because of incessant media reports about his role in ordering the surveillance of his opponents and then covering it up. The Senate investigating committee hearings, the impeachment hearings, and the battles waged by the president, independent prosecutors, and the U.S. Supreme Court over access to tape recordings and documents kept the Watergate crisis, as the press dubbed it, before the public for more than two years. The unfolding of the misdeeds and the drama of new revelations prolonged the story, giving Nixon's opponents ample time to convince the public that he was lying. Eventually, the Watergate issue was framed as a struggle between upholders of the Constitution and those who would subvert it for political gain.

Public opinion was a major force in Nixon's resignation from office. The president understood that the Republicans in the U.S. Senate would not support him, primarily because the public no longer supported him. The media's principal contribution to changing public opinion was their extensive coverage of critical events in ways that were essentially unfavorable to President Nixon. The Langs conclude that "there could have been no real public opinion on Watergate without the media. They alone could have called into being the mass audience of 'bystanders.' It was the media that, by reporting and even sponsoring [public opinion] polls, presented the cast of political actors in Watergate with a measure of public response to their every move. . . . The impression of public support made it easier to move against Nixon." [60]

Passionate public responses to issues are unusual, but they have far-reaching effects. Public policies may be changed quickly when large segments of the public rally to support or oppose issues of high salience. Politicians feel compelled to act rather than face a disgruntled, even angry, citizenry. One reason the public seldom becomes aroused is that public officials are adept at anticipating serious problems and responding to them before people get angry.

Problems that are widely recognized as serious by the public generate anxiety and often lead to demands for action. Government funding for research to find a cure for AIDS jumped by more than 200 percent after public opinion polls revealed widespread fear about the epidemic.[61] State lawmakers toughened laws against drunk driving in dozens of states in the wake of polls revealing public outrage at the trivial penalties given to drunk drivers responsible for vehicular homicides.

Given the weight assigned to public opinion in the myth and reality of American politics, it is perhaps surprising that strongly held public preferences are sometimes ignored. Politicians are known to use public opinion polls when they support their point of view and to ignore or denounce them as unreliable when they bring unfavorable, unwanted, or inconvenient news. Public officials often believe that poll results put them in an embarrassing position. If they follow public opinions as recorded in the surveys, cherished positions may have to be abandoned. If they ignore the polls, their opponents or journalists may chastise them for disregarding the will of the people. Fortunately for politicians, journalists seldom call attention to public officials who fail to respond to sentiment expressed in public opinion polls.

As intermediaries between the public and political leaders, the media influence policy choices and the evaluation of programs. Policy makers are preoccupied with managing the news because the media command public attention in a way that no elected officials or interest group possibly can. More than half of the senior federal government policy makers contacted in a recent survey reported that the press has *substantial* effects on federal policy. One official in ten believed the press is *the* dominant influence on policy. To some extent, press influence has become a self-fulfilling prophecy: "If policy makers themselves believe the press is influential, then by definition it is." [62]

Managing the press and responding to it often becomes a surrogate for managing public opinion and responding to it. Interactions among the media, public opinion, and public officials affect public policies in subtle ways. According to Linsky, extensive press coverage oversimplifies and nationalizes stories, forces quick responses, pushes decisions up the bureaucratic chain of command, and creates supportive climates for some options and excludes others.[63] Two case studies illustrate the dynamic relationships that are part of living room politics and their influence on government policies.

Love Canal

In the late 1970s, state and local health officials discovered that between 1942 and 1952, Hooker Chemical Company had deposited 21,000 tons of hazardous chemicals in an abandoned canal in Love

Canal, New York.[64] The Environmental Protection Agency commissioned pilot studies to ascertain the possible health and environmental threats posed by chemicals that were leaching into the groundwater, yards, and basements of homes around the canal. President Carter declared the Hooker site at Love Canal a national emergency, and hundreds of residents were evacuated from the area. Media attention to the problems at Love Canal influenced these decisions.

After Love Canal became a national issue, a consultant was hired by the EPA to examine the possible genetic effects of the leaking chemicals. The consultant examined individuals who had experienced serious health problems, such as cancer or birth defects. By first selecting people with known health problems, the consultant hoped to determine whether a more thorough investigation was warranted. Research uncovered chromosomal aberrations in twelve of the thirty-six people tested. Without more rigorous and comprehensive tests, however, it was not possible to establish a definite link between the chemicals dumped in the canal and the health problems experienced by people in the pilot study.

Fearing that the preliminary study would be leaked to the press, White House officials decided they would release the report and promise further investigation. But before they could act, the report was published in the *New York Times*. Love Canal was hot news. In the ten days following the publication of the findings, the *Times* printed thirty-one articles on Love Canal, including eight front-page stories and three editorials. Other newspapers and the television networks ran dozens of related stories describing serious threats to health from the uncontrolled dumping of hazardous wastes.

To put an end to stories about government insensitivity to the problems of Love Canal's residents, the White House decided to relocate 710 individuals. The pressure to respond so as not to appear callous and indifferent had been intensified by media coverage. Ironically, the complete review of the EPA pilot study was finished the same day that the relocation decision was announced. It concluded that there was "inadequate basis for any scientific or medical inferences from the data (even of a tentative or preliminary nature) concerning exposure to mutagenic substances because of residence in Love Canal." If the Love Canal story had not been framed by the media as a dangerous health threat to hapless victims, the government might have undertaken a lengthier investigation and might not have spent millions to relocate the families.

Like many instances of press and public involvement in the policy process, the Love Canal story had far-reaching effects. The spotlight was focused on one example of a national problem—the cleanup of abandoned hazardous waste dumps. The publicity that resulted from the Love Canal incident helped focus public attention on this lingering problem. Soon after, new environmental legislation to clean up abandoned waste dumps was enacted by Congress.

Disability Reviews

An Office of Management and Budget investigation of the Social Security disability insurance program launched during the Carter administration estimated that 20 percent of the people receiving benefits were ineligible for such assistance.[65] Disability payments are reserved for individuals who cannot work because of physical or mental problems. The preliminary review indicated that some able-bodied people were "ripping off" the program. Based on this information, the Social Security Administration initiated a comprehensive effort to rid the program of ineligibles who might be costing the government as much as $2 billion annually. The Reagan administration accelerated the review process, and some local news stories suggested that people were losing benefits despite legitimate claims. Public awareness of the issue increased dramatically when CBS televised a story about a man who had committed suicide and left a note blaming the SSA for cutting off his payments and "playing God." Other network and newspaper stories soon followed, emphasizing that deserving people had been wronged by careless government bureaucrats.

Bolstered by negative media stories, members of Congress, editorial writers, and advocates for the disabled stepped up pressure on the Reagan administration to revise or drop the disability reviews. A television special, hosted by Bill Moyers of CBS, featured a cerebral palsy victim who had lost his disability assistance for what appeared to be inappropriate reasons. Other stories reported that people had died from disabilities that the government deemed not serious enough to keep them enrolled in the program. The television program "Real People" ran a story about a wounded Vietnam veteran—a recipient of the Congressional Medal of Honor—who was about to have his disability checks cut off.

Administration officials claimed that the stories of deserving people wrongfully dropped from the disability assistance rolls were exaggerated, unrepresentative, and even false. They noted that some of these people were working full time, yet were still claiming benefits. Eventually, senior White House staff members concluded that the rising tide of negative stories left the impression that Reagan's budget cuts were inhumane and unfair and that such publicity undermined the president's efforts to achieve further spending reductions. The only way to mute the criticism was to suspend the reviews and that is exactly what they did. A few months later, legislation revising procedures for removing individuals from the program swept through Congress.

Choosing Policies in the Voting Booth

Referenda and initiatives give millions of Americans a direct say on policy issues, and liberal and conservative groups have been equally successful with the voters. A study of nearly 200 initiatives approved between 1977 and 1984 revealed that 44 percent of the 79 proposals backed by liberals were approved, and 45 percent of the 74 conservative-sponsored initiatives were approved. (The remainder were classified as not having ideological content.)[66]

Tax and government spending limitations have been aggressively pursued by use of the statewide initiatives. "No other issue cluster . . . has faced popular scrutiny more often. Win or lose, the tax cut movement has . . . been deciding the bounds of political debate on tax and fiscal policy," wrote Patrick McGuigan, the author of an authoritative newsletter on referenda and initiatives.[67] The modern tax revolt began with California's Proposition 13, which reduced property tax revenues by 57 percent and limited future tax increases to no more than 2 percent annually.

Between 1976 and 1984, however, only three states of the nine that voted on Proposition 13-type initiatives approved them, as shown in Table 8-1. But voters in eleven states approved moderate tax and spending measures referred to them by state legislatures that were trying to head off more Draconian revenue cuts. Alaskans dropped the income tax; North Dakotans reduced the income tax bite; and Washingtonians eliminated the state inheritance tax.[68]

In the 1990 election, initiatives proposing government spending and tax limitations did not fare very well. Voters in Massachusetts, Colorado, Montana, and Utah said "no" to proposals that would have required legislators to roll back or curtail taxes. Public officials, public employees and teachers, and others who would be negatively affected by budget cuts have rallied enough voter support to defeat efforts to further shrink state and local governments.[69]

What followed passage of Proposition 13 shows that a state need not have a strong initiative process to be affected by initiatives passed in other states.[70] In fact, legislators in states without the initiative process interpreted the rash of tax and spending initiatives as a message they must heed. They thought voters wanted lower taxes and changes in the methods of taxation. In 1965 less than half of the electorate thought that taxes were too high. By 1983, nearly 75 percent were complaining that taxes are excessive. And eight Americans in ten thought that government funds are often wasted.[71]

Even a defeated initiative may trigger a remedial or preemptive policy response. In South Dakota the Public Utilities Commission ap-

Table 8-1   Tax and Spending Cut Initiatives and Referenda,
1976 to 1984

State	Proposition 13 tax cuts	Limited tax and spending cuts
Alaska		passed (1980, 1982)
Arizona	failed (1980)	passed (1978)
California	passed (1978)	failed (1980), passed (1982)
Colorado		failed (1978)
Hawaii		passed (1978)
Idaho	passed (1978)	
Maine		passed (1982)
Massachusetts	passed (1980)	
Michigan	failed (1980)	failed (1976, 1984)
Missouri		passed (1980)
Montana		passed (1980)
Nevada	passed (1978) failed (1980, 1984)	failed (1984)
North Dakota		passed (1978)
Ohio		failed (1983)
Oklahoma		failed (1979)
Oregon	failed (1978, 1980, 1982, 1984)	
South Carolina		passed (1984)
South Dakota	failed (1980)	
Texas		passed (1978)
Utah	failed (1980)	
Washington		passed (1979, 1981)

Source: Patrick B. McGuigan, *The Politics of Direct Democracy in the 1980s* (Washington, D.C.: Free Congress Research and Education Foundation, 1985), 52, 54, 55. Reprinted by permission.

proved special rates for the elderly and the poor two years after the defeat of a similar but more comprehensive rate initiative.[72] The California state legislature responded to an antinuclear initiative while the campaign for it was still under way. One week before the scheduled election, the legislature approved a weaker version of the antinuclear initiative, which was subsequently rejected by the voters. The defeated initiative had served as a catalyst, prodding politicians to act before the voters took matters into their own hands.

In California, according to most observers, legislators still debate the state's public policy agenda, but the focus has shifted from the legislature to the initiative process. In the 1990 election, California voters were asked to weigh twenty-eight ballot issues, ranging from sweeping environmental policy changes to alcohol taxes. California citizens have already set major policy directions on insurance rates, the environment, and the levels of spending for education. "It [the initiative] is a force that has produced occasional benefits, but at enormous cost—an erosion of responsibility in the executive and legislative branches," says Eugene C. Lee of the University of California.[73]

Public ballot proposals have also given voters a voice on issues of social policy.[74] Voters have cut abortion funding in Colorado, but voters defeated similar proposals in Arkansas, Oregon, Washington, and Rhode Island. Following the 1989 Supreme Court decision that gave states more latitude in regulating abortions, Oregon voters rejected a proposal that would have required parents to be notified when teenagers sought an abortion. Citizens rejected stricter regulations on the sale of pornographic materials in Maine and Utah, endorsed prayer in the public schools in West Virginia, and repealed the Massachusetts law requiring the use of seat belts. Laws restricting the disposal of radioactive waste were strengthened in Montana, Oregon, and Washington. Maine voters rejected a proposal to shut down a nuclear power plant and threw out laws requiring large stores to close on Sunday. More stringent environmental protection laws were endorsed by voters in California, New Jersey, and Massachusetts. California voters declared English the state's official language and rejected a plan to quarantine victims of AIDS.

Citizens have used the ballot box to register dismay over U.S. foreign and defense policies. State and local governments have no control over foreign policy, and state initiatives and referenda are not binding on the federal government. Nevertheless, activists frustrated with U.S. foreign policy have used this tactic to goad the president and Congress to halt the production and deployment of nuclear weapons.[75] With nearly 20 million people voting, the so-called nuclear freeze referenda were the closest the nation has come to a national referendum on a policy issue. Similarly worded proposals calling for a halt to the arms race were approved by comfortable margins—averaging 60 percent—in ten of the eleven states and thirty-one of thirty-two communities where balloting occurred in 1982. Perhaps the measure won easily because freeze supporters encountered almost no organized opposition (except in Arizona where the measure failed) and outspent their opponents thirteen to one nationwide. Still, the vote can be considered a measure of the desire for reduced tensions in the arms race.

Policy from the Grass Roots

Grass-roots political movements grow out of the frustration citizens feel about the pace of reform or their outrage at decisions that threaten their way of life. Seeking relief from the government, citizen groups have denounced U.S. foreign policy and pestered legislators, administrators, and judges to alter policies on a host of moral issues—from prayer in public schools to the siting of garbage incinerators.

The success of minority groups in quickening the pace of change is noteworthy. What began as an effort to secure basic rights evolved into a broad-based effort to increase economic opportunities. The ability of leaders to mobilize minorities beyond protest and get them into the voting booth had positive effects on the appointment and election of minority officeholders, expanded employment opportunities for minorities in city governments, and enlarged programs for the minority community.[76]

Since the late 1960s, hundreds of national and local environmental groups have also achieved considerable success in translating widespread public support for environmental conservation and protection into political action and policy results. Statutes have been passed governing air and water quality, control of toxic pollution, and the disposal of industrial, agricultural, and urban wastes. Regulatory agencies have been established at the state and national levels. Billions of dollars have been allocated to environmental protection and cleanup. Environmental interest groups are represented in Washington and in state capitals. Obviously, these sweeping reforms were not stimulated entirely by ordinary citizens, but grass-roots environmental organizations were powerful agents for change.[77]

Environmental groups have effectively organized to stop construction of nuclear power plants, dams, and toxic waste incinerators. When the New Jersey Department of Environmental Protection announced it would transfer 15,000 barrels of radium-contaminated dirt to a quarry near the rural town of Vernon, local residents rallied to thwart the plan. Thousands of people protested the decision, and hundreds followed Governor Thomas Kean (1982-1990) around the state, interrupting his speeches; they also picketed his home. Locals prepared for civil disobedience and violent acts of sabotage. Fearing for the safety of citizens and state troopers alike, Kean reversed the decision and directed the department to find another site for the dirt.[78]

Majority Rule and Minority Rights

Who benefits from living room politics? Who are the winners and the losers? Because living room politics concerns issues that arouse the public and galvanize ordinary citizens into action, one might glibly conclude that the public wins. Unfortunately, figuring out who benefits from living room politics is considerably more complicated than that.

Living room politics can be the expression of majority sentiments, and public officials are inclined to heed the will of the people when public preferences are clear and reflect a broad-based consensus. When the majority of the public supports a controversial course of action, however, policy makers may ignore it, especially if the public's wishes would infringe on minority interests. Suppose that public opinion polls show that most people favor isolating AIDS victims from the rest of the population. Political institutions, especially the courts, are unlikely to be guided by such opinions because the basic rights of a disadvantaged minority would be violated in an attempt to allay the fears of the majority.

Well-organized and well-financed groups are more likely to have their views heeded than are those who are economically disadvantaged. Those who are better off are generally more successful in directing media and public attention to their concerns. It is no accident that many ballot initiatives are of greater interest to white, middle-class voters than they are to minorities and the poor. Disadvantaged Americans are more likely to go to the courts for help than to the ballot box (see Chapter 7).

A central dilemma of democracy is the clash of majority rule and minority rights. Basic issues, such as war, civil rights, morality, public health and safety, are most likely to stimulate public concern and foster intense, divergent beliefs. Individuals with diametrically opposed positions on controversial issues, such as abortion, women's rights, or nuclear plant safety, usually do not find the alternative point of view acceptable.

When people are divided over an issue that arouses strong feelings, public officials search for Solomonic compromises that might satisfy the losers as well as the winners. However, finding such answers is often impossible. When accommodation fails, the public policy process grinds to a halt because neither side is willing to compromise. Elected officials and government administrators either ignore the problem as long as they possibly can or pass the buck to another institution—the judiciary or the president. They may even pass the buck to the voters, hoping to find an answer in the majority will expressed via referenda.

When majority preferences are honored, the losers may be angry, feel alienated, and resort to unconventional methods, including civil disobedience and violence. Indeed, many of the most violent or potentially violent episodes in American political history took place when the losers felt the political system no longer cared about them. Riots and violence over racial segregation and injustice in the 1950s and 1960s and demonstrations against the Vietnam War that ended in violent confrontations between marchers and police and national guardsmen are but two vivid examples. More recently, individuals opposed to the U.S. Supreme Court's legalization of abortions have bombed abortion clinics. Environmental activists have sabotaged chemical plants and physically blocked the construction of nuclear power plants and hazardous waste disposal facilities.

Well-organized, sophisticated segments of the citizenry benefit most from living room politics, but when minority concerns are trampled on, the potential for political instability increases. It is perhaps for this reason that politicians fear citizen participation in the government process. Once citizens are drawn into the conflict, they demand satisfaction, and once the genie is out of the bottle, it is hard to get it back in again.

A Potent Weapon of Democracy

Whether through the informal plebiscite of public opinion polls or through active participation, citizens can have a powerful influence on the implementation and impact of public policies. Public pressure may be brought to bear concerning the tactics and pace of program administration. The public's evaluation of government policies, institutions, and political actors, which is shaped by the media, may influence financial support for a program or cause its cancellation. Public perceptions of a specific leader's popularity may embolden or intimidate other political leaders. Finally, angry citizens can force radical changes in public policy.

Public and Media Evaluations of Government Policy

Americans are generally skeptical about government programs and institutions. Such perceptions are based partly on personal experience, such as frustration with the IRS, a state department of motor vehicles, or the local building code enforcement officer. For the most part, however, the public's understanding of politics and policy comes to it via newspapers and television, which not only reflect this skeptical attitude about government but also encourage it.

As messengers of public concern and guardians of the public interest, reporters often deserve high praise. Journalists criticize weak government policies and inform the public about crises and conflicts, fraud and corruption. Journalists root out corrupt public officials and call attention to the insensitivity and injustice of public institutions. Media scrutiny, followed by public anger, can spur an indifferent, cautious, or incompetent agency or legislature to positive action in the public interest.

The contributions of media organizations and journalists to policy implementation can be a mixed blessing, however. Media publicity can divert administrators from important tasks and induce them to attend to relatively trivial matters. One recent summer, for example, federal, state, and local officials were perplexed about how to deal with an ordinary garbage barge that had been the subject of many news reports. The barge posed little or no threat to public health, but the wave of stories about it had generated fear about what was on it. The barge *Mobro* had picked up 3,186 tons of normal household refuse and waste from construction sites in Islip Township on Long Island. The tugboat *Break of Dawn* towed the barge to North Carolina where the crew expected to unload its cargo, but local officials refused to grant the necessary permits. Subsequent attempts to dock and unload were rebuffed in Mississippi, Alabama, Florida, Texas, Louisiana, New York, and three foreign countries. Meanwhile, environmental regulators and elected officials at all levels of government wrangled over where to unload it. Eventually, the contents of the barge were buried in a landfill near the original source of the refuse. Public anxiety and a crisis atmosphere had been created, and political grandstanding had been encouraged, mostly by the media.

On balance, the intense interest in the pariah garbage barge was probably a useful contribution to public education. The tale of the *Mobro* and the *Break of Dawn* highlighted a genuine problem—the disposal of solid waste in a country that is running out of landfill sites. Environmentalists and government officials had been trying, largely without success, to increase public awareness about the mounting problem of finding safe, efficient methods of recycling and disposing of trash. The barge provided an unexpected but welcome boost for their cause. "For anybody who works with waste, the barge has been like a religious experience," observed Gerald Boyd of New York's Legislative Commission on Solid Waste.[79]

According to some analysts, the media's influence on elected officials and the public is pernicious. Timothy Cook argued that members of Congress are less concerned with the public interest than with what will sell with the media.[80] Obsession with the way things appear in the press, he maintained, drives elected officials to search for overly simple answers to complicated questions. The need to explain one's position in a thirty-second spot on television encourages legislators to latch onto symbols and slogans, rather than to seek carefully crafted solutions. As a case in point, Cook cited the Gramm-Rudman-Hollings Deficit Reduction Act, which mandated across-the-board spending cuts to reduce government spending. The measure was simple and straightforward, but it did not solve the budget deficit problem. Since the law was passed in 1985, Congress and the president have failed to find a politically acceptable formula for achieving real spending reductions.

The attitudes news organizations have toward government institutions and programs color their reporting. According to Lewis Wolfson, a former reporter and editor, the press is "not inherently interested in what's involved in developing a policy or administering a program or what impacts these decisions may have at the grass roots." If a policy fails, journalists "rush to discover what went wrong, looking more for incompetence or corruption than for shortcomings of the policy-making process that may have compromised the approach from the start." [81] In consequence, the public may be led down the path to ignorance rather than understanding.

The pervasive role of the media in shaping the public's view of politics helps explain why it is difficult to galvanize the public to support some issues. People trust and understand what they can see more than what they hear.[82] It is impossible to show in visual terms that deficit spending harms the nation's economy or that the depletion of the ozone layer can cause the earth's temperatures to rise dangerously. These limitations of mass communication circumscribe the issues that engender broad public participation.

Government policies and the financial practices of hundreds of banking institutions led to a near collapse of the savings and loan industry and the costliest government financial rescue in the history of this country. It is estimated that when all is said and done the price will amount to upward of $500 billion—$2,000 for every, man, woman, and child in America. Despite the enormous consequences, the mass media were very late in grasping the significance of what was going on, reporting it to the public, and thus arousing public interest in the nature of the problem or the proposed solutions. It is a classic example of how the media falter when a political and policy story cannot be reduced to the bare essentials of good guys and bad guys. According to one observer, "given its complexity and its lack of identifiable heroes, the S&L debacle may have become the inert issue of the 1990s." [83]

In contrast, when the media can readily sensationalize administrative shortcomings and the foibles of public officials, otherwise effective programs may be damaged and their base of public and political support eroded. Consider the media's role in the implementation of the Comprehensive Employment and Training Act.[84] The law called for CETA administrators to take on some nearly impossible tasks. Press accounts criticized the hiring of ineligible workers, blatant political patronage, and programs of doubtful value. Although such practices were the exception rather than the rule, the public and political officials responsible for its administration believed the program to be riddled with fraud, waste, and abuse. In fact, CETA's problems were caused as much by congressional pressure to spend money too rapidly as they were by unscrupulous or incompetent administrators. Nevertheless, a negative image plagued CETA, and its public service jobs component was ultimately terminated.

By ridiculing the National Aeronautics and Space Administration for failing to launch on schedule, the media may have contributed to the space shuttle disaster in 1986. Elected and appointed officials bristle at media criticism and try to avoid it. At times, their thin skins cause irresponsible behavior, such as the decision to launch the Challenger despite warnings about faulty O-rings and inclement weather.

On the evening of January 27, 1986, the television news networks announced that the launch had been delayed for a third time. Following are the remarks of Dan Rather of CBS on the decision to "scrub" the flight:

> Yet another costly, red-faces-all-around-space-shuttle-launch delay. This time a bad bolt on a hatch and bad weather bolt from the blue are being blamed. What's more, a rescheduled launch for tomorrow doesn't look good either. Bruce Hall has the latest on today's hi-tech low comedy.[85]

The other networks were equally harsh. And the *New York Times* described the situation as a "comedy of errors."

The following morning, NASA launched the space shuttle and seven astronauts perished. Ultimately, NASA must accept responsibility for the disaster. Its flight schedule was unrealistic, and it should have resisted pressure for a premature launch. The reality of media pressure is undeniable, however. As one NASA official put it:

> Every time there was a delay, the press would say, "Look, there's another delay.... Here's a bunch of idiots who can't even handle a launch schedule...." You think that doesn't have an impact? If you think it doesn't, you're stupid.[86]

The media's relentless unfavorable portrayal of political institutions, public officials, and government programs fosters negative public attitudes about the public sector.[87] Media analyst Michael Robinson calls these feelings about the political world "video-malaise."[88] Cynical views about government and political figures are conveyed not only by news and public affairs programs, but by soap operas and drama series as well.

Contempt for the political world is pervasive on entertainment television. There is no television series in which political figures are cast in positive roles. Television regularly portrays "heroes" doing battle with evil politicians.

In earlier sections we discussed the politics of getting proposals on the ballot and voted upon. Now we turn our attention to assessing the impact that initiatives and referenda have on public policy.

The Impacts of Initiatives and Referenda

Initiatives and referenda probably have had profound impacts on the shape of social, political, and economic change. Voters have halted restrictions on the sale of pornographic literature, rolled back state laws requiring that drivers wear seat belts, and imposed stronger criminal penalties for the use of illegal substances. Initiatives and the political fallout generated by them have restrained public spending. Voters have mandated expenditure limitations and tax policies that have altered the economies of more than a dozen states. Resources for public institutions, the poor, and minority groups have been cut, while property owners have retained a larger portion of their income.

Public officials often are unable to implement public ballot decisions because the decisions are not clear or call for significant policy adjustments.[89] In 1986, California's Proposition 65 required the state government to reduce substantially the flow of toxic chemicals into the state's water supply. Administrators found it extremely difficult to identify and classify all the chemicals that might harm the water supply, to determine safe standards, and finally to establish a system for monitoring thousands of chemical manufacturers and users. After more than five years of costly lawsuits to determine which substances the state would list as toxic, the impact of Proposition 65 finally began to be felt in California in the early 1990s.[90]

Nuclear freeze referenda and initiatives clearly revealed the public's anxieties about a nuclear holocaust, but the measures have had little practical impact. Most freeze propositions required state and local officials to communicate with the president and Congress about the deployment of nuclear weapons. The results were not binding on federal officials, and no freeze on deployment has been imposed. The initiatives constituted a symbolic victory, however.

Like any other method of decision making, initiatives and referenda have their strengths and weaknesses.[91] On the positive side, initiatives give citizens an opportunity to raise issues that elected leaders and interest groups might just as soon ignore. Initiatives can also help overcome stalemates in the legislative process. Taking policy choices to the voters can be an effective method of legitimating controversial decisions.

On the negative side, initiatives and referenda are blunt instruments. It is not possible to reduce complicated questions to one-line statements. Ballot questions—with the choices restricted to yes or no—lack the deliberation and accommodation of legislative institutions and administrative agencies. For example, California voters approved a proposition in 1987 that requires that at least 40 percent of the state's general funds go to the public schools. As a result, the flexibility of the legislature and the governor to respond to changing priorities is severely limited.

Moreover, initiatives and referenda may not be as sensitive to minorities as the courts might be. Evidence suggests that interest groups and political officials are seizing the tools of direct democracy to seek victories that they were unable to gain through mainstream institutions. The practice of direct democracy is becoming professionalized and costly and, therefore, may be moving beyond the reach of volunteers. Finally, the opportunity to evade difficult decisions may encourage irresponsible behavior by public officials. Rather than assume duties they were elected to perform, they may wait for voters to send a clear signal. By then it may be too late.

Summary

Living room politics is a unique, important, but often misunderstood part of democratic government. High school civics books and Independence Day speeches may exaggerate citizen control of the policy process, but many sophisticated observers also may underestimate the power the public wields in policy making.

For most ordinary citizens, politics and public policy are another form of entertainment. They find it interesting to tune in now and then, but not to stay tuned. From time to time, however, large segments of the public hold strong opinions on public issues, and an enraged, out-of-control public is a formidable threat to political stability. In full force, the power of public opinion and citizen participation has driven high officials from office, changed the course of American foreign and domestic policy, and stopped countless government proposals from ever getting off the ground.

The mass media are particularly important players in living room politics. Newspapers, television, and radio are the principal sources of information about politics and government for most Americans. The power of the media derives not from a conspiracy to lead American policy in a particular direction, but from the fact that most people have no other way of conjuring up a political reality.

Legislators, chief executives, bureaucrats, corporate leaders, and even judges are sensitive to the need for public understanding and support because without it government can lose its legitimacy—the very foundation of governance. Public officials must not only understand but also manage public opinion in order to build support for their cherished programs and to maintain control of the political process.

Notes

1. W. Lance Bennett, *Public Opinion in American Politics* (New York: Harcourt Brace Jovanovich, 1980).

2. As quoted in Leo Bogart, *Polls and the Awareness of Public Opinion*, 2d ed. (New Brunswick, N.J.: Transaction Books, 1985), 3.

3. See, for example, W. Russell Neuman, *The Paradox of Mass Politics* (Cambridge, Mass.: Harvard University Press, 1986); and Benjamin Ginsberg, *The Captive Public* (New York: Basic Books, 1986).

4. Martin Linsky, *Impact: How the Press Affects Federal Policymaking* (New York: W. W. Norton, 1986), 36-37.

5. E. E. Schattschneider, *The Semi-Sovereign People* (New York: Holt, Rinehart and Winston, 1960).

6. Neuman, *The Paradox of Mass Politics*.

7. The concepts of top-down and bottom-up public opinion are borrowed from Cliff Zukin of the Eagleton Institute of Politics at Rutgers University.

8. Bennett, *Public Opinion in American Politics*.

9. V. O. Key, Jr., *Public Opinion and American Democracy* (New York: Alfred A. Knopf, 1961), 14.

10. Bennett, *Public Opinion in American Politics*, 367.

11. Robert Weissberg, *Public Opinion and Popular Government* (Englewood Cliffs, N.J.: Prentice-Hall, 1976), 213.

12. Richard E. Neustadt, *Presidential Power: The Politics of Leadership from FDR to Carter* (New York: John Wiley, 1980). See also Samuel Kernell, *Going Public* (Washington, D.C.: CQ Press, 1986).

13. Paul West, "The Never-Ending Campaign," *Governing* 3 (March 1990): 52-53.

14. Linda Greenhouse, "Silence Is Heartening to Democrats," *New York Times*, June 19, 1987, A20.

15. Neuman, *The Paradox of Mass Politics*.

16. *The Book of the States, 1984-1985* (Lexington, Ky.: Council of State Governments, 1984), 167-169, 225.

17. Ellen Torelle, comp., *The Political Philosophy of Robert M. La Follette* (Westport, Conn.: Hyperion Press, 1975), 173-174.

18. Michael Nelson, "Power to the People: The Crusade for Direct Democracy," in *The Clash of Issues*, 7th ed., ed. James Burkhart, Samuel Krislov, and Raymond L. Lee (Englewood Cliffs, N.J.: Prentice-Hall, 1981), 25-28.

19. Patrick B. McGuigan, *The Politics of Direct Democracy in the 1980s* (Washington, D.C.: Free Congress Research and Education Foundation, 1985); and Patrick B. McGuigan, ed., *Initiative and Referendum Report*, December 1986-January 1987.

20. Carol Matlack," Where the Big Winner Was the Status Quo," *National Journal*, November 10, 1990, 2748-2749.

21. Barry Commoner, "A Reporter at Large: The Environment," *New Yorker*, June 15, 1987, 46-71.

22. Bogart, *Polls and the Awareness of Public Opinion*, 198.

23. See, for example, Linsky, *Impact*; Stephen Hess, *The Ultimate Insiders: U.S. Senators and the National Media* (Washington, D.C.: Brookings Institution, 1986); and Austin Ranney, *Channels of Power: The Impact of Television on American Politics* (New York: Basic Books, 1983).

24. Leon V. Sigal, *Reporters and Officials: The Organization and Politics*

of Newsmaking (Lexington, Mass.: D. C. Heath, 1973), 186.

25. Schattschneider, *The Semi-Sovereign People*, 2-3.

26. Donald L. Shaw and Maxwell E. McCombs, *The Emergence of American Political Issues: The Agenda-Setting Function of the Press* (St. Paul, Minn.: West, 1977).

27. Sigal, *Reporters and Officials*, 12.

28. See, for example, David E. Price, "Policymaking in Congressional Committees: The Impact of Environmental Factors," *American Political Science Review* 72 (June 1978): 548-574.

29. Linsky, *Impact*, 90.

30. Sigal, *Reporters and Officials;* and Shaw and McCombs, *The Emergence of American Political Issues.*

31. Timothy E. Cook, "P.R. on the Hill: The Evolution of Congressional Press Operations," in *Legislative Politics*, ed. Chris Deering (Homewood, Ill.: Dorsey Press, 1989).

32. As quoted in Steven V. Roberts, "A Most Important Man on Capitol Hill," *New York Times Magazine*, September 22, 1985, 48.

33. Gladys Engel Lang and Kurt Lang, *The Battle for Public Opinion: The President, the Press, and the Polls During Watergate* (New York: Columbia University Press, 1983), 58-61.

34. As quoted by Timothy E. Cook, "Marketing the Members: The Ascent of the Congressional Press Secretary" (Paper presented at the annual meeting of the Midwest Political Science Association, Chicago, April, 1985), 15.

35. See, for example, Edward Jay Epstein, *News from Nowhere: Television and the News* (New York: Vintage Books, 1983); W. Lance Bennett, *News: The Politics of Illusion* (New York: Longman, 1983); and Sigal, *Reporters and Officials.*

36. Sigal, *Reporters and Officials*, 186.

37. See Christopher J. Bosso, "Mass Media, Mass Politics: Making the Ethiopian Famine a Public Problem" (Paper presented at the annual meeting of the Midwest Political Science Association, Chicago, April, 1987).

38. "How Safe Are America's Roads and Highways?" *National Journal*, April 14, 1990, 919.

39. Linsky, *Impact;* and Sigal, *Reporters and Officials.*

40. Linsky, *Impact*, 94.

41. Edward Jay Epstein, *Between Fact and Fiction: The Problem of Journalism* (New York: Vintage Books, 1975).

42. Sigal, *Reporters and Officials*, 188.

43. Herbert J. Gans, *Deciding What's News* (New York: Pantheon Books, 1979).

44. Donald C. Baumer and Carl E. Van Horn, *The Politics of Unemployment* (Washington, D.C.: CQ Press, 1985).

45. Victor Cohn, "Fear of AIDS Is Spreading Faster than the Disease," *Washington Post* national weekly edition, September 16, 1985, 37.

46. Laurence I. Barrett, "Giving the Public What It Wants," *Time*, October 23, 1989, 34.

47. Reported in "Liberals, Conservatives Share Initiative Success," *Public Administration Times*, February 15, 1985, 1, 12.

48. James A. Barnes, "Losing the Initiative," *National Journal*, September 1, 1990, 2049.

49. Ruth S. Jones, "Financing State Elections," in *Money and Politics in the*

United States, ed. Michael J. Malbin (Chatham, N.J.: Chatham House, 1984), 206-207.

50. Manning J. Dauer and Mark Sievers, "The Constitutional Initiative: Problems in Florida Politics," in *State Government: CQ's Guide to Current Issues and Activities, 1986-1987,* ed. Thad Beyle (Washington, D.C.: Congressional Quarterly, 1986), 29-32.

51. David B. Magleby, *Direct Legislation: Voting on Ballot Propositions in the United States* (Baltimore: Johns Hopkins University Press, 1984).

52. Barnes, "Losing the Initiative," 2050-2051.

53. McGuigan, *The Politics of Direct Democracy,* 93-106.

54. Ibid., 58-59.

55. Ibid., 63.

56. Doris Graber, "Say It with Pictures: The Impact of Audio-Visual News on Public Opinion Formation" (Paper presented at the annual meeting of the Midwest Political Science Association, Chicago, April, 1987).

57. David Halberstam, *The Powers That Be* (New York: Alfred A. Knopf, 1979); and Peter Braestrup, *Big Story* (New York: Doubleday Anchor, 1978).

58. Peter M. Sandman and Mary Paden, "At Three Mile Island," in *Media Power in Politics,* ed. Doris Graber (Washington, D.C.: CQ Press, 1984), 267; and Christopher Flavin, "Reassessing Nuclear Power," in *The State of the World, 1987,* ed. Lester R. Brown, William V. Chandler, Christopher Flavin, Jodi Jacobson, Cynthia Pollock, Sandra Postel, Linda Starke, and Edward C. Wolf (New York: W. W. Norton, 1987), 57-80.

59. Lang and Lang, *The Battle for Public Opinion.*

60. Gladys Engel Lang and Kurt Lang, "The Media and Watergate," in *Media Power in Politics,* 209.

61. Cohn, "Fear of AIDS Is Spreading."

62. Linsky, *Impact,* 84.

63. Ibid., 86.

64. This case study adapted from Linsky, *Impact,* 71-78.

65. This case study adapted from ibid., 49-60.

66. "Liberals, Conservatives Share Initiative Success," 1.

67. McGuigan, *The Politics of Direct Democracy,* 46.

68. Ibid., 45-66.

69. Matlack, "Where the Big Winner was the Status Quo," 2748.

70. David B. Magleby, "Legislatures and the Initiative: The Politics of Direct Democracy," *State Government* (Spring 1986): 31-39.

71. Susan Hansen, "Extraction: The Politics of State Taxation," in *Politics in the American States,* ed. Virginia Gray, Herbert Jacob, and Kenneth N. Vines (Boston: Little, Brown, 1983), 441-442.

72. William Gormley, Jr., *The Politics of Public Utility Regulation* (Pittsburgh: University of Pittsburgh Press, 1983), 208.

73. As quoted in Barnes, "Losing the Initiative," 2047.

74. McGuigan, *The Politics of Direct Democracy;* and McGuigan, *Initiative and Referendum Report,* December 1986-January 1987.

75. McGuigan, *The Politics of Direct Democracy,* 67-92.

76. See, for example, Rufus P. Browning, Dale Rogers Marshall, and David H. Tabb, *Protest Is Not Enough: The Struggle of Blacks and Hispanics for Equality in Urban Politics* (Berkeley: University of California Press, 1984).

77. Commoner, "A Reporter at Large: The Environment"; Daniel A. Mazmanian and Jeanne Nienaber, *Can Organizations Change? Environmental*

Protection, Citizen Participation, and the Corps of Engineers (Washington, D.C.: Brookings Institution, 1979); and Lynton Caldwell, Lynton R. Hayes, and Isabel M. MacWhirter, *Citizens and the Environment* (Bloomington: Indiana University Press, 1976).

78. Carl E. Van Horn, "It's Just Dirt: A Case Study of Radium-Contaminated Dirt in Montclair, New Jersey" (New Brunswick, N.J., Eagleton Institute of Politics, Rutgers University, May 1987), photocopy.

79. As quoted in Neal R. Pierce, "Hats Off to the Pariah Barge Mobro," *Public Administration Times*, June 15, 1987, 2.

80. Cook, "P.R. on the Hill."

81. Lewis Wolfson, *The Untapped Power of the Press: Explaining Government to People* (New York: Praeger, 1986).

82. Graber, "Say It with Pictures."

83. James A. Barnes, "Pinning the Blame," *National Journal*, September 22, 1990, 2259-2263.

84. See Baumer and Van Horn, *The Politics of Unemployment*, 198-199.

85. As quoted by David Ignatius, "Maybe the Media Did Push NASA to Launch the Challenger," *Washington Post* national weekly edition, April 14, 1986, 19.

86. Ibid.

87. Linsky, *Impact*, 146-147.

88. Michael J. Robinson, "Public Affairs Television and the Growth of Political Malaise: The Case of the 'Selling of the Pentagon,'" *American Political Science Review* 70 (June 1976): 409-432.

89. Magleby, "Legislatures and the Initiative," 32.

90. Robert Guskind, "Big Green Light," *National Journal*, October 6, 1990, 2403.

91. Magleby, *Direct Legislation*.

FROM POLICY DOMAINS
TO POLICY RESULTS

PART III

The six chapters of Part II examined policy making in a number of different institutional settings, which help define different kinds of politics. The various politics can be compared and contrasted in terms of their scope and the intensity of conflict, the complexity of the problems to be dealt with, and the public salience of the issues. Political institutions, with their characteristic political environments, have their own distinctive styles for approaching policy issues and for formulating and adopting policy responses. *Describing* and *analyzing* the politics and policies of these various institutional settings was the purpose of Part II.

In Part III the questions are more normative and evaluative. Having studied how the public policy process works, the reader should begin to ask how well it works. Explaining and evaluating the performance of political institutions, and the value of the policies themselves, are formidable tasks that require judgments about complex conditions and outcomes that are difficult to measure. How well do government institutions preserve national ideals? Are government institutions excessively resistant to change? How much progress has the United States made in reducing racial discrimination? These questions have to be answered with considerable caution and care and some degree of uncertainty. The intention of the last three chapters is to stimulate constructive thinking about indisputably important matters.

Chapter 9 explores the functioning of American political institutions. Several questions are considered: How well do government and private sector institutions and their leaders respond to society's problems? To what extent do public officials lead, as opposed to follow, in the resolution of public problems? Will reforms in the structures and process of American politics make a difference? In short, the chapter raises broad questions about the relationships between governance and policy consequences and between the performance of American political institutions and the policy process.

Chapter 10 explores the subject of political change, and how American political institutions both promote and inhibit it. The broad question being examined is one of political feasibility; that is, how can agents of political change secure satisfactory responses from political institutions? A number of strategies for realizing institutional responsiveness are identified and evaluated in this effort to promote a clearer understanding of the relationship between political institutions and effective policy action.

Chapter 11 is a description and an evaluation of the consequences of American public policies. Several critical questions are addressed, including: What is known about the actual effects of major public policies? How effective are public policies in achieving announced objectives? How are public benefits and costs distributed in American society? What conception or definition of fairness or justice can be applied to this distribution? Although these questions cannot be answered definitively, evidence is provided for readers to consider in reaching their own judgments.

9 Institutional Performance

Politicians and ordinary citizens in the United States believe that properly structured political institutions are essential to freedom, democracy, and prosperity. The Constitution reflects this view in that it prescribes certain relationships among these institutions and between them and the citizens. Characteristic of the political culture of the United States is an unquestioning support for the election of legislatures and chief executives, an independent judiciary, and federalism. Despite the symbolic reverence for government institutions, they are continually examined and criticized by citizens and politicians alike. Explanations and evaluations of the government's performance are another political tradition.

The principal observations and conclusions offered in Part 2 provide a useful starting point for an explanation of institutional performance.

1. Corporations focus primarily on one goal, company profits, and boardroom politics is highly centralized—dominated by top executive officers—although pressure is growing to increase the number of actors involved and to consider other goals. Corporate decisions, made privately, have far-reaching consequences for society.

2. Bureaucracies like to define issues so that they are compatible with standard methods of operation. Policy decisions are made at various levels in the organization by administrative officials who are subject to a number of outside influences, including legislative committees, interest groups, chief executives, and courts. The standards for bureaucratic decisions are often explicit, but they can be quickly and dramatically changed by outsiders.

3. Legislatures react to many issues but are often slow to make decisions. Decision making is decentralized and subject to many influences, most notably well-organized, well-financed interests. Majorities rule when they are assembled, but the institutional structure of most American legislatures does not encourage the formation of decisive working majorities. Issue characteristics and contextual factors have a great impact on whether decisions are incremental, innovative, gridlocked, or symbolic, and on whether the decision-making process is slow or rapid, decentralized or centralized.

4. Chief executives address highly visible issues and dominate public perceptions about government, but the policy significance of a chief executive's term may be quite different from its image. The essence of chief executive leadership is the ability to persuade other policy makers, especially legislators, to transform chief executive priorities into policy. This part of the policy process is always difficult, even for presidents making foreign policy.

5. Courts consider a more restricted range of issues but are capable of taking decisive policy actions that sometimes have significant effects on society. The politics of judicial policy making is controlled by clear, specific procedures and criteria. The independence of the courts is rarely challenged.

6. Public opinions are influential in American politics. When highly salient issues are the subject of debate, the public may directly change public policy by acting through grass-roots organizations and expressing opinions via initiatives or referenda. But there are also instances in which public opinions are manipulated by media elites and government officials. The public, therefore, can be an active agent of democracy or a fairly weak, passive part of the policy process. Although it would be going too far to assert that media and governmental elites conspire to keep the public passive, political elites enjoy much more latitude in their policy actions when the public is passive.

Do these disparate observations form some larger picture? The answer is that American political institutions reflect rather faithfully their historical and philosophical roots. Their performance can be explained fairly well by reference to the free market/procedural democracy model of politics discussed in Chapter 2. American political institutions perform different roles in striving to uphold the basic principles of the market paradigm and the ideals of procedural democracy. Understanding these differences is the key to explaining institutional behavior. Boardroom politics and living room politics expand the system's repertoire of policy-making processes in interesting and important ways, some of which push the political process beyond the limits of procedural democracy.

An Analysis of Conventional Political Institutions

Courts and Legislatures

This analysis begins with a comparison of two very different political institutions: the Supreme Court and Congress. The Court acts on the basis of a philosophical view of procedural democracy; Congress understands procedural democracy on a more personal level. Why has the Court been the political institution most inclined to act decisively to secure the rights of disadvantaged minorities? The reason is that the

Supreme Court justices, in their role as interpreters of the Constitution, have been forced to define in legal terms what the main principles of this document mean in specific circumstances. The nature of the judicial process—using written opinions to establish precedents that guide future decisions—induces justices to take a philosophical look at constitutional principles. The logic of the Constitution is derived from a school of thought that places importance on certain procedural values. In the case of disadvantaged minorities, the guiding principle is equality of opportunity, and the specific means to achieve equality of opportunity are the equal protection and due process clauses of the Fourteenth Amendment. The context in which the Court makes decisions, and the process employed, encourage it to be decisive about the core principles of procedural democracy.

Supreme Court interpretations of constitutional principles have done a great deal for advantaged minorities as well as the disadvantaged. This outcome of Court decision making can be seen as another indication of the pervasiveness of the market paradigm, which discourages a distinction between market participants. An interesting example of the Court's adherence to market principles is the freedom granted to the press. The press has continually invoked the Constitution on behalf of its right to publish or display all sorts of misleading and distasteful material. Anyone who has stood in a check-out line at a grocery store can testify to the alluring, but false, headlines used by some newspapers and magazines. By defining libel and slander restrictively, the Court has allowed the press to continue printing sensational material. The courts believe there should be a marketplace of ideas in a free society and that valid ideas persist and invalid ideas perish in such a setting. Therefore, the Court protects and promotes economic and information markets.

The Court's strength depends on its adherence to the central principles of the Constitution, and the Court is generally reluctant to increase the number or expand the meaning of these principles. When the Court breaks new constitutional ground, however, as it did several times under Chief Justice Earl Warren, it is difficult for it to ignore subsequent cases pursuing related questions. Still, to venture too far into politics is to risk confrontation with Congress or the president, as has nearly occurred over issues such as busing and school prayer. The Court's role in the American system is to define and protect the rules of the game, but the game of politics and economics, for the most part, is played elsewhere. Nevertheless, gridlock and indecisiveness on the part of elected officials have made the Court a more prominent political player.

The Court must understand the rules of procedural democracy because it is their principal guardian. To perform this guardianship well, it must be somewhat removed from popular passions. Citizens and politicians

often fail to grasp some of the unpleasant nuances of procedural democracy—for example, that Communists and Nazis have the right of free
speech. The Court is not a very good vehicle for popular participation,
although class action suits and other advocacy efforts have made it a
forum in which some popular causes have been advanced. The Court will
never lead the way to radical social changes such as wealth redistribution,
public ownership of industry, or income guarantees, but it sometimes
forces the system to live up to its ideals, as when it required that public
schools admit children of all racial backgrounds.

The market paradigm fits well with cloakroom politics. Citizens
register their preferences for representatives who then try to give their
constituents what they want at the lowest political cost. Those who are
successful in retaining elected offices are, in most cases, efficient producers of political goods. Citizen preferences can be expressed individ-
ually or through political parties or interest groups. It is not surprising
that citizens prefer interest groups over individual action or parties.
Individual political action is often regarded as quixotic, and many
Americans find parties constraining—they do not always like their allies
within party coalitions. Interest groups are effective, aggressive, and
self-interested; they operate as if politics were a market where each
person's pursuit of self-interest is justified because it is part of a system
that maximizes collective welfare. The idea that interest group competition produces policies that serve the public interest is accepted by most
politicians and by many political scientists.[1]

Why, then, does Congress specialize in policies that carry particularized benefits, created in decentralized settings where interest groups are
accepted participants? Why is meaningful congressional policy action
difficult to bring about on matters that do not carry clear benefits for
constituents? The answer is that the legislative version of the market
paradigm encourages such behavior. Like businesses in a market, legislators like to make a profit, and their profits are measured in votes. To
secure comfortable electoral margins, they hand out benefits. Who gets
the benefits? Those who can pay with money or votes. Should the
legislators view this posture as improper or unethical? Not really. The
existence of winners and losers is quite consistent with the dominant
political philosophy of the nation, with the culture, and with the
institutional environment in which Congress operates. If one assumes
that the political marketplace is open, it is fair and just to respond to
articulated demands and to maximize voter satisfaction. Congress can
be compared with network television in that people seem to like most of
the programs on television, and they usually admire their representatives, but there are widespread complaints about the overall product.

It is alleged that one of the advantages of a free market economic system is its self-correcting tendency. If producers churn out too much of a product, its price falls; then new buyers are attracted, and eventually the price stabilizes. If only a little is produced of a product people want, its high price attracts the interest of potential producers. Periods of vigorous consumer spending generate rising prices and high levels of production, which eventually result in overstocked inventories and falling prices. These self-correcting factors are not purely automatic; rather, they are linked to government monetary and fiscal policies. But what about political markets? Are they self-correcting?

Recent American history suggests that congressional self-correction mechanisms do not function very well. Congress practiced dispensing benefits in exchange for votes from the 1950s through the late 1970s. Federal spending and taxes grew to the point that they became highly salient issues. Deficit spending provided a temporary refuge, but soon the deficits became an issue. Various reforms were tried, but none of them broke the pattern, and Congress now faces difficult, painful choices. This situation has helped somewhat to curb further fragmentation and has encouraged more centralized, party-based decision making. The failure of self-correcting mechanisms in markets and politics is a reminder of the necessity to maintain the distinction between theory and reality. Just as free markets do not always work as they are supposed to because entry is restricted, or because consumer knowledge is imperfect, large producers conspire, or various other distortions occur, political markets also have flaws. Voter knowledge of issues and candidates is not what it should be. Some groups, such as the poor, are not represented in a way that reflects their numerical significance. Some politicians engage in deceptive advertising and get away with it. Because elected politicians establish the rules of politics, it is not surprising that they use the rules for their own advantage and distort political markets. Political reform is always needed in a system that depends on periodic corrections of destructive tendencies.

Chief Executives and the Bureaucracy

The bureaucracy resembles the courts in some ways and the legislatures in others. It resembles the courts in having formal and specific decision-making criteria, though not so specific or complete as to eliminate discretion. The courts have laws, the Constitution, and legal precedents to guide their decisions, and bureaucratic agencies have written statutes and rules. The agencies resemble legislatures because they are highly vulnerable to politics. Agencies can be battered by citizen groups, legislators, chief executives, or judges, and their vulnerability has led them to assume a defensive posture toward the outside world. Standard procedures, public hearings, citizen advisory councils, bureaucratic hierarchy, and participation in subgovernments are all forms of defense. Even innovation, which bureaucracies are quite capable of, is usually a response to a threatening political environment.

American bureaucracies are highly political, not because they want to be, but because they are forced to be in order to defend themselves against stronger political institutions. The pluralist ethic operates in the administrative state. Bureaucratic officials know they cannot succeed if they offend powerful interests, and they need to know who are their agencies' friends and enemies in the legislature and the office of the chief executive. Agencies are increasingly conscious of their public image, but administrative policy makers cannot depend on voter satisfaction. They must be prepared—with defensible procedures and services—in case political headhunters start looking in their direction.

Chief executives are the principal agents of majoritarian rule in pluralist politics. They are the main corrective force against the potentially harmful effects of fragmentation toward which legislatures drift if left to their own devices. Chief executives often try to define a public interest that is separate and distinguishable from the sum of the parochial interests. They set certain goals—a cleaner environment, better schools, less poverty—and try to figure out ways to achieve them. The problem is that they have limited authority to act on their own, and convincing legislators to follow a clear and consistent policy path is extremely difficult.

The nature of this difficulty should be apparent by now. Legislators have their own relationships with voters and they do not like having them disrupted by chief executives. Legislators sometimes can be convinced that departure from their cherished mode of operation—giving subsidies to those who are organized—is necessary if a crisis is to be avoided, but they require a good deal of proof that conditions warrant such extraordinary action; they also need to be skillfully coaxed and made aware of public pressure. Some chief executives are able to provide the proof, the coaxing, and the pressure; others are not.

The strength of chief executives lies in their ability to command attention. Their efforts to assemble ruling coalitions and resolve crises provide most of the action and drama in politics, and the media find action and drama irresistible. People identify with chief executives and, for the most part, with their legislators, but not with the legislature as a whole. This interest and loyalty give chief executives a certain amount of leverage that can be used to pursue policy objectives. The greatest weakness of chief executives is their lack of power, influence, and authority over other political elites, which stems from the independence of government institutions and the weak party system.

The strength of the bureaucracy lies in its staying power. Bureaucracies are essential to the operation of government, and elected officials recognize this when they stop to think about it. Bureaucracies can be decisive, even innovative, but most show a marked preference for stability and continuity. The weakness of bureaucratic agencies is their formal and informal subservience to political institutions and interests. They can usually defend themselves against abolition, but they have to be constantly on their guard. The bureaucracy is the punching bag of American politics; it takes many blows but somehow remains intact.

Alternatives to Conventional Politics

Politics and public policies are not captives of government institutions. Private institutions also shape public policy, as do individual citizens and grass-roots organizations. Boardroom politics and living room politics reflect contrasting philosophical principles and cultural values.

For most corporate decision makers the market paradigm is the world view of utmost importance. They have no doubt about the value of the pursuit of private gain because it is accepted as an essential part of a system that maximizes social welfare by translating free market competition into overall economic efficiency and productivity. This world view is part of what enables corporate decision makers to lay off thousands of reliable skilled workers in Michigan, Pennsylvania, and Texas while they commit funds to new automobile and steel plants in Mexico, Taiwan, and South Korea. They argue that market forces should dictate wages, plant locations, and, ultimately, living patterns. Many corporate leaders understand that markets can be cruel to human beings, and they sympathize with the plight of their workers.

Rhetoric and reality are frequently at odds in the boardroom. Government intervention is abhorred when it costs money, but eloquently defended when it protects or subsidizes. Herbert Simon's pioneering work on corporate decision making demonstrates that private sector decision making is neither simple nor automatic.[2] Economic theory holds that businesses attempt to maximize their profits. Simon showed that in practice, large corporations with many decision makers normally choose options that satisfy as many interests as possible, rather than seek optimal profits in every circumstance. In this way, corporations resemble legislatures and public bureaucracies because bargaining and accommodation figure in their decision making. This kind of decision making is found particularly in publicly owned corporations, those that are subject to a great deal of government regulation, and those that are controlled by public officials. In such institutions decision makers are sometimes forced to confront the fact that the pursuit of private gain and the enhancement of society's well-being may not be synonymous.

"We the people," the opening phrase of the Constitution, conveys an unmistakable message: Government should be controlled by the citizenry. Certain Americans throughout the nation's existence have taken this message seriously. They have attempted to make the public an active instrument of policy making, to establish a more participatory mode of democracy. Their successes—town meetings, initiatives, referenda, recall, grass-roots movements—add important elements to American politics. Clearly, many Americans believe there is an important difference between pursuing private gain and serving organized interests, and the achievement of collective well-being. Because of this belief, living room politics is very much alive.

Living room politics, in its ideal form, comprises those occasions when politicians take a back seat to citizens, when popular feelings are registered in a clear, unmistakable way. This activism is what Jean-Jacques Rousseau saw as essential to democracy, and what contemporary advocates of participatory democracy would like to see strengthened in American politics. It would be naive to think that the dominant forces could be removed from any arena of politics, however. The mass media and communication technology have shown themselves to be both friend and foe of democratic reformers and activists. The media reach people, but they also bring their own priorities, procedures, and prejudices to the information they transmit. Grass-roots leaders and mainstream politicians sometimes find, to their mutual surprise, that they have much in common because they both have to deal with the media to succeed and they at times find this difficult and frustrating.

Direct democracy is easily perverted by demagoguery or captured by elite interests because symbolism and showmanship are so much a part of its practice in modern societies. Living room politics springs from the genuinely democratic impulse to allow people to determine the rules under which they will live. But we must be ever mindful of the gap between the ideal and reality in politics. Just as real markets are often woefully inadequate representations of the free market paradigm, initiatives, referenda, and grass-roots movements can be a far cry from the ideals of unitary or strong democracy.[3]

Performance Appraisal

The preceding brief analysis of American political institutions shows that these institutions are driven by philosophical principles, constitutional prescriptions, cultural traditions, and economic forces. Here the focus shifts to evaluation. How well do American political institutions work? Should Americans be satisfied with their performance? One way of approaching these questions is to take a broad look at society and examine how satisfied people are with it. American society has both positive and negative characteristics:

—individual freedom of thought, movement, religion, life-style, and consumption
—widespread prosperity, but a persistent underclass
—real and symbolic violence
—great cultural, educational, residential, and aesthetic diversity
—a materialistic, pragmatic value orientation
—a pervasive belief in the importance of individual and group competition
—a tradition that people have a recognized right to participate in politics

Some positive aspects of institutional behavior were pointed out in Part 2. Corporate boards are more representative and less incestuous than they used to be; some companies are innovative and public-spirited. Modern bureaucracies are seldom "captured" by narrow interests, and most listen to a wide variety of interests. Chief executives can be powerful agents of change and usually are given the leeway they need to be effective in crises. Even legislatures are capable of achieving major breakthroughs when political and economic conditions are ripe. The courts address some of society's most troublesome controversies in a forthright and reasonable manner, and they can, over time, foster significant changes. Public opinion, once aroused, has played a constructive role in disputes such as the Vietnam War and environmental protection.

Those who want a society that is more cohesive, peaceful, humanistic, cooperative, and democratic would be inclined to give American political institutions a less favorable overall evaluation. But such critics would acknowledge that the dominant forces in society—legal, social, political, and economic—have been pushing in a direction that is quite different from one they advocate; that is, toward a strong private sector and a government that acts cautiously to correct the problems that private sector competition leaves behind. American political institutions were not designed to be strong enough to chart an independent course for national development because the Founders feared what unchecked political institutions might do.

Nevertheless, Americans generally impose high standards of performance on their political institutions. They expect them to be open, efficient, and caring, in part because politicians make absurd claims about what government can accomplish. When the institutions fail to live up to these expectations (as they frequently do), citizens become disappointed, cynical, and distrustful.

These attitudes are reinforced by media attention to corruption in government. Coverage of allegations, investigations, indictments, and convictions conveys the sense that corruption is widespread in American government. In the 1980s some top officials of the Reagan administration were investigated, and in some cases removed, for committing improprieties or illegalities. Speaker of the House Jim Wright was hounded from office in 1989 because of his questionable financial arrangements and practices. More recently, five senators have been implicated in the affairs of convicted California savings and loan executive Charles Keating. Corruption, real or perceived, is a constant in American politics and can have significant effects on government.

In addition to facing a demanding audience, government institutions confront many difficult problems. Some of these problems, such as poverty, unemployment, pollution, and crime, may be unsolvable in a society with a dominant private sector and an ever-changing economy. But these are matters with which government is expected to grapple. The number of intractable problems at the top of the agenda seems to be increasing rather than decreasing, however. The New Deal bit off some of the easier problems: providing a reasonable income for the elderly and the disabled, guaranteeing worker rights, and building a physical infrastructure for economic development. Since the 1960s, the government has directed attention and money to the more difficult problems, such as poverty, but the returns have been disappointing. With budget deficits looming, policy makers have less ammunition to attack these problems. It is not only the nature of the institutions but the nature of the problems themselves that makes effective government action difficult.

Americans are fixers. If something is not working properly, the American instinct is to find a cure, usually through technology. This fix-it mentality is evident in almost every aspect of American life, including government and politics. Perceived malfunctions of government generate suggestions for reform. Americans, therefore, have established a civil service to correct the evils of the spoils system; created regulatory agencies to curb private sector abuses; reorganized the executive branch to make departments more responsive to chief executive preferences; and instituted initiative and referendum procedures to make government more responsive to citizens. There is an obvious and natural link between performance assessments and proposals for institutional reform.

Assessing institutional performance on the basis of broad societal outcomes—how healthy, wealthy, and wise a society is—leads to endless debates of questions that are difficult to answer with any precision. For this reason, it is necessary to introduce some guidelines and standards into an evaluative discussion. Six criteria of political institutions—

stability, representativeness, responsiveness, public awareness, efficiency, and competence—are identified as positive characteristics in the discussion that follows.

Stability

Government stability may be the most important standard by which to judge the success or failure of political institutions, and the American system would get high marks on anyone's stability scale. From a world perspective, the peaceful transfer of power from one regime, usually defined by its leader, to the next is still one of the most difficult problems for countries to solve. The U.S. constitutional prescriptions regarding presidential succession have passed all tests, including the Watergate crisis, with flying colors. Furthermore, when the institutions are unresponsive to strongly felt public desires, there are other mechanisms, such as living room politics, through which discontent can be expressed without threatening the stability of the system. The Founders believed that having a stable government was more important than having an enlightened one, and the performance of American institutions has generally reflected this priority.

Economic markets are not expected to be stable in the same way that governments are. Indeed, the private sector is supposed to be dynamic, innovative, and ever changing. But changing private sector markets can have profoundly painful human consequences, and liberal reformers have sought to smooth the rough edges of business cycles through economic planning and joint public and private ventures. The idea is that planning and partnerships can make less wrenching the transitions caused by declining industries, changing raw material costs, or population migrations.

Pennsylvania, and several other states, have formed economic planning and development groups to bring together representatives of business, labor, and government in efforts to avoid sudden, disruptive dislocations of workers and to improve business conditions.[4] At the national level, some Democrats in Congress have proposed the creation of an industrial development bank to encourage promising new industries and subsidize the modernization of older ones, and an economic cooperation council, composed of representatives of business, labor, and government, that would look at the position of American industries from a world perspective and advise businesses how best to compete with foreign enterprises. These institutional innovations are part of what has been called an industrial policy (see Chapter 10).[5] Legislation to establish such a bank or council has failed repeatedly to go very far in Congress, however, because Democrats and Republicans alike are wary of government involvement in capital investment decisions.[6]

Interest in these new kinds of institutional arrangements is, to a large extent, an outgrowth of the widespread recognition during the late 1970s that wages in core industries could not go higher if American companies were to stay competitive in world markets. In fact, the wages of many industrial workers have declined steadily since 1970, and the two questions that are asked with increasing frequency are: Will management share profits and the power to make operational and investment decisions with labor? Will profit sharing and cooperative management produce demonstrably better products and enhance worker productivity? This type of sharing would represent a major institutional change in boardroom politics.

Representativeness

A simple way of approaching the representativeness of political institutions is to ask: Who gets into policy-making circles and who does not? The answer to this question has been that well-educated white professional men, especially lawyers, tend to get in; women, blacks, the poor, and those with limited education do not. Despite years of effort to change the skewed demographic composition of policy-making groups, little progress has been made. Legislatures used to be biased in favor of rural areas, but much of this bias has been corrected by Supreme Court rulings upholding the principle of one person, one vote.[7] That public officials are better educated than the average citizen is not surprising, and it is not a primary concern of most critics. But other aspects of the leadership profile are troubling, as is the fact that the demographic patterns are quite consistent across institutions.

Women are drastically underrepresented in every institutional arena. They constitute about 7 percent of the members of Congress, top bureaucratic officials, and federal judges; 6 percent of the governorships; 3 percent of the mayoralties; and less than 1 percent of corporate chief executive officers. Women have made substantial gains in middle management in both the public and private sectors; more than half of the boards of directors of major companies include at least one woman.[8] Women have made their greatest gains in state legislatures and city councils, where their proportion rose from 5 percent in the early 1970s to 17 percent in the late 1980s.[9]

Blacks (12 percent of the population) and Hispanics (9 percent) have fared somewhat better. The proportion of blacks in top federal policy-making posts—in Congress, the courts, and the bureaucracies—is about 6 percent; the proportion of Hispanics is about 3 percent. Blacks have been elected to 5 percent of the state legislative seats and one governorship (Douglas Wilder of Virginia).[10] There were two Hispanic governors in the 1980s, Toney Anaya of New Mexico and Robert Martinez of

Florida (who is now the Bush administration's director of drug policy). Like women, blacks and Hispanics are still virtually absent from the tops of corporate hierarchies, but they have made significant advances in middle management; about one-third of all corporate boards have a minority member. A bright spot in minority representation is the steady election of black and Hispanic mayors in such major cities as Atlanta, Chicago, Detroit, Los Angeles, Newark, Kansas City, New Orleans, New York, Philadelphia, and San Antonio.

Women and ethnic minorities still face an uphill struggle in obtaining policy-making positions. This situation is long standing and will likely improve as the pool of women and minorities with the qualifications traditionally sought for top institutional positions—advanced degrees, relevant work experience, and favorable references—gradually expands.[11] Still, the preferences and commitments of those making appointments can make a big difference. Jimmy Carter made the appointment of more women and blacks to the federal courts a priority, and 30 percent of his appointments went to these groups. Ronald Reagan did not share this commitment; less than 15 percent of his court appointments went to women and blacks, although he did appoint the first woman to the Supreme Court.[12] In the late 1980s, a few historically male-dominated companies like International Harvester (now Navistar International), Nabisco, and R. J. Reynolds Tobacco (now RJR Nabisco, Inc.) broke with their own traditions and appointed women vice presidents.[13]

The selection processes are obviously different for elected officials. A critical problem for women is recruitment—getting women into state and local party organizations, getting some of them elected to state and local offices, and then supporting female candidacies for more visible, powerful offices. Racial prejudice seems an important reason blacks are not selected. White voters have shown a clear, sustained disinclination to vote for black candidates at all levels of government. For the most part, black candidates win only where blacks are the majority or near majority of voters. For example, in Jesse Jackson's second bid for the presidency in 1988, he ran ahead of all the other Democratic candidates in primaries where the electorate was more than 20 percent black (receiving more than 90 percent of the black vote and 38 percent overall), but he ran well behind Michael Dukakis (46 percent to 28 percent) in states where less than 20 percent of the Democratic voters were black.[14]

Responsiveness

Democratic political systems are supposed to be responsive to popular needs and preferences. Critics fault the U.S. government for not being more responsive to problems such as the spread of AIDS, ozone depletion, soaring medical costs, and homelessness. Many would argue that the federal government has a responsibility to take the lead in diagnosing and making plans to avert potential catastrophes because the private sector cannot be relied on to do so. Judgments about which problems are the most important at any given time are difficult to make with certainty, however. Some problems turn out to be less serious than they first appeared, and government institutions are seen as justified in having given them scant attention. Moreover, small steps may eventually yield substantial returns. Still, it seems to many that major American institutions often ignore problems for which no popular and easy solution is apparent, and they do so to the detriment of society as a whole.

One of the political reforms demanded most by ordinary citizens, scholars, and politicians concerns the ever-increasing amounts of money spent to get people elected and to influence officials once they are in office. Critics allege that politicians have to spend so much of their time attending to money matters—giving speeches to donor groups, attending fund-raisers, meeting with contributors, planning media promotions—that they have little time for the public's business. This problem is prevalent at the national and state levels. For most politicians, simply maintaining their positions in the highly competitive political world is almost a full-time job. In such an environment, politicians can be responsive to money, but to little else.

A variety of campaign finance reform proposals have been advanced, considered, and in some cases passed, by Congress since the mid-1980s, but none have been enacted into law. Democrats and Republicans have basic differences with regard to campaign financing that have prevented final action on reform legislation. Democrats have generally favored creation of some sort of public financing system, with spending limitations and possibly free television time and mailing privileges for major party candidates. Republicans abhor public financing. They favor giving political parties a larger role in campaign financing (allowing larger party contributions and more coordinated spending), and have recently shown an interest in eliminating political action committees altogether. Democrats, well aware of the Republicans' superior ability to raise money and of PACs' increasing contributions to incumbents, find little to like in the Republican proposals.

Beyond these basic differences lie many complexities. Since the Supreme Court has ruled that candidates cannot be forced to limit their spending,[15] it would seem that the resources (such as money and television time) available to candidates under a full-scale or modified public financing scheme would have to be ample enough to convince most candidates not to run outside the system, where they could raise and spend unlimited amounts. And would the public be willing to pay the hundreds of millions of dollars that would be required by public financing systems? Severe restrictions on PACs might also attract the interest of the Court, which in past cases has tended to view these organizations as important instruments of political expression. A multitude of constitutional and political issues must be resolved before serious federal campaign finance reform can be implemented.

If one of the principal concerns about campaign financing is the advantage incumbents have in raising money and getting reelected, then imposing limitations on the number of terms members of Congress can serve might be an attractive reform. Indeed, this idea gained popularity in the early 1990s, as several states (California, Colorado, and Oklahoma) passed term limitation proposals in referenda and President Bush publicly endorsed it.[16] A potential disadvantage of this reform is the possibility that Congress would be less able to compete with presidents in battles over public policy because of a lack of seasoned legislators.

Efforts to make corporations more responsive have included citizen protests and lobbying efforts by unions, churches, public interest groups, and grass-roots organizations. These protests have brought to the attention of corporate managers and boards, politicians, and the public such examples of corporate abuse and social irresponsibility as conduct of business operations in South Africa, discrimination against blacks and women, and the exposure of workers and the public to dangerous chemicals. Many of these efforts have stimulated changes in corporate policy and, perhaps more important, have served to politicize corporations. The once sedate stockholder meetings have been turned into forums for discussions of a wide range of political and social issues and of shareholder or proxy resolutions.

This movement has spawned a number of corporate reform proposals, most of which aim to make managers more accountable to individual and institutional investors and to the public. These proposals include giving all shareholders, regardless of the size of their investment, one vote on proxy resolutions; taking the selection of directors out of the hands of management and putting it into the hands of shareholders; and requiring that corporate boards include government or other outside representatives.[17] Although there have been a limited number of clear victories, the accountability movement has made corporate decision makers more aware of their public responsibilities. Because they are sympathetic to genuine expressions of public sentiment, some corporate managers willingly make policy changes, as long as the changes do not threaten profitability.

Public Awareness

The picture of the public's role in the political process presented thus far has not been entirely complimentary. Public opinion is often manipulated by political and media elites. Many expressions of public opinion suggest that Americans are concerned mainly about the economic well-being of their families and communities, that they are unreasonably impatient with government, and that they are ignorant of many aspects of national and international politics.

Proposals for greater public involvement in public policy decisions should be scrutinized carefully. The political education of citizens is not a high priority in the United States. Americans seem content to speak through their votes in elections and then to allow political elites representing various interests to hammer out the details of public policy. Some observers, however, believe that the ignorance, apathy, and parochialism of the American public are best viewed as a result, not a cause, of a political system that does not value democratic participation and does not encourage civic education.

Over the years many reforms have been advanced that are aimed at increasing the quantity and quality of citizen participation in American government. Political scientist Benjamin Barber and others believe that a comprehensive system of citizen education is needed to make American democracy work. He has proposed extensive reforms that begin with institutionalized neighborhood assemblies. According to Barber, Americans have no place to meet where they can learn about and discuss issues. Therefore, all neighborhood groups ranging from 5,000 to 25,000 citizens should have a facility that can be used for regular public meetings to discuss local and national issues. Once established, these assemblies could vote on local issues and choose local officials (in some cases by lot), be tied in to a national civic education electronic network, and eventually vote on national issues through electronic referenda. Barber also would establish universal citizen service requirements, democratize the workplace, and generally reorient society to focus on communal concerns and civic responsibilities.[18]

A more modest proposal along these lines is to institute a national referendum. State referenda have proven very popular—polls show that 70 percent to 75 percent of the public support them—and a majority of Americans favor the adoption of a national referendum.[19] A national referendum, which could be established by constitutional amendment, could be used to discourage or break deadlocks within Congress or between Congress and the president. If national institutions were deadlocked, the voters could settle disputed issues at the next election. Most other Western democracies have national referenda, and their use, which is infrequent, has not disrupted the process of government.

Having more television coverage of court proceedings might be another means of encouraging civic education. The presence of television cameras in Congress is now accepted, and they have not disrupted or fundamentally altered the legislative process. The audience usually is small, but not insignificant. Court proceedings in Florida have been televised since the late 1970s. The results have been generally positive—lawyers and judges do not play to the camera, and witnesses and jurors are not confused or intimidated by the cameras' presence. The response from citizens indicates a genuine fascination in seeing how the judicial process really works, a development that advocates of participatory democracy would no doubt applaud.[20]

Efficiency

American government is far from efficient in the way it makes and implements policies; many of the inefficiencies stem from basic tenets of the Constitution such as the separation of powers, bicameralism, and federalism. If stability is the strongest virtue of American government, inefficiency is probably its greatest vice.

That inefficiency is demonstrated by the difficulty Congress has in making controversial policy decisions and its penchant for policies that are symbolic, vague, weakened by compromise, and internally inconsistent. When Congress cannot decide, problems are either left unresolved or settled by the courts or the state governments. Bureaucratic implementation of ambiguous statutes frequently leads to new problems, and then to ongoing cycles of legislative patchwork, discretionary enforcement, public or interest group complaints, and more patchwork. Chief executives have trouble making government more efficient because legislatures often refuse to cooperate. Chief executives cannot force cooperation because legislators are virtually immune to sanctions that might lead to cohesive action. National and state policy is all too often a mishmash of statutory actions taken by small groups of legislators whose principal aim in formulating the statutes is to serve the interests of organized groups or of the localities they represent. Almost everyone gets something, but there is no clear policy direction and a great deal of duplication and lack of coordination occurs.

The solution? Students of the problem suggest some combination of discipline and central control. They see strong political parties, such as those found in Western Europe, as the best source of discipline. Political scientist Leon Epstein, however, believes that disciplined parties are unlikely ever to take hold in the United States because candidate-centered elections are deeply rooted in the culture and supported by elected officials. He does see value in reforms that would increase the role of parties in the control of campaign financing because raising money and providing campaign services are functions that American parties could potentially perform well.[21] Invigorated national parties might also push the government to act more efficiently.

Another approach to discipline is what political scientist Theodore Lowi has called "juridical democracy." [22] What Lowi had in mind was that Congress should be prevented from passing so many ambiguous laws. The Supreme Court could take the first step by resurrecting the reasoning it used in declaring unconstitutional Franklin Roosevelt's National Industrial Recovery Act. The Court said that policies that delegate power to administrative agencies without defining the precise standards that should be used during implementation are invalid under the Constitution.[23] Lowi would like to see this logic applied to modern statutes that fail to specify the rules of implementation and therefore convey vast discretionary power to administrative agencies. Presidents could take a step in this direction by refusing to sign vague bills into law. These types of actions, Lowi believes, would force Congress to discipline itself to enact statutes with clear standards. He also would have Congress periodically review all its laws to prevent overlap and other inefficiencies.[24]

Another reform proposal that would complement the strengthening of parties by enhancing the power of presidents is to increase the term of House members from two years to four and possibly to decrease Senate terms to four years. The idea is to tie congressional electoral fortunes more directly to those of presidents, who have an obvious stake in emphasizing party loyalty. Perhaps more important, it would do away with midterm elections, which almost invariably contribute to gridlock among policy makers, because the president's party tends to lose seats. Such a change would encourage a more national outlook among House members and should reduce their obsession with reelection, casework, and pork-barrel policies.

A different gridlock-breaking device is the line-item veto. Governors in forty-three states have this power, and many presidents have sought it. To date, proposals to give the president a line-item veto have failed to get very far in Congress, in large part because of the continuing partisan division between the two institutions. State-level experience with the line-item veto is difficult to apply to the national government for two reasons. The line-item veto powers of governors vary from state to state, and most states are constitutionally bound to balance their budgets.[25] Nevertheless, the line-item veto would be a powerful addition to the presidential arsenal of policy-making weapons. It would give presidents the threat to veto pet projects of legislators and thereby enhance presidential bargaining power. Whether this change would result in greater government efficiency and spending reductions is less clear and would depend on the presidential policy objectives. Governors have used the line-item veto most frequently when they faced majorities of the opposition party; such usage confirms the suspicion that a presidential line-item veto would be used mainly for partisan purposes.[26]

Competence

In evaluating the competence of institutional actors, we ask whether American policy makers are knowledgeable and skilled enough to accomplish their tasks. Most elected officials are lawyers or business-men, which means that, on average, they are well educated. State and local politics traditionally serve as the first test of aspiring politicians' interest and ability; the more successful move on to Congress or state executive positions. Those who make it that far tend to stay in politics a long time. They are career politicians and policy makers.

Legislatures. The U.S. Congress stands out among the national legislatures in the world for the low turnover of its members and its preponderance of lawyers. Nearly 50 percent of the members of recent Congresses have been lawyers, whereas in most West European countries lawyers constitute about 20 percent of the legislatures. Most West European legislatures include more journalists, teachers, intellectuals, and blue-collar workers than does the U.S. Congress.[27] Low turnover among legislators would seem to earn Congress low marks for representativeness and accountability, but high marks for competence, although much depends upon what kind of competence is sought. American legislators know a good deal about their specialized committee decisions, but they tend to be weak when it comes to formulating long-term answers to major national or international questions.

Bureaucracies. The American bureaucracy is not generally regarded as one of the the most professional or competent in the world. The civil service system ensures a certain level of competence, but training for public service is not taken as seriously in the United States as it is in Western Europe, nor are career civil service positions prized as highly. In France, for example, top civil service jobs have been controlled for years by the members of elite Parisian families, who go to special schools and see themselves as guardians of the national interest.[28] Except for officers of the Foreign Service, most American administrators see themselves as employees of a specific agency or department, rather than as members of a corps of public servants. The prevailing public view is that the American civil service system encourages mediocrity rather than excellence. The public's view is neatly captured in a survey of individuals who had recently dealt with a bureaucratic agency. Seventy-one percent of those polled thought their particular problem had been handled well, but only 30 percent had a generally favorable impression of bureaucratic performance.[29]

Bureaucratic reforms at the national and state levels typically revolve around the same themes: providing incentives for better performance, making it easier for managers to fire unproductive employees, establishing clear lines of authority, and improving the image of public employees. The results of bureaucratic reforms at the national level have been modest. In 1978, at President Jimmy Carter's behest, Congress passed a major civil service reform act that created a Senior Executive Service (SES) composed primarily of career executives with outstanding records who were willing to trade tenure and job security with a particular agency for the chance to get large bonuses and faster promotions by filling in wherever they were needed most in the executive branch. The new law also required agencies to make performance assessments of all their employees and to use these appraisals as the basis for firing incompetents and rewarding strong performers.

Those who have assessed the results of these changes agree that they have been minor. The SES has not been used consistently by presidents and department secretaries as a source of talented, neutral managers, mostly because top executive branch officials were not looking for neutral managers to help them run their agencies. A distressingly high percentage of senior executives have been successfully recruited by the private sector in what some regard as a serious government "brain drain." [30] The employee performance assessments have been difficult to develop, are viewed negatively by nearly all federal workers, and have not resulted in noticeably higher firing rates. Merit pay systems have been very difficult to implement, especially in agencies undergoing budget cuts, and merit pay does not appear to be a primary motivator for employees.[31]

Courts. The power and prestige of American courts are unrivaled in the world. They do far more than merely apply laws to specific cases; the courts often make policy, especially when other institutions are unwilling to do so. One way to ensure judicial competence is to improve the quality of appointments to the bench. Chief executives can appoint advisory panels to make recommendations; groups of citizens and legal professionals then can narrow the list of potential nominees to candidates with outstanding records and abilities. The use of advisory panels would not eliminate partisan considerations, but it could ensure that only truly competent individuals are considered. President Carter created panels of this sort to assist him in making circuit court appointments, but the panels were dropped by President Reagan. President Bush has relied on the Justice Department to help him screen nominees, and his slowness in filling vacancies has been criticized by several members of the Senate Judiciary Committee.[32]

The proper connection between the law and science is increasingly of interest in modern society, and the competence of judges is tested when they confront highly technical questions. Agencies like the Environmental Protection Agency make complex scientific assessments about what industries can and should do to comply with environmental statutes, and their assessments are often contested in court. These cases can be difficult for judges. Although they are inclined to defer to agency expertise on technical matters, they maintain a role for themselves in taking a "hard look" at the evidence and the procedures an agency employed in making its assessment.[33]

Appeals court judge Harold Leventhal, who had extensive experience with such matters, proposed that judges hire scientific experts in highly technical cases. The experts would not judge the adequacy of agency rulings but would assist judges "in understanding problems of scientific methodology and in assessing the reliability of tests conducted by the agency in light of specific criticisms." [34] Such individuals would be similar to special consultants or law clerks, in that their advice to judges would not be a matter of legal record, and they would not normally be cross-examined.[35] Similar proposals have been made with regard to the interpretation and use of social science evidence to help judges make informed decisions about conditions in mental health facilities, prisons, and schools.[36]

Chief executives. If national politics are the leading edge of American politics, then presidential experiences should shed some light on the future for governors and mayors. One problem is that the public relations aspects of the job have become so dominant in the media age that competence is now what good looks used to be—a desirable quality, but not necessary. Chief executives can be, and are, packaged and sold all over the country. The more salient the politics, the more likely it is that public relations specialists will dominate. In the United States, chief executive politics is the most visible form of politics and, therefore, the most prone to deceptive appearances.

Successful chief executives must be able to perform their many difficult political and administrative tasks with the knowledge that many people are watching and waiting to exploit every failing, both public and private. Furthermore, because they lack the authority to do everything they would like, their leadership is often more a matter of symbolism than substance. The ability to convincingly utter symbolic rhetoric in front of huge, but usually remote, audiences is rapidly becoming the primary qualification for chief executives.

Thus far most states and localities have benefited from more visible and competitive politics. It was not all that long ago—prior to 1940—

that state governments were weak and, in many cases, corrupt. Governors' powers were limited; their offices were poorly staffed; money and favor-trading pervaded legislatures; and the bureaucracy was filled with patronage appointees who did more political work than government work. A good deal of progress has been made since then. Governors have been granted broader powers, and they exercise them more vigorously. State legislatures sit longer, and legislators are better paid and less corrupt. Bureaucracies have been enlarged and revamped, with most appointees governed by merit systems. Innovative policies are coming from the states: education reform, far-reaching environmental statutes, welfare-for-work programs, requirements that businesses provide day-care for their employees' children, joint public and private economic development efforts, and others. Most big city governments have also become more professional in outlook and practice. But many mayors, as well as governors, are beginning to experience the public relations demands presidents know all too well, with the result that symbolism tends to be elevated over substance.

Boardrooms. Private sector competence and effectiveness are difficult to characterize in general terms. The nation has experienced a steady stream of economic difficulties since the 1960s, and at least some of these problems can be attributed to private sector decisions and practices. The most important recent example was the creation of the junk bond market and the free-wheeling practices of deregulated savings and loan executives, which together led to the rapid escalation of real estate prices and then to the collapse of real estate markets in many parts of the country. These ill-advised private sector activities have cost the public, and especially many individual investors, billions of dollars. Still, in comparison with most of the rest of the world, Americans enjoy a very high standard of living, and there are consistent signs of innovation and vitality in the private sector.

American industry has depended for years on the high-volume manufacture of standardized products by workers who performed repetitive tasks for union-negotiated wages. Consensus is growing that this production style cannot compete effectively against West European and Japanese systems that are more flexible and yield higher-quality products, or against cheaper systems, organized along American lines, in developing countries. The difficulties of the American steel and auto industries are attributed by most analysts to the failure of corporate leaders to modernize plants and change their product orientation soon enough to avert disaster. Problems of this sort are to be expected in market economies, however, and they can even provide valuable lessons for the future.

The experience of the steel and automobile industries, for example, seems to have led to a new consensus about the importance of investment in infrastructure, research and development, and methods to improve worker productivity. By the early 1990s, manufacturing accounted for 23 percent of the GNP, up from 20 percent in 1982. This increase was attributable to very high productivity rates in the 1980s because the number of jobs in manufacturing did not increase.[37] Most Americans believe the future of U.S. industry rests with high-technology products, precision manufacturing, telecommunications, and farming, in which the United States has what economists call a "comparative advantage." The private sector has become much more attentive to international markets, a fitting development because that is where the fate of American industry will be determined.

Summary

The competence of American policy makers is not the main issue with regard to institutional performance. The more fundamental issue is political will or the lack thereof. Overall, one of the greatest failings of American public institutions is their indecisiveness. This failing is obvious to anyone who has studied the workings of Congress, where indecision in the form of stalling, ambiguous statutory language, symbolic responsiveness, and passing the buck has been raised to an art. Former Ohio State football coach Woody Hayes always explained his reluctance to use the forward pass by saying, "There are three things that can happen when you pass—completion, incompletion, and interception—and two of them are bad." This philosophy captures the essence of legislators' attitudes: faced with the choice between taking forceful action to resolve a problem, which could be ineffective or unpopular, or using one of their polished methods of delay, obfuscation, and pacification, they will invariably choose the latter.

Indecisiveness is not simply a product of the fear of making mistakes. It also stems from the fixation that elected officials have with public opinion and the extraordinary role played by interest groups in American politics. The socialization of conflict and increased public and group participation in decision making have produced, in a political system of fragmented power, more gridlock than direction, which is another way of saying that democratic decision making is cumbersome. Powerful groups in society often disagree about the steps that should be taken to resolve problems. The government apparatus is designed to reflect such disagreement, and it does, in the form of inaction. This inaction then becomes the target of reformers and other critics because chief executives are almost always unsuccessful in charting a clear course of government policy, bureaucrats are paranoid because they never know when elected officials are going to turn on them, and the public is confused and disillusioned.

In the 1990s the effects of gridlock and indecision at the national level are placing increasing demands on the states. The inability of presidents and Congresses to chart a clear course for national policy are forcing states to make tough decisions about everything from social welfare and taxes to the environment. Inaction by representative institutions at all levels of government has also increased the significance of living room politics (initiatives, referenda, and grass-roots movements) and courtroom politics. The growing conservativism of the U.S. Supreme Court further adds to the importance of state-level politics, particularly the importance of state supreme court decisions.

But overly harsh judgments about the performance of American political institutions may not be fully justified. In this postindustrial age, government institutions of all sorts face vastly expanded policy agendas. The rapidity of change in society denies policy-making institutions any opportunity to rest on their laurels. A steady stream of demands can be heard from groups who want more or less from government, as technological and social developments alter the environment within which they operate. As the government has taken on new tasks and sought to satisfy more demands, its old responsibilities have not withered away. Instead, the earlier commitments usually have become permanent. The inability to shed old baggage is another reason why government institutions are reluctant to take on new problems. This reluctance to act has a positive side: It reduces the chances of making serious mistakes.

The reform impulse enjoys continuing popularity in the United States because it offers methods for overcoming governmental problems that will not cause a great deal of pain. Americans are always searching for a "quick fix." But the reality of change is that it is slow and that it is a cumulative process rather than a single decisive act. Some of the most significant reforms, such as equal rights for women and minorities, have followed a long, painful course.

In many ways the question is whether private sector performance is rewarding enough to justify a government that is so timid that it rarely acts in a disruptive way. Whenever such a question is posed, the answer that almost invariably comes forward is that "the people" should decide. But are the people in any position to decide? Are alternatives stated in a way that people can understand and make reasoned judgments about what is in society's best interest? In general, the answer to these questions is no, primarily because a good deal of what the people know has been packaged for them by people who have a vested interest in keeping things much as they are. Nevertheless, history makes clear that when conditions get bad enough, decisive popular action is likely. In a free society, widespread suffering can lead to strong expressions of citizen preference and significant changes in institutions and policies. Citizen inattentiveness to politics and government and policy gridlock are an indication of relative prosperity. Perhaps there is some wisdom in letting peoples' sense of economic well-being, or lack of it, determine the government's policy.

Notes

1. For the classic statements of pluralist theory, see Robert A. Dahl, *Who Governs?* (New Haven, Conn.: Yale University Press, 1963); or Nelson W. Polsby, *Community Power and Political Theory* (New Haven, Conn.: Yale University Press, 1963). For the classic critiques of the pluralist position, see Peter Bachrach and Morton S. Baratz, "Two Faces of Power," *American Political Science Review* 56 (December 1962); or Theodore J. Lowi, *The End of Liberalism*, 2d ed. (New York: W. W. Norton, 1979).

2. See Herbert A. Simon, *Administrative Behavior: A Study of Decision-Making Processes in Administrative Organizations* (New York: Macmillan, 1957); or James G. March and Herbert A. Simon, *Organizations* (New York: Wiley, 1964).

3. Jane Mansbridge, *Beyond Adversary Democracy* (Chicago: University of Chicago Press, 1983); Benjamin R. Barber, *Strong Democracy: Participatory Politics for a New Age* (Berkeley: University of California Press, 1984).

4. See Walter H. Plosila and David N. Allen, "State Sponsored Seed Venture Capital Programs: The Pennsylvania Experience," *Policy Studies Review* 6 (February 1987): 529-537; Walter H. Plosila, "A Comprehensive and Integrated Model: Pennsylvania's Ben Franklin Program," *Technological Innovation*, ed. D. O. Gray and W. Hetener (Amsterdam: New Holland, 1986), 261-272; and David Osborne, *Laboratories of Democracy* (Boston: Harvard Business School Press, 1990), chap. 2.

5. For the most widely recognized statement of the industrial policy position, see Ira C. Magaziner and Robert B. Reich, *Minding America's Business: The Decline and Rise of the American Economy* (New York: Harcourt Brace Jovanovich, 1982).

6. See Ross K. Baker, "The Bittersweet Courtship of Congressional Democrats and Industrial Policy" (Paper presented at the annual meeting of the Midwest Political Science Association, Chicago, April 1986).

7. The most important case in this area was *Baker v. Carr*, 369 U.S. 186 (1962).

8. For figures on the bureaucracy, see Randall B. Ripley and Grace A. Franklin, *Congress, the Bureaucracy, and Public Policy*, 5th ed. (Pacific Grove, Calif.: Brooks/Cole, 1991), 30; for Congress, see *Congressional Quarterly Weekly Report*, November 10, 1990; on the courts, see Everett Carll Ladd, *The American Polity*, 2d ed. (New York: W. W. Norton, 1987), 290; and Sheldon Goldman and Thomas Jahnige, *The Federal Courts as a Political System*, 3d ed. (New York: Harper & Row, 1985), 55. Corporate figures were taken from *Business Week*, June 22, 1987, 72-78, and April 5, 1991, 52-60; *Wall Street Journal*, July 17, 1987, 21; and Dell Mitchell, "The Boardroom: Still a Frater-

nity?" *New England Journal of Public Policy* 6 (Spring-Summer 1990): 91-97.

9. Robin Toner, "Gains Predicted for Women in Races for Statewide Office," *New York Times*, May 19, 1986, A1, B7; and Cathleen Douglas Stone, "Women and Power: Women in Politics," *New England Journal of Public Policy* 6 (Spring-Summer 1990): 157-161.

10. Figures were taken from Ripley and Franklin, *Congress, the Bureaucracy, and Public Policy*, 30; *Congressional Quarterly Weekly Report*, November 10, 1990, 3835; Goldman and Jahnige, *The Federal Courts*, 55; and *The State of Black America* (New York: National Urban League), 1987.

11. See *Business Week*, June 22, 1987, 72-78.

12. See Goldman and Jahnige, *The Federal Courts*, 55.

13. See *Business Week*, June 22, 1987, 72-78.

14. Rhodes Cook, "The Nominating Process," in Michael Nelson, ed., *The Elections of 1988* (Washington, D.C.: CQ Press, 1989), 53.

15. *Buckley v. Valeo*, 424 U.S. 1 (1976).

16. The term limitation measures passed in Oklahoma and California apply only to state legislators, but members of Congress were included in the Colorado measure. Legal scholars doubt that it is constitutional for states to limit the terms of federal officials in this way.

17. See David Vogel, *Lobbying the Corporation* (New York: Basic Books, 1978), 219-220.

18. Benjamin R. Barber, *Strong Democracy* (Berkeley: University of California Press, 1984), chap. 10.

19. See David Magleby, "Legislatures and the Initiative: The Politics of Direct Democracy," *State Government* 59 (Spring 1986): 34; and James L. Sundquist, *Constitutional Reform and Effective Democracy* (Washington, D.C.: Brookings Institution, 1986).

20. See Norman Davis, "Television in Our Courts: The Proven Advantages, the Unproven Disadvantages," *Judicature* 64 (August 1980): 85-92.

21. Leon D. Epstein, *Political Parties in the American Mold* (Madison: University of Wisconsin Press, 1986), chap. 9.

22. Lowi, *The End of Liberalism*, 298.

23. *Schechter Poultry Co. v. United States*, 295 U.S. 495 (1935).

24. Lowi, *The End of Liberalism*, chap. 11.

25. In some states governors can veto not only appropriations, but also statutory language included in appropriations bills; in other states they can only veto appropriations. In some of the cases where statutory language is covered by the line-item veto, the veto can be used only to strike language from the bill; in other cases it can be used to change the language. Some states even allow governors to change appropriations figures, not just to veto them. Additional variations exist. See James J. Gosling, "Wisconsin Item-Veto Lessons," *Public Administration Review* 46 (July-August 1986): 292-300.

26. See ibid., 293; and Glen Abney and Thomas Lauth, "The Line-Item Veto in the States: An Instrument of Fiscal Restraint or an Instrument of Partisanship?" *Public Administration Review* 45 (May-June 1985): 1110-1117.

27. Lawyers and businessmen usually make up a large percentage of West European conservative party legislators; the other parties have many educators, journalists, and political organizers as candidates. See J. Blondel, *Comparative Legislatures* (Englewood Cliffs, N.J.: Prentice-Hall, 1973), 76-91; and *Guardian*, London, England, May 29, 1987.

28. See Ezra Suleiman, *Politics, Power, and Bureaucracy in France* (Prince-

ton, N.J.: Princeton University Press, 1974).

29. See Daniel Katz, Barbara A. Gutek, Robert L. Kahn, and Eugenia Barton, *Bureaucratic Encounters: A Pilot Study in the Evaluation of Government Services* (Ann Arbor, Mich.: Institute for Social Research, 1975), 120-121.

30. See Howard Rosen, *Servants of the People: The Uncertain Future of the Federal Civil Service* (Salt Lake City: Olympus, 1985), 76.

31. Ibid., 80-81.

32. See Joan Biskupic, "Bush Lags in Appointments to the Federal Judiciary," *Congressional Quarterly Weekly Report*, January 6, 1990, 38-42.

33. Harold Leventhal, "Environmental Decisionmaking and the Role of the Courts," *University of Pennsylvania Law Review* 122 (January 1974): 514.

34. Ibid., 550.

35. Ibid., 550-555.

36. See Peter W. Sperlich, "Social Science Evidence in the Courts: Reaching Beyond the Adversary Process," *Judicature* 63 (December-January 1980): 280-289; and David M. O'Brien, "The Seduction of the Judiciary: Social Science and the Courts," *Judicature* 44 (June-July 1980): 8-21.

37. Sylvia Nasar, "American Revival in Manufacturing Seen in U.S. Report," *New York Times*, February 5, 1991, A1, D8.

10   Political Feasibility

A key feature of the American political system is the slow pace of change. Our political institutions were designed to inhibit change, not to facilitate it. Nevertheless, significant policy changes have occurred in recent years, at all levels of government, in such areas as welfare policy, educational policy, and environmental policy. The challenge that confronts public policy activists, whether inside or outside government, is how to develop strategies that facilitate political success. Depending on one's perspective, success may consist of dramatic change, incremental change, or perpetuation of the status quo.

In this chapter, we examine political institutions and their role in both promoting and undermining political feasibility. We develop a perspective of political feasibility that differs somewhat from the prevailing norm, which is to view political feasibility analysis, for the most part, as the study of constraints in the political system.[1] Although we acknowledge the importance of constraints, we also stress that political institutions may be viewed as presenting opportunities and that they should be viewed as manipulable. Political feasibility analysis is more than identifying obstacles in an obstacle course.

After establishing that institutions may both facilitate and undermine political feasibility, we discuss several strategies for enhancing political feasibility. Here we draw on examples from a variety of settings, including the boardroom, the living room, and the familiar corridors of power. Our central theme is that a keener understanding of political institutions is essential to effective policy action.

Alternative Perspectives on Institutions

Institutions as Constraints

Political institutions impose constraints on those who wish to shape public policy. The structures, rules, and norms of American politics must be understood by those who seek to work successfully within the system. Even protestors, who work outside the system to some extent, must understand political institutions well enough to avoid lost causes and squandered resources.

The fragmented congressional committee system illustrates the constraints that political institutions present. Congress is divided and subdivided into numerous committees and subcommittees, with overlapping jurisdictions. The diffusion of responsibility on Capitol Hill makes it extremely difficult to get meaningful legislation passed in certain policy areas. For example, twenty-one committees and forty-three subcommittees of Congress have significant energy policy jurisdiction.[2] Under such circumstances, it is small wonder that the United States has no energy policy, according to some critics. Congressional fragmentation does not preclude major change but it does make change quite difficult. Thus the reauthorization of the Superfund program, which provides funding to clean up hazardous waste sites, took a total of three years. Each step of the authorization process seemed agonizingly slow. The appointment of House conferees was delayed a few months because of a squabble between the Energy and Commerce Committee and the Public Works Committee over which conferees would have jurisdiction over leaking underground storage tanks and other issues.[3] These obstacles were eventually overcome but only after the perspectives of five House committees were taken into account. The result—a patchwork of compromises—failed to satisfy many critics.

Federalism, a hallmark of our political system, presents a similar set of challenges, though they are somewhat more concentrated at the policy implementation stage. We normally think of federalism as requiring the consent of two or three sets of actors (federal, state, and sometimes local governments). In practice, however, major federal programs must be funneled through regional federal administrators and sometimes locally based federal administrators as well. Both cities and counties may be involved. And in education policy, environmental policy, and other issue areas, special districts, such as school districts and sewerage districts, also have a role to play. When Jeffrey Pressman and Aaron Wildavsky studied the implementation of a federal economic development program in Oakland, California, they concluded that seventy different agreements, involving dozens of different actors, were needed for the program to work. With tongues only partly in cheek, they estimated that if the probability of agreement at each stage were 95 percent (an extraordinarily optimistic assumption), the combined probability of the program's working as planned would be .00395.[4] Not surprisingly, the program did not work as planned.

Serious implementation problems often arise when implementing grant programs or making case-by-case decisions. But administrative rule making presents formidable constraints as well. At the federal level, since 1946, administrative rules must be formulated through a "notice and comment" process spelled out in the Administrative Procedure Act.

At first glance, these requirements appear to be quite modest. Yet if an issue attracts considerable interest, hearings and deliberations may drag on for months, even years. In one notorious instance, the Federal Trade Commission took nearly twelve years to define peanut butter. Since the early 1970s administrative adoption of "major rules" has become even more cumbersome. Under Office of Management and Budget requirements that have evolved in the course of several presidencies, most federal agencies must submit a proposed rule to OMB. The final rule must also be submitted to OMB for its approval. OMB may delay approval of the proposed rule or the final rule indefinitely, with only token opportunities for review. Not surprisingly, this development has discouraged administrative rule making.[5]

Some institutional constraints are structural, others are procedural, and still others are, in effect, intellectual or conceptual. A good example of the last category is the courts' long-standing reliance on precedent as the basis for much judicial decision making. This emphasis on precedent has its roots in the common law tradition of Anglo-Saxon jurisprudence, and it has become institutionalized in the doctrine of *stare decisis* (let the decision stand). Attorneys who argue before juridical tribunals must be able to cite a precedent (decision in an earlier case) to justify a favorable decision in the current case. The extent of this adherence varies from court to court. For example, federal appeals court judges view their role in somewhat more expansive terms than do federal district court judges.[6] Even federal appeals court judges rely heavily on precedent, however.[7] Thus, precedents impose real constraints on litigants who seek redress from the courts.

Institutions as Opportunities

Just as institutions impose constraints, they also present opportunities. To some extent this may be described as the "ruby slippers" phenomenon—the sudden recognition of powers that we have had for a long time. After wearing her ruby slippers throughout many misadventures in the land of Oz, Dorothy eventually learned how to use them to good advantage. Similarly, all of us can take advantage of our political institutions if we are perceptive enough to recognize extraordinary opportunities embedded in our political structures, rules, and norms.

A good example of such an opportunity is the initiative, which has been available to citizens in twenty-one states for several decades. During the 1970s and 1980s citizens began to take advantage of the initiative, by placing proposals on ballots in record numbers. Many of these initiatives were successful. In particular, initiatives in California and other states helped to launch a taxpayers' rebellion that culminated in property tax limitations of considerable importance.

Another example of institutional opportunities has been the growing reliance upon state supreme courts to sustain and expand the scope of civil rights and civil liberties. During the 1980s, the U.S. Supreme Court began to restrict its interpretation of the Bill of Rights, especially in criminal justice cases. Some civil libertarians immediately recognized that they might instead do battle in state courts, where state constitutions might be properly interpreted by state judges, with perspectives that differed from those of the Supreme Court.[8] These lawsuits have resulted in some significant victories at the state level.

State court judges who are elected are more responsive to public opinion, especially on highly salient issues, than their appointed counterparts. James Kuklinski and John Stanga found that some state judges gave harsher sentences in marijuana cases after local referenda revealed support for tougher criminal penalties for the use of that drug. In contrast, other state judges gave lighter sentences in marijuana cases after local votes calling for less severe penalties or outright decriminalization.[9] In short, elected judges present different opportunities than appointed judges.

As the preceding example suggests, one person's constraint is another person's opportunity. Thus the same institutional configuration will be interpreted quite differently by those who favor and those who oppose change—liberals and conservatives, Democrats and Republicans. The classification of a given institutional arrangement as a constraint or an opportunity is a matter of interpretation. As the old adage reminds us, "Where you stand depends on where you sit."

Institutions as Manipulable Variables

Political institutions, like other institutions, change over time, sometimes suddenly. Institutions can be shaped and reformed to suit the needs or hopes of political activists. And new institutions can be created, ranging from new modes of channeling citizen complaints (such as ombudsmen) to new modes of delivering public services (such as privatization).

Among the more interesting institutional transformations of recent years has been the professionalization of state legislatures. Most state legislatures today consist of full-time legislators, who meet every year, are reasonably well paid, and are supported by capable legislative staffs. For better or for worse, turnover is lower than it used to be. This may mean greater expertise but less responsiveness. Political power is also more decentralized than it used to be. More legislators participate in a more meaningful way in the policy-making process. Consensus is more difficult to achieve, however. All of these changes have occurred quite rapidly and in most states.

Although most state legislatures have moved more or less in the same direction, other institutions have followed a less direct evolutionary path. Consider, for example, standing to sue or the right to take a case to court. During the 1970s, the U.S. Supreme Court relaxed standing requirements, allowing environmental groups, welfare groups, and consumer groups to represent the interests of broad, diffuse interests in court.[10] During the 1980s, the Supreme Court moved in the other direction, tightening standing requirements and reducing access to the federal courts. In both instances, the federal judiciary reformed itself by changing important rules of the game.

Institutional change may be either broader or narrower than these examples suggest. Some institutional transformations redefine the very role of government, whereas others concentrate on a particular aspect of the policy-making process. Privatization is a particularly interesting reform because it redefines the boundaries between the public and the private sectors. In many instances, it provides for public funding but private production of services. This arrangement is often referred to as "contracting out." For years, state and local governments have contracted out a wide variety of services, such as data processing and trash collection. The federal government also relies heavily on contracting, as when the Defense Department purchases weapons systems from for-profit firms.

Increasingly, privatization is being proposed—and tried—in more controversial settings. For example, some have proposed the privatization of medium-security and maximum-security prisons. At the moment, all such facilities are managed by government officials. But the privatization of juvenile detention homes, immigrant detention centers, and even minimum-security prisons is now common. Other forms of privatization are also receiving considerable attention. The Bush administration has promoted privatization experiments in housing policy, education policy, and other areas. The desirability of privatization has been debated with some vehemence. But there is considerable evidence that privatization, for better or for worse, has important consequences for public policy.[11]

Among the more novel reforms of recent years have been innovations in environmental policy, such as the environmental impact statement. Established in 1970 as a mechanism for sensitizing federal agencies to environmental concerns, an environmental impact statement serves as an "action-forcing" mechanism. Under the National Environmental Policy Act of 1970, federal agencies must issue an environmental impact statement for all major actions "significantly affecting the quality of the human environment." If a citizens' group believes the environmental impact statement to be inadequate, it may take the agency to court. Anxious to avoid this possibility, agencies have hired environmental experts to prepare defensible environmental impact statements and to formulate defensible environmental policies.[12] This is more or less what proponents of the impact statement had expected and hoped would occur.

Sometimes one reform begets another. The environmental impact statement requirement has encouraged not just environmental sensitivity but environmental litigation. And many critics believe that litigation is not the best way to resolve disputes.[13] In recent years, mediation and arbitration have emerged as important alternatives to litigation, in environmental policy and in other fields. One recent study identified 161 environmental cases that were referred to a mediator. The overwhelming majority of these cases was successfully resolved with the mediator's help.[14] Here also we can see how institutions may be reshaped and redesigned to reflect changing circumstances.

Institutional reform is not a panacea. Reforms seldom work as intended and some reforms do more harm than good.[15] Also, reform proposals sometimes become bargaining chips in a high-stakes game. Franklin Roosevelt often seemed less interested in achieving administrative reform than in using the threat of administrative reform to achieve other political goals.[16] Nevertheless, this illustrates our more general point that reform may be used strategically to enhance political feasibility. We turn now to several strategies employed by political activists in a wide variety of contexts. These strategies rely, to varying degrees, on inclusion, exclusion, and persuasion.

Inclusionary Strategies

Consultation

It is vital that politicians, especially those from different branches of government, confer with one another on matters of shared responsibility, preferably before positions begin to harden. The need for consultation is especially strong when divided government exists, that is, when different parties control different branches of government. As studies have shown, presidents fare worse on Capitol Hill when Congress is controlled by members of the other party.[17] The same is true of governors and state legislatures, although one-party states in the South pose a special set of problems.[18]

Unfortunately, presidents have not always appreciated the need to confer with members of Congress and specifically to confer with them as equal partners in a common enterprise. Jimmy Carter, for example, presented a comprehensive energy plan in the spring of

1977 without first conferring with congressional leaders. The result was a savage legislative attack on virtually every aspect of the Carter energy plan. Although an energy bill did pass in 1978, it was a far cry from the "moral equivalent of war" Carter had originally proposed.

Consultation is important not only between institutions but within institutions as well. It takes different forms in different settings. In legislative bodies, consultation is primarily oral, which facilitates bargaining and the making of intensely personal appeals. In judicial settings, consultation usually includes the circulation of memos or drafts of opinions on pending cases. These norms must be understood by those who wish to succeed in a particular policy area. A legislator who inundates colleagues with memos will be shunned as assuredly as a judge who explicitly offers a deal in return for a vote.

Coalition Building

Some policies do not require a coalition, as when a president or governor issues an executive order. But most policy proposals are doomed to failure unless their architects devote considerable time, effort, and skill to coalition building. It is particularly important to piece together a broad coalition when major new initiatives are being proposed. In pushing for new child-care legislation, the Children's Defense Fund spearheaded an Alliance for Children that encompassed approximately 100 labor, religious, and public interest groups. In late 1990 that coalition prevailed and won approval of the first federal child-care bill since World War II.

Although politicians and lobbyists are the most conspicuous coalition builders in American politics, coalition building is not confined to legislative corridors and cloakrooms. Appeals court judges, who decide cases in groups, must enlist the support of a majority of their colleagues before promulgating an opinion. And chief executives of corporations must enlist the support of sympathetic board members before launching major new initiatives.

Successful coalition building requires considerable patience and sensitivity. Former Supreme Court justice William Brennan, who crafted numerous successful coalitions under three different chief justices, once circulated ten drafts of an opinion until he won over a majority of his colleagues.[19] Senator Bill Bradley, a former New York Knicks basketball star, helped the cause of tax reform by playing pickup basketball with several colleagues in the House gym. According to journalists Jeffrey Birnbaum and Alan Murray, Bradley "took care not to humiliate his less-athletic rivals."[20]

Compromise

Few major initiatives succeed without some give and take. The willingness to compromise distinguishes reformers from gadflies. The passage of federal child-care legislation in 1990, mentioned earlier, would not have been possible were it not for key concessions by the Children's Defense Fund and other children's lobbyists. For example, the Children's Defense Fund eventually abandoned its insistence on strong federal regulation of child-care facilities and its opposition to funds for church-run facilities in order to secure passage of a bill. In contrast, supporters of parental leave legislation dug in their heels during the same session of Congress. Specifically, they were unwilling to compromise on key issues, such as whether leave should apply to parents of newborn children (tough to oppose politically) or to the broader category of persons with family health problems (easier to oppose on the grounds that it opens up a Pandora's box of leave opportunities). Not surprisingly, the family leave bill did not become law.

Though compromise is often important, it may not always be possible in a particular institutional setting. Once an initiative is on the ballot, for example, voters must approve or disapprove. They cannot redraft the language before the election. Although judges have greater control over the text of an opinion, they are not always in a position to devise a "win-win" situation. Technically, one side loses while the other side wins. A judicial compromise often concerns not the outcome of a dispute but the reasoning behind the outcome.

Exclusionary Strategies

Bypass

One of the most beguiling strategies, when one faces a major obstacle, is to bypass that obstacle, thereby avoiding or postponing a fight. This permits a tentative agreement on a complex problem before critics have a chance to shoot it down. A bypass strategy seems to have worked in 1983, when a small group of legislators and political executives met to try to forge an agreement on social security reform. Known informally as "the Gang of Nine," these individuals were pragmatists who felt they could make substantial progress without the distracting presence of more ideological colleagues. The Gang of Nine, meeting in a private home, developed a good enough rapport that they were able to resolve numerous disagreements among themselves. Their proposal, with modifications, won the support of the National Commission on Social Security Reform and eventually became law.[21]

Bypass, however, is a risky strategy. Consider, for example, the budget summit convened in late 1990 as a last-ditch effort to resolve the annual budget impasse on Capitol Hill. Rather than bargain with the many congressional leaders who could claim a legitimate interest in budget determinations, the White House convened a budget summit consisting of a select group of congressional leaders and top White House aides. To seal off the summiteers from rancorous debate and political deals, their meetings were held at Andrews Air Force Base, behind closed doors. The hope was that a small group of responsible leaders would reach an agreement that could then be sold to the full congressional membership.

That hope was realized, in a superficial way, when the summiteers announced an agreement calling for higher taxes and cuts in social programs, including Medicare. The deal was unacceptable to many members of Congress, however, including members of the president's own party, who promptly denounced the summit package. Many members of Congress were rankled as much by the highly exclusionary procedure as by the substance of the plan. Despite strong support from the White House and congressional party leaders, the budget agreement was defeated in the House of Representatives and the federal government briefly shut down, while puzzled tourists tried to figure out how to spend a weekend without having access to the Smithsonian museums, the National Zoo, and the Washington Monument. Eventually, a more inclusionary budget process resulted in a last-minute agreement. But the bypass strategy left behind bruised egos, deep intraparty divisions, and tarnished reputations. From the perspective of the White House, it was a public relations disaster.

Although the budget summit was unusual—and unlikely to be repeated—another bypass strategy has become quite common. As Beth Fuchs and John Hoadley have noted, Congress in recent years has placed a variety of important measures on a legislative fast track, bypassing the usual labyrinth of congressional procedures.[22] On the surface, this strategy of expedited procedures has succeeded, in that Congress has been able to pass some important legislation. Much of the health legislation of the 1980s, for example, was enacted this way, as part of the annual budget reconciliation process. But the fast track strategy has resulted in sweeping policy changes that were dimly understood by most members of Congress and that did not sufficiently anticipate implementation problems. In one instance, a catastrophic health insurance bill passed by the 100th Congress was promptly repealed by the 101st Congress after the elderly complained bitterly about its repercussions. Ultimately, the price of an expedited legislative process may be poor legislation.

Secrecy

Secrecy, sometimes found in conjunction with bypass, is aimed at excluding journalists in particular from the policy-making process. Secrecy is a much less viable strategy in legislative settings than it used to be, as a result of legislative reforms mandating open committee hearings unless committee members vote openly to close their doors. Secrecy is also less possible in the bureaucracy, as a result of sunshine laws mandating open meetings. The courts have managed to preserve considerable secrecy through closed meetings and informal norms against premature leaks.

Secrecy, though troublesome to many observers, was a successful strategy in the Persian Gulf War of 1990-1991. President Bush and his military advisers were intent on keeping their plans hidden from their adversary, Saddam Hussein. After major deployments of military personnel to the Gulf area were successfully completed, a war had to be planned and conducted. Journalists from all over the world complained about their lack of access to battlefield sites and the packaged information they were being given by General H. Norman Schwarzkopf and his aides. In the end, the details of the ground assault on Iraq were kept secret long enough for the allied forces to overpower the Iraqi army in very short order. Along the way, though, the public was less well informed than it might have been.

Deception

Even less acceptable than secrecy as a strategy is deception, which may range from an outright lie to the simple suppression of pertinent information. Deception can be quite damaging if it involves outright lies that are subsequently disclosed. The Reagan administration's policy of selling arms to Iran and diverting the proceeds to support Nicaraguan contras, or rebels, triggered a public outcry, a major congressional investigation, and prosecutions in the federal courts. Congress reacted severely in this case not just because it opposed the administration's policies but because it depends on the honesty of, and accurate information from, the executive branch in order to play its own constitutionally guaranteed role in foreign policy. The American people also react negatively to deception. What offended many people about President Bush's support for taxes late in 1990 was not just the policy but the fact that he had broken a campaign promise: "Read my lips. No new taxes."

Like other strategies, deception is more acceptable in some institutional settings than in others. In the courts, deception by an attorney is a serious matter indeed. If discovered, it may result in a contempt citation or even disbarment. In other institutional settings, deception is sometimes tolerated, though it matters a great deal who is deceiving whom.

For example, a New Mexico state legislator, summarizing legislative norms, reports that a legislator may deceive a lobbyist but not a fellow legislator. And a lobbyist who deceives a legislator risks ostracism and unemployment.[23]

Advertising consumer products frequently involves some degree of deception. In the 1990s, environmental awareness has grown to the point that nearly 30 percent of consumers questioned say that advertisements or labels suggesting environmental benefits affect their choice of products. Of course, this development has not escaped the attention of corporate decision makers. Gillette now describes its cans of Foamy shaving cream as "ozone friendly—no CFCs," and the producers of Lemon Pledge make a similar claim, even though the use of chlorofluorocarbons as aerosol propellants has been prohibited by the federal government since 1978.[24] In effect, these companies are deceiving consumers by implying that they are doing more than what is required by law.

Persuasive Strategies

Rhetoric

Rhetoric is fundamental to political success, especially when politicians seek to expand the scope of conflict by bringing an issue into American living rooms. Congressman Dan Rostenkowski, chairman of the House Ways and Means Committee, used rhetoric effectively in a televised speech on tax reform in the spring of 1985. After describing in a folksy way what his blue-collar constituents think about taxes, Rostenkowski appealed to viewers to express their support for significant tax reform. In closing remarks, he urged taxpayers to write to R-O-S-T-Y in Washington, D.C., and tell him what they thought. More than 75,000 letters flowed in to "Rosty's" office, including a package containing a two-by-four with which to paddle the special interests. Rostenkowski's speech—a smashing success—helped to generate support for an unprecedented tax reform bill.[25]

In recruiting supporters, proponents of a policy proposal are sometimes tempted to exaggerate the proposal's significance. In the short run, this serves a useful purpose, for it helps to generate interest and mobilize support. Unfortunately, however, exaggeration may become detrimental in the long run, as proponents attempt to move beyond agenda setting to policy formulation and policy adoption. The paradox, which seems obvious except in the heat of battle, is that exaggerated claims intensify support but also intensify opposition. When the consent of a majority is needed, that is not much of a bargain.

Jane Mansbridge illustrates this paradox nicely in her discussion of how the women's movement lost the struggle for state ratification of the equal rights amendment.[26] In an effort to recruit supporters and sustain their ideological zeal, feminist leaders exaggerated the probable impact of the ERA. They claimed that the amendment would require the military to send women into combat, despite court rulings to the contrary. They argued that the ERA would significantly narrow wage differentials between men and women, even though it would apply only to public sector wages, leaving private sector wages more or less intact. They also contended that the ERA would require states to fund medically necessary abortions. These exaggerated claims appealed to hard-core activists but frightened and ultimately alienated potential allies in the state legislatures. Thanks in part to their own hyperbole, ERA supporters were unable to convince three-fourths of the state legislatures to ratify the amendment.

According to Mansbridge, the ERA experience highlights a more general paradox that afflicts social movements. She points out that "Organizing on behalf of the general interest usually requires volunteers, and mobilizing volunteers often requires an exaggerated, black or white vision of events to justify spending time and money on the course." [27] To motivate supporters, leaders of social movements often go overboard in portraying what to them is a utopian vision of a just society. In doing so, they are embarking on a dangerous course. Successful social movements depend not just on internal solidarity but also on external support. Exaggerated claims may strengthen the former, but they run the risk of undermining the latter.

Policy Analysis

Although rhetoric matters, especially in highly salient issue areas, evidence also matters, especially in highly complex issue areas. Policy analysis, based on rigorous empirical research, can make a difference. Martha Derthick and Paul Quirk have shown, for example, that economic analysis and empirical research contributed significantly to the wave of deregulation that took place during the late 1970s. They concluded that "ideas" often count as much as "interests." [28]

The circumstances that led to airline deregulation, trucking deregulation, and telecommunications deregulation were somewhat unusual. Almost all the studies of deregulation had pointed to the same conclusion—that it would promote competition and efficiency. And the timing was right. As Martha Feldman has shown, however, policy analysis can be useful even when the timing is not right. The Department of Energy "stockpiles" policy reports for a rainy day. When a crisis erupts, department officials can select from their inventory a policy report that nicely analyzes the present situation and offers options or even remedies.[29] In this way, the Department of Energy, like other bureaucracies, overcomes the timing problem by preparing, in effect, for a variety of contingencies.

Legislative bodies, whose members have wide-ranging interests and pressing deadlines, are less able to stockpile policy reports for a rainy day. Although numerous policy reports are produced (by the General Accounting Office, the Office of Technology Assessment, and other bodies), they often must be used quickly if they are to be used at all. Their use depends on the nature of the issue,[30] the comprehensibility of the report,[31] and the extent of interaction between legislators and analysts.[32]

Protest

In some issue areas, factual disputes matter less than value disputes and evidence counts less than political muscle. Under such circumstances, protest can be an effective strategy, especially when public opinion is favorable. A good example of successful protest was the late Mitch Snyder's continuing crusade for the homeless residents of the District of Columbia. Snyder, a former Wall Street stockbroker, staged sleep-ins on city streets and erected a tent city to dramatize the plight of the homeless. When these tactics failed, he began a hunger strike, eventually winning the right to run a shelter in an empty school building. Snyder's victory was short-lived. As a result of health and safety violations in the building, Snyder's constituents were evicted. But another hunger strike enabled Snyder to pry loose federal funds just in time to prepare for another winter.[33]

Protest is a powerful weapon in political combat, but it is also a dangerous one, precisely because it arouses such a strong emotional response, either positive or negative. Antiwar protestors may trigger a backlash if people believe that the protestors are unpatriotic (a charge hurled at Jane Fonda when she posed with North Vietnamese troops at the height of the Vietnam War). Persian Gulf War protestors tried to avoid these problems by distinguishing, for the most part, between the war (which they opposed) and the warriors (whom they supported). This enabled them to maintain a delicate balance, in Albert Hirschman's words, between "voice" (protest) and "loyalty" (patriotism).[34]

Forum Shifting

A central theme of this book is that institutional settings or policy domains materially affect the outcome of policy disputes. Recognizing this, proponents and opponents of policy change seek to shift a policy dispute from one domain, or forum, to another or to prevent such a shift if it is contrary to their interests. E. E. Schattschneider has observed that policy activists seek to expand or limit the scope of conflict.[35] Building on these insights, Frank Baumgartner and Bryan Jones have emphasized the dynamic character of the policy-making process: "The image of a policy and its venue are closely related. As venues change, images may change as well; as the image of a policy changes, venue changes become more likely." [36]

A good example of forum shifting is nuclear power. In a perceptive case study, Baumgartner and Jones demonstrate how the public image of nuclear power was transformed from extremely positive to extremely negative in a fairly short period of time. The key to that transformation was the successful shift of the nuclear issue by nuclear power critics from one forum to another—from the private sector to the bureaucracy in the mid-1960s, from the bureaucracy to Congress and the courts in the early 1970s, and to the front pages of American newspapers in the late 1970s. In the terms used in this book, the nuclear issue shifted among domains—from corporate boardrooms to bureaucratic hearing rooms to congressional cloakrooms to courtrooms and eventually to American living rooms. Nuclear power critics thus effectively expanded the scope of the conflict and contributed to the creation of an increasingly negative public image of the nuclear power industry. They demonstrated a keen awareness of the gravitational pulls of different political institutions and exploited them to good advantage.

The nuclear power case involved both a gradual expansion of the scope of the conflict and a sequential shift from one forum to another. More often, however, issues are considered simultaneously in more than one forum, the scope of conflict widens and narrows, and the receptivity of a particular forum to a particular plea or protest changes over time. Abortion illustrates all of these phenomena. The U.S. Supreme Court, Congress, and numerous state legislatures are all considering the abortion issue, though the framing of the issue differs in each case. A generally salient issue, abortion becomes even more salient when the Supreme Court hands down a major opinion, such as *Webster v. Reproductive Health Services* (1989) or *Rust v. Sullivan* (1991). And the preferred venue for a given perspective changes too. In the 1980s, pro-life activists sought relief from Congress, whereas pro-choice activists preferred a resolution by the Supreme Court. For all intents and purposes, that pattern is now reversed.[37]

To a considerable extent, forum shifting is ad hoc, tentative, and improvisational. But some forum shifting is more permanent, as when jurisdiction over an issue is formally transferred from one administrative agency to another. When Congress transferred jurisdiction over pesticides from the Department of Agriculture to the Environmental

Protection Agency, it anticipated—correctly—that this change of venue would prove favorable to environmental interests.[38] The USDA, which was created as a clientele agency, was highly responsive to farmers; the EPA, of course, had a strong mandate to protect the environment. Pesticide disputes still shift from the EPA to Congress, to the state governments, and occasionally to the courts. But this example shows that it is possible to achieve a relatively permanent forum shift that may benefit one set of interests over another.

Summary

Political feasibility analysis is more an art than a science, which may explain why scholarly commentary on the subject has been so scarce. And like both art and science, success is much more easily recognized retrospectively than prospectively. In any effort to change public policy there is probably no reliable substitute for trial and error. Those seeking change should be prepared with multiple strategies, geared toward the peculiarities of different institutional domains, and use as many such strategies as are needed to achieve their objectives. This may involve working in several arenas simultaneously. Clearly, complicated, far-flung political change efforts can be very costly, which means that what may be politically feasible for one group may not be feasible for another. As we have noted throughout this book, the American political system consistently favors well-organized, well-financed political causes or movements.

We have stressed that political institutions should be viewed not only as having constraints but also as presenting opportunities and being manipulable. Political activists should study political feasibility not simply to identify mines in a mine field but also to identify opportunities. And if significant obstacles exist, they may be removable through institutional reform. In either case, we need to reclaim feasibility analysis from those who would portray it as the art of determining what is not possible. Institutions designed to inhibit change do not necessarily prevent it. And few institutions remain impervious to reform.

Notes

1. Ralph Huitt, "Political Feasibility," in Austin Ranney, ed., *Political Science and Public Policy* (Chicago: Rand McNally, 1968), 263-275; Arnold Meltsner, "Political Feasibility and Policy Analysis," *Public Administration Review* (November-December 1972): 859-867; and David Webber, "Political

Feasibility and Policy Analysis," *Policy Studies Journal* (June 1986): 545-553.

2. Charles Jones and Randall Strahan, "The Effect of Energy Politics on Congressional and Executive Organization in the 1970s," *Legislative Studies Quarterly* 10 (May 1985): 151-179.

3. Barry Rabe, "Legislative Incapacity: The Congressional Role in Environmental Policy-Making and the Case of Superfund," *Journal of Health, Politics, Policy, and Law* 15 (Fall 1990): 571-589.

4. Jeffrey Pressman and Aaron Wildavsky, *Implementation* (Berkeley: University of California Press, 1973), 107.

5. The number of rules issued annually by federal agencies declined during the 1980s from 7,745 to 4,711. See Office of Management and Budget, "Regulatory Program of the U.S. Government, April 1, 1990-March 31, 1991" (Washington, D.C.: Government Printing Office, August 1990), 651.

6. Robert Carp and Ronald Stidham, *Judicial Process in America* (Washington, D.C.: CQ Press, 1990), 291.

7. Ibid., 258.

8. Kenneth Gormley, "Ten Adventures in State Constitutional Law," *Emerging Issues in State Constitutional Law* (Washington, D.C.: National Association of Attorneys General, 1988).

9. James Kuklinski and John Stanga, "Political Participation and Government Responsiveness: The Behavior of California Superior Courts," *American Political Science Review* 73 (December 1979): 1090-1099.

10. The Supreme Court, however, steadfastly refused to relax standing requirements for taxpayers.

11. William Gormley, ed., *Privatization and Its Alternatives* (Madison: University of Wisconsin Press, 1991); and John Donahue, *The Privatization Decision: Public Ends, Private Means* (New York: Basic Books, 1990).

12. Daniel Mazmanian and Jeanne Nienaber, *Can Organizations Change? Environmental Protection, Citizen Participation, and the Corps of Engineers* (Washington, D.C.: Brookings Institution, 1979).

13. See, for example, Donald Horowitz, *The Courts and Social Policy* (Washington, D.C.: Brookings Institution, 1977).

14. Gail Bingham, *Resolving Environmental Disputes: A Decade of Experience* (Washington, D.C.: Conservation Foundation, 1986), 30-31.

15. For a discussion of how reforms aimed at eliminating bureaucratic pathologies have created another set of bureaucratic pathologies, see William Gormley, *Taming the Bureaucracy: Muscles, Prayers, and Other Strategies* (Princeton, N.J.: Princeton University Press, 1989).

16. James March and Johan Olsen, *Rediscovering Institutions: The Organizational Basis of Politics* (New York: Free Press, 1989).

17. George Edwards, *At the Margins: Presidential Leadership of Congress* (New Haven, Conn.: Yale University Press, 1989).

18. Sarah Morehouse, *State Politics, Parties, and Policy* (New York: Holt, Rinehart and Winston, 1981), 246-252, 294-297.

19. David O'Brien, *Storm Center: The Supreme Court in American Politics* (New York: W. W. Norton, 1986), 249.

20. Jeffrey Birnbaum and Alan Murray, *Showdown at Gucci Gulch* (New York: Random House, 1987), 120.

21. Paul Light, *Artful Work: The Politics of Social Security Reform* (New York: Random House, 1985), 177-195.

22. Beth Fuchs and John Hoadley, "The Remaking of Medicare: Congres-

sional Policymaking on the Fast Track" (Paper presented at the annual meeting of the Southern Political Science Association, Savannah, Georgia, November 3, 1984); and Beth Fuchs and John Hoadley, "Reflections from Inside the Beltway: How Congress and the President Grapple with Health Policy," *PS* 20 (Spring 1987): 212-220.

23. José Garcia, "New Mexico: Traditional Interests in a Traditional State," *Interest Group Politics in the American West*, ed. Ronald Hrebenar and Clive Thomas (Salt Lake City: University of Utah Press, 1987), 100.

24. John Holusha, "Coming Clean on Products: Ecological Claims Faulted," *New York Times*, March 12, 1991, D1, D10.

25. Birnbaum and Murray, *Showdown at Gucci Gulch*.

26. Jane Mansbridge, *Why We Lost the ERA* (Chicago: University of Chicago Press, 1986).

27. Ibid., 61.

28. Martha Derthick and Paul Quirk, *The Politics of Deregulation* (Washington, D.C.: Brookings Institution, 1985).

29. Martha Feldman, *Order Without Design: Information Production and Policy Making* (Stanford: Stanford University Press, 1989).

30. David Whiteman, "The Fate of Policy Analysis in Congressional Decision Making," *Western Political Quarterly* 38 (June 1985): 294-311.

31. Christopher Mooney, "Pushing Paper: The Flow and Use of Written Information in State Legislative Decision-Making," unpublished Ph.D. dissertation, University of Wisconsin, Madison, Wisconsin, 1990, 148-184.

32. David Rafter, "Policy-Focused Evaluation: A Study of the Utilization of Evaluation Research by the Wisconsin Legislature," unpublished Ph.D. dissertation, University of Wisconsin, Madison, Wisconsin, 1982.

33. Lyn Stolarski, "Right to Shelter: History of the Mobilization of the Homeless as a Model of Voluntary Action," *Journal of Voluntary Action Research* 17 (January-March 1988): 36-45.

34. Albert Hirschman, *Exit, Voice, and Loyalty* (Cambridge, Mass.: Harvard University Press, 1970).

35. E. E. Schattschneider, *The Semi-Sovereign People* (New York: Holt, Rinehart and Winston, 1960).

36. Frank Baumgartner and Bryan Jones, "Agenda Dynamics and Policy Subsystems," *Journal of Politics* 53 (November 1991).

37. E. J. Dionne, Jr., "Court Could Revive Abortion as '92 Issue," *Washington Post*, May 25, 1991, 17.

38. Christopher Bosso, *Pesticides and Politics: The Life Cycle of a Public Issue* (Pittsburgh: University of Pittsburgh Press, 1987), 143-177.

11   Assessing American Public Policy

The political struggle that yields public policies is not just a game about the exercise and maintenance of power. Whether governments and private corporations produce effective policies and programs profoundly affects the nation and its citizens. At stake are national survival, the quality of life, and the nature of justice in society.

Public policies are developed and implemented by private corporations, courts, legislatures, chief executives, administrative agencies, and citizens. Chapter 10 demonstrated how policy entrepreneurs can use political institutions to good advantage to secure enactment and implementation of public policies. In this chapter we consider fundamental questions of governmental performance. How well do public policies serve the needs and wants of the American people? Does the United States live up to the ideals proclaimed by elected leaders and set forth in the Constitution? Is the nation better off or worse off in the 1990s than it was fifty, twenty-five, or ten years ago? What pressing problems has the nation failed to grapple with effectively? These are difficult questions to answer. A selective report card on the nation's policy accomplishments and failures is offered here; more questions are raised than answered.

Choosing Yardsticks

What criteria should be applied in an assessment of public policy? What evidence is available to measure policy performance? Against what standards can progress and failure be judged? The question is not just whether the public policy "glass" is half full or half empty, but which glasses should be examined. There are many inherent difficulties in assessing public policy. Following is a discussion of a few of them and how they might be handled.

Principal Policy Goals

Before evaluating any public policy, one must decide what questions to ask, which is not as simple as it sounds. What is important to one observer may not be important to another. People in different circumstances have distinct views of the world and its problems. The inner-city resident and the suburban homeowner whose dwellings may be less than an hour apart have different expectations about what government should do to help them. The city dweller is more likely to be concerned about crime, public transportation, air quality, overcrowding, and housing. The suburban homeowner is more interested in the state highway system, the availability of safe drinking water, and recreational opportunities.[1]

Public policy concerns are also shaped by the nature of the times. Some goals, such as peace and prosperity, always command attention. Issues such as drug abuse or education, may seem urgent one year, but less pressing the next. Circumstances change; policies change; new problems arise, or new aspects of old problems are recognized. During the late 1950s, for example, policy makers debated whether black Americans had the right to enjoy the same public facilities, schools, mass transportation, restaurants, and parks as white Americans. In the 1990s, the policy issues center on how far the government should go in promoting economic and social opportunities for minority groups.

Conceptions of the proper role of government in the lives of American citizens are highly controversial and provide a framework for evaluations of public policy. Should the government permit employers to require individuals to stop smoking, even if they only smoke when not on the job? Should the government be able to require individuals to use mass transportation and stop using outdoor grills in order to cut air pollution? Should government provide subsidies for families whose children attend private elementary and secondary schools, when public schools are available? Should the United States continue to play a central role in policing the "new world order," or should other nations begin to play a larger role in defending the interests of Western democracies? Because people disagree about what government ought to do, they often disagree about what governments actually accomplish.

Despite disagreement about whether government should increase its involvement, its reform programs, or get out of the way, there is fundamental agreement on the nation's principal public policy aspirations.[2] They are (1) to defend the nation; (2) to achieve sustained economic growth; (3) to ensure equal opportunity; (4) to provide a "safety net" for the disadvantaged and senior citizens; and (5) to protect the environment. The stability of these central policy goals over the last several decades reflects a widespread consensus about government responsibilities in American political culture. In the United States, in contrast to other nations, political battles usually take place over means, not ends. Public officials fight fiercely about how basic values will be expressed and defined in practice, but almost always there is little conflict over core values.

What is at stake in these struggles is not whether public policies should help the poor, for example, but how much and in what way. Lawmakers often fight over subtle differences in the language of a statute or a bill because they know that their decisions may one day have profound consequences. Only in rare instances, such as the New Deal of President Franklin Roosevelt, do major changes occur quickly.

Weighing Evidence

How does one know whether government policies and programs are effective? Reliable, objective information is available for the evaluation of many policies. Government agencies and public and private analysts monitor unemployment, inflation, trade balances, life expectancy, race relations, the quality of the environment, and so on. Knowledge about the effectiveness of public policies has increased substantially since the 1960s. Policy makers can be better informed than ever before about conditions in society and the possible effects of their actions.[3]

In spite of these gains, policy makers still may not know enough about the effectiveness of public policies to reach sound conclusions. Too often they are unwilling to use the information that is available. It is embarrassing to discover that a once-ballyhooed policy does not work; therefore, many lawmakers do not ask probing questions, authorize careful evaluations, or listen to disconcerting evidence. Politicians usually are more concerned about who gets what, when, and how than with evaluations of program performance.

Establishing cause-and-effect relationships between a government action and a societal consequence is very difficult. If millions of Americans suffer from heart disease and high blood pressure, is the U.S. health care system to blame, or is it because Americans refuse to eat properly, quit smoking, and take care of themselves? If minorities increase their membership in the professions, should credit accrue to civil rights laws, or are there simply more minority applicants who are better prepared? Because a single government policy cannot be isolated from other events, trends, or policies, the specific impacts of government decisions may go undetected.

Making Judgments

After evidence is gathered about the impacts of a particular policy, standards must be applied to judge success or failure. For example, the unemployment rate among Americans is carefully calculated and reported each month, but the raw data do not speak for themselves. Is a 6 percent unemployment rate alarming or acceptable? Sound public policy conclusions should not be based on the optimism or pessimism of the observer, but where do analysts turn for standards that yield reasonable judgments?

The determination of standards begins with an examination of the objectives of governmental policy. One must be careful to distinguish between pronouncements and results, however. Public laws, regulations, and judicial decrees state objectives; they are not automatically translated into positive outcomes. Political leaders frequently engage in hyperbole, claiming that new laws and policies will solve long-standing problems. But the proposed solution may not work in practice, or the problem may be much more difficult than originally envisioned. Therefore, careful observers ignore the rhetoric and examine the impacts of policies on people, institutions, and society.

A thorough evaluation of public policy also requires looking beyond contemporary policy debates. Policy makers should anticipate and address problems before they become unmanageable crises or potential catastrophes. Only governments have the broad powers to act on behalf of an entire state or nation. Scientists warn, for example, that the ozone layer that shields the earth from harmful ultraviolet rays is gradually diminishing, causing the earth's temperature to rise. They predict that unless the use of ozone-depleting chemicals is curtailed, the earth's fragile ecology may be severely damaged.

Public perceptions should be carefully considered in judging policy performance, but it is misleading to rely solely on public satisfaction. Public opinions about government policies are often based on fragmentary or unreliable information. Policies should not be judged exclusively according to whether an individual feels personally better off than before. The perspective of most citizens is narrow, limited to their families, jobs, and neighborhoods. What is good for one family may not be good for another family or for the community as a whole. Majority preferences may be insensitive to minority rights and needs. Indeed, disadvantaged minorities often receive benefits they would probably be denied if public policies were based exclusively on majority sentiment.

Perspectives on the effectiveness of public policy are possible when meaningful comparisons can be made to put the naked evidence into perspective. Placing current policy performance in historical perspective is particularly valuable. Taken as a raw number, a 6 percent unemployment rate does not reveal much. Its significance is established only by comparison with peak levels of nearly 11 percent in 1982 and with the lower than 6 percent rate of the previous three decades. The 6 percent unemployment rate in 1991 is lower than the historical post-World War II high, but it is still troubling.

Comparing U.S. policy performance with experiences in other countries may also be useful, if handled with care. For instance, the fact that infant mortality rates are higher in the United States than in seventeen other countries suggests that Americans have inadequate access to health care. Conversely, there may be little comfort from the fact that U.S. toxic waste cleanup efforts lead in comparison with those of other nations, because most would still judge U.S. efforts inadequate.

Comparisons of different states, communities, and population subgroups may also yield insights. Ideally, analysts would like to know what conditions would have been like without a public policy or program. Because such knowledge is often unattainable, analysts compare states that have programs with those that do not or compare groups in the population that have received services with those that have not. In this way, it may be possible to understand what difference the program made in people's lives.

In the following review of five principal policy goals, we examine how the United States measures up by comparing current performance with announced objectives and by looking at historical and crossnational comparisons where appropriate. The impacts of public policies on different groups of Americans are highlighted. In each section we consider accomplishments, failures, and unanswered questions. The summary is a discussion of the challenges facing the nation and its leaders in the years ahead.

Defend the Nation

The U.S. Constitution declares that a primary purpose of government is to "provide for the common defense." Nothing could be more fundamental than ensuring the survival of the nation, protecting its vital economic interests, and preserving the freedom of its citizens. Americans and their leaders have had grave concerns about the nation's security since World War II. These anxieties derive from the perception that in the age of nuclear weapons and dependence on foreign oil supplies, the Soviet Union and other foreign powers are potential adversaries capable of seriously threatening U.S. economic interests and national security.

Consequently, since the late 1940s, a bipartisan consensus has existed in favor of maintaining sufficient military power to deter the Soviet Union and other nations from pursuing hostile intentions.[4] The American commitment extends beyond defending U.S. soil, citizens, and overseas investments. U.S. policy makers believe that military force and the threat of nuclear retaliation must be used to protect allies and to counter attempts by hostile nations to expand their influence. American lives and military resources were spent defending Korea and Vietnam from communist regimes and in protecting Middle East oil supplies during the Persian Gulf War. In 1991 more than $14.8 billion in U.S.

foreign and military aid was distributed throughout the world—to Israel, Egypt, Saudi Arabia, Afghanistan, Nicaragua, and dozens of other countries.

Soldiers and Dollars

Disputes over national security policy have often been heated. When should U.S. military forces be involved in hostile actions? American involvement in Vietnam provoked one of the most damaging internal political conflicts in the nation's history, and it has had lasting effects. How much conventional military and nuclear weaponry does the country need? Critics argue that the military establishment and many U.S. politicians exaggerate the threats posed by the Soviet Union and other nations and that the defense budget is larger than necessary. Supporters of a large defense budget maintain that it is the price that must be paid to protect U.S. interests at home and abroad. The swift military victories in Grenada, Panama, and Iraq helped vindicate U.S. defense policy makers who argued that overwhelming U.S. military power could be used effectively without great costs in terms of American lives.

National security policy not only affects the nation's survival and prosperity, it also influences domestic priorities and is influenced by them. The funds that remain after defense spending requirements have been met determine what else the government can do; defense spending consumed more than $300 billion of the $1.4 trillion federal budget in 1991. Strong national security requires the fostering of industries to design and manufacture ships, submarines, tanks, airplanes, and nuclear weapons.

The strength and self-reliance of a nation's economy shapes the strategies that must be taken to defend it. The United States is one of the most independent and self-sustaining nations in the world; it has abundant raw materials necessary for survival and adequate food supplies for the entire population. Yet, the United States depends on other nations for oil and other materials, and it sells its products and services around the world. Hence, U.S. policy makers must be concerned with the political, military, and economic situations in dozens of other nations. The U.S. reaction to Iraq's invasion of Kuwait and the possible threat to oil supplies was swift and decisive. In contrast, the United States did not confront the Soviet Union when it invaded Afghanistan, a relatively resource-poor nation.

Unlike inflation, air pollution, or crime, national security problems are not "experienced" by large segments of the American public, except in times of war. A segment of the population also must serve in the military. Since the mid-1970s, U.S. armed forces personnel have been volunteers—a change that reshaped the composition of the military substantially. Soldiers in the modern volunteer army are more likely than in the past to come from low-income, poorly educated, and minority backgrounds.[5]

Since the end of World War II, American political leaders have convinced the public that the Soviet Union poses a serious threat to the nation and its allies, but this perception has been clouded by Soviet behavior in the late 1980s and early 1990s. The public favors arms control agreements and greater efforts to reduce tensions, but it has been willing to pay for a large defense establishment until such time as arms control agreements are concluded.[6]

The size of the defense budget is based on perceptions of risk and assumptions about the strategies that will be most effective in minimizing those risks. Unlike the planning of government entitlement programs, where needy populations can be precisely defined and spending determined accordingly, the task of constructing defense budgets is a deadly guessing game. If military power is inadequate to protect vital economic interests, the problem may not be apparent until it is too late to do anything about it. How serious is the military threat posed by the Soviet Union and other foreign powers? To what extent should the United States shield other nations against military attack? Should the United States respond to all situations in which potential adversaries wield military power?

The ups and downs of U.S. military expenditures since the end of World War II reflect changing perceptions of the threat to U.S. interests at home and abroad. From 1945 through the 1960s, military spending constituted nearly 9 percent of the gross national product. By the 1970s the defense budget had dropped to 6 percent of the GNP, despite the expenses connected with the Vietnam War. By 1980, the end of Jimmy Carter's administration, defense spending had fallen to 5.3 percent of the GNP.[7] Defense spending accounted for more than 50 percent of the federal budget in 1960, 42 percent in 1970, and only 23 percent in 1980.[8]

During Reagan's presidency, the United States accomplished the largest sustained peacetime expansion of military spending in its history. By fiscal year 1988, the military budget had more than doubled over the fiscal 1980 outlays. The military's share of the federal budget rose from 23 percent in 1980 to 32 percent in 1988; in the same period, its share of the GNP jumped from 5.3 percent to 6.4 percent.[9] In fiscal year 1990, following improvements in relationships with the Soviet Union in the late 1980s, defense spending fell slightly to 22 percent of overall federal spending. These outlays are 24 percent lower than 1985 outlays for defense programs in real terms.[10]

How Much Is Enough?

Is the United States more capable of protecting itself and projecting its influence around the world than it was before the military expansion? Were the benefits worth the costs? Officials of the Reagan and Bush administrations have argued that the massive military buildup of the 1980s brought the Soviet Union to the bargaining table and resulted in an arms control agreement—the first to result in the destruction of an entire class of nuclear weapons. They have further argued that U.S. military dominance allowed the United States to conduct the war effectively in the Persian Gulf with few American casualties.

Critics maintain, however, that the Soviet Union was willing to bargain because of its need to reduce defense spending and to improve relations with the rest of the industrialized world. Despite the reductions in intermediate-range nuclear weapons, the strategic nuclear defense arsenal on the ground, in submarines, and in bombers remains incredibly destructive. They also argue that the massive military buildup of the 1980s increased the likelihood that U.S. policy makers would resort to deadly force in situations when diplomacy and economic sanctions would work just as effectively and without great loss of lives. Finally, military might does little or nothing to deter suicidal terrorist attacks on U.S. citizens and military personnel.

American politicians are always reluctant to engage U.S. forces in armed conflict, especially if there is a risk of confrontation with the Soviet Union. The Soviet Union continued its occupation of Afghanistan despite U.S. protests and the government's refusal to sell the Russians grain. President Reagan was unable to convince the public and Congress that substantial military aid to the opponents of the government of Nicaragua was justified as a means to protect vital U.S. interests. U.S. intervention in the Persian Gulf was favorably received by the public largely because Americans perceived that a vital economic interest—the supply of oil—was at stake and because the war lasted less than two months. Public opinion ran strongly against military involvement when World War II began in Europe; U.S. troops were not committed until after the Japanese attacked Pearl Harbor in late 1941. Large segments of the public opposed subsequent military actions involving American armed forces in Korea and Vietnam,[11] as well as the Persian Gulf. In fact, one legacy of the war in Southeast Asia is the so-called Vietnam syndrome—a deep distrust of U.S. military involvement in other nations. Such concerns continue to shape public opposition to U.S. involvement in Lebanon, Nicaragua, and the Persian Gulf.[12] President Bush claims that this skepticism was removed by successful conduct of the Persian Gulf War. It is more likely, however, that public distrust of U.S.

troop commitments in armed conflicts will continue to shape U.S. foreign policy.

Achieve Sustained Economic Growth

Sustained economic growth, like national security, is a central policy goal of all governments. This broad goal subsumes several specific economic objectives: rising standards of living and wealth, low levels of unemployment and inflation, increasing productivity of the work force, and expanding exports. Policy makers of all stripes want to promote economic growth and vitality. For more than a decade, the sharpest partisan and ideological disputes have revolved around the extent to which the government can and should manage the economy.

The achievement of economic goals depends, perhaps more than any other policy objective, on the policies and financial resources of both the government and the private sector. In general, government involvement in fostering a healthy economy takes two forms: *macroeconomic policy* decisions and decisions about *investment* in human capital and the nation's physical infrastructure. Macroeconomic policy encompasses matters such as the government's spending and tax policy, the supply and cost of money, and trading policies with other nations. When the economy is functioning at less than full employment, the government can increase public and private spending through fiscal and monetary stimulation, which in turn generates greater demand for goods and services and puts more people to work.[13] Federal Reserve Board decisions that establish the size of the money supply and the level of interest rates profoundly influence the rate of inflation in the price of goods and services and the ability of individuals and corporations to raise capital.

Government-sponsored education and research strategies also affect the ability of the nation to achieve its economic goals. Education and training programs translate directly into improvement in the quality and productivity of the work force. America's colleges and universities have produced one of the most highly educated populations in the world, but the supply of qualified individuals is not meeting the demand in some fields. The American Electronics Association estimated, for example, that between 1983 and 1987, only half of the 200,000 electrical engineers and computer scientists needed by business and industry would be available to meet demand.[14]

Government-sponsored research and development activities often generate new products and increase economic growth. More than half of the money spent on research and development in the United States is supplied by the federal government—the sum was more than $75 billion in 1991. Since 1962, government research in the aerospace industry has yielded numerous products and productivity improvements. For example, the demand for lightweight, reliable circuitry helped spawn the development of microchips that eventually led to the development of the personal computer. Historically, countries with the highest rates of growth in research and development expenditures have also experienced greater gains in productivity and had higher GNPs.[15]

Finally, the quality of the nation's infrastructure is vital to a prosperous economy. But the level of the government's investment in infrastructure declined by 40 percent per capita between 1965 and 1984. Bridges, roads, and water systems are simply wearing out. A distinguished advisory panel estimated that planned government spending on infrastructure will have to increase by $450 billion before the end of the century to meet urgent needs. Most of the funds for this massive undertaking will be raised and spent by state governments.[16]

Effective government policies promote a prosperous, competitive economy, but many factors are beyond government control. Private sector decisions have a direct influence on the size and health of the U.S. economy (see Chapter 3). Private businesses generate nearly two-thirds of the nation's gross domestic product and control virtually all major industrial activities. Therefore, the cumulative impact of corporate decisions is significant. If General Motors decides to locate a plant to manufacture automobiles for the U.S. market in Mexico rather than in Atlanta, the decision costs Americans thousands of high-paying jobs. Because IBM is the leading manufacturer of computers, its decision to develop faster computer-processing equipment enhances the ability of the U.S.-based manufacturers to make faster, more reliable computers that can compete effectively in the world market.

Economic growth also depends on the behavior of investors, workers, and consumers. Workers' productivity and wage demands are important factors in economic expansion. The preference of American consumers for imported products, such as Japanese automobiles and electronic equipment, means that billions of American dollars flow to other nations. Japanese consumers also prefer Japanese-manufactured products, even when U.S. products are superior.[17]

Mixed Success and an Uncertain Future

The United States has been the world's dominant economic power since the 1950s. American living standards have risen substantially during this period; the per capita income of Americans has doubled.[18] Americans are enjoying more leisure time, and they are retiring at a younger age than previous generations. By many standards the United States remains an economic powerhouse. Nevertheless, it seems proper to conclude that the record is mixed and the future is uncertain.

Despite its strong showing, the U.S. economy has not always outperformed those of other nations. Since the mid-1960s, the economies of several countries, including Japan, France, the former West Germany, Italy, Austria, and Norway, have grown at faster rates than the U.S. economy.[19] Japan's economy has expanded at roughly twice the U.S. growth rate. The spendable earnings of American workers have been declining since 1960.[20] By the mid-1980s, the wages of workers employed in the manufacturing sector in Sweden, West Germany, the Netherlands, and Belgium had surpassed the earnings of American workers in the same industries.[21]

Although the American standard of living remains high in absolute terms, it is gradually declining relative to those of other industrialized countries. Life expectancy is lower in the United States than in fourteen other nations. Infant mortality rates are higher in the United States than in seventeen other countries,[22] although they have improved in this country since the early 1960s as a result of the introduction of medical assistance for the poor. The U.S. economy has been plagued by several recessions—periods of either no growth or decline. Severe recessions, bringing high levels of unemployment, occurred in 1954, 1958, 1975, 1979, 1982, and 1991. Since the late 1960s, U.S. unemployment levels, on average, have exceeded those of several other nations, including Germany and the United Kingdom.[23]

Since 1972, more than 20 million new jobs have been created to absorb the expanding work force, but despite that impressive record, not everyone who has wanted to work has been able to find a job.[24] During the 1950s and 1960s, unemployment averaged 4.6 percent; during the 1970s, the average climbed to 6.2 percent. The average for the 1980s was 7.3 percent. During the 1982 recession, unemployment reached 10.8 percent—the highest level since World War II. More than 12 million Americans were unable to find jobs.[25]

The aggregate figures do not reveal all the underlying problems. Not counted in the official unemployment statistics are the more than 1 million "discouraged workers"—people who have given up looking for work because they do not believe any jobs are available—and 6 million part-time workers who would rather be working full time.[26] The reported unemployment figures therefore understate the magnitude of the real demand for jobs by Americans.

Older workers who have lost long-term stable jobs because of changes in the structure of the U.S. economy present another vexing problem. Although the service sector (telecommunications, insurance, banking, and restaurants) grew during the 1980s, the manufacturing sector did not. As a result, many workers have been displaced—that is, they lost their jobs permanently. It has not been uncommon for displaced workers to take positions offering lower pay, longer hours, and reduced benefits. Steel, automobile, textile, and machinery workers account for more than half of the estimated 2 million displaced workers. Most of these people live in one of the eight states where the economy is dominated by heavy industry—Illinois, Indiana, Michigan, New Jersey, New York, Ohio, Pennsylvania, and Wisconsin.[27]

The United States has also struggled with inflation in the prices of goods and services for several decades. From 1950 to the mid-1960s prices increased, on average, no more than 2 percent or 3 percent annually. From 1968 to 1973, prices rose at a 4.6 percent average rate; from 1973 to 1980 the average rate was 8.9 percent.[28] Double-digit annual inflation rates were reached in 1974 and 1975 and in 1980 and 1981.[29] A car that cost $2,000 in 1968 cost more than $15,000 in 1990.

Since reaching peak levels, inflation has fallen to levels of little more than 5 percent per year. The underlying factors contributing to higher prices include the price of fossil fuels and agricultural commodities, mortgage interest rates, and wage demands. The collapse of the oil cartel and the rapid decline in the price of crude oil accounted for nearly half of the decline in inflation from 1980 to 1985.[30] When Middle East oil-exporting countries increase prices or become embroiled in war, energy prices and inflation shoot up again.

The New Economic Agenda

American policy makers are grappling with two relatively new economic difficulties, the burgeoning federal budget deficit and the decline of America's competitive position in the world economy. Government policy makers and American citizens will be living with the consequences of these problems for many years, and neither problem will be easily resolved.

In less than a decade, the federal deficit, which used to be a relatively minor problem, has assumed gargantuan proportions. Between 1981 and 1988, the total national debt doubled, to more than $2.3 trillion; it had taken nearly 200 years to accumulate the first trillion dollars of debt.[31] It is estimated that by 1992, the total federal debt will have reached $4 trillion.[32]

In 1968 the federal government ran a deficit of $25 billion in a $178 billion budget.[33] In 1983 the deficit exceeded $200 billion in an $800 billion budget. In 1988, after concerted efforts were made to reduce spending, the deficit still exceeded $145 billion.[34] By fiscal year 1991, the deficit had grown to $318 billion of the $1.4 trillion federal budget.[35]

Interest payments to government creditors are the largest contributor to the growth of deficits and constitute one of the fastest-growing portions of the federal budget. In 1979 interest on the debt was $43 billion; by 1991 it had ballooned to $197 billion. In general, two-thirds of the money borrowed each year by the Treasury is used merely to meet interest payments. Because larger and larger portions of the annual budget must be set aside to pay investors, the funds available for productive federal spending have diminished.[36]

During the 1980s, the federal government paid out about five dollars for every four it collected. In simple terms, Americans got more from government than they paid for. The government borrowed the rest from American and foreign investors. The long-term consequences of continued high deficits go beyond the restriction of federal spending. Brookings Institution scholars have warned:

> If continued over the long run, large budget deficits would either reduce domestic investment [in plant, equipment, and other forms of capital] or be financed by increasingly uncertain, and potentially reversible, capital inflow from abroad. In either case, living standards of U.S. citizens would fall.[37]

Despite repeated attempts during the 1980s to bring them under control, budget deficits have continued to grow. The president and Congress have been unable to find the politically acceptable balance between program cuts and additional revenues that would arrest the continuing upward spiral in the federal budget. Budget deficits are required to decline as a result of agreements reached under the Deficit Reduction Act of 1990, but it remains to be seen whether the will to reduce government spending will be sufficient to produce results. Future generations of policy makers and citizens may be saddled with the responsibility of paying these huge debts.

The struggle of the United States to remain competitive in the world economy may pose an even more difficult problem. America is facing some of the most serious economic challenges in its history. Its rate of technological advance has fallen behind those of many other industrial nations and even some Third World countries. Once the world's leading exporter, the United States now regularly experiences trade deficits of more than $100 billion.[38] By the 1980s, the United States was importing more than half of its televisions, radios, tape recorders, and phonographs. One automobile in four and one-fourth of the steel purchased in the United States were made abroad. During the 1960s, foreign competitors supplied no more than 10 percent of the U.S. market for these products. During the 1970s, the U.S. share of the world market for manufactured goods declined by nearly 25 percent, while every other industrialized nation either maintained or increased its share of the world market.[39]

The United States work force is plagued by declining productivity and skills shortages. During the 1950s and early 1960s, productivity increased at the healthy rate of more than 3 percent per year. During the 1970s, the productivity rate plunged to just over 1 percent, and by 1979 the productivity rate actually had declined. During the 1980s, worker productivity rebounded slightly, increasing on average 1.2 percent per year.[40] Aggressive businesses of industrialized nations, such as Japan and Germany, have been joined by efficient new companies in Korea, Hong Kong, Taiwan, and Brazil. Competition from abroad and ineffective public and private policies could lead to a U.S. economy that produces fewer jobs, more low-level (lower-paying) jobs, and a reduced standard of living for Americans.

Although there is bipartisan agreement that the U.S. economy faces serious challenges, little consensus has been reached on an appropriate response by the government and private sector.[41] Some argue that America's competitive weakness proves that government should restructure its policies to encourage corporate Darwinism—the survival of the fittest. Others contend that more government planning and management of the economy is needed to match the efforts of overseas competitors. Some insist that U.S. industries will compete more effectively on the world scene when government subsidies and trade restrictions are removed. Others maintain that government trade policies should either force foreign countries to open up their markets to U.S. products or shut them out of U.S. markets entirely. The search for the correct approach to these problems may well dominate America's economic and political agenda for some time to come.

Ensure Equal Opportunity

Since the founding of the nation, America's leaders have espoused a commitment to equality of opportunity. But when Thomas Jefferson wrote in the Declaration of Independence that "all men are created equal," he did not include blacks, women, and native Americans. Over time, government policies have gradually extended political, social, and economic opportunities to groups originally denied them. The Constitution has been amended to ensure political rights for blacks and women. Statutes prohibiting discrimination on the basis of race, gender, ethnicity, age, and disability have been applied to education, employment, housing, voting, and public accommodations.

The nation's moral credo rejects discrimination and advocates equal opportunity, but living up to this code and giving it practical meaning have been as difficult to accomplish as any aspect of American public policy. The battle over racial equality was marked by lynchings, bombings of black churches, and other ugly incidents. The uncomfortable chasm between American ideals and the actual distribution of opportunities and benefits has properly been called an American dilemma.[42] Americans place a high value on individual initiative and self-reliance. But there is a growing awareness that even in a democracy, prosperity that is not shared is prosperity soon disdained. Working toward and giving people a sense of fairness is the glue that holds a democratic society together. Economist Arthur Okun commented that U.S. society awards prizes that allow the big winners to feed their pets better than the losers can feed their children. Such is the double standard of a capitalist democracy, professing and pursuing an egalitarian political and social system and simultaneously generating gaping disparities in economic well-being.[43]

The achievement of equal opportunity raises four difficult questions about what equal opportunity means and how the government should promote it:

1. Should government guarantees of equal opportunities encompass both the political system and the economic system?
2. To what extent is the government obligated to redress past discrimination against particular groups of Americans?
3. Should government promote greater equality in the distribution of wealth and other social benefits?
4. Does meaningful affirmative action require a quota system?

Unfulfilled Promises

The United States has made significant strides, especially since the early 1960s. Women, blacks, and other minorities are no longer denied the right to vote or hold office. The U.S. armed forces no longer places black and white Americans in separate fighting units. The Supreme Court has declared that all children in a particular community should be educated in the same schools, regardless of race. Congress has determined that Americans must not be discriminated against because of their race, gender, disabilities, or ethnic origin when they apply to colleges and universities, seek employment or housing, and apply for insurance and bank loans. White Americans have become more racially tolerant.[44]

Despite these significant accomplishments, America remains a society in which millions do not fully enjoy the nation's political, social, and economic benefits.[45] Poverty, homelessness, and hunger remain serious problems in one of the world's most affluent nations. After dropping to 11 percent in 1973 from 22 percent in 1960, poverty gradually increased in the 1980s. In 1989 more than 31 million people, or 13 percent of the population, could not afford the basic necessities of life as defined by government standards. The poverty rate for children was even higher.[46]

Income and wealth are unequally distributed. The bottom 20 percent of all U.S. families received only 3.8 percent of the total money income in 1986; the top 20 percent received more than ten times as much, or 46.1 percent of the total.[47] Inequities in the distribution of income have not improved since World War II.[48] "There has been an increase in income inequality in the United States during the last decade and a half," according to Census Bureau official Gordon Green.[49] The equity of income distribution in America ranks eighth among the eleven members of the Organization for Economic Cooperation and Development, which includes the United Kingdom, Japan, Canada, Australia, Sweden, and other nations.[50] The ownership of wealth is even more unevenly distributed than income; more than three-quarters of all the privately owned wealth is in the hands of 20 percent of the population.[51]

Federal, state, and local tax systems do little to redistribute income, and in some ways they increase inequities. According to Benjamin Page:

> The federal income tax is more egalitarian than other taxes. But the progressivity of the actual effective rates—as contrasted with the nominal schedule rates—is rather mild and has been eroded over time. Taxes on the rich are not very high.... Various exclusions and exemptions and deductions from taxable income greatly benefit the rich.[52]

The tax code revision of 1986 eliminated millions of poor and near-poor Americans from the tax rolls, but even after these major changes tax laws remain inequitable.

People earning the same income often pay very different amounts in federal taxes. High-income Americans may pay less in taxes than people who earn a great deal less. Inequities persist because the tax code contains a host of exclusions, preferences, and deductions. For example, homeowners are permitted to deduct all of the interest they pay on mortgages for their primary residence and for a vacation home. The owner of a $60,000 house and the owner of a $5 million mansion can deduct the entire amount of their interest payments from their tax liability. The home mortgage deduction amounts to a direct subsidy of more than $40 billion to high-income individuals. People who rent or have modest mortgage payments receive little or no tax benefits.[53]

If federal income taxes do little to redistribute income from the rich to the poor, payroll taxes and state and local income taxes accomplish the opposite: the more money a person is paid, the lower the percentage of income paid to the government. Social Security taxes, for example, are withheld at a flat rate and only on $55,000 in income. The $250,000-a-year investment banker on Wall Street pays the same amount in Social Security taxes as the $45,000-a-year civil engineer. State and local taxes, which rely heavily on the sales tax, are regressive. People with low incomes pay the same tax rate as those with high incomes. But a larger share of the poor person's income is used to purchase the goods and services necessary for survival.[54]

These disparities are especially difficult to justify in a society where economic hardship is not random. Minorities are much more likely to be poor, unemployed, and otherwise disadvantaged than white Americans. In 1989 the poverty rate was 31 percent for blacks, but it was only 10 percent for whites. Unemployment rates follow a similar pattern. In December 1990, for example, the unemployment rate for white adults was 6 percent, but it was 12 percent for blacks and 11 percent for Hispanics. The picture is even bleaker for young people. During the same month in 1990, 15 percent of white teens were unemployed, as opposed to 36 percent of black and Hispanic teenagers.[55]

Women head more than half of all poor families, continuing a trend that has been called the feminization of poverty.[56] Most poor women are widowed or divorced and have been left without economic support for themselves and their children, and many are unwed mothers. Eighty percent receive no financial support from the child's father. Teen pregnancy rates have jumped by 20 percent since 1970; two-thirds of those mothers will spend at least some time in poverty. Many women are poor even though they work at full-time, year-round jobs. Because of inflation, the purchasing power of their minimum-wage jobs eroded by one-quarter in the period 1980-1985.[57]

Progress for minorities has been slow because in many ways, the United States remains a racially segregated society. Minority groups are concentrated in metropolitan areas; they may be kept from living in suburban communities by discriminatory real estate sales practices or the lack of affordable housing for moderate- and low-income individuals. Efforts to desegregate the schools have had limited success. Although the number of black children attending predominantly black schools in the South dropped from 81 percent in 1968 to 57 percent in 1980, black children attending predominantly black schools in the North increased from 7 percent to 80 percent during the same period.[58]

Women have not achieved economic and political parity with men. Women have increased their participation in the work force from 42 percent in 1970 to more than 58 percent in 1990,[59] and laws guaranteeing equal pay for equal work have been passed in many states.[60] But women earn on average sixty-three cents for every dollar earned by men.[61] Women are concentrated in several occupations (teaching, nursing, and clerical positions) that pay less than occupations predominantly held by men (accountants, salespeople, and laborers), even though the female-dominated jobs require similar skills and training. Although women constitute more than half of the U.S. population, there are few women in leadership positions in business and industry or government.

Prospects for Change

Strategies promoting social, political, and economic equity have been highly controversial and only moderately successful. The women's movement has failed to obtain ratification of an equal rights amendment to the Constitution. Although the Supreme Court has endorsed the strategy of affirmative action, the practice is still subject to legal challenge and to resistance by many institutions. Inequities in the distribution of income and wealth were not addressed by the tax policy changes of the Reagan or Bush administrations and the Democratic party has not advanced any bold or promising initiatives to redistribute income in America.

A major impetus for change may come from the desire of American business and industry to remain competitive in the world economy. Business and political leaders are beginning to realize that the nation must fully use available human resources. For the foreseeable future, a significant portion of entry-level workers will consist of minorities, immigrants for whom English is a second language, and other low-income individuals.[62] This surge of disadvantaged workers may prompt greater efforts to bring them into the mainstream of the American economy.

Provide a Safety Net

The power of government has not been exercised in an attempt to achieve a radical redistribution of income and wealth, but American policy makers have erected a network of programs that provide financial support and health care to millions of citizens. These measures may not always lift the poor out of poverty, but they keep people from falling farther into it. Initiated by liberal Democratic president Franklin D. Roosevelt in the 1930s, these New Deal social insurance and welfare programs were considered an essential social "safety net" even by conservative Republican president Ronald Reagan.[63]

The vast array of programs that support elderly, poor, unemployed, and disabled Americans consume the largest proportion of the federal budget. It has grown so quickly since the 1950s that politicians are beginning to ask some very tough questions. Can Americans afford these programs? Can the country afford to be without them? How can these programs be made more efficient and equitable?

Income-Support Programs

Since the New Deal, the basic structure of the American welfare state has expanded to encompass new classes of beneficiaries and to authorize more generous benefits. Once a small fraction of the budget, income-support programs now account for approximately 40 percent of federal outlays and constitute a huge portion of state and local spending. Income-support programs amounted to less than 3 percent of the GNP in 1960; by 1990 they amounted to nearly three times as much. Federal expenditures have increased tenfold in less than thirty years.[64] During the 1980s, the trend of extending eligibility and expanding benefits slowed, but safety net spending continued its upward trend.[65]

The number of Americans benefiting from the safety net has grown by leaps and bounds. Social Security—which aids retirees, the children of deceased workers, and disabled workers—is the largest federal program, with expenditures of $248 billion in 1990.[66] In 1990, one American in six received Social Security retirement checks, and 90 percent of the working population contributed through payroll tax deductions to the program. An average of 2.7 million Americans received unemployment compensation each week during 1990 at an annual cost of $19 billion, and most of the nation's more than 100 million workers are employed by companies that contribute to the insurance system. Approximately 20 million people receive food stamps. Nearly 4 million American families receive public assistance.[67]

Income-support programs come in two forms: programs dispensed according to need and programs distributed without regard to need. Many income-support programs are called "entitlement" programs because people receive benefits as a matter of statutory right. The largest income-support programs, including Social Security and unemployment insurance, are available to eligible recipients no matter what their income or assets may be. Therefore, most income-support programs are not subject to a means test: full benefits are extended to rich and poor alike. About 90 percent of the funds reserved for older Americans do not require applicants to demonstrate financial need.[68]

Social Security and unemployment insurance replace part of the income lost due to retirement, disability, or unemployment. Retirees who made $1,000 per month during their working years receive about a 60 percent replacement.[69] A typical unemployed worker is paid about $450 per month or about a 40 percent replacement of income. Unemployment insurance lasts only a few months; during the recessions of the early 1980s and 1991, less than half of the unemployed were receiving unemployment insurance checks.[70]

Social Security and unemployment insurance are based on the concept of social insurance. During their working years, individuals contribute about 7 percent of their income into the Social Security trust fund to help cover the cost of benefits they may eventually receive. Employers pay into an insurance trust fund from which workers receive benefits during periods of unemployment.

Intended as a partial supplement to private pension plans and family incomes, Social Security provides a financial base for those who could not adequately prepare for retirement. Social Security is the nation's strongest antipoverty program and, along with medical insurance for senior citizens, it has contributed substantially to reducing the number of older Americans who are poor. Once the elderly were a disadvantaged group: in 1960 more than 25 percent of the nation's senior citizens lived in poverty. Today, just over 10 percent of the elderly are poor. Median family incomes of the elderly have more than doubled since 1960. In fact, their incomes have increased faster than the incomes of the rest of the population. The average Social Security check for a retired couple in the late 1980s was higher than $700 per month, which by itself provides sufficient income to live above government-defined poverty levels.[71]

The biggest challenges for administrators of the Social Security program have been controlling growth and keeping the system solvent. The earlier retirements and longer life-spans of Americans have imposed new strains on the Social Security trust fund. Since the mid-1970s, benefit payments have increased at regular intervals as a result of legislated cost-of-living adjustments and thus roughly keep pace with inflation.

Proposals for trimming Social Security benefits in the early 1980s met a firestorm of criticism from Democrats and senior citizen groups, who form a large, politically powerful constituency. A bipartisan reform commission made several short- and long-term changes in the program, but virtually all the modifications increased the funds for distribution, rather than curtailing existing benefits.[72] In the future, changing demographics and the need to maintain a sound insurance system may force policy makers to tighten up eligibility criteria. Then, older Americans with higher incomes might receive lower benefit payments.

The balance of the federal and state income-support programs are reserved for poor Americans. Aid to Families with Dependent Children and food stamps are made available only after individuals have proved they need assistance. A woman must have children and no other means of support in order to be considered for AFDC payments. She must not earn more than $3,000 in any given year and must have few personal assets.

The AFDC program is paid for by the states and the federal government and administered by states and localities. Benefit levels vary widely. For example, in 1987 the monthly payment for a family of four in Alabama was $147, whereas in Alaska it was $833.[73] In 1989 the combined benefits of AFDC and food stamps came to less than 60 percent of poverty-level income in eight states and within 20 percent of poverty-level income in only sixteen states.[74] The typical welfare recipient is a white female who remains on welfare for less than two years and works part time.

Welfare and food stamps consume fewer federal dollars and constitute much smaller portions of the federal budget—less than 5 percent—than the non-means-tested entitlement programs. Welfare and nutrition aid for the poor cost the federal government approximately $35 billion in fiscal year 1990—less than 15 percent of the cost of Social Security alone.[75] Food stamps are the fastest-growing component of these programs. In less than two decades the cost of food stamps has increased nearly twentyfold.[76]

Unlike Social Security, which is widely regarded as a successful, but expensive, program, AFDC is disliked by taxpayers and recipients alike. Even though only a small percentage of funds is spent on ineligible people, opinion polls consistently show that the public perceives the program as awash in corruption and abuse. Welfare recipients and others complain that AFDC payments are stingy and that the system encourages recipients to remain poor and discourages their self-reliance.

The widespread perception that the welfare system was "broken" led to significant welfare reform in 1988.[77] Congress endorsed a major overhaul of the system, modeled after successful state initiatives.[78] Under the Family Support Act, welfare will no longer penalize those who want to work their way off welfare. The new programs are designed to encourage or require recipients to seek full-time employment and get off welfare by providing them with extended health benefits and child-care assistance after they find jobs.

Health Care

America's income-support programs were spawned primarily by the New Deal. The health-care programs—Medicare for the elderly and Medicaid for the poor—were the offspring of Lyndon Johnson's War on Poverty. When Medicare was adopted in 1965, the Social Security Administration estimated that it would cost the government $8.2 billion in 1983. The estimate was terribly wrong. Medicare cost more than $98 billion in 1990; Medicaid cost another $40 billion. Government health insurance pays nearly half of the hospital costs and doctor bills for the entire nation.[79] Although government support for health care in the United States still trails that of other industrialized nations, the commitment has increased rapidly. When private contributions to health care spending are included, the United States leads the world in the amount of its GNP devoted to health care.[80]

Elderly and poor Americans are the principal beneficiaries of government health care programs. Medicare serves all Americans over the age of 65 regardless of need. Program participants pay for part of the cost of physician visits and hospital care, but most of the tab is picked up by the government. Medicaid is reserved for the poorest of the poor. Approximately one-third of America's poor population is not poor enough to qualify for Medicaid.[81] Millions of Americans who are not old or not very poor have inadequate medical insurance or none at all.

Health care costs and government expenditures for health programs have skyrocketed, driven by three factors: demographics, third-party reimbursement, and the complexity of medical care. Increases in the aging and poor populations have resulted in greater outlays in these entitlement programs. Medical consumers and medical professionals are not motivated to keep costs down because three-fourths of all medical bills are borne by third parties, namely, the government or private insurance companies.[82] Consumer goods currently cost four times as much as they did in the late 1950s, but medical care costs have increased eightfold.[83] The enormous increase in government outlays for medical procedures and hospitalization has generated demands for a less costly health care system.

In many ways, Medicare and Medicaid meet their legislative objectives. Medicare provides financial assistance for a critical need of elderly citizens. Medicaid serves as an adjunct to food stamps and public assistance for the poor, the blind, and the disabled. Despite these accomplishments and burgeoning budgets, government health care programs have not substantially reduced many serious health care problems. Simply increasing health care expenditures does not necessarily lead to better health.[84] Infant mortality rates have declined, but they still exceed those in many other industrialized nations. For black Americans, the number of deaths per 1,000 births is higher than in Jamaica, Cuba, Brunei, and twenty-eight other countries.[85] Access to affordable, high-quality medical care remains a serious problem for millions of Americans, including many covered by Medicare and Medicaid. Medicare, for example, does not fund extended care in nursing homes—one of the most serious problems of the elderly. Older persons must exhaust their financial resources before they can turn to Medicaid for help.[86]

Most important, American health insurance programs do little to help prevent serious health problems.[87] Significant public health gains were realized in the first half of the twentieth century through government-sponsored measures to improve sanitation, water quality, and immunization against communicable diseases. Government-sponsored research contributes significantly to the treatment of serious diseases, but many health policy analysts argue that government policy should be changed to encourage Americans to take more responsibility for their own health. Some of the leading causes of death—smoking, alcohol consumption, and faulty diet—are influenced by personal choices. According to the surgeon general of the United States, smoking is "the chief, single avoidable cause of death in our society and the most important public health problem of our time." [88] Not only does the government do little to stop smoking (such as banning cigarettes and cigars), it actually subsidizes the production of tobacco in several states.

Protect the Environment

Conserving the nation's resources and protecting its environment yield immediate, tangible benefits and long-term, intangible benefits. The primary purpose of environmental controls is improved public health—lower mortality and morbidity rates and reduced medical expenses. The long-term benefits derived from protecting the environment are less tangible and more diffuse, but critically important. President Carter's Commission for a National Agenda for the Eighties posed this question: "What value can be placed on public enjoyment of purer air, cleaner water, or protected wilderness, or more importantly, on preserving the long-term integrity of natural life support systems?" [89]

Compared with other goals, preserving and protecting the environment has been a central policy goal in the United States for a short period of time. Prior to the 1960s, concern for the environment centered on preserving the natural environment. Landmark policies adopted during the early decades of the twentieth century established national parks, forests, and wilderness refuges. The federal government is the nation's largest landholder: it owns 700 million acres or one-third of the entire country. [90] Environmental measures—such as the Refuse Act of 1899—were adopted to blunt the most egregious results of urbanization.

Although conservation goals have not been abandoned, environmental policies since the early 1960s have constituted reactions to the consequences of an industrialized, chemically dependent society. For decades, American consumers and businesses took environmental quality for granted. Vast quantities of hazardous and toxic wastes and chemicals were dumped on the land and in the water and released into the air. Perhaps more than any other single event, the publication of Rachel Carson's *Silent Spring* in 1962, promoted an awareness of the fragility of the environment. Carson's book documented that the use of the chemical DDT in farming destroyed wildlife and threatened humans. Ten years later, the production of DDT was banned for use on American soil.

Concern over the deterioration of the environment generated widespread public support (marked by Earth Day 1970) for stronger environmental laws. Americans are frequently reminded of potentially harmful substances lurking in the air and water. The poisoning of the food chain with cancer-causing PCB (polychlorinated biphenyl), the presence of noxious fumes and smog in urban communities, and the contamination of water due to leaking toxic waste dumps are the price exacted for the casual attitudes of the past. According to environmental scholar Walter Rosenbaum, "We are practically the first generation in the world's history with the certain technical capacity to alter and even to destroy the fundamental biochemical and geophysical conditions for societies living centuries after ours." [91]

More than twenty major environmental protection laws were enacted at the federal level during the 1970s—the "environmental decade." Among the landmarks were the National Environmental Protection Act, which established a process of assessing the environmental impact of federal projects; the Water Pollution Control Act; the Clean Water Act; the Clean Air Act; the Insecticide, Fungicide, and Rodenticide Act; the Toxic Substances Control Act, which regulates the production and handling of toxic waste; the Resource Conservation and Recovery Act, which regulates the disposal of solid waste; and the Comprehensive Environmental Response, Compensation, and Liability Act, commonly called Superfund, which established procedures for cleaning up toxic waste dumps. Hundreds of state and local laws were also adopted during this period. Standards for improving the quality of the air, water, and land were established, along with government agencies to monitor and enforce compliance. Driving this surge of government regulation was the need to correct the harmful practices of private businesses and individuals.

A Legacy of Contempt

The laws and agencies created during America's environmental awakening set ambitious goals, but decades of contempt for the environment have proved difficult and costly to rectify. Citizens and policy makers began to realize that improving environmental quality will require years of sustained effort, billions of dollars, and profound changes in the way Americans do business and live. The United States has stepped up its attack on environmental problems, but much remains to be done.

Water Quality

Water quality laws enacted during the 1960s and 1970s were supposed to ensure safe drinking water and to clean up polluted rivers, streams, and lakes. The National Technical Advisory Committee on Water Quality Controls reported, however, that there has been little improvement in water quality during the 1980s, according to measurements of five standard pollutants.[92] Pollution generated by individuals and industry continues to flow into surface and ground waters at alarming rates. The $100 billion spent on water pollution control measures has not significantly cut dangerous levels of toxic chemicals, bacteria, nitrates, and phosphorus in the water supply. A national survey of the nation's harbors and lakes in the mid-1980s revealed almost no improvement. Some important bodies of water, such as Lake Erie and the Chesapeake Bay, remain seriously polluted.[93]

Air Quality

Lawmakers hoped that the standards and enforcement mechanisms established by the Clean Air Act of 1970 would significantly reduce air pollution in five years. Despite some progress, those hopes are yet to be fulfilled. On the positive side, by the mid-1980s, dangerous lead emissions had dropped 86 percent, largely as a result of banning the use of high-lead gasoline. Particulate and dust pollution had declined by one-third since the early 1960s. Overall, however, air quality improved by only 13 percent between 1975 and 1985. The air is still fouled with sulfur dioxide and carbon monoxide, which harm the respiratory system. These persistent problems finally resulted in new air pollution legislation in 1990.

Toxic Waste

Notable success in protecting the public from the negative effects of toxic chemicals has been achieved by imposing sharp restrictions on the production and use of several cancer-causing products, including DDT, PCBs, and dioxin. Federal laws governing the handling of toxic wastes established procedures for assessing chemical hazards and disposing of them properly. Government agencies responsible for cleaning up abandoned toxic waste dumps have identified hundreds of dangerous situations and eliminated or curtailed many threats to the environment and public health.

Unfortunately, toxic waste problems are growing in complexity and scope. Many possibly toxic chemicals are being introduced so fast that the government is unable to test them all for potential hazards. American industry generates 265 million metric tons of hazardous waste every year—more than one ton for each citizen. Up to one-third of these wastes, most often in the form of "dirty water," are released untreated into the environment.[94] Little progress has been made in curtailing the flow of poisonous chemicals.

Progress in implementing the Superfund cleanup program has been slow and disappointing. According to the Office of Technology Assessment, there are 30,000 toxic waste dumps in the United States, thousands of which pose serious health threats. The OTA estimates that cleanup measures could cost more than $50 billion.[95] The Environmental Protection Agency identified more than 1,000 priority toxic dumps for remedial action, but less than 10 percent of them have been completely cleaned up. The $8 billion fund available under the Superfund program will not be adequate for the task. Often the health effects of toxic chemicals are impossible to detect accurately; the technology for defusing toxic bombs and neutralizing toxic soups is still in its infancy.

From React and Cure to Anticipate and Prevent

America's first two decades of serious environmental regulation were marked by uneven progress. Much effort and billions of dollars have yielded important but modest improvements. The problems that have been discovered and addressed await resolution, but the environmental threats in the immediate future may be even more intractable. An EPA task force reported that "newer" environmental problems, such as "indoor radon, global climatic change, . . . acid precipitation, and hazardous waste," will be difficult to evaluate and may "involve persistent contaminants that move from one environmental medium to another, causing further damage even after controls have been applied." [96]

Enormous expenditures and upheavals in industrial production practices will be needed to clean up and preserve the environment. These economic and social costs must be borne today, but most of the benefits will accrue to future generations. Thus far, private and public policy makers have been unwilling to take the necessary steps: The pressures for immediate economic growth have been too powerful to resist. The so-called greenhouse effect illustrates the trade-offs. Increased accumulation of carbon dioxide and other gases in the upper atmosphere has caused global temperatures to rise by three to four degrees in the last 100 years. Scientists project that similar temperature increases could occur by the year 2030, causing drastic changes in the earth's climate, severe flooding, drought, and famine on a scale unparalleled in human history. Reversing or slowing this trend will require reductions in the use of fossil fuels and unprecedented cooperation among the nations of the world.[97]

Compared with many other parts of the world, the United States has an admirable environmental protection record. The industrialized communist nations have relatively poor environmental records. Levels of sulfur dioxide emissions from the Soviet Union are three times greater than the levels emitted from the United States. Hundreds of thousands of people were exposed to dangerous radiation levels in the aftermath of the world's worst nuclear power plant disaster at Chernobyl in the Soviet Union.[98] Environmental degradation is widespread in the Third World, where the pressures for development to support exploding populations are intense. Twenty-eight million acres of ecologically valuable rain forests—an area roughly the size of Pennsylvania—are destroyed every year. If this destruction continues unchecked, the loss of the rain forests could become "an ecological disaster of major proportions." [99]

Clearly, public policy makers in this country and around the world must do better. The World Commission on Environment and Development concluded that

> many present development trends leave increasing numbers of people poor and vulnerable while at the same time degrading the environment. How can such development serve next century's world of twice as many people relying on the same environment?. . . [T]he react and cure environmental policies that governments have pursued are bankrupt. . . . Anticipate and prevent is the only realistic approach.[100]

Achieving a sustainable environment in the face of enormous worldwide development pressures will be extremely difficult, but the very survival of the planet depends on it.

Summary

Any fair assessment of American public policy would conclude that great progress has been made toward fulfilling the nation's goals and values. The United States is, in many ways, better off than it was fifty, twenty, or ten years ago. Some significant arms control agreements have been signed, and the prospects for more far-reaching controls look better than they have in many years. Despite several difficult recessions in the 1980s and in 1991, the economy remains vital and growing with relatively low inflation and modest unemployment levels. The most egregious forms of racial and gender-based discrimination have been curtailed or at least identified. The social safety net of income support and health care for the elderly and disadvantaged has survived attempted reductions. The first steps have been taken to preserve and protect the air, water, and land necessary for survival.

But U.S. public policies are not as effective as they should be. Massive increases in defense spending have not produced a country that is significantly less vulnerable to thermonuclear war or terrorist attacks. The rising tide of economic recovery has failed to lift all boats.

In one of the world's most affluent nations, millions are unemployed, homeless, and hungry. The gaps between rich and poor, black and white have grown wider. Discrimination based on race, gender, age, and disability is still pervasive. The costs of income security and health care programs have risen so rapidly that their solvency is threatened, but benefits for poor people are barely adequate for their survival, and the health of Americans has not improved significantly. The water and air remain dangerously polluted by automobile exhaust, industrial waste, and toxic chemicals.

Much, therefore, remains to be done. The problems facing policy makers and citizens are as intractable as any the nation has faced. Among the most pressing are:

—reducing the budget deficit
—keeping America competitive in the world economy
—redressing discrimination against minorities and women
—bringing poor people into the mainstream of society
—improving the social safety net
—meeting unprecedented threats to the environment
—accommodating an increasingly diverse population

If the past is prologue, there is reason to be deeply concerned about the willingness and ability of American political institutions to meet these challenges. Extraordinary skills, leadership, and cooperation will be required in the years ahead.

Notes

1. Center for Public Interest Polling, *Images III: The Quality of Life in New Jersey* (New Brunswick, N.J.: Eagleton Institute of Politics, Rutgers University, 1985).

2. See, for example, President's Commission for a National Agenda for the Eighties, *A National Agenda for the Eighties* (Englewood Cliffs, N.J.: Prentice-Hall, 1980).

3. See, for example, Carol Weiss, *Evaluation Research* (Englewood Cliffs, N.J.: Prentice-Hall, 1972); Peter Rossi and Howard E. Freeman, *Evaluation: A Systematic Approach*, 3d ed. (Beverly Hills, Calif.: Sage, 1984); and Arnold J. Meltsner, *Policy Analysts in the Bureaucracy* (Berkeley: University of California Press, 1976).

4. John D. Steinbruner, "Security Policy," in *The New Direction in American Politics*, ed. John E. Chubb and Paul E. Peterson (Washington, D.C.: Brookings Institution, 1985), 343-364.

5. B. Guy Peters, *American Public Policy: Promise and Performance* (Chatham, N.J.: Chatham House, 1986), 287-289.

6. Steinbruner, "Security Policy," 345.

7. Henry J. Aaron, Harvey Galper, Joseph A. Pechman, George L. Perry, Alice M. Rivlin, and Charles C. Schultze, *Economic Choices, 1987* (Washington, D.C.: Brookings Institution, 1986), 75.

8. *Economic Report of the President* (Washington, D.C.: Government Printing Office, 1985); and John L. Palmer and Isabel V. Sawhill, *The Reagan Record: An Assessment of Changing Domestic Priorities* (Cambridge, Mass.: Ballinger, 1984), 8.

9. Steinbruner, "Security Policy," 349.

10. Executive Office of the President, Office of Management and Budget, *Budget of the United States Government, Fiscal Year 1991* (Washington, D.C.: Government Printing Office, 1990), 183.

11. Leo Bogart, *Polls and the Awareness of Public Opinion*, 2d ed. (New Brunswick, N.J.: Transaction Books, 1985), 89-96.

12. W. Lance Bennett, "Marginalizing the Majority: Conditioning Public Opinion to Accept Managerial Democracy" (Paper presented at the annual meeting of the Midwest Political Science Association, Chicago, April, 1987), 16.

13. Joseph A. Pechman, *Federal Tax Policy*, 4th ed. (Washington, D.C.: Brookings Institution, 1983), 27-28.

14. U.S. Congress, Joint Economic Committee, *The 1985 Joint Economic Report* (Washington, D.C.: Government Printing Office, 1985), 67-68.

15. Executive Office of the President, Office of Management and Budget, *Budget of the United States Government, Fiscal Year 1992* (Washington, D.C.: Government Printing Office, 1991), 35.

16. Joint Economic Committee, *The 1985 Joint Economic Report*, 70-71.

17. Bruce R. Scott, "U.S. Competitiveness: Concepts, Performance, and Implications," in *U.S. Competitiveness in the World Economy*, ed. Bruce R. Scott and George C. Lodge (Boston: Harvard Business School Press, 1985), 61.

18. Ibid., 38.

19. Ibid., 36-37; and Robert Kuttner, *The Economic Illusion: False Choices between Prosperity and Social Justice* (Boston: Houghton Mifflin, 1984), 291.

20. Scott, "U.S. Competitiveness," 35-36.

21. Ibid., 39; and Robert B. Reich, *The Next American Frontier* (New York: Times Books, 1983), 118.

22. Reich, *The Next American Frontier*, 118-119.

23. Kuttner, *The Economic Illusion*, 291.

24. Reich, *The Next American Frontier*, 207.

25. Donald C. Baumer and Carl E. Van Horn, *The Politics of Unemployment* (Washington, D.C.: CQ Press, 1985), 2-3.

26. Ibid., 3-4.

27. Joint Economic Committee, *The 1985 Joint Economic Report*, 36.

28. Kenneth M. Dolbeare, *Democracy at Risk: The Politics of Economic Renewal*, rev. ed. (Chatham, N.J.: Chatham House, 1986), 60.

29. Joint Economic Committee, *The 1985 Joint Economic Report*, 97.

30. Ibid., 25. Inflation rates for 1980-1990 are from the *Economic Report of the President* (Washington, D.C.: Government Printing Office, 1991), 351 (Table B-58). Current figures are from the *New York Times*, August 15, 1991, D1.

31. Joint Economic Committee, *The 1985 Joint Economic Report*, 47.

32. *Economic Report of the President*, 1991, 375.

33. Executive Office of the President, Office of Management and Budget,

Budget of the United States Government, Fiscal Year 1986 (Washington, D.C.: Government Printing Office, 1985).

34. Executive Office of the President, Office of Management and Budget, *Budget of the United States Government, Fiscal Year 1987* (Washington, D.C.: Government Printing Office, 1986).

35. Executive Office of the President, Office of Management and Budget, *Budget of the United States Government, Fiscal Year 1992.*

36. Ibid.

37. Aaron et al., *Economic Choices, 1987,* 4.

38. *Economic Report of the President,* 1991, 402 (Table B-102).

39. Reich, *The Next American Frontier,* 121-122.

40. *Economic Report of the President,* 1991, 339.

41. See, for example, Scott and Lodge, *U.S. Competitiveness in the World Economy;* Reich, *The Next American Frontier;* and Sidney Blumenthal, "Drafting a Democratic Industrial Plan," *New York Times Magazine,* August 28, 1983.

42. Gunnar Myrdal, *An American Dilemma* (New York: Harper & Row, 1944).

43. Arthur M. Okun, *Equality and Efficiency: The Big Tradeoff* (Washington, D.C.: Brookings Institution, 1975), 1.

44. William Schneider, "People Watching," *National Journal,* January 12, 1985, 63.

45. See, for example, Okun, *Equality and Efficiency;* Dolbeare, *Democracy at Risk;* and Kuttner, *The Economic Illusion.*

46. *Economic Report of the President,* 1991, 320.

47. Robert Pear, "Poverty Rate Dips as the Median Family Income Rises," *New York Times,* July 31, 1987, A12.

48. Harrell R. Rodgers, Jr., *The Cost of Human Neglect* (Armonk, N.Y.: M. E. Sharpe, 1982), 29.

49. Pear, "Poverty Rate Dips."

50. Benjamin I. Page, *Who Gets What from Government* (Berkeley: University of California Press, 1983), 191.

51. Rodgers, *The Cost of Human Neglect,* 28.

52. Page, *Who Gets What from Government,* 22-23.

53. Pechman, *Federal Tax Policy,* 60-128.

54. Page, *Who Gets What from Government,* 35-41.

55. *Economic Report of the President,* 1991, 320, 330-331.

56. Pear, "Poverty Rate Dips."

57. Isabel V. Sawhill, "Anti-Poverty Strategies for the 1980s," discussion paper (Washington, D.C.: Urban Institute, December 1986), photocopy.

58. Editorial Research Reports, *Education Report Card: Schools on the Line* (Washington, D.C.: Congressional Quarterly, 1985), 13.

59. *Economic Report of the President,* 1991, 328.

60. Renée Cherow-O'Leary, *The State-by-State Guide to Women's Legal Rights* (New York: McGraw-Hill, 1987).

61. Linda Tarr-Whelan and Lynne Crofton Isenee, eds., *The Women's Economic Justice Agenda: Ideas for the States* (Washington, D.C.: National Center for Policy Alternatives, 1987).

62. National Alliance of Business, "Employment Policy Issues for the End of the Century and the Year 2000" (Washington, D.C.: National Alliance of Business, November 22, 1985), photocopy.

63. David Stockman, *The Triumph of Politics* (New York: Harper & Row, 1986), 8.

64. James R. Storey, "Income Security," in *The Reagan Experiment*, ed. John L. Palmer and Isabel V. Sawhill (Washington, D.C.: Urban Institute Press, 1982), 364-365.

65. R. Kent Weaver, "Controlling Entitlements," in *The New Direction in American Politics*, 308.

66. Executive Office of the President, Office of Management and Budget, *Budget of the United States Government, Fiscal Year 1992*, part 4, 3.

67. Baumer and Van Horn, *The Politics of Unemployment*, 9; Weaver, "Controlling Entitlements," 307; and *Economic Report of the President*, 1991, 333.

68. *Economic Report of the President*, 1991, 167.

69. Peters, *American Public Policy*, 214.

70. Kuttner, *The Economic Illusion*, 149; and Baumer and Van Horn, *The Politics of Unemployment*, 14.

71. Pear, "Poverty Rate Dips."

72. Weaver, "Controlling Entitlements," 320.

73. James W. Fesler and Donald F. Kettl, *The Politics of the Administrative Process* (Chatham, N.J.: Chatham House, 1991), 254.

74. *Congressional Quarterly Weekly Report*, May 20, 1989, 1192.

75. Executive Office of the President, Office of Management and Budget, *Budget of the United States Government, Fiscal Year 1992.*

76. Executive Office of the President, Office of Management and Budget, *Budget of the United States Government, Fiscal Year 1986*, part 5, 116.

77. Sawhill, "Anti-Poverty Strategies for the 1980s."

78. See, for example, Julie Kosterlitz, "Reforming Welfare," *National Journal*, December 6, 1986, 2926-2931.

79. *Economic Report of the President*, 1991, 135-137 and 376-377 (Table B-77); and Executive Office of the President, Office of Management and Budget, *Budget of the United States Government, Fiscal Year 1992.*

80. Peters, *American Public Policy*, 188.

81. Ibid., 186.

82. Weaver, "Controlling Entitlements," 323.

83. *Economic Report of the President*, 1991, 351-354, Tables B-58, B-59, B-60.

84. Ibid.

85. Peters, *American Public Policy*, 185.

86. Ibid., 192.

87. *Economic Report of the President*, 1991, 139.

88. Ibid.

89. *A National Agenda for the Eighties*, 49.

90. Congressional Quarterly, *The Battle for Natural Resources* (Washington, D.C.: Congressional Quarterly, 1983), 2.

91. Walter A. Rosenbaum, *Environmental Politics and Policy* (Washington, D.C.: CQ Press, 1985), 100.

92. Barry Commoner, "A Reporter at Large: The Environment," *New Yorker*, June 15, 1987, 51.

93. Ibid.; and Victoria Churchville, "Clean Water Laws Didn't Save the Bay," *Washington Post* national weekly edition, July 7, 1986, 99-111.

94. Commoner, "A Reporter at Large," 52.

95. Office of Technology Assessment, *Technologies and Management Strategies for Hazardous Waste Control* (Washington, D.C.: Government Printing Office, 1983), 7ff.

96. Environmental Protection Agency, "Unfinished Business: A Comparative Assessment of Environmental Problems" (Washington, D.C.: EPA, February 1987), photocopy, xiii.

97. Commoner, "A Reporter at Large," 54.

98. William U. Chandler, "Designing Sustainable Economies," in Lester R. Brown, William U. Chandler, Christopher Flavin, Jodi Jacobson, Cynthia Pollock, Sandra Postel, Linda Starke, and Edward C. Wolf, *The State of the World, 1987* (New York: W. W. Norton, 1987), 187-190.

99. Editorial Research Reports, *Earth's Threatened Resources* (Washington, D.C.: Congressional Quarterly, 1986), 163.

100. World Commission on Environment and Development, *Our Common Future: From One Earth to One World* (New York: Oxford University Press, 1987), 4.

Index

A. H. Robins, 79
Abortion, 178, 250
  forum-shifting of, 306
  public opinion of, 235-236
  referenda, 228, 247
  Supreme Court and, 36, 158, 202, 306
Acid rain, 133, 182, 228
Acquired immune deficiency syndrome (AIDS). *See* AIDS
Adams, Walter, 71
Administrative adjudication, 101, 102-103
Administrative agencies. *See* Bureaucracies
Administrative law, 190, 192-193
  constitutions and, 198
  "hard look" doctrine, 197
  minorities and, 206-208
  versus constitutional law, 208
Administrative law judges, 102-103
Administrative Procedure Act of 1946 (APA), 102, 192, 198, 208, 294-295
Administrative rule making, 11, 59, 294-295
Administrative state, 87
Advertising, deception in, 303
Advisory opinions, 103
Advisory panels, 284
Aerospace industry, 319-320
Affirmative action, 12-13, 62, 92-93, 145, 204-205, 328
Afghanistan, Soviet invasion of, 157, 182-183, 316, 318
Africa, famine in, 232
Agenda building, 231-232
Agent Orange, 129
Agriculture, U.S. Department of (USDA), 94, 306-307

Aid
  block grants, 14-15, 48
  categorical programs, 14, 48
  EDA grants program, 140
  grants-in-aid, 14, 40, 47-48, 160
  intergovernmental, 14-15
AIDS (acquired immune deficiency syndrome), 133, 236, 242, 247
Aid to Families with Dependent Children (AFDC), 14, 87, 109, 330-331
Airplane accidents, 233
Air pollution, 128, 215, 335
Alabama prison reform, 195, 210, 216-217
Allen-Bradley, 71, 80
Alliance for Children, 299
American Bar Association, 107
American Civil Liberties Union (ACLU), 199, 205
American Electronics Association, 319
American Enterprise Institute, 65
American Federation of Labor-Congress of Industrial Organizations (AFL-CIO), 16
American Telephone and Telegraph Co. (AT&T), 58, 63, 195
Amtrak, 78, 127-128
Anaya, Toney, 276
Anderson, George, 180
Antitrust laws, 190
Appellate courts, 209
Apple Computers, 62
Arbitration, 298
Arms control, 247, 317, 318
Army Corps of Engineers, 94, 100, 106, 140, 211, 213-214
Assault weapons, 171-172
Auto emission standards, 133

Automobile industry, 286-287, 323

Babbitt, Bruce, 10
Baker, Howard, 43
Baker, James, 168, 170
Bankruptcy, 78
Barber, Benjamin, 280
Barber, James David, 169
Bargaining, 133-134, 165-168
Baum, Lawrence, 212
Baumgartner, Frank, 306
Bazelon, David, 197
Belew, Wendell, 143
Bell Laboratories, 75-76
Benefit-to-cost ratios, 100
Biden, Joseph, 18
Bieber, Owen, 69
Big Green, 238
Bill of Rights, 201-203
Bird, Rose, 194
Birnbaum, Jeffrey, 299
Bismarck, Otto von, 134
Black, Hugo, 197, 200
Blacks, 325. *See also* Minorities
   infant mortality rates, 332
   policy making and, 163, 276-277
   poverty, 44, 181, 327
   public opinion and, 36
   school desegregation, 212
   unemployment, 77, 327
   voting, 30, 147, 178-179, 212-213
Blanchard, Jim, 178
Block grants, 14-15, 48
Boardroom politics, 24-25, 57-59,
   271-272, 276
   agenda, 59-65
   benefits, 75-77
   competence, 286-287
   corporate governance, 65-70
   decision making, 265
   policy consequences, 77-79
   policy implementation, 74-75
   strategies and policies, 70-74, 79-
   81
Bork, Robert, 199
Boston school desegregation, 12, 195,
   210, 215, 216, 217
Bottle deposits, 237
Boyd, Gerald, 251
Bradley, Bill, 299
Brady, Nicholas, 170

Brennan, William, 299
Brock, James, 71
Brookings Institution, 323
Brown, Lawrence, 141
Brown v. Board of Education
   (1954), 198, 201, 212
Budget deficit, 43, 44, 142-144, 147,
   236-237, 322-323
Budget summit (1990), 301
Bureaucracies, 87-88, 179-180, 273
   chief executives and, 183-184,
   269-271
   competence, 283-284
   courts and, 206-208
   decision making, 99-101, 206-208,
   265
   efficiency, 281
   policies, 101-109, 115-116
Bureaucratic politics, 24, 25, 87-88
   agenda, 88-93
   benefits, 107-109
   change and, 105-107
   cross-pressured bureaucracy, 93-
   101
   decision making, 99-101
   leadership, 96-99
   low game, 88-93
   policy consequences, 109-117
   power, 94-96
   rules and regulations, 101-109
   symbolism, 104-105
Bureaucrats, 87-88
   leadership, 96-99
   policy making and, 10-11
   types of, 97
Burford, Anne, 96
Burger, Warren, 196
   Burger Court, 196, 201-202, 204,
   206
Burke, Edmund, 223
Burroughs Wellcome Company, 73
Bush, George, 34, 43, 107, 127
   budget, 136-137, 144, 160
   campaign promises, 302
   environmental issues, 128, 158
   executive power, 167
   foreign policy, 156, 157
   grants-in-aid, 14
   judicial appointments, 199, 284
   new federalism, 184

Persian Gulf War, 5-6, 164, 175-
176, 234, 302, 318-319
  policies, 59, 175, 178, 318
  privatization, 58, 297
  public opinion, 226
  staff, 169-170, 277
  symbolism, 175
  taxes, 136-137, 302
Business interests, 207, 238. *See also*
  Boardroom politics
Business Roundtable, 16
Busing, 201, 209, 210-211, 214-217
Bypass strategy, 300-301

Cabinet, 10
Cable News Network (CNN), 234
Cable television, 64
California Coastal Act, 111
California Coastal Commission, 110-
111, 116
California Coastal Initiative, 115
California Energy Conservation
  Commission, 74
*California Federal Savings and
  Loan Assn. v. Guerra* (1987), 204
Campaign financing, 17, 128, 168,
  237, 278-279
Campaign GM, 63
Campaign promises, 174, 175, 302
Canada, 47
Capitalism, 31
Capital punishment, 202
Capture theory, 107-108
Cargill, Inc., 64, 67
Carson, Rachel, 333
Carter, Jimmy, 101, 107, 111
  affirmative action, 92-93
  appointments, 199, 277, 284
  campaign promises, 174, 175
  civil service reform, 284
  defense spending, 317
  disability review incident, 244
  energy program, 182, 298-299
  environmental issues, 333
  executive branch reorganization,
    183-184
  executive power, 166, 167
  foreign policy, 157, 182-183
  Iran hostage incident, 157
  legislature and, 9
  Love Canal, 243

media coverage of, 18
  policies, 42-43, 58, 171, 178
  staff, 169
Casework, 8, 126
Catastrophic health insurance, 301
Categorical programs, 14, 48
CBS, 62, 66, 149, 234, 244, 253
Ceaser, James, 176
Celeste, Richard, 226
Centrists, 196
CETA (Comprehensive Employ-
  ment and Training Act), 111-116,
  252-253
Chandler v. Florida (1981), 203
Charitable contributions, 76-77
Chase, Chevy, 238
Chen, Steve, 75
Cheney, Richard, 170
Chernobyl, Soviet Union, 240, 337
Chicago Sun-Times, 19
Chief administrative officers, 170
Chief executive officers (CEOs), 61
Chief executive politics, 24, 25, 155-
156
  agenda, 156-163, 172-179
  benefits, 177-179
  constitutions and, 155
  crisis situations, 157-158, 163-164,
    170-171, 176
  leadership, 168-170
  noncrisis situations, 164-165, 171
  persuasion strategy, 163-172
  policy consequences, 179-184
  policy implementation, 179-184
  policy making, 157-165, 170-172,
    266
  power, 165-168
  symbolism, 173-176
Chief executives, 9-10, 273
  budget, 172-173
  bureaucracies and, 183-184, 269-
    271
  competence, 285-286
  constituents, 167-168, 177-179
  decision making, 170-172
  efficiency, 281
  innovative policies, 176-177
  legislatures and, 9-10, 128-129,
    137
  management and, 183-184
  media and, 155, 167-168

public opinion and, 225-226
staff, 169-170
taxes, 158-160, 168
Child-care legislation, 299, 300
Children's Defense Fund, 299, 300
Chlorofluorocarbons, 68, 303
Chrysler Corporation, 62, 67-68, 69, 72, 78
Cigarette sales, 133
Circuit courts of appeals, 193, 200
City of Pleasant Grove v. United States (1987), 204
Civil Aeronautics Board (CAB), 58, 107
Civil liberties, 197, 199, 202, 203, 296
Civil rights, 65, 141, 161, 175, 178. *See also* Minorities
courts and, 296
public opinion and, 36, 240
symbolism and, 175
Civil Rights Act of 1964, 141, 175
Civil Service Reform Act of 1978, 184
Civil service system, 184, 283-284
Clean Air Act of 1970, 103, 128, 133, 141, 145, 334, 335
Clean Water Act, 129, 334
Clinton, Bill, 157, 166
Cloakroom politics, 24, 25, 123-124
agenda, 124-130
characteristics of, 137-144
market paradigm and, 268-269
policy making, 130-137, 144-150
Coalition-building, 133-134, 196, 299
Coastal Initiative, 110
Code of Federal Regulations, 102
Coelho, Tony, 136
Collins, Martha Layne, 75
Commission for a National Agenda for the Eighties, 333
Commissions, 11
Communications industry, 61, 213
Community Action Program, 41
Community Development Block Grant program, 15
Comparable worth, 210
Competition, 31, 71, 276, 322, 323-324
Comprehensive Coastal Plan, 111

Comprehensive Employment and Training Act (CETA), 111-116, 252-253
Comprehensive Environmental Response, Compensation, and Liability Act (Superfund), 149-150, 294, 334, 336
Compromise, 133-134, 300
Computer-aided design/computer-aided manufacturing (CAD/CAM), 80
Computer-integrated manufacturing, 71
Conflict, scope of, 306
Congress
committee system, 294
compared with Supreme Court, 266-269
efficiency, 281, 282
102d, 124, 125
Congressional Budget Office (CBO), 129-130
Congressional Research Service (CRS), 129-130
Conrail, 78, 127-128
Conservation. *See* Environmental issues
Conservatism, 34-35, 245
"new conservatism," 37
Supreme Court and, 206
Constitution, U.S., 13, 33, 205-206
Constitutional law, 190-192
minorities and, 203-206, 208
versus administrative law, 208
Constitutions, 198
administrative law and, 198
chief executive politics and, 155
initiatives, 23
Consultation, 298-299
Consumer movement, 105-106
Consumer Product Safety Commission, 82
Contracting, 58, 205, 297
Cook, Timothy, 251
Corporate governance, 20-22, 65-70
decision making, 68-70
leadership styles, 67-68
powerholders, 65-67
Corporate raiders, 22, 66
Corporations. *See also* Boardroom politics

adaptability, 70-71
corporate governance, 20-22, 65-70
decision making, 20-22, 68-70, 265, 271-272, 320
image, 71-72
leadership, 67-68
profitability, 59-61, 72-74
public-private spectrum of, 63-65
reform, 279
responsiveness, 279
symbolism, 71-72
takeovers, 62, 66, 72
Cost-benefit analysis, 100
Court decrees, 215-217
Courtroom politics, 24, 25, 189
court decrees, 215-217
decision making, 201-203
issues, 189-194
judicial coalitions, 194-200
policy consequences, 212-215
policy implementation, 208-212
symbolism, 200-201
Courts
appellate, 209
bureaucracies and, 206-208
case selection, 194
chief judge, 197
chief justice, 197
circuit courts, 193, 200
competence, 284-285
environmental issues, 199, 207-208, 213-215
foreign policy and, 193
funding, 210
media and, 203, 209-210, 211, 281
minorities and, 203-208, 210, 212-213
neglected issues, 193
policy making, 266
power of, 195
precedent, 12, 198, 200, 208, 211, 295
state courts, 296
state supreme courts, 13, 195, 202-203
television coverage of, 281
Cronkite, Walter, 234
Cross-media ownership, 61
Crossover sanctions, 15
Cuban missile crisis, 180

Culture, political. See Political culture
Cuomo, Mario, 166

Dahl, Robert, 22, 204
Dalkon Shield, 79
D'Amato, Alfonse, 127
Dames & Moore v. Regan (1981), 193
Daughters of the American Revolution (DAR), 239
DDT, 334, 335
Death penalty, 36
Deception strategy, 302-303
Decision making
bureaucracies, 99-101, 206-208, 265
chief executives, 170-172
corporate, 20-22, 68-70, 265, 271-272, 320
cost-benefit analysis and, 100
incremental, 26, 99-100, 105
information and, 99
judicial, 197-203
legislative, 265
private, 20-22, 25, 26, 286-287
public, 19-20, 22-23, 24, 26
rational model of, 100-101
Declaration of Independence, 32
Defense, 312, 315-319
Defense Department, U.S., 63
Deficit. See Budget deficit
Deficit Reduction Act of 1990, 323
Demand function, 31
Democracy, 19-20, 30, 250
direct, 237-239
juridical, 282
participatory, 33-34
policy making in, 19-20
procedural, 30-33, 266-269
representative, 19, 31, 223
unitary, 33-34
Democratic party, 37
judges, 199
liberalism and, 35, 161
New Deal, 177-178
Democratic Policy Committee, 136
Deregulation, 11, 46-47, 58-59, 182, 304
Derthick, Martha, 304

Desegregation. *See* School deseg-
regation
Deukmejian, George, 177
Dingell, John, 133
Dioxin, 335
Disability review incident, 244
Discouraged workers, 321
Displaced workers, 321-322
Distributive policies, 140
Dole, Robert, 136
Douglas, William, 200
Downs, Anthony, 97
Drexel Burnham Lambert, 79
Drug abuse, 129, 160, 235, 240-241
Drug tests, 127-128
Drunk driving, 147, 202, 242
Dukakis, Michael, 160, 177, 277
Du Pont Company, 68

Eagle Forum, 239
Earth Day, 334
Economic cooperation council, 275
Economic Development Administration (EDA), 140
Economic development program,
294
Economic growth, 312, 319-324
Economic indicators, 38, 41
Economic Recovery Tax Act, 43
Economy
cloakroom politics and, 141
defense and, 316
domestic versus foreign, 44, 45-
47, 320-321
government role in, 38-41
minorities and, 328
policy making and, 37-38, 44-48
political culture and, 41-44
stability, 275-276
Western Europe, 41, 45-46
EDA (Economic Development Ad-
ministration), 140
Edie, David, 98
Education, 205, 319
reform, 159, 170-171, 182
Eisenhower, Dwight, 48, 166-167
Electoral accountability, 8
Electric utilities, 80
Electronic referenda, 280
Eli Lilly, 79
Employment

government, 87, 89
private, 58
public, 59, 87, 89
Energy, U.S. Department of, 304-
305
Energy policy, 182, 294, 298-299
England, representative government
in, 33
Engler, John, 178
Entitlement programs, 329
Entrepreneurial politics, 130-137
Environmental Defense Fund, 199
Environmental groups, 68, 105-106,
199, 207-208, 248, 250
Environmental impact statement,
138, 211, 213-214
Environmental issues, 60-61, 149-
150, 312
acid rain, 133, 182, 228
advertising, 303
air pollution, 128, 215, 335
arbitration and mediation, 298
courts and, 199, 207-208, 213-215
greenhouse effect, 336
litigation, 298
media and, 238
policy, 147, 158, 297-298
solid waste, 250-251
toxic waste, 144, 150, 242-244,
248, 315, 335-336
water quality, 228, 254, 335
Environmental protection, 333-337
air quality, 335
legislation, 247, 334
toxic waste, 335-336
water quality, 335
worldwide, 336-337
Environmental Protection Agency
(EPA), 95, 96, 131, 243, 307, 336
Epstein, Leon, 281
Equal opportunity, 312, 324-328
Equal Rights Amendment (ERA),
239, 304
Europe, Western
civil service system, 283
economy, 41, 45-46
industry, 286
legislators, 283
legislatures, 8
political parties, 281
standard of living, 41

Evidence, judicial decision making and, 198-199
Exclusionary strategies, 300-303
    bypass, 300-301
    deception, 302-303
    secrecy, 302
Exclusionary zoning, 202, 213
Executive Order 11246 (1965), 62
Executive power, 165-168
Exports, 39, 323

Fair Labor Standards Act, 103
Fairness doctrine, 213
Family Support Act, 331
Family Support Administration, 92
Federal Communications Commission (FCC), 11, 58, 61, 91, 213
Federal government, 10-11, 13-14
    aid. *See* Aid
    budget, 40, 142-144, 322-323
    employees, 87, 89
    federalism, 13-14
    intergovernmental relations, 14-15
    land holdings, 333
    policy making and, 47-48
    shutdown, 301
    spending, 46, 89, 245
Federal Home Loan Bank Board, 91
Federalism, 13-14, 48, 179, 294
Federal Power Commission (FPC), 107
Federal Railway Administration (FRA), 127
Federal Register, 46, 102
Federal Reserve Board, 42, 44, 319
Federal Trade Commission (FTC), 73, 103, 106, 107, 295
Federation of Women's Clubs, 239
Feldman, Martha, 304
Firestone Tire and Rubber Company, 73
First Amendment, 199, 200
Fishel, Jeff, 173, 174
Florida Medical Association, 238
Florida Power & Light, 80
Florio, Jim, 157, 171-172
Foley, Thomas, 5, 136
Fonda, Jane, 238, 305
Food and Drug Administration (FDA), 82, 91

Food stamps, 109, 329, 330-331
Ford, Gerald, 42, 111, 169
Ford, Henry, II, 70
Ford Foundation, 64-65
Ford Motor Company, 62, 70-71, 79
Foreign aid, 315-316
Foreign policy, 156-157, 182-183, 247
    courts and, 193
    media and, 234
Fortune magazine, 60, 61
Forum-shifting, 305-307
Foundations, 64-65
Fourteenth Amendment, 12, 197, 201, 203
Fourth branch, 11, 87
France, gross domestic product (GDP), 46, 58
Frankfurter, Felix, 200
Fraser, Douglas, 72
Freedom of the press, 203, 267
Free market, 21-22, 100, 266-269, 271
    political culture and, 30-33, 45-46
Fuchs, Beth, 301
Furman v. Georgia (1972), 202

Galanter, Marc, 206
Gang of Nine, 300
Gans, Herbert, 235
Garbage barge incident, 250-251
Garrity, Arthur, 12, 195, 210, 215, 216, 217
General Accounting Office (GAO), 129-130, 140, 148-149, 305
General Motors, 63, 71, 72, 320
Gideon v. Wainwright (1963), 198
Gillette, 303
Ginsburg, Douglas, 199
Golden parachute, 72
Goldsmith, James, 66
Goodyear, 66
Gormley, William, 106, 108
Gorsuch, Anne, 96
Goss v. Lopez (1975), 209, 214
Government, 47
    benefits of, 146, 177-179
    citizen participation, 280-281
    competence, 283-287
    corruption in, 274
    efficiency, 281-283

job-creation programs, 142
job-training programs, 77-78, 109
performance, 265-266
public-private spectrum, 64
public trust in, 35-36
reorganizations, 183-184
responsiveness, 277-279
role in economy, 38-41
spending, 245
stability, 275-276
Government contracts, 58, 205, 297
Government subsidies, 22
Governors, 155
budgets, 173
issues, 158
line-item veto, 165-166
minority, 276
policy making, 157
power, 165-166
staff, 170
taxes, 158-160
Graham, Bob, 175
Gramm, Phil, 127
Gramm-Rudman-Hollings Deficit
Reduction Act, 143, 251
Grants-in-aid programs, 14, 40, 47-
48, 160
Grass-roots politics, 228-229, 239-
240, 247-248, 272, 279
Great Britain, 47, 189
Great Society, 47, 94, 141, 156
Green, Gordon, 326
Greene, Harold, 195
Greenhouse effect, 336
Greenmail, 66
Gridlock, 142-144, 282-283
Griffiths, Martha, 178
Grogan, Fred I., 174
Gross domestic product (GDP), 46,
57-58
Gross national product (GNP), 39,
40, 287, 317, 329, 332
Gun control, 36, 141, 171-172
Gunderson, Steven, 130-131

Hall, Bruce, 253
Hall, Monty, 134
Halperin, Morton, 99
"Hard look" doctrine, 197
Hart, Gary, 18
Hayes, Woody, 287

Hazardous waste. See Toxic waste
Head Start, 109, 138, 181
Health care, 331-333
legislation, 301
Health insurance, 331-332
Heritage Foundation, 65
Highways, 129, 183
Hillman, Henry, 67
Hirschman, Albert, 305
Hispanics, 44, 276-277, 327
Hoadley, John, 301
Hobson v. Hansen (1967, 1968), 198
Holmes, Oliver Wendell, 200
Homeless people, 305
Home mortgage deduction, 326
Honda, 70
Hooker Chemical Company, 242
Hoover, J. Edgar, 97, 98
Horowitz, Donald, 189
Hostile takeovers, 66, 72
House Agriculture Committee, 131,
132
House Ways and Means Committee,
131
Housing, 213, 327
Hughes, Charles Evans, 196
Human service spending, 91-92
Hussein, Sadaam, 6, 164, 233, 302

Iacocca, Lee, 67-68
IBM, 58, 72, 76, 320
Icahn, Carl, 66
Immigration, 11, 129, 145
Immigration and Naturalization Ser-
vice (INS), 11
Imports, 39, 41, 320, 323
Inclusionary strategies, 298-300
coalition-building, 299
compromise, 300
consultation, 298-299
Income, per capita, 320
Income distribution, 326
Income support programs, 329-331
Income taxes, 40, 326
Incrementalism, 26, 99-100, 105,
139
Independent party, 37
Individualism, 29, 32
Industrial development bank, 275
Industrial policy, 275-276
Industry, 286-287

Industry groups, 207-208
Infant mortality rates, 314-315, 321, 332
Inflation, 37-38, 42, 43, 322
Informal rule making, 102
Information, decision making and, 99
Infrastructure, 319, 320
Initiatives, 224, 272, 280-281, 295, 296
    constitutions and, 23
    impact of, 254-255
    living room politics and, 227-228, 237-239, 245-247
In re Gault (1967), 198, 214
Insecticide, Fungicide, and Rodenticide Act, 334
Institutional reform, 214, 215-217
Institutions, political. *See* Political institutions
Insurance
    catastrophic health insurance, 301
    disability insurance, 244
    health insurance, 331-332
    liability insurance, 79
    national health insurance, 35, 178
Insurance companies, 79
Intellectual leaders, 197
Interest groups, 268, 279
    bureaucratic politics and, 94-95
    chief executive politics and, 166-167
    cloakroom politics and, 128, 132
    courts and, 198-199
    environmental, 68, 105-106, 199, 207-208, 248, 250
    industry, 207-208
    policy making and, 15-18, 41-42
Interest payments, 143, 322-323
Interest rates, 41, 42
Intergovernmental relations, 14-15
Interlocking directorates, 69
Internal Revenue Service (IRS), 11, 103, 180, 193
International Harvester, 277
Interstate Commerce Act of 1887, 87
Interstate Commerce Commission (ICC), 87, 107
Intervenor funding, 199
Investigative reporting, 19

Investment, 319
Iran-contra scandal, 10, 157
Iran hostage incident, 157, 159
Issue networks, 15, 132

Jackson, Andrew, 30
Jackson, Jesse, 277
Japan, 39, 46
    economy, 41, 45-46, 321
    industry, 60, 286
Jarvis, Howard, 239
Jefferson, Thomas, 32, 324
Job Corps, 148
Job-creation programs, 142
Jobs, Steve, 62
Job-training programs, 77-78, 109
Johns Manville, 79
Johnson, Frank, Jr., 12, 195, 210, 216-217
Johnson, Lyndon, 156, 176
    campaign promises, 174, 175
    executive power, 166
    Great Society, 47, 94, 141, 156
    new towns program, 179, 181
    policies, 35, 62, 161
    public opinion and, 23
    War on Poverty, 14, 108-109, 181, 331
Johnson & Johnson, 72-73
Johnson v. Santa Clara County (1987), 12-13, 204
Jones, Bryan, 306
Jones, Charles, 141
Judd, Orrin, 216
Judges, 26, 194-195
    administrative law, 102-103
    decision making, 197-200
    federal district court, 215-217
    leadership, 195-197
    lobbying for, 17
    personal values, 200
    policy making and, 12-13
    political parties and, 199
    scientific cases, 285
    symbolism, 200-201
Judicial restraint, doctrine of, 200
Junk bond market, 286
Juridical democracy, 282
Justice Department, U.S., 92

Kean, Thomas, 248

Keating, Charles, 274
Kennedy, Anthony, 199
Kennedy, Edward, 127
Kennedy, John F.
    campaign promises, 174, 175
    Cuban missile crisis, 180
    policies, 161, 178
    space program, 182
    staff, 169
Key, V. O., Jr., 225
King, Martin Luther, Jr., 10, 228,
    240
Kissinger, Henry, 156
Korean conflict, 315, 318
Kuklinski, James, 296
Kunin, Madeleine, 141, 160

Labor Department, U.S., 103
    public service employment pro-
        grams and, 111-116
Labor force, 41
Labor unions, 16, 60, 279
La Follette, Robert M., 227
Lane, Mel, 114
Lang, Gladys, 231, 241
Lang, Kurt, 231, 241
Lasswell, Harold, 57
Lautenberg, Frank, 127
Lavelle, Rita, 96
Law. See also Administrative law;
    Constitutional law; Private law;
    Public law; Statutory law
    judicial decision making and, 198
    science and, 285
Lawyers, 16, 283
Lawyers' Committee for Civil
    Rights under Law, 65
Lead emissions, 335
League of Nations, 156
League of Women Voters, 239
Learnfare program, 87
Lee, Eugene C., 247
Legal aid societies, 198
Legislators, 126-128
    campaign financing, 128
    competence, 283
    Europe and U.S., compared, 8
    policy making and, 7-9, 135
    public opinion and, 225-226
    terms, 126-127, 228, 279, 282

Legislatures, 123-124, 128-130, 266-
    269, 273
    bargaining and compromise, 133-
        134
    chief executives and, 9-10, 128-
        129, 137
    committees and subcommittees, 8,
        124, 127-128, 131-133, 149
    competence, 283
    deadlines, 134-135
    decision making, 265
    gridlock, 142-144
    incrementalism, 139
    innovation, 140-142
    leadership, 135-137
    oversight, 147-150
    policy delegation, 144
    policy impact, 147
    policy implementation, 145-147
    policy making, 130-137, 144-150
    pork-barrel policies, 140
    power, 131-133
    professionalization, 296
    staff, 129-130
    symbolism, 137-138
Leventhal, Harold, 197, 285
Liability insurance, 79
Libel, 201, 267
Liberalism, 34-37, 161, 205, 206, 245
Life expectancy, 321
Light, Paul, 160
Lincoln, Abraham, 223
Lindblom, Charles, 20, 57
Line bureaucrats, 95
Line-item veto, 10, 165-166, 282-
    283
Linsky, Martin, 233, 242
Lipsky, Michael, 99
Litigation, 298
Living room politics, 24, 25, 223-
    224, 266
    benefits, 248-250
    citizens and, 229-230
    democracy and, 250
    direct democracy, 237-239
    grass-roots politics, 247-248
    initiatives and referenda, 227-228,
        237-239, 245-247, 254-255
    issues, 231-235
    leadership, 239-240

media and, 229-230, 231-235, 240-244, 250-253
minorities and, 248-250
policy implementation, 250-253
policy making, 245-247, 271-272
politicians and, 229-230
public opinion and, 224-229, 235-237, 240-244, 250-253
Lobbying, 16, 17, 75, 279, 303
Local government, 47
federal aid and, 14-15
lobbying, 16
policy making, 13-14
Long Island State Park Commission, 97
Love Canal, 242-244
Lowi, Theodore, 282
Lynn, Laurence, 92

McComas, Maggie, 61
McGovern, George, 241
McGuigan, Patrick B., 245, 246
MacMillan, Whitney, 67
McNamara, Robert, 180
Macroeconomics, 38-39, 193, 319
Madison, James, 223
Magleby, David, 238
Magnuson, Warren, 107
Management strategies, 80-81
Managerial capitalism, 21
Mansbridge, Jane, 33, 303-304
Manufacturing, 39, 41, 286-287, 321-322
Mapp v. Ohio (1961), 209, 210, 214
Marijuana, 228
referenda, 296
Market paradigm, 30-33, 268-269. See also Free market
Marshall Plan, 182
Martinez, Robert, 276-277
Masters, 216
Mayors, 155
issues, 158
minority, 276-277
policy making, 157
power, 165-166
staff, 170
Mecham, Evan, 10
Media, 61, 75, 224. See also Living room politics
African famine issue, 232

chief executives and, 155, 167-168
corruption in government and, 274
courts and, 203, 209-210, 211, 281
disability review incident, 244
environmental issues, 238
fairness doctrine, 213
foreign policy and, 234
freedom of the press, 203, 267
garbage barge incident, 251
issues, 231-232
Love Canal, 242-244
neutrality of, 234-235
Persian Gulf War, 233-234
policy making and, 18-19, 266
public opinion and, 240-244
secrecy and, 302
space shuttle disaster, 253
Watergate scandal, 241
Mediation, 298
Medicaid and Medicare, 41, 109, 331, 332
Metro Broadcasting v. FCC (1990), 204
Michigan v. Long (1983), 202, 204
Midterm elections, 282
Military aid, 315-316
Miller, James, 107
Minimum wage laws, 176, 178
Minneapolis, Minnesota, 76
Minorities, 312, 324-328
administrative law and, 206-208
constitutional law and, 203-206, 208
courtroom politics and, 203-208
courts and, 203-208, 210, 212-213
economy and, 328
governors, 276
housing, 213
living room politics and, 248-250
mayors, 276-277
in policy making, 276-277
Supreme Court and, 203-205, 266-267
Miranda v. Arizona (1966), 204, 209, 211, 212
Missouri v. Jenkins (1990), 211
Mitchell, George, 128, 136
Mondale, Walter, 18, 130
Monitoring committees, 216-217
Monks, Robert, 69

Monopolies, 21
Moses, Robert, 96-98
Moyers, Bill, 244
Murray, Alan, 299
Muskie, Edmund, 141

NAACP Legal Defense Fund, 65
Nader, Ralph, 22, 63, 105, 240
National Aeronautics and Space Administration (NASA), 78-79, 94, 253
National Association for the Advancement of Colored People (NAACP), 65, 199, 205
National Association of Counties, 16
National Commission on Social Security Reform, 300
National Conference of State Legislatures, 16
National debt, 142-144, 322-323. See also Budget deficit
National Environmental Policy Act (NEPA), 138, 213-214, 297
National Environmental Protection Act, 334
National Governors' Association, 16
National health insurance, 35, 178
National Highway Traffic Safety Administration (NHTSA), 73, 82
National Industrial Recovery Act, 282
National Labor Relations Board (NLRB), 88, 91
National League of Cities, 16
National Organization for Women (NOW), 205, 239
National referendum, 280
National Rifle Association, 141, 172
National security, 312, 315-319
National Technical Advisory Committee on Water Quality Controls, 335
National Transportation Safety Board (NTSB), 127
Natural gas companies, 64, 107
Natural monopolies, 63
Natural Resources Defense Council, 199
Navistar International, 277
Navy, U.S., 180
NBC, 232

Neely, Richard, 13
Negligence suits, 238
Neighborhood assemblies, 280
Nelson, Benjamin, 178
Neustadt, Richard, 165, 167, 225
New conservatism, 37
New Deal, 9, 30, 35, 47, 176, 274, 313, 328, 331
    Democratic party and, 177-178
    Resettlement Program, 146, 181
New federalism, 48
New institutionalism, 6
Newspapers, 19, 61, 201. See also Media
New towns program, 179, 181
New York State Council of Parks, 97
New York Times, 129, 226, 231, 243, 253
New York Times v. Sullivan (1964), 201
New York v. Quarles (1984), 204
Nixon, Richard
    campaign promises, 174, 175
    executive branch reorganization, 183
    foreign policy, 156-157
    management strategy, 10
    media and, 19, 241
    new federalism, 14, 15, 48, 184
    policies, 35, 42
    public opinion, 23, 241
    staff, 169
    wage and price controls, 193
    Watergate scandal, 19, 157, 241, 275
"Not in My Back Yard" (NIMBY) syndrome, 229
Nuclear freeze referenda, 247, 254
Nuclear power, 18-19, 74, 106, 240, 246, 247, 306
Nuclear Regulatory Commission (NRC), 74, 106
Nuclear weapons, 318
Nucor Inc., 71

Obey, David, 137
Occupational Safety and Health Administration, 82
O'Connor, Sandra Day, 199
Office of Communication of the United Church of Christ, 213

Office of Management and Budget (OMB), 59, 93, 244, 295
Office of Technology Assessment (OTA), 129-130, 305, 336
Oil, economy of, 44, 316, 322
Okun, Arthur, 325
Old Age Survivors Disability Insurance (OASDI), 40
Omnibus Budget and Reconciliation Act, 43
O'Neill, Thomas P. (Tip), Jr., 231
O'Neill, William, 160
Open meetings law, 302
Oraflex, 79
Oregon Taxpayers United, 239-240
Organization, hierarchical model of, 66-67
Organization for Economic Cooperation and Development, 326
Organization of Petroleum Exporting Countries (OPEC), 44
Organized labor, 16, 60, 178, 279
Orr, Kay, 178

Pacific Gas and Electric Company (PG&E), 74
Page, Benjamin, 326
Parental leave legislation, 300
Partial preemptions, 15
Participatory democracy, 33-34
Patient rights
  mentally ill, 197
Payroll taxes, 326
PCB (polychlorinated biphenyl), 334, 335
Peace Corps, 97
Peck, Gregory, 238
Penn Central, 69, 78
Perot, H. Ross, 71, 72
Perpich, Rudy, 157
Persian Gulf War, 5-6, 157, 164, 175-176, 226, 305, 315-316, 318-319
  media coverage, 230, 233-234
  secrecy and, 302
Personal freedom, 29
Persuasive strategies, 303-305
  policy analysis, 304-305
  protest, 305
  rhetoric, 303-304
Pertschuk, Michael, 107

Pesticides, 306-307, 334, 335
Peters, Thomas, 81
Phillips, Ray, 239-240
Pickens, T. Boone, 22, 66
Pittsburgh, Pennsylvania, 76
Pittsburgh Press, 210
Plessy v. Ferguson (1896), 201
Pluralism, 179, 270
Policy analysis, 304-305
Policy domains, 24-26, 305-307
Policy gridlock, 142-144
Policy makers, 7
  bureaucrats, 10-11
  chief executives, 9-10
  interest groups, 15-18, 41-42, 128, 132, 140
  judges, 12-13
  legislators, 7-9
  media, 18-19
  political parties, 15-18
Policy making
  bureaucratic, 95-96
  federalism and, 13-14
  incrementalism, 99-100, 105
  intergovernmental relations, 14-15
  media and, 18-19, 250-253
  politics and, 5-7, 23-26
  private, 20-22, 271-272, 286-287
  public, 22-23, 272
  public opinion, 22-23, 250-253
  representativeness, 276-277
  scope of conflict, 19-23
Policy reports, 304-305
Policy statements, 103
Political action committees (PACs), 75, 140, 168
  funding by, 168, 278-279
Political culture, 29-37, 44-48, 225
  assessing, 34-37
  courts and, 205-206
  definition, 29
  economy and, 41-44
  free market and, 30-33, 45-46
  participatory democracy, 33-34
  procedural democracy, 30-33
Political-economic problems, 41-44
Political feasibility, 293
  exclusionary strategies, 300-303
  forum-shifting, 305-307
  inclusionary strategies, 298-300

institutions, 293-298
persuasive strategies, 303-305
Political institutions, 6
alternative perspectives, 293-298
analysis of, 266-271
change and, 293, 296-298
as constraints, 293-295
criteria of, 274-287
evaluation, 272-287
exclusionary strategies, 300-303
inclusionary strategies, 298-300
as opportunities, 295-296
performance, 265-266
persuasive strategies, 303-305
policy domains, 305-307
political feasibility and, 293
reform, 296-298
Political parties, 281-282
judges and, 194-195
judicial decision making and, 199
policy making and, 15-18
Politics. *See also* Boardroom politics;
Bureaucratic politics; Chief executive politics; Cloakroom politics;
Courtroom politics; Living room
politics
conventional, alternatives to, 271-
272
policy and, 5-7, 23-26
Pomper, Gerald, 174
Pork-barrel policies, 140
Pornography, 247
Postal Service, U.S., 64
Postmaterialist values, 36-37
Poverty, 39, 40, 43, 108-109, 179,
325-326, 327, 328, 330
Prayer in public schools, 36, 247
Precedent, 12, 198, 200, 208, 211,
295
Preemptions, 15
Presidential Power, 165
Presidents, 155
campaign promises, 174, 175, 302
foreign policy, 156-157
military policy, 156-157
Pressman, Jeffrey, 294
Price, David, 142
Price controls, 42
Prison reform, 195, 210, 216-217
Prisons, privatization of, 297
Private law, 189-190

Private sector, 45-46
decision making, 20-22, 25, 26,
286-287
gross domestic product, 46, 57-58
Privatization, 58, 297
Procedural democracy, 30-33, 266-
269
Productivity, 38, 41, 60, 320, 323-
324
Product safety, 72-73
Profitability, 59-61, 72-74
Progressives, 23, 227
Property taxes, 202
Proposition 13 (California), 239, 245
Proposition 20 (California), 110,
113-114
Proposition 65 (California), 254
Proposition 128 (California), 238
Protest, 305
Public awareness, 280-281
Public law, 190
Public opinion, 223-224, 266, 273,
280-281, 314
bottom-up, 226-229
disability review incident, 244
Love Canal, 242-244
media and, 240-244
policy making and, 22-23
polls, 227, 231, 234, 235-237, 242
soft opinions, 235
state court judges and, 296
top-down, 224-226
Public policy, 44-48, 223
assessment criteria, 311-315
effectiveness, 313
goals, 311-313
standards, 313-315
defense, 315-319
economic growth, 319-324
environmental protection, 333-
337
equal opportunity, 324-328
social programs, 328-333
Public sector, 46-47
decision making, 19-20, 22-23, 24,
26
regulatory agencies, 46-47
Public service employment programs, 146
Labor Department and, 111-116

Public utilities, 21, 63-64, 71, 74, 105-106, 192-193, 207, 209-210

Quirk, Paul, 304
Quotas, 204, 205

Radio, 11. *See also* Media
Radioactive waste, 247
Rain forests, 158, 337
Rand McNally, 76
Rather, Dan, 253
Rational model of decision making, 100-101
RCA, 70
Reader's Digest, 113
Reagan, Nancy, 129
Reagan, Ronald, 34, 42-43, 101, 107, 127, 148, 156
  affirmative action, 93
  appointments, 96, 199, 207, 277, 284
  budget, 43, 142, 160, 182
  campaign promises, 174, 175
  conservatism, 161
  corruption in administration, 274
  defense spending, 317
  disability review incident, 244
  Environmental Protection Agency, 96
  executive power, 166, 167
  foreign policy, 157, 183
  grants-in-aid, 14, 15, 48
  Iran-contra scandal, 10, 237, 302
  legislature and, 9, 136
  management strategy, 10
  media and, 18, 167-168, 231
  military policy, 318
  new federalism, 48, 184
  Nicaragua, 158, 318
  policies, 30, 58, 129, 140, 171, 178
  public opinion, 226
  slogans, 173
  social programs, 328
  staff, 169
  taxes, 43, 130-131, 164-165
  veto, 140
Real estate market, 286
Real interest rates, 44
Reason Foundation, 65
Recessions, 38, 43, 321
Referenda. *See* Initiatives

Reform, 274, 280-281
  bureaucratic, 284
  campaign financing, 278-279
  civil service, 284
  corporate, 279
  education, 159, 170-171, 182
  institutional, 214, 215-217, 296-298
  taxes, 130-131, 159, 168, 180, 303, 326
  welfare, 177, 331
Refuse Act of 1899, 333
Regan, Donald, 65
Regulations, 88-92. *See also* Bureaucratic politics
  crossover sanctions, 15
  partial preemptions, 15
Regulatory agencies, 46-47
  courts and, 206-207
Rehnquist, William H., 12, 193, 199
  Rehnquist Court, 12, 196, 204-205
Reich, Robert, 72
Religion, 36
Representative democracy, 19, 31, 223
Republican party, 34, 37
  judges, 199
Research and development, 319-320
Resettlement Program, 146, 181
Resource Conservation and Recovery Act, 334
Retail politics, 134, 168
Rhetoric, 138, 173-175, 271, 303-304
Richmond v. Croson (1986), 205
Rickover, Hyman, 97
Right-to-die, 202
Ripley, Randall, 135
RJR Nabisco, Inc., 277
Robinson, Michael, 253
Roe v. Wade (1973), 202
Roosevelt, Franklin D., 9, 30, 142, 156, 161, 165. *See also* New Deal
  administrative reform, 298
  executive branch reorganization, 183
  executive power, 166-167
  National Industrial Recovery Act, 282
  policies, 178
  staff, 169
  Supreme Court and, 196

Rose, Richard, 59
Rosenbaum, Walter, 334
Rosenthal, Alan, 137, 165
Rostenkowski, Dan, 130, 168, 303
Rousseau, Jean-Jacques, 33, 272
Ruckelshaus, William, 96
Rural Electrification Administration
   (REA), 176
Rust v. Sullivan (1991), 306

Salamon, Lester, 181
Sales tax, 228, 327
SALT I agreement, 156
*San Antonio Independent School
   District v. Rodriguez* (1973), 202
Sarnoff, Robert, 70
Sasser, James, 226
Savings and loan industry, 78, 163,
   252, 274, 286
Scalia, Antonin, 199
Schaefer, William, 141
Schattschneider, E. E., 6, 22, 81,
   224, 306
Schick, Allen, 142
Schlafly, Phyllis, 239, 240
School desegregation, 201, 205, 211,
   212, 214-215, 327
   Boston, 12, 195, 210, 215, 216, 217
School prayer, 36, 247
Schwarzkopf, H. Norman, 302
Search warrants, 202
Sears, 69
Secrecy, 302
Securities and Exchange Commis-
   sion (SEC), 63, 103
Senate Democratic Conference, 136
Senate Labor and Human Resources
   Committee, 131, 132
Senior citizens, 312, 330
   employment, 321-322
Senior Executive Service (SES), 284
Service delivery programs, 88-92,
   109
Service industry, 41, 321-322
Sexual harassment, 12-13
Shearson Lehman Hutton, 79
Shepherd, Cybill, 238
Shriver, Sargent, 97
Sierra Club, 199
Sigal, Leon, 230
Silent Spring , 333

Simon, Herbert, 271
"60 Minutes," 19, 149
Slander, 267
Sleeper effects, 181-183
Smith, Adam, 31, 33
Smith, Robert, 140
Snyder, Mitch, 305
Social Security, 35, 40-41, 109, 180,
   183, 329-330
   disability insurance program, 244
   Medicaid/Medicare, 41, 109, 331,
      332
   Old Age Survivors Disability In-
      surance (OASDI), 40
   poverty and, 40
   reform, 300
   Supplemental Security Income
      (SSI), 40-41
   taxes, 326-327
Social Security Act of 1935, 35, 140-
   141
Social Security Administration
   (SSA), 88, 207, 244, 331
Social service programs, 91-92, 108-
   109, 247, 304, 312, 328-333
Society, characteristics of, 273
Soft opinions, 235-237
Solid waste disposal, 250-251
Souter, David, 199
South Africa, 129
South Carolina v. Katzenbach
   (1966), 212
*Southern Burlington County
   NAACP v. Township of Mt. Lau-
   rel* (1975), 202
Soviet Union, 315, 317, 318
   Afghanistan invasion, 157, 182-
      183, 316, 318
   arms control agreements, 183
   Chernobyl, 240, 337
   environmental protection, 337
Space shuttle disaster, 253
Stagflation, 42
Standard of living, 39, 41, 320-321
Standing to sue, 297
Stanga, John, 296
Stare decisis, 12, 211, 295
State Department, 180
State government, 47-48, 176-177
   bureaucracy, 10-11
   chief executives, 9-10

economy and, 275
federal aid and, 14-15
federalism and, 13-14
lobbying, 16
reorganizations, 183
supreme courts, 13, 195, 202-203
State legislatures, 124, 137
innovation, 141
pork-barrel policies, 140
professionalization, 296
State of the State address, 9
State of the Union address, 9
State supreme courts, 13, 195
innovative decisions, 202-203
Statutory language, 113-114
Statutory law, 190
Steel industry, 286-287, 323
Steiger, Janet, 107
Stigler, George, 107
Stockholders, 22
Stockman, David, 134, 140
Stock market, 22, 143
Stone, Geoffrey, 204
Stone, Harlan, 197
Subcommittees, 132-133
Subgovernments, 15
Subnational governments, 47
Substitution, 112, 115
Sudafed, 73
Sue, right to, 297
Sunshine laws, 302
Sununu, John, 170
Superfund Toxic Waste Cleanup
Law, 149-150, 294, 334, 336
Supplemental Security Income (SSI),
40-41
Supreme Court, U.S., 74, 192, 193,
200, 282
abortion, 306
Burger Court, 196, 201-202, 204,
206
case selection, 194
chief justice, 197
civil rights, 296
compared with Congress, 266-269
conservatism, 206
constitutional law, 208
federal agency decisions, 206
market paradigm and, 267-269
minorities and, 203-205, 266-267
nominees, 199

Rehnquist Court, 12, 196, 204-205
standing requirements, 297
stare decisis, 12
state supreme courts and, 195,
202-203
Warren Court, 12, 200, 201, 204,
206
Surface Mining Control and Reclamation Act of 1977, 15
*Swann v. Charlotte-Mecklenburg
Board of Education* (1971), 209
Swing voters, 196
Symbolism
bureaucratic, 104-105
chief executive politics, 173-176
corporate, 71-72
courtroom politics, 200-201
legislative, 137-138

Takeovers, corporate, 62, 66, 72
Taxes, 236-237, 245, 326-327
courts and, 193
initiatives, 295
revenues from, 46
Tax increases, 236-237
Tax reform, 130-131, 159, 168, 180,
303, 326
Tax Reform Act, 130
Television, 253. *See also* Media
advertising, 237
court proceedings, 281
Tennessee Valley Authority (TVA),
64, 176
Think tanks, 65
Thin-slab casting, 71
Third World, 44
Thompson, Tommy, 75, 165-166
Three Mile Island, 106, 240
Tiananmen Square, 234
Tobacco industry, 238
Tocqueville, Alexis de, 123
Torts, 190
Town meetings, 34, 228, 272
Toxic Substances Control Act, 334
Toxic waste, 144, 150, 242-244, 248,
315, 335-336
Toyota, 75
Trade deficit, 39, 44
Traffic fatalities, 233
Transfer payments, 46

Tri-City Herald (Washington), 18-19
Truman, Harry, 172, 178, 182, 183
Turner, Ted, 62, 66
Tylenol, 72-73

Unemployment, 37-38, 41-43, 77-78, 115, 236, 314, 321-322, 327
Unemployment insurance, 88, 142, 329-330
Union Carbide, 75
Unitary democracy, 33-34
United Auto Workers, 69, 72
United Church of Christ v. FCC (1966, 1969), 213
United Kingdom, gross domestic product (GDP), 46, 58
U.S. Conference of Mayors, 16
U.S. Steel, 60, 72, 77
United States v. Brignoni-Ponce (1975), 204
United States v. Carolene Products (1938), 197
United States v. Cortez (1981), 204
United States v. Paradise (1987), 204
University of Pennsylvania v. EEOC (1990), 204
Upward Bound, 109
Used-car dealers, 73
USX, 60, 72
Utility, 32

Values, 34-37
Veterans, 129
Veterans Affairs, U.S. Department of, 94
Veto, 9-10
   line-item, 10, 165-166, 282-283
Vietnam syndrome, 318
Vietnam War, 129, 156, 240, 249-250, 305, 315-318
Volcker, Paul, 42
Volunteer army, 316-317
Voter turnout, 237
Voting rights, 212-213
Voting Rights Act of 1965, 147, 175, 204, 212-213

Wages, 42, 276, 320
Wagner Act of 1935, 87-88

Walker, Jack, 65
Wallace, George, 178-179, 210, 217
Wards Cove Packing Co. v. Atonio (1989), 204-205
War on Poverty, 14, 108-109, 181, 331
War protestors, 305
Warren, Earl, 12, 267
   Warren Court, 12, 200, 201, 204, 206
Washington Post, 19, 130, 149, 231
Watergate scandal, 19, 157, 241, 275
Waterman, Robert, 81
Water pollution, 228, 254, 335
Water Pollution Control Act, 334
Water quality, 335
Water Quality Act of 1987, 140
Waxman, Henry, 133
Wealth distribution, 44, 326
Wealth of Nations, The, 31
Weaver, James, 140
Weber, Max, 66
Webster v. Reproductive Health Services (1989), 158, 306
Weicker, Lowell, 128
Weissberg, Robert, 225
Welfare, 329, 331
   reform, 177, 331
Wendy's Hamburgers, 62
Wenner, Lettie, 207
Wholesale politics, 134, 168
Wildavsky, Aaron, 294
Wilder, Douglas, 138, 276
Willowbrook, 214, 216, 217
Wilson, Pete, 157-158
Wilson, Woodrow, 131, 156
Wisconsin Department of Health and Social Services, 87, 98-99
WLBT-TV (Jackson, Mississippi), 213
Wolfson, Lewis, 252
Women, 30, 204, 205, 325
   equal pay, 327-328
   equal rights, 228
   in labor force, 41, 327-328
   in policy making, 276-277
   poverty, 327
   voting, 30
Women's movement, 304
Woolard, Ed, 68
Worker's compensation, 199

Workfare, 92
World Commission on Environment
   and Development, 337
World market, 323
World War II, 318

Wright, Jim, 136, 274

Zero-based budget, 101
Zero-sum game, 76-77